Technological Resources for Second Language Pronunciation Learning and Teaching

Technological Resources for Second Language Pronunciation Learning and Teaching

Research-based Approaches

Edited by Shannon McCrocklin

LEXINGTON BOOKS
Lanham • Boulder • New York • London

Published by Lexington Books
An imprint of The Rowman & Littlefield Publishing Group, Inc.
4501 Forbes Boulevard, Suite 200, Lanham, Maryland 20706
www.rowman.com

86-90 Paul Street, London EC2A 4NE

British Library Cataloguing in Publication Information Available

Library of Congress Cataloging-in-Publication Data Available

ISBN 978-1-66690-229-7 (cloth : alk. paper)
ISBN 978-1-66690-230-3 (electronic)

♾™ The paper used in this publication meets the minimum requirements of
American National Standard for Information Sciences—Permanence of Paper
for Printed Library Materials, ANSI/NISO Z39.48-1992.

Contents

PART 5: CORPUS-BASED APPROACHES

Figures

Tables

Acknowledgments

I would like to gratefully acknowledge all of the authors who contributed to this book and worked with me to peer review chapters. Authors also put in remarkable work revising their own chapters in order to help make this book a success.

I would also like to thank John Levis, Veronica Sardegna, and Jennifer Foote for taking the time to talk with me about this book and help me navigate this process. Dr. Foote also helped by supplementing the peer reviews by providing a review of one of the chapters.

Part 1

GETTING STARTED WITH TECHNOLOGY IN SECOND LANGUAGE PRONUNCIATION LEARNING AND TEACHING

Chapter One

Exploring Technologies Available for Teaching and Learning Second Language Pronunciation

Shannon McCrocklin

INTRODUCTION

As the field of language learning and teaching has changed over time, the status of pronunciation has also shifted. Research has continued to show that learners must be engaged communicatively and negotiate meaning for successful acquisition of a second language (L2) (Ellis 2005; Long 1996), which has led to widespread adoption of communicative language teaching approaches. This has, at times, left the area of pronunciation teaching to struggle to find its place (Levis and Sonsaat 2017). Today, though, there is a recognition that both meaning-focused interaction and form-focused instruction are key elements of language instruction (Ellis 2005; Nation and Newton 2008) and there are resources to help teachers and learners approach pronunciation in conjunction with communicative approaches, such as Celce-Murcia, Brinton, and Goodwin (2010).

Along with these changes, recognition of the importance of pronunciation in L2 learning has grown in the last twenty years. With the development of conferences such as Pronunciation in Second Language Learning and Teaching (PSLLT), journals such as the *Journal of Second Language Pronunciation*, and books such as *Pronunciation Fundamentals* (Derwing and Munro 2015) and *Second Language Pronunciation: Bridging the Gap between Research and Teaching* (Levis, Derwing, and Sonsaat-Hegelheimer 2022), L2 pronunciation has become increasingly visible as an important area of second language learning, teaching and research. Despite incredible gains in pronunciation research, L2 pronunciation teaching has often lagged behind and often relies on traditional models of pronunciation teaching that prioritize controlled, not communicative, activities such as listen and repeat (Carey,

Sweeting, and Mannell 2015). Further, the lack of attention to pronunciation, starting in the 1970s, but continuing well into the 1990s (Levis and Sonsaat 2017) has left the field of L2 pronunciation with many areas to address, including instructors' lack of training and comfort in teaching pronunciation and limited time devoted to pronunciation in second language classes (Foote, Holtby, and Derwing 2011).

Technology is likely to play a key role in the resurgence of pronunciation as it can enrich and augment traditional methods of teaching (Fouz-González 2015; O'Brien et al. 2018) by offering more individualized feedback and training (Hincks 2015). Further, it can reduce the burden on teachers to provide feedback and support autonomous learning (McCrocklin 2016). Technology has been especially important in the last few years as schools around the world shut down due to COVID-19 (UNESCO.org 2020) and teachers were thrust into online instruction (Herold 2020; Pastor 2020).

Despite the growing number of resources available focused on L2 pronunciation, technology in L2 pronunciation has received much less concentrated attention. Levis (2018) noted that while technology has been a "consistent" strand of L2 pronunciation research, it is also somewhat "invisible" (173). Indeed, research has examined a wide variety of technologies such as language-learning platforms, speech visualization software, and Automatic Speech Recognition. Despite the abundance of research, it can be difficult to gain a full sense of work in this area given the lack of a comprehensive and consolidated resource or reference. Popular reference books for L2 pronunciation (e.g., Derwing and Munro 2015; Kang, Thomson, and Murphy 2018; Pennington and Rogerson-Revell 2019; Reed and Levis 2015) dedicate only one or two chapters to technology. Similarly, numerous computer-assisted language learning reference books dedicate limited, if any, attention to pronunciation (Chapelle and Sauro 2017; Farr and Murray 2016; Stanley 2013; Walker and White 2013).

OVERVIEW OF THE BOOK

This book endeavors to fill that gap and make L2 pronunciation technologies more visible by providing teachers and researchers an introduction to research in a wide variety of technologies that can support pronunciation learning. This book brings together original research in technology for pronunciation learning and a practical interest in applications for teaching. While working to introduce new practitioners to numerous technologies available, it also dives into the research-basis for their use by providing new studies and data featuring a wide variety of languages and learning contexts. Generally, each chapter focuses on a specific technology, or set of technological resources, providing a literature review to provide background information and describing a new research study that examines the use of technology in L2 pronunciation learning or teaching. Each chapter ends by turning attention to implications of current research and suggestions for integration of the specific technologies in pronunciation classrooms.

As part of getting the book started, chapter 2 shows how not only can a language's pronunciation be seen as a complex system, given the dynamic interaction of multiple layers of pronunciation features, but how language learning itself can be seen as a complex system as variables such as first language and identity interact in the language learning process. The authors, Di Liu and Marnie Reed, argue that given the intricacy of the pronunciation system and language learning process, we should see technology as an indispensable resource to better support pronunciation learning as it can support more individualized learning, provide stealth assessment tools, and increase engagement through game-based approaches.

The second section focuses on web-based resources, tools, and language-learning platforms. Within this section, the first two chapters introduce a variety of resources and tools. Chapter 3, by Lara Wallace and Julia Choi, investigates a pedagogical phonology course in which prospective teachers explored a wide range of resources for teaching L2 pronunciation, highlighting successes and challenges along the way. Similarly, chapter 4, by Hseuh Chu Chen and Jing Xuan Tian introduces a range or tools. For their study, however, the authors created a package utilizing five major educational web-based tools, examining prospective teachers' evaluations of the tools in supporting their own L2 pronunciation improvement. Within the second section, the final two chapters focus on specific language-learning resources. Chapter 5, by Vivian Flanzer and Veronica Sardegna, focuses on an open educational resource, ClicaBrasil, which provides a catalogue of Portuguese learning materials and activity ideas. The authors' study shows how meaningful, content-focused materials can be used to heighten learners' pronunciation awareness. Finally, the last chapter in this section (chapter 6), by Mariko M. Wei, Mayu Miyamoto, Namiko Uchida, Atsushi Fukada, and Jessica L. Sturm, focuses on the usefulness of a language-learning platform, SpeakEverywhere, for task-based pronunciation assessment in Japanese, finding the new assessment system better aligned with learner goals and supported a greater sense of achievement.

The third section of the book focuses on a range of studies focusing on Automatic Speech Recognition (ASR) for pronunciation feedback. Chapter 7, by Karen Acosta and Michelle Ocasio, transitions from the previous section by assessing another language-learning platform, Transparent Language, for its wide range of activities. The study found that several of the speaking activities that used ASR were found to be the most useful practice activities in students' Spanish learning. Aurore Mroz, in chapter 8, continues the section by exploring not only speech-to-text (ASR) technologies, but also text-to-speech technologies. Her study shows that these technologies can be useful in advancing French learners' intelligibility and proficiency. Chapter 9, by Solène Inceoglu, focuses on multiple technologies and learning activities, ASR dictation along with technology-supported shadowing practice. Her study suggests that the technologies may complement each other by focusing on different pronunciation-learning skills. The last chapter of this section, chapter 10 by Shannon McCrocklin, Rachel Stuckel, and Eugenie Mainake, provides an exploratory study of a VR application, Mondly VR, which, at its core, uses Automatic Speech Recognition to support immersive simulated language learning experiences. While learners reported focusing on speaking, listening, and pronunciation during practice, the study raises concerns about the feedback provided and the lack of evidence that learners were able to improve their pronunciation through practice with the program.

The fourth section of the book focuses on speech visualization in pronunciation learning. Chapter 11, by Debra M. Hardison and Tomoko Okuno, inspects L2 production of Japanese, focusing on vowel durations following perception training with either auditory-only or auditory-visual input using waveforms to emphasize durational differences. Although previous research has shown benefits of waveform perception training, this study raises questions about the optimal nature of such training and best length of training to promote benefits. Heather Offerman and Daniel J. Olson, in chapter 12, continue by looking at learner attitudes regarding the visual feedback generated through Praat for L2 Spanish learning. Their study finds a learner preference for active instructor involvement leading them to recommend both software training and explicit instruction in interpreting and using visual feedback. Finally, the last chapter in this section, chapter 13 by Ivana Rehman and Anurag Das, explores a different form of visual feedback, vowel plotting. Their study finds that vowel plotting can be useful in providing individualized learning and promoting greater noticing and makes recommendations for the development of vowel plotting resources, including audio exemplars and useful guidance needed to navigate such technologies.

The final section wraps up the book by looking at corpus-based approaches. While chapter 14, by Idée Edalatishams, focuses on the ways that teachers can use corpora in researching pronunciation features and identifying useful exemplars to bring into the classroom, chapter 15, by Suzanne Franks and Mai M. Eida, describes a study on classroom implementation of corpora for pronunciation learning. Notably, in chapter 14, Edalatishams introduces her new Corpus of Teaching Assistant Classroom Speech (CoTACS), examining the ways the corpus can be used to identify and illustrate L2 prosodic phenomena. Franks and Eida then show the ways that learners could use corpora in the classroom, evaluating a mini-corpus project as part of a speaking/pronunciation course for International Teaching Assistants in order make suggestions for future teachers.

Although the overview of technologies provided by this book is not exhaustive, readers will be introduced to many well-established veins of research in Computer-Assisted Pronunciation Teaching. Practitioners will further find many accessible and affordable technologies and resources that can be integrated into the pronunciation classroom, along with research to help understand the ways the technologies may or may not be useful.

REFERENCES

Carey, Michael David, Arizio Sweeting, and Robert Mannell. 2015. "An L1 Point of Reference Approach to Pronunciation Modification: Learner-Centred Alternatives to 'listen and repeat.'" *Journal of Academic Language and Learning* 9 (1): A18–A30.

Celce-Murcia, Marianne, Donna M. Brinton, and Janet M. Goodwin. 2010. *Teaching Pronunciation: A Course Book and Reference Guide.* Cambridge, UK: Cambridge University Press.

Chapelle, Carol and Shannon Sauro, eds. 2017. *The Handbook of Technology and Second Language Teaching and Learning.* Hoboken, NJ: Wiley-Blackwell.

Derwing, Tracey and Murray Munro. 2015. *Pronunciation Fundamentals: Evidence-based perspectives for L2 teaching and research.* Philadelphia, PA: John Benjamins.

Ellis, Rod. 2005. Principles of instructed language learning. *System,* 33, no. 2, 209–224.

Farr, Fiona and Liam Murray, eds. 2016. *The Routledge Handbook of Language Learning and Technology.* New York, NY: Routledge.

Foote, Jennifer A., Amy K. Holtby, and Tracey Derwing. 2011. "Survey of the teaching of pronunciation in adult programs in Canada 2010." *TESL Canada Journal,* 29, no. 1, 1–22.

Fouz-González, Jonás. .2015. "Trends and directions in computer-assisted pronunciation training." In *Investigating English pronunciation: Trends and directions,* edited by Jose A. Mompean and Jonás Fouz-González, 314–342. London, UK: Palgrave Macmillan.

Herold, Benjamin. 2020. "The scramble to move America's schools online." *Education Week.* https://www.edweek.org/technology/the-scramble-to-move-americas-schools-online/2020/03.

Hincks, Rebecca. 2015. "Technology and learning pronunciation." In *The handbook of English pronunciation,* edited by Marnie Reed and John Levis, 505–519. Malden, MA: Wiley-Blackwell.

Kang, Okim, Ron Thomson, and John M. Murphy, eds. 2018 *The Routledge Handbook of Contemporary English Pronunciation*. New York, NY: Routledge.

Levis, John. 2018. "Technology and second language pronunciation." *Journal of Second Language Pronunciation*, 4, no. 2, 173–181.

Levis, John, Tracey Derwing, and Sinem Sonsaat-Hegelheimer, eds. 2022. *Second Language Pronunciation: Bridging the Gap between Research and Teaching*. Hoboken, NJ: John Wiley and Sons, Inc.

Levis, John and Sinem Sonsaat. 2017. "Pronunciation teaching in the early CLT era." In *The Routledge Handbook of English Pronunciation*, edited by Okim Kang, Ron I. Thomson & John M. Murphy, 267–283. New York, NY: Routledge.

Long, Michael. 1996. "The role of the linguistic environment in second language acquisition." In *The Handbook of Second Language Acquisition*, edited by William C. Ritchie and Tej K. Bhatia, 413–468. San Diego, CA: Academic Press.

McCrocklin, Shannon. 2016. "Pronunciation learner autonomy: The potential of automatic speech recognition." *System*, 57, 25–42.

Nation, I. S. P. and Jonathon Newton. 2008. *Teaching ESL/EFL Listening and Speaking*. New York, NY: Routledge.

O'Brien, Mary Grantham, Tracey Derwing, Catia Cucchiarini, Debra Hardison, Hansjörg Mixdorff, Ron I. Thomson, Helmer Strik, John M. Levis, Murray J. Munro, Jennifer A. Foote, and Greta M. Levis. 2018. "Directions for the future of technology in pronunciation research and teaching." *Journal of Second Language Pronunciation*, 4, no. 2, 182–207. https://doi.org/10.1075/jslp.17001.obr.

Pastor, Cherish K. 2020. "Sentiment analysis on synchronous online delivery of instruction due to extreme community quarantine in the Philippines caused by COVID-19 pandemic." *Asian Journal of Multidisciplinary Studies*, 3, no. 1, 1–6.

Pennington, Martha C. and Pamela Rogerson-Revell. 2019. *English Pronunciation Teaching and Research: Contemporary Perspectives*. London, UK: Palgrave Macmillan.

Reed, Marnie and John Levis, eds. 2015. *The Handbook of English Pronunciation*. Malden, MA: Wiley-Blackwell.

Stanley, Graham. 2013. *Language Learning with Technology: Ideas for integrating technology in the classroom*. Cambridge, UK: Cambridge University Press.

Walker, Aisha and Goodith White. 2013. *Technology Enhanced Language Learning: Connecting Theory and Practice*. Oxford, UK: Oxford University Press.

UNESCO. 2020. "Education: From disruption to discovery." *United Nations Educational, Scientific and Cultural Organization (UNESCO)*. https://en.unesco.org/COVID-19/educationresponse.

Chapter Two

From Technology-enhanced to Technology-based Language Teaching

A Complexity Theory Approach to Pronunciation Teaching

Di Liu and Marnie Reed

COMPLEXITY THEORY

Complexity Theory (CT), also commonly referred to as Complex Dynamic System Theory (CDST) and Chaos Theory, is a transdisciplinary theoretical approach widely applied in Physics (Kwapień and Drożdż 2012; Liu and Barabási 2016), Engineering (Ottino 2004; Sheard and Mostashari 2009), Computer Science (Mitchell 2006), Economics (Foster 2005), Biology (Kaneko 2006; Loscalzo, Kohane, and Barabasi 2007), and Applied Linguistics (Larsen-Freeman and Cameron 2008). Complexity Theory views the research entity as an open, dynamic, nonlinear, adaptive, and spontaneous system. While some people may think that a complex system must be a complicated system encompassing a large number of variables, it can also be as simple as two to three elements, such as a double pendulum (Shinbrot et al. 1992) or the three-body problem (Vasiliev and Pavlov 2017). One crucial characteristic of a complex dynamic system is its nonlinearity, which does not satisfy the superposition principle (Gudder 1970). In other words, the solution of a nonlinear system cannot be expressed as a linear sum of independent components. As Larsen-Freeman (2017) stated, "it is from the components and their relationships that the system we are trying to understand emerges. If we isolate components artificially, we lose the essence of the phenomena we are attempting to describe" (p. 29).

PRONUNCIATION AS A COMPLEX DYNAMIC SYSTEM

Pronunciation is a complex dynamic system. First, pronunciation encompasses multiple variables, including segmental (consonants and vowels) and suprasegmental features (intonation, stress, pauses, and rhythm). Second, the relationship among segmental and suprasegmental features is dynamic and nonlinear. Third, pronunciation is open and adaptive as learners constantly use environmental inputs to elaborate and further develop their pronunciation systems.

The complexity of the system of pronunciation can be investigated from multiple layers. The first layer consists of multiple sub-systems. For example, *sentence stress*, which is also commonly referred to as *primary stress* (Hahn 2004), *focus* (Grant 2006), *pitch accent* (Pierrehumbert 1980), *emphasis* or *prominence* (Celce-Murcia, Brinton, and Goodwin 2010) is a perceptual phenomenon associated with three pronunciation features—*pitch, duration, intensity,* and *vowel quality.* The expression of sentence stress, however, cannot be reduced to a simple combination of the changes of each of these features. For example, a stressed word typically has raised pitch level, increased intensity, and extended duration (Celce-Murcia, Brinton, and Goodwin 2010; Ito, Speer, and Beckman 2004). However, the relationship among these three features is not prescribed by a fixed rule or correlation. Even if such a correlation exists, say increase pitch by 30 percent if duration is increased 50 percent, learners would likely struggle to use the rule to signal sentence stress.

The complexity extends beyond the boundary of a sub-system. For instance, to use sentence stress appropriately, a user will need to address both its production and its placement. The former relates to other sub-systems at different levels—*word stress* or *stressed syllable* and the latter concerns pragmatic functions and information structure (Liu and Reed 2021). *Sentence stress* is also closely associated with intonation, which, in a narrower sense, describes "the use of pitch structure over the length of a given utterance" (Pickering 2018, p. 2) and in a broader sense, can be viewed as "the grammatical system that includes our use of pitch, pause, and prominence (or sentence stress) . . . (Pickering 2018, p. 3).

Viewed dynamically across time, the complexity of the pronunciation system exists at the second language development level. Specifically, the second language acquisition process has been researched as a complex and dynamic system (De Bot et al. 2007; Larsen-Freeman 2018) in which multiple variables—L1 (Larsen-Freeman 2006), identity (Sade 2009), motivation (Hiver and Papi 2019; Pigott 2012), and many others interact and shape learners' L2 dynamically.

CHALLENGES IN PRONUNCIATION
TEACHING AND LEARNING

Due to the complexity of the pronunciation system, pronunciation features can often be defined and understood from different perspectives. For example, scholars may choose different terms to denote a similar or the same pronunciation feature or sub-systems. What is referred to as *pitch accents* (Pierrehumbert 1980, Pierrehumbert and Hirschberg 1990) in research is often called *prominence, emphasis,* or *focus* in textbooks. The definitions of the same feature also vary. For example, Halliday (2015) stated that "intonation was analysed as a complex of three phonological systems, or (more accurately) systemic variables: tonality, tonicity and tone . . ." (p. 31). Levis and Wichmann (2015) defined intonation as "the use of pitch variations in the voice to communicate phrasing and discourse meaning in varied linguistic environments" (p. 139). Ladd (2008) used intonation to refer to "the use of suprasegmental phonetic features to convey 'postlexical' or sentence-level pragmatic meanings in a linguistically structured way" (p. 4). Bolinger (1989), with the focus on the paralinguistic aspect of intonation, stated that "Intonation manages to do what it does by continuing to be what it is, primarily a symptom of how we feel about what we say, or how we feel when we say" (p. 1).

The fact that different terms and definitions were used to represent similar concepts or phenomena derives from scholars' approaches and pursuit of precision. It also indicates the inherent complexity of the underlying system— there are multiple ways to analyze a phenomenon, depending on the contexts and the focus of the investigation. However, different terms and definitions may lead to varying conceptualizations of the system of pronunciation in teacher cognition. In an earlier study, we collected twenty-eight pronunciation related terms from fourteen empirical studies published between 2007 and 2016, three teacher training resource books (Celce-Murcia et al. 2010, Wells 2006, and Underhill 2005), and three student textbooks (Gilbert 2012, Grant 2016, Hahn and Dickerson 1999). These terms can be categorized by three themes: phrasing, prominence, and pitch contour.

Phrasing: Chunks, Phrasing, Tonality, Tone unit, Intonational phrases, Pauses
Prominence: Primary stress, Pitch accents, Focus, Nucleus, Stressed syllable, Unstressed syllable, Emphasis
Pitch Contour: Pitch contour, Final intonation, Pitch, Rhythm, Tune, Boundary tone, Pitch range, Phrase accents, F0, Prosody, Intonation, Melody, Key

We presented these terms to six experienced ESL teachers and asked them to put the same or related words together and explain the relationships among them. Teachers were generally consistent in their categorization of terms at the sub-system level. For instance, all participants categorized *primary stress*, *emphasis*, *stressed syllable*, and *unstressed syllable* in one category. However, we found significant variability in teachers' categorization and conceptualization of the selected terms, particularly at the large-scale pronunciation system level, as one pronunciation feature may be related to multiple concepts and features. One teacher, for example, put *pitch, pitch range, pitch accents*, and *pitch contour* together because they are all about *the pitch*. Another teacher associated *pitch* with *intonation, intonational phrases, tonality, final intonation, pitch accents, and pitch range* because they are closely related concepts.

Teachers' different categorization of terms reflects their conceptualization of the relationship among pronunciation features, which can be traced back to the complexity of the system of pronunciation. As one teacher shouted out loud when sorting the terms, "They are all kind of related!"

The question is: can we teach pronunciation features separately, and should we? The answer to the first half of the question is obvious—we can separate individual pronunciation features to a certain extent, and it is probably ben-

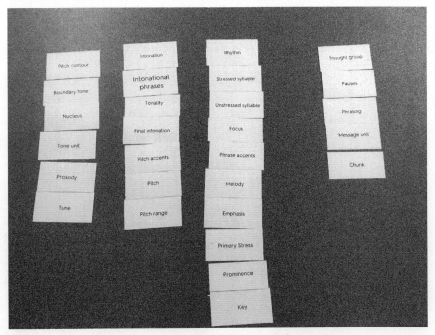

Figure 2.1. Sample teacher categorization of pronunciation terms.
Di Liu & Marnie Reed

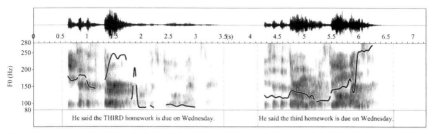

Figure 2.2. Waveform of the sentence "He said the THIRD homework is due on Wednesday." and "He said the third homework is due on WEDNESDAY."
Di Liu & Marnie Reed

eficial to focus on one feature when first introducing learners to the system of pronunciation. But it is not enough, as the interconnectivity among features makes it particularly challenging for learners to apply features learned in isolation to continuous speech. To use *sentence stress* in spontaneous speech, for example, learners need to manage all variables that are directly used to signal sentence stress and shift the whole intonation contour in a way that is consistent with the placement. In the sentence "He said the third homework is due on Wednesday" we can emphasize different words to carry different meanings. However, if we alter the placement of the emphasis, what gets changed is not only the word that is stressed but the whole intonation contour (See figure 2.2).

Although pronunciation features like *sentence stress* can be analyzed and taught as isolated sub-systems, features analyzed in isolation may be different from the same features used in a dynamic system. As De Bot, Lowie, and Verspoor (2007) stated when investigating second language development, "the system is in constant complex interaction with its environment and internal sources. Its multiple interacting components produce one or many self-organized equilibrium points, whose form and stability depend on the system's constraints" (p. 14). If we isolate the variables, we miss the essential connection between the feature we investigate and other interrelated features or processes used in spontaneous speech production. Further, as we discussed earlier, a complex system cannot be reduced to a combination of individual variables. Thus, even if learners can use a pronunciation feature in isolation, they could still have difficulties using it in a dynamic system—manifested as the lack of transferability from classroom examples to spontaneous speech.

PARADIGM SHIFT: FROM CAPT TO CBPT

One of the major questions that many teachers have is how to apply complexity theory in teaching practice. Our answer is technology. It is extremely difficult and time-consuming, if not totally impossible, for a teacher to monitor fifteen learners' use of a number of pronunciation features in their learning trajectories. Not to mention that some teachers need to teach a class with thirty or more students. Technology can assist teachers in managing the inherent complexity of the pronunciation system in language development.

Technology has already played an essential role in pronunciation teaching and research (Levis 2007; O'Brien et al. 2018). Specifically, automated speech recognition (ASR) has been used in pronunciation pedagogy for teaching (Elimat and AbuSeileek 2014), assessment (Cucchiarini and Strik 2018) and feedback (McCrocklin 2019; McCrocklin and Edalatishams 2020; Neri, Cucchiarini, and Strik 2001), speech visualization has been used to teach intonation (Hardison 2004; Levis and Pickering 2004), and text-to speech (TTS) has been used to provide models for language learners (González 2007; Mixdorff et al. 2009). Websites with high-variability phonetic training (HVPT) have been developed to expose learners to different varieties of segmental models, allowing learners to establish a more robust perceptual representation of segments (Thomson 2018).

The application of technology in pronunciation teaching, however, remains peripheral. While all existing technological tools effectively improve pronunciation teaching, systematic integration of technology in pronunciation teaching remains scarce. In other words, pronunciation teaching is still dominated by the computer-*assisted* pronunciation teaching (CAPT) model, in which technology is used optionally and occasionally. However, due to the inherent complexity of the subject matter and language development process, the role of technology is essential. Thus, we need a paradigm shift and creation of pedagogical and technological models under the computer-*based* pronunciation teaching (CBPT) framework.

COMPUTER-BASED PRONUNCIATION TEACHING

Computer-based pronunciation teaching (CBPT) requires innovations in multiple aspects, from teacher training to pedagogy. The following section lists some of the areas that would benefit from this paradigm shift, changes that we recommend, and potential technological resources.

Preparing Pronunciation Teachers with TPACK

One of the most influential areas in teacher cognition that has long been investigated is teacher knowledge. Shulman (1987) stated that "A teacher knows something not understood by others, presumably the students. The teacher can transform understanding, performance skills, or desired attitudes or values into pedagogical representations and actions. . . . Thus, teaching necessarily begins with a teacher's understanding of what is to be learned and how it is to be taught" (p. 7). In the past few decades, the role of technology in language teaching has become increasingly prominent. Built upon Shulman's (1987) seven categories, scholars have developed new systems categorizing and understanding teacher knowledge. One of the most influential frameworks is the technological pedagogical content knowledge (TPACK) framework developed by Mishra and Koehler (2009), which consists of three major components: Content Knowledge (CK), Technological Knowledge (TK), and Pedagogical Knowledge (PK). The overlap of these three categories leads to four other categories of knowledge including Technological Content Knowledge (TCK), Technological Pedagogical Knowledge (TPK), Pedagogical Content Knowledge (PCK), and Technological Pedagogical Content Knowledge (TPACK). TPACK is a general framework. To put it in the context of second language pronunciation teaching and learning will lead to a more specific definition of each of its components. Table 2.1 lists the components of the TPACK framework and the definition of each component in the context of pronunciation teaching.

In CBPT, the roles of TK, TCK, TPK, and TPACK become central. More supports in the form of workshops and courses are needed to help teachers in developing these categories of knowledge (Mainake and McCrocklin 2021). Efforts are also needed to translate research findings into optimal teaching practice using technological resources in teaching practice. For instance, when preparing teachers to teach segmental features, ideally teachers would be provided with knowledge about technological tools such as *English Accent Coach*[1] and *Google Voice Typing* to assess and improve learners' segmental perception and production. Teachers should also be given opportunities to discuss and develop pronunciation teaching lesson plans and curricula with systematic integration of technological tools, requiring them to develop TCK, TPK, and TPACK.

Using Short Videos to Address the Research-Practice Gap and Enhance Metalinguistic Awareness

The theory to practice gap has been recognized for half a century (Allen 1971; Levis 1999). Professional development funding for traditional delivery mechanisms like conferences is competitive and limited. Practitioner perceptions that research-oriented journals are conceptual but not practical limit their reach and impact. Short-form user videos such as TikTok can spark the inspiration for a series of short YouTube-like videos with embedded links to

Table 2.1. Definition of TPACK Components in the Second Language Pronunciation Context

Components	Definitions	Examples
Content Knowledge (CK)	Teachers' knowledge about the system of pronunciation, the sub-systems, and the related features.	A teacher understands that intonation is used primarily to describe the change of pitch but is also closely related to prominence, meaning, and pragmatic functions.
Pedagogical Knowledge (PK)	Teachers' knowledge about the methods and strategies in teaching pronunciation features.	A teacher knows to use a transcription system such as IPA for teaching segmental features.
Technology Knowledge (TK)	Teachers' knowledge about the technological resources in pronunciation teaching.	A teacher knows how to use *Praat* to visualize pitch.
Pedagogical Content Knowledge (PCK)	Teachers' knowledge about teaching methods, strategies, and techniques appropriate for teaching a particular pronunciation feature.	A teacher chooses to use rubber bands to teach stressed and unstressed syllables.
Technological Content Knowledge (TCK)	Teachers' knowledge about the correspondence between technological tools and the pronunciation features that the tools are targeting or could be used to address.	A teacher knows that *YouGlish* can be used to facilitate the teaching of connected speech processes.
Technological Pedagogical Knowledge (TPK)	Teachers' knowledge about the use of technological tools in optimizing teaching of a particular pronunciation feature.	A teacher uses *English Accent Coach* in teaching and assessing learners' perception of segmental features.
Technological Pedagogical Content Knowledge (TPACK):	Integration and optimization of strategies, approaches, and technological tools to facilitate the spontaneous production of pronunciation features.	A teacher systematically integrates multiple technological resources into the curriculum to assess, improve, and promote spontaneous production of speech.

Source: Di Liu & Marnie Reed

relevant research, which can be used as an alternative venue and enticement to access the scholarship.

Short videos can also be beneficial in the improvement of learners' metalinguistic awareness, which has been found by researchers to be a crucial aspect in pronunciation teaching (Liu 2018; O'Brien 2019; Reed and Michaud 2015). Without awareness of the importance of intonation and its functions, learners may "walk out of the class without having accepted the system at all. Or they may think intonation is simply decorative" (Gilbert 2014, p. 125). To date, it is still the teachers' responsibility to raise learners' metalinguistic awareness. Short videos have the potential to ease the burden from teachers in enhancing learners' metalinguistic awareness in widely accessible platforms such as *TikTok* and *Instagram*.

For example, the /j/ and /dʒ/ segmental difference can be illustrated with depiction of law school student presentations of Supreme Court profiles, declaring that all but one of the sitting Justices went to either Harvard or "jail." The link includes this quote: "The most important sounds are the ones that can change the meaning of words" (Carley and Mees 2021, p.1). Similarly, a short video as follows can be created to demonstrate the connection between intonation and meaning.

Setting:
- Classroom: Teacher at desk in front of a chalkboard
- Chalkboard: Agenda: Assignment due. See syllabus for Late Penalty

Characters:
- Student—requesting a homework extension
- Teacher—responding using affirmative words with implicational intonation

Scene

Student: (*Affect:* anxious; reads from excuse cards, concludes:) Can I turn in my assignment late?

Teacher: You *can. . .*

Student: (*Affect:* relieved) Thank you! (takes seat, all smiles)

Teacher: Looking confused (Wait . . . what ? ? ?)

Conclusion: Intonation carries meaning. "Intonation has the power to . . . undermine the words spoken" (Wichman 2005. p. 229)

Teaching Tip: Provide instruction that "teaches the student to think in terms of the speaker's intention in any given situation" (Allen 1971, p. 1)

Using Agile/Scrum as a Pedagogical Model

To manage the complexity inherent to pronunciation and language development, it is recommended that the Agile/Scrum model be used (Schwaber and Beedle 2002). The Agile/Scrum model originated in software development and has been widely adapted to many different fields including project management (Pries and Quigley 2010) and higher education (Jurado-Navas and Munoz-Luna 2017). It is characterized by a number of short cycles known as *Sprints*. In each *Sprint* cycle, the team optimizes one aspect of the product in a relatively short period of time (typically one or two weeks) and iterates the process to make continuous improvement to the product.

Suppose we want to build an automobile. We have two options. One way to do it is to design and optimize different parts separately and put them together at the end of the development cycle. Another way to do it is to develop a prototype that can run in the shortest time frame. Then, improve individual sub-systems and test them in the running car. The former is called a Waterfall Model (Petersen et al. 2009) and the latter is the Agile/Scrum model.

Similar to automobile manufacturing, pronunciation teaching can be done either by (1) separating different features and improving them in isolation, or (2) improving students' use of individual features within the interlanguage system (Selinker 1972). We recommend that teachers begin with learners' interlanguage system, focus on individual features in Sprints, and assess learners' use of pronunciation features within the system at the end of each Sprint (see figure 2.3).

As figure 2.3 shows, pronunciation teaching can be broken down into recursive Sprint cycles, each focusing on a sub-system such as vowels, intonation, stress, and chunking (thought groups). Each cycle begins with an individualized task-based assessment (discussed below). Based on the assess-

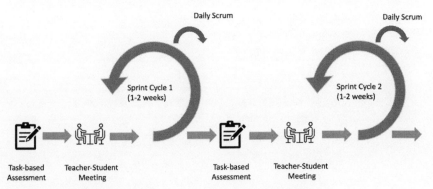

Figure 2.3. Agile/Scrum Sprint Cycle in Pronunciation Teaching
Di Liu & Marnie Reed

ment results, the teacher and student will meet and set up the objectives for the next Sprint. Each Sprint will take approximately 1–2 weeks with daily scrums focusing on smaller issues.

For example, in the pre-assessment, a teacher may identify that a learner has problems with some segments and also consonant clusters. Then, the teacher will design the first Sprint cycle targeting on the segments that have the highest functional load. The first Sprint cycle can focus on consonants and the first daily scrum can be, for example, distinguishing /l/ and /r/. Technological tools will be implemented with the focus on these two sounds. For instance, using *English Accent Coach* to train learners' perception of just /l/ and /r/. After the daily scrum, assessment on learners' spontaneous production will be conducted and the focus will move to another problematic area in the next daily scrum. The following Sprint cycle can focus on consonant clusters and the daily scrum can be /sk/ (school), /st/ (stop), etc. The Agile/Scrum approach differs from the current approach in several aspects:

1. The Agile/Scrum assesses students' spontaneous or extemporaneous speech and uses it as an indicator of learners' pronunciation development. Out-of-context practices of individual features are seen as scaffolding steps rather than developmental progress.
2. Pronunciation teaching is individualized in several ways: (a) errors are detected and analyzed based on individual students; (b) teaching is individualized by focusing on individual errors, contexts, and goals of learning; (c) Sprint cycles are individualized based on different errors and development.
3. Agile/Scrum breaks the barrier between classroom teaching and self-directed learning. Classroom time is used for strategic planning and awareness raising. Learners are encouraged to use technology for self-directed learning (Lai 2013).
4. The role of the teacher shifts from a model of pronunciation and a provider of exercises to an advisor and project manager who, based on his or her expertise, designs the optimal learning strategies and practical learning plans with learners.

Integrating Task-based Language Learning and Game-based Learning

The key to pronunciation teaching from a Complexity Theory perspective is spontaneous production. Teachers provide communication opportunities for students to reinforce and apply what they learn in class in order to transfer explicit knowledge to implicit skills. Task-based language teaching, which situates language teaching in particular tasks, is particularly suitable as a pedagogical approach, promoting "language learning by focusing not only on fluency but also on accuracy and complexity" (González-Lloret 2015, p. 4). The core of TBLT is a "task." That is: "A workplan that requires the learner to process language pragmatically in order to achieve an outcome that can be evaluated in terms of whether the correct and appropriate propositional content has been conveyed" (Ellis 2003, p. 16). Teachers may design teaching activities that facilitate language use. For instance, Willis (1996) proposed a three-stage model which includes a pre-task stage, a task cycle, and a language focus stage.

To implement TBLT, teachers need a platform. Games-based learning can provide a platform that is diverse and accessible to language learners. Researchers found that game-based learning increases learner motivation (Butler 2017; Li et al. 2021) and fosters flow, generally described as "a state of total mental engagement in an activity or endeavor" (Franciosi 2011, p. 12). Further, game-based learning provides a complex and dynamic virtual environment for meaningful interaction and communication, making it particularly suitable for TBLT. For instance, teachers may situate pronunciation teaching in Face-to-Face games, in which each student creates their avatar and completes tasks like ordering food, buying groceries, seeing a doctor, and meeting with a professor. Teachers can further enrich the learning experience by leveraging a virtual reality environment such as *Mondly VR*, which offers simulated task-based language learning experiences like checking into a hotel through pseudo-dialogs using ASR. Using game-based learning and TBLT, a teacher "engage[s] learners with the language in productive and creative ways and with a purpose beyond language practice per se" (González-Lloret 2015, p. 7).

Using Artificial Intelligence and Machine Learning for Stealth Pronunciation Assessment

The intelligibility principle (Munro and Derwing 1995; Munro and Derwing 2015) is one of the most fundamental and revolutionary changes in pronunciation teaching in the past 30 years. It has now become the gold standard for pronunciation teaching and assessment. While both researchers and teachers agree that mutual intelligibility should be the goal for pronunciation teaching, assessment in class remains an issue. Typically, intelligibility is measured by the percentage of correct words that native listeners write down and comprehensibility is determined by a seven- or nine-point Likert scaler judgment task with "1" being "extremely easy to understand" and "9" being "extremely difficult to understand" (Derwing and Munro 2005). It is not easy for teachers to implement in language classrooms because it is hard to find native speakers to transcribe students' speech and rate students' comprehensibility. What further complicates the issue is that raters' background characteristics, including their familiarity with the accent, content, attitudes, and linguistic awareness, can all influence the result of a judgment task. Thus, teachers' judgment may be biased because the teacher is familiar with their students (Yan and Ginther 2017).

Stealth assessment is "a methodology that utilizes machine learning (ML) for processing unobtrusively collected data from serious games to produce inferences regarding learners' mastery level" (Georgiadis et al. 2020, p. 180). As Shute (2011) stated, "[s]tealth assessment is intended to support learning and maintain flow, defined as a state of optimal experience, where a person is so engaged in the activity at hand that self-consciousness disappears, sense of time is lost, and the person engages in complex, goal-directed activity not for external rewards, but simply for the exhilaration of doing" (p. 504–505).

As discussed in earlier sections, automated speech recognition (ASR) has been used as an assessment and feedback tool and has the potential to be a tool for stealth assessment. For instance, teachers may ask students to use *Windows Speech Recognition* or *Google Voice Typing* in online teaching or a discussion activity. Students' speech will be automatically transcribed, and assessment can be done based on the transcript. However, because most ASR applications are not designed for pronunciation teaching, the feedback often focuses on segmental aspects, and suprasegmental feedback is insufficient (Garcia, Nickolai, and Jones 2020). Automated scoring systems are either bounded by the activities or language proficiency test evaluation criteria such as fluency and grammatical accuracy (Chen et al. 2018). Teachers need a system that has the following capabilities:

1. Allows teachers to conduct stealth assessments without interrupting the flow and pace of teaching and learning activities.
2. Assesses learners' intelligibility and comprehensibility in a way comparable to human raters.
3. Generates reports that help teachers to identify learners' errors on both segmental and suprasegmental features such as pitch, stress, and chunking.
4. Recommends learning strategies focusing on the errors and practice exercises.

CONCLUSION: ENVISIONING PRONUNCIATION TEACHING IN 10 YEARS

Due to the transient nature of speech, technology has been used to facilitate pronunciation teaching for many years. The complex and dynamic nature of the pronunciation system requires pronunciation to move one step forward from "Computer-Assisted Pronunciation Teaching" to "Computer-Based

Pronunciation Teaching." The CBPT model is a paradigm shift that includes changes in teacher training, awareness-raising, stealth assessment, game-based learning, and task-based learning. Recent development has already witnessed some of the changes (Okim, Johnson, and Kermad 2021). By situating pronunciation teaching in more extensive use of technology, pronunciation teaching will take a different form within 10 years. We envision the following:

1. Video skits on social media platforms will attract learners. These skits also increase learners' metalinguistic awareness of the importance of pronunciation, particularly suprasegmental features.
2. Teachers can use YouTube videos created by researchers in which pronunciation features are clearly defined and explained. Teachers can also watch the videos first and then explain them in class.
3. Learners' intelligibility and comprehensibility are assessed using stealth assessment tools based on machine learning and artificial intelligence, and teachers would not need to spend extra time designing and implementing pronunciation assessment activities. Teachers will be able to personalize learners' learning based on the assessment results.
4. Teachers use game-based and task-based language teaching within Sprint cycles to create meaningful contexts that lead to spontaneous language use.
5. Students are constantly assessed by the stealth assessment tool during each Sprint cycle. Reports with progress and areas that still need to be improved are generated. Teachers and learners review and discuss reports at the end of each Sprint cycle. Then, teachers and learners jointly decide the goals for the next Sprint and enter the next cycle. Learners' pronunciation is improved recursively.

This paradigm shift will require joint efforts from researchers, teachers, and software developers. We hope that this chapter can shed light on a potentially productive future avenue for pronunciation teaching.

NOTE

1. https://www.englishaccentcoach.com/.

REFERENCES

Allen, Virginia French. 1971. "Teaching intonation, from theory to practice." *TESOL Quarterly* 5, no.1: 73–81.

Bolinger, Dwight, and Dwight Le Merton Bolinger. 1989. *Intonation and its uses: Melody in grammar and discourse.* Stanford University Press.

Butler, Yuko Goto. 2017. "Motivational elements of digital instructional games: A study of young L2 learners' game designs." *Language Teaching Research* 21, no. 6: 735–750.

Carley, Paul, and Inger M. Mees. 2021. *American English Phonetic Transcription.* Routledge.

Celce-Murcia, Marianne, Donna M. Brinton, and Janet M. Goodwin. 2010. *Teaching Pronunciation: A Course Book and Reference Guide (2nd Ed.).* New York: Cambridge University Press.

Chen, Lei, Klaus Zechner, Su-Youn Yoon, Keelan Evanini, Xinhao Wang, Anastassia Loukina, Jidong Tao et al. 2018. "Automated scoring of nonnative speech using the speechrater sm v. 5.0 engine." *ETS Research Report Series* 2018, no. 1: 1–31.

Cucchiarini, Catia, and Helmer Strik. 2017. "Automatic speech recognition for second language pronunciation training." In *The Routledge Handbook of Contemporary English Pronunciation*, edited by Okim Kang, Ron I. Thomson, & John Murphy. 556–569. London: Routledge.

De Bot, Kees, Wander Lowie, and Marjolijn Verspoor. 2007. "A dynamic systems theory approach to second language acquisition." *Bilingualism: Language and Cognition* 10, no. 1: 7–21.

Derwing, Tracey M., and Murray J. Munro. 2005. "Second language accent and pronunciation teaching: A research-based approach." *TESOL Quarterly* 39, no. 3: 379–397.

Elimat, Amal Khalil, and Ali Farhan AbuSeileek. 2014. "Automatic speech recognition technology as an effective means for teaching pronunciation." *JALT CALL Journal* 10, no. 1: 21–47.

Ellis, Rod. 2003. *Task-based Language Learning and Teaching.* Oxford University Press.

Foster, John. 2005. "From simplistic to complex systems in economics." *Cambridge Journal of Economics* 29, no. 6: 873–892.

Franciosi, Stephan J. 2011. "A comparison of computer game and language-learning task design using flow theory." *Call-Ej* 12, no. 1: 11–25.

Garcia, Christina, Dan Nickolai, and Lillian Jones. 2020. "Traditional versus ASR-based pronunciation instruction: An empirical study." *Calico Journal* 37, no. 3: 213–232.

Georgiadis, Konstantinos, Giel van Lankveld, Kiavash Bahreini, and Wim Westera. 2020. "On the robustness of stealth assessment." *IEEE Transactions on Games* 13, no. 2: 180–192.

Gilbert, Judy B. 2012. *Clear Speech Teacher's Resource and Assessment Book: Pronunciation and Listening Comprehension in North American English.* Cambridge University Press.

Gilbert, Judy. 2014. "Intonation is hard to teach." In *Pronunciation myths: Applying second language research to classroom teaching*, edited by Grant, Linda. pp. 107–137. University of Michigan Press.

González, Dafne. 2007. "Text-to-speech applications used in EFL contexts to enhance pronunciation." *TESL-EJ* 11, no. 2: 1–11.

González-Lloret, Marta. 2015. *A Practical Guide to Integrating Technology into Task-based Language Teaching*. Georgetown University Press.

Grant, Linda. 2016. *Well said (4th Ed.)*. Cengage Learning.

Gudder, Stanley P. 1970. "A superposition principle in physics." *Journal of Mathematical Physics* 11, no. 3: 1037–1040.

Hahn, Laura D. 2004. "Primary stress and intelligibility: Research to motivate the teaching of suprasegmentals." *TESOL Quarterly* 38, no. 2: 201–223.

Hahn, Laura D., and Wayne B. Dickerson. 1999. *Speechcraft: Discourse Pronunciation for Advanced Learners*. University of Michigan Press.

Halliday, Michael Alexander Kirkwood. 2015. *Intonation and Grammar in British English*. De Gruyter Mouton.

Hardison, Debra M. 2004. "Generalization of computer assisted prosody training: Quantitative and qualitative findings." *Language Learning & Technology* 8, no. 1: 34–52.

Hiver, Phil, and Mostafa Papi. 2019. "Complexity theory and L2 motivation." In *The Palgrave Handbook of Motivation for Language Learning*, edited by Lamb, Martin, Kata Csizér, Alastair Henry, & Stephen Rya. pp. 117–137. Palgrave Macmillan, Cham.

Ito, Kiwako, Shari R. Speer, and Mary E. Beckman. 2004. "Informational status and pitch accent distribution in spontaneous dialogues in English." In *Speech prosody 2004, international conference*.

Jurado-Navas, Antonio, and Rosa Munoz-Luna. 2017. "Scrum Methodology in Higher Education: Innovation in Teaching, Learning and Assessment." *International Journal of Higher Education* 6, no. 6: 1–18.

Kaneko, Kunihiko. 2006. *Life: An introduction to complex systems biology*. Springer.

Kang, Okim, David O. Johnson, and Alyssa Kermad. *Second Language Prosody and Computer Modeling*. Routledge, 2021.

Koehler, Matthew, and Punya Mishra. 2009. "What is technological pedagogical content knowledge (TPACK)?." *Contemporary Issues in Technology and Teacher Education* 9, no. 1: 60–70.

Kwapień, Jarosław, and Stanisław Drożdż. 2012. "Physical approach to complex systems." *Physics Reports* 515, no. 3–4: 115–226.

Ladd, D. Robert. 2008. *Intonational phonology*. Cambridge University Press.

Lai, Chun. 2013. "A framework for developing self-directed technology use for language learning." *Language Learning & Technology* 17, no. 2: 100–122.

Larsen-Freeman, Diane. 2006. "The emergence of complexity, fluency, and accuracy in the oral and written production of five Chinese learners of English." *Applied Linguistics* 27, no. 4: 590–619.

Larsen-Freeman, Diane. 2017. "Complexity theory: The lessons continue." In *Complexity Theory and Language Development*, edited by Ortega, Lourdes, and Zhaohong Han. 11–50. Amsterdam: John Benjamins.

Larsen-Freeman, Diane, and Lynne Cameron. 2008. *Complex Systems and Applied Linguistics*. Oxford: Oxford University Press.

Larsen-Freeman, Diane. 2018. "Second Language Acquisition, WE, and language as a complex adaptive system (CAS)." *World Englishes* 37, no. 1: 80–92.

Levis, John M. 1999. "Intonation in theory and practice, revisited." *TESOL Quarterly* 33, no. 1: 37–63.

Levis, John. 2007. "Computer technology in teaching and researching pronunciation." *Annual Review of Applied Linguistics* 27: 184–202.

Levis, John, and Lucy Pickering. 2004. "Teaching intonation in discourse using speech visualization technology." *System* 32, no. 4: 505–524.

Levis, John M., and Anne Wichmann. 2015. "English intonation—Form and meaning." *The Handbook of English Pronunciation,* edited by Reed, Marnie, and John Levis. 139–155. West Sussex, UK: Wiley-Blackwell.

Li, Rui, Zhaokun Meng, Mi Tian, Zhiyi Zhang, and Wei Xiao. 2021. "Modelling Chinese EFL learners' flow experiences in digital game-based vocabulary learning: The roles of learner and contextual factors." *Computer Assisted Language Learning* 34, no. 4: 483–505.

Liu, Di. 2018. "Leveraging Metalinguistic Awareness and L1 Prosody in the Learning of L2 Prosody: The Case of Mandarin Speakers Learning English Sentence Stress." PhD diss., Boston University.

Liu, Di, and Marnie Reed. 2021. "Exploring the complexity of the L2 intonation system: An acoustic and eye-tracking study." *Frontiers in Communication* 6: 51.

Liu, Yang-Yu, and Albert-László Barabási. 2016. "Control principles of complex systems." *Reviews of Modern Physics* 88, no. 3: 035006.

Loscalzo, Joseph, Isaac Kohane, and Albert-Laszlo Barabasi. 2007. "Human disease classification in the postgenomic era: a complex systems approach to human pathobiology." *Molecular Systems Biology* 3, no. 1: 124.

Mainake, Eugenie, and Shannon M. McCrocklin. 2021. "Indonesian Teachers' Perceived Technology Literacy for Enabling Technology-Enhanced English Instruction." *New Horizons in English Studies* 6.

McCrocklin, Shannon. 2019. "Dictation programs for second language pronunciation learning: Perceptions of the transcript, strategy use and improvement." *Konińskie Studia Językowe* 7, no. 2: 137–157.

McCrocklin, Shannon, and Idée Edalatishams. 2020. "Revisiting popular speech recognition software for ESL speech." *TESOL Quarterly* 54, no. 4: 1086–1097.

Mitchell, Melanie. 2006. "Complex systems: Network thinking." *Artificial Intelligence* 170, no. 18: 1194–1212.

Mixdorff, Hansjörg, Daniel Külls, Hussein Hussein, Shu Gong, Guoping Hu, and Si Wei. 2009. "Towards a computer-aided pronunciation training system for German learners of Mandarin." In *ISCA International Workshop on Speech and Language Technology in Education Development (2009)* edited by Luo, Dean, Nobuaki Minematsu, Yutaka Yamauchi, and Keikichi Hirose.

Munro, Murray J., and Tracey M. Derwing. 1995. "Foreign accent, comprehensibility, and intelligibility in the speech of second language learners." *Language Learning* 45, no. 1: 73–97.

Munro, Murray J., and Tracey M. Derwing. 2015. "Intelligibility in research and practice: Teaching priorities." *The Handbook of English Pronunciation* edited by Reed, Marnie, and John Levis. 375–396. West Sussex, UK: Wiley-Blackwell.

Neri, Ambra, Catia Cucchiarini, and Helmer Strik. 2001. "Effective feedback on L2 pronunciation in ASR-based CALL."

O'Brien, Mary Grantham. 2019. "Attending to second language lexical stress: Exploring the roles of metalinguistic awareness and self-assessment." *Language Awareness* 28, no. 4: 310–328.

O'Brien, Mary Grantham, Tracey M. Derwing, Catia Cucchiarini, Debra M. Hardison, Hansjörg Mixdorff, Ron I. Thomson, Helmer Strik et al. 2018. "Directions for the future of technology in pronunciation research and teaching." *Journal of Second Language Pronunciation* 4, no. 2: 182–207.

Ottino, Julio M. 2004. "Engineering complex systems." *Nature* 427, no. 6973 (2004): 399–399.

Petersen, Kai, Claes Wohlin, and Dejan Baca. 2009. "The waterfall model in large-scale development." In *International Conference on Product-Focused Software Process Improvement*. 386–400. Springer, Berlin, Heidelberg.

Pickering, Lucy. 2018. "*Discourse intonation*." Ann Arbor, MI: University of Michigan Press.

Pierrehumbert, Janet Breckenridge. 1980. "The phonology and phonetics of English intonation." PhD diss., Massachusetts Institute of Technology.

Pierrehumbert Janet and Julia Hirschberg. 1990. "The meaning of intonational contours in the interpretation of discourse." *Intentions in Communication* 271.

Pigott, Julian. 2012. "A call for a multifaceted approach to language learning motivation research: Combining complexity, humanistic, and critical perspectives." *Studies in Second Language Learning and Teaching* 2, no. 3: 349–366.

Pries, Kim H., and Jon M. Quigley. 2010. *Scrum project management*. CRC Press.

Reed, Marnie, and Christina Michaud. 2015. "Intonation in research and practice: The importance of metacognition." *The Handbook of English Pronunciation* edited by Reed, Marnie, and John Levis. 454–470. West Sussex, UK: Wiley-Blackwell.

Sade, Liliane Assis. 2009. "Complexity and identity reconstruction in second language acquisition." *Revista Brasileira de Linguística Aplicada* 9, no. 2: 515–537.

Schwaber, Ken, and Mike Beedle. 2002. *Agile Software Development with Scrum*. Vol. 1. Upper Saddle River: Prentice Hall.

Selinker, Larry. 1972. "Interlanguage." *International Review of Applied Linguistics* 10: 209–231.

Sheard, Sarah A., and Ali Mostashari. 2009. "Principles of complex systems for systems engineering." *Systems Engineering* 12, no. 4: 295–311.

Shinbrot, Troy, Celso Grebogi, Jack Wisdom, and James A. Yorke. 1992. "Chaos in a double pendulum." *American Journal of Physics* 60, no. 6: 491–499.

Shulman, Lee. 1987. "Knowledge and teaching: Foundations of the new reform." *Harvard Educational Review* 57, no. 1: 1–23.

Shute, Valerie J. 2011. "Stealth assessment in computer-based games to support learning." *Computer Games and Instruction* 55, no. 2: 503–524.

Thomson, Ron I. 2018. "High variability [pronunciation] training (HVPT): A proven technique about which every language teacher and learner ought to know." *Journal of Second Language Pronunciation* 4, no. 2: 208–231.

Underhill, Adrian. 2005. *Sound foundations*. Macmillan Education.

Vasiliev, N. N., and D. A. Pavlov. 2017. "The computational complexity of the initial value problem for the three body problem." *Journal of Mathematical Sciences* 224, no. 2: 221–230.

Yan, Xun, and April Ginther. 2017. "Listeners and raters: Similarities and differences in evaluation of accented speech." *Assessment in Second Language Pronunciation,* edited by Kang, Okim and April Ginther: 67–88. Oxford, England: Routledge.

Wells, John Christopher. 2006. *English intonation: An introduction*. Cambridge University Press.

Willis, Jane. 1996. "A flexible framework for task-based learning." *Challenge and Change in Language Teaching* 52: 62.

Part 2

WEB-BASED RESOURCES, TOOLS, AND LANGUAGE-LEARNING PLATFORMS

Chapter Three

Preparing Second Language Educators to Teach Pronunciation with Technology

Lara Wallace and Julia Choi

INTRODUCTION

The rise of pronunciation teaching and research has grown in tandem with the accessibility of technology for language teaching (Levis 2007, 184–202; Thomson & Derwing 2015, 338–340). While pronunciation has traditionally received less focus than other language skills—commonly decried as the Cinderella of its sister-skills, it recently has become "The Belle of the Ball" in applied linguistics in terms of the attention it has gotten in research and teaching methods (Derwing 2019, 17–25). Nonetheless, while there is a growing consensus that intelligibility and comprehension can be improved through explicit teaching (Lee, Jang, and Plonsky 2014, 353–363; Thomson & Derwing 2015, 338), there is often a disconnect when it comes to applying research to the classroom (Couper 2017, 836–837; Levis 2016, 425). While many researchers agree that, theoretically, pronunciation should be part of the language curriculum, many second language teachers are still finding ways to practically incorporate it into their classrooms (Couper 2017, 820–843; Jones 2016, xi). The following chapter aims to reflect on the choices of teachers in training as they learn to teach pronunciation and utilize technology to do so.

REVIEW OF THE LITERATURE

Pronunciation teaching has received more attention in research in recent years, but it is still often underprioritized in the second language classroom (Jones 2016, xi). The reasons pronunciation may be omitted from a language curriculum are complex. First and foremost, teachers may feel underqualified to teach pronunciation and lack confidence in their ability to model good pronunciation (Couper 2017, 829–831; Levis et al. 2016, 894–931; Sardegna 2020, 232). This may be especially true for non-native ESL teachers, although research has found that both native and non-native teachers can be successful in improving second language (L2) students' pronunciation (Levis et al. 2016, 910–914). Additionally, many second language teachers feel that they have received inadequate training in pronunciation teaching (Couper 2017, 829–831). Couper (2017, 835–837) found that these gaps in knowledge can lead to teachers neglecting or even avoiding pronunciation teaching. Even when teachers do receive training in pronunciation, the focus may be more theoretical than pedagogical (Couper 2017, 830; Murphy 2018, 303–304). ESL teacher training programs may include courses on phonetics or phonology but likely lack classes on applying knowledge of pronunciation to practical teaching. However, teachers are not the only ones who struggle with focus on pronunciation during language education classes.

Further barriers to teaching pronunciation include time constraints and student attitudes toward practicing pronunciation in class. While second language acquisition theory has recently favored "intelligibility" as a goal over sounding like a native speaker, unrealistically high standards for production may intimidate learners (Levis et al. 2016, 914–915; Murphy 2014, 259). Students might feel self-conscious practicing in front of their classmates and receiving public judgment on their speaking (Fouz-González 2015, 316). Motivation to improve pronunciation may also be lowered by repetitive and outdated classroom activities. Despite effective and engaging practice activities such as shadowing (Foote & McDonough 2017, 44–47), mirroring (Meyers 2018, 1–2), and voice over (Henrichsen 2015, 272) classroom exercises may be limited to "outdated" (Carey, Sweeting, and Mannell 2015, 22) listen and repeat activities that do little to motivate the learners. A final consideration is that improving pronunciation does not only require a knowledgeable teacher, but it also calls for opportunities for students to practice extensively (Thomson & Derwing 2015, 331). These time constraints, learner hesitation, and need for engaging speaking activities call for creative and novel approaches to teaching pronunciation.

A solution to the anxieties of both teachers and students regarding pronunciation in the classroom could be using technology effectively in support of pronunciation learning. Computer assisted pronunciation teaching (CAPT) has long been viewed as a practical solution to ESL pronunciation training (Levis 2007, 184–202). Teaching pronunciation with technology has many benefits including extended opportunities for learners to produce language and access to tools that can visualize sound (O'Brien et al. 2018, 183–195). Computer assisted pronunciation training also offers the opportunities for learners to practice privately, overcoming some of the anxieties L2 learners experience when speaking in a classroom setting (Fouz-González 2015, 316). Teaching pronunciation with technology also provides benefits to educators. Through using YouTube videos, authentic audio materials, and recording devices, teachers can not only provide learners with a variety of input, but also have more time to assess their students' pronunciation (Fouz-Gonzalez 2015, 316–319; O'Brien et al. 2018, 183). For both learners and teachers, if used correctly, CAPT may make pronunciation pedagogy more user-friendly and less anxiety-inducing. As risk taking has long been considered an essential part of language learning (Rubin 1975, 46), CAPT has the potential to make risk taking and creativity safer for both students and teachers.

Despite its potential, CAPT is not without its challenges. The process requires training for both the learners and the teachers (Hubbard 2013, 165; Kessler & Hubbard 2017, 278). Hubbard (2013, 164–165) suggests that learner training is necessary to maximize the effectiveness of a Computer Assisted Language Learning (CALL) tool. Language teachers should also not assume that all learners have the technological proficiency to incorporate CAPT seamlessly into their language learning (Hubbard 2013, 165). Like learners, teachers also require tech training and an openness to adapt to the rapidly changing field of CALL (Kessler & Hubbard 2017, 285–287). Finding the specific tech tool for a class may require some trial and error. Although many technological tools exist for language teachers to try, not every available tool has pedagogical value (Fouz-González 2015, 330). This suggests second language teachers may benefit from having freedom to explore tech tools and try them out before they are implemented in the classroom. A final essential consideration in using technology in a classroom is that regardless of how ubiquitous it may seem in our lives, access to technology is not necessarily universal. The COVID-19 pandemic brought light to the digital divide that exists in education. In 2020, research showed that 17 percent of high school students in the United States were unable to complete homework for online classes because they lacked the proper technological tools (Anderson and Perrin 2020). When selecting pronunciation tools for a classroom, it is important for a teacher to envision the process from the perspective of a learner. By considering the technological limitations of learners and the necessity of learner training, language teachers may be able to incorporate technology into their classes more seamlessly.

Research has established that both pronunciation and technology play important roles in the language learning classroom (Derwing 2019, 17–25; Levis 2007, 184–202; O'Brien et al. 2018, 194–199; Thomson & Derwing 2015, 1–20). However, research into second language teacher cognition has shown that more teacher training specific to pronunciation would be useful for improving confidence and competency in pronunciation teaching (Couper 2017, 829–831). The current study explores the intersection between technology and pronunciation in a language teacher course. While current research has suggested that technology tools have a valuable role to play in pronunciation teaching (Fouz-Gonzalez 2015, 316–319; O'Brien et al. 2018, 183), few studies have examined how using technology in the classroom influences teachers' confidence in pronunciation teaching. Additionally, more research into how teachers choose technology and the challenges they face while implementing it into pronunciation lessons may be valuable to both teachers and teacher training programs.

THE STUDY

The current study aims to examine how MA students in a pedagogical phonology class incorporated technology into their pronunciation teaching after a half semester of theory and training. Specifically, we analyze their experiences in choosing and using technology as both teachers and learners in a half-semester project called the Private Teaching and Learning Experience (PTLE). By considering their choices—what worked and where they struggled—more teachers may be encouraged to bring pronunciation into the classroom, and teacher trainers can better equip them to do so.

Research Questions

The questions that guided this study were:

RQ 1: Which instructional technology tools did the student teachers use for both teaching and learning pronunciation?
RQ 2: Which uses of technology did the student teachers find the most effective for pronunciation teaching?
RQ 3: What challenges did participants face with technology?
RQ 4: What were the student teachers' opinions regarding their skills and confidence of teaching pronunciation with technology after taking the course?

METHODOLOGY

Participants

The participants were graduate students in a two-year Linguistics MA program at a midwestern state university in the United States. All of them graduated with their degree and both a CALL and TEFL (Teaching English as a Foreign Language) certificate. They were required to take the Pedagogical Phonology course in their final semester. Of the fourteen students enrolled in the course, ten students consented to participate in the current study but only eight were able to complete interviews after their graduation. To allow for proper triangulation of data, only the data from the eight participants were used.

These eight participants were between the ages of 25 and 37 and were from seven different countries: China (Tynn), Colombia (Chirru), Ghana (Bodhi), Iraq (Jen), Jordan (Cassi), South Korea (Galen), and two from the United States (Bazey and Lyra) (names are pseudonyms). Before beginning the MA program, all of them had experience teaching English in some capacity (tutor, teacher, college instructor) with the total years of experience ranging from three to nine years. Some had experience teaching their native languages as well. On the topic of pronunciation, only Bazey, the participant who had been teaching for nine years and was CELTA certified, had experience and felt prepared to teach pronunciation; the rest had no notable pronunciation teaching training beyond professional development workshops. For those who did have some experience, it was limited to choral repetition.

Course Design and Assignments

The Pedagogical Phonology course focused on the teaching of English pronunciation and honored the diversity of its students by applying pedagogical concepts to teaching and learning in other languages as well. This flexibility was particularly important since there were multiple foreign language TAs in the class and not all students planned on teaching English as a profession.

Because of COVID, the course met online only. The live, synchronous classes were twice weekly: one day was for discussion of concepts, the communicative framework presented in the textbook (*Teaching Pronunciation* by Celce-Murcia, Brinton, and Goodwin 2010), and other relevant readings and videos. The second day was used to build practical skills. Discussion days centered around the students' doubts and delights from the material that they viewed before. Practical days relied heavily on participation and were used for teaching demonstrations and Tech Show and Tell. While students were credited for attendance, their teaching demonstrations were ungraded to encourage risk-taking and learning.

Technology was infused throughout the course. Discussion of how technology for teaching pronunciation could be integrated into teaching, the importance of teacher familiarity with tech, and learner training were frequent topics. Tech was a feature of both the teacher-led and the student-led demonstrations in the practical classes. In the final third of the semester, a class was dedicated to a Tech Show and Tell, where each student shared an app or tool for learning, discussing how it could be used along with its benefits and limitations. These tech tools were then added to the course resource list on the Learning Management System (LMS). Finally, students were required to incorporate technology into the private teaching and learning experience project (PTLE).

There were three graded items in the course: the Applied Experience Project (AEP), the midterm, and PTLE. For the AEP, students applied what they learned in the course toward something that could advance their career or further their understanding. Two participants wrote tech reviews that they submitted for publication (Bazey on Screencastify and Galen on SpeakPulse), Cassi and Tynn wrote conference proposals that incorporated technology and pronunciation into their language classrooms, and Bodhi wrote a concept paper around technology in pronunciation teaching. The remaining two participants chose tech-free projects (a book review and a case study).

Throughout the second half of the semester, participants paired up for a private teaching and learning experience project (PTLE) in which they became both teacher and student. This was done to synthesize their experience in a personal way and expand their skills as teachers by exploring how to use technology to support their partner's pronunciation learning. As teachers, they conducted a needs assessment. This then informed their design and delivery of four lessons in which they were required to meaningfully incorporate technology into half of these lessons. They reflected on the teaching process throughout both privately and as part of the forms that they submitted. As learners, they wrote student-perspective reports and reflected on each lesson, also privately and as part of a submitted form. The project culminated in a creative synthesis demonstration in which they explored and integrated these experiences, expressing how their pronunciation teaching may be shaped moving forward.

Data Collection and Analysis

This is an intrinsic case study on the experiences of Linguistics MA students' technology use for teaching pronunciation as part of the required Pedagogical Phonology course during Spring semester 2021. Intrinsic case studies, according to Stake (2005, 443–445), are conducted to understand the specific experiences of participants in a case, without seeking to generalize. This is appropriate for the current study as it is exploratory in nature. "Technology" here broadly encompasses CALL (Computer-Assisted Language Learning), CAPT (Computer-Assisted Pronunciation Teaching), and any app or electronic tool used for teaching, whether on a computer, tablet, or smartphone. The researchers analyzed data from the individual PTLE assignment forms that participants submitted as electronic documents and transcribed interviews with individual participants that were conducted a month after completing the course.

To gather data ethically from these class assignments, IRB protocol was observed.[1] Students were given the option to sign an informed consent form at the beginning of the study. The form and the principal investigator (P.I.) (also the instructor of the course) made it clear that participation in the study was independent of their grades, that there was nothing additional that participants needed to do during the semester, and they were free to decide whether to participate in the interview that would take place after the grades for the semester were submitted. Data was anonymized.

The primary source of data collection and analysis were the interviews. Transcriptions of the audio were completed by Otter.ai and corrected by the researchers as they were prepared for coding. Data was then aggregated categorically and assigned codes for direct interpretation. The researchers analyzed these data for emergent themes by searching for "recurring regularities in the data," distinguishing them from data that diverged, following Patton's discussion of coding and classifying in qualitative research (Patton 2002, 465–466). They then checked for consistency by triangulating these findings with instructor's (the P.I.'s) private notes from the course, notes taken during the interviews, and the other data that participants submitted as part of the class—specifically, the PTLE written assignment and synthesis demonstration (done with partners, many of whom did not participate in the study, so only some of these were examined), and finally with the participants themselves. This final step was for member checking. Glesne (2006, 38) defines "member checking" as sharing the results with the participants to make sure that the researchers "represent[ed] them and their ideas accurately."

Researcher Positionality

The authors have unique perspectives and positions related to this study. Wallace designed and instructed the Pedagogical Phonology course with the intention of technology being an integral part of these student teachers' formation. Choi was a student in the course who, upon being asked to participate in the study, also expressed interest in joining as a researcher at the conclusion of the semester. Since the course was taught remotely in the participants' final semester, Choi's role was also instrumental in the ability to maintain contact with participants to secure and jointly conduct the follow-up interviews after graduation.

RESULTS

RQ 1: Technology Tools Used for Teaching and Learning

Participants made use of a trove of technology. Following are the technology instructional tools they found useful, classified by their uses for teaching and learning:

Curated Content and Created Materials

- EnglishCentral
- Fluent American YouTube channel
- LearnAkan.com
- Playaling
- Self-created materials with Google Suite, Office 365, Camtasia, Zoom
- Tech tutorials
- YouGlish
- YouTube

Participants found it helpful to use ready-made resources as content, when possible, although more often they created their own materials. For instance, participants appreciated the PowerPoints that their PTLE teachers created both during class and for something to refer to afterward. These slides often included images and diagrams from the internet, tongue twisters, and more. Cassi explained her use by saying "some students wouldn't get it, but if they see it, they would understand—especially visual learners. And it's also useful as a reference, if they want to practice again, they can just like have the slides and check them later." Of her PTLE partner's use of PowerPoint slides, she described them as "really interactive, because he would have it written and then we would listen to the audio. And then he would ask which sound it is." Galen created an instructional video of the Korean vowels. His reason was:

> It's kind of like showing them instead of telling them. Um, so I think it's a bit more effective than [lecturing]. What I'm saying is just giving them an opportunity to just receive the idea more in a visual way. It'll be useful for visual learners, and auditory learners because I'm speaking, I'm narrating.

Videos featured into many lessons. While participants found videos from many different sources such as YouGlish and Playaling (for Arabic), Bazey turned to a trusted source. "Having worked with Geoff Anderson before, I trusted the thoroughness of the Fluent American video content and was pleased with how well Chirru engaged with it." Her partner concurred, saying "Bazey used an excellent video of a guy who she worked with and has appropriate videos for my level." Videos were also useful for tech tutorials, and there are many pre-made tutorials available. Jen notes that with these tutorials, "you don't have to worry if you are struggling with something—it's fine. There's something else to help you. You just have to learn how to use it."

Models of Authentic Speaking

- Edpuzzle
- Playaling (Arabic)
- Speech Accent Archive
- YouGlish
- YouTube
- podcasts

Apart from instructive content, videos and other sources were used as models of authentic speaking. With YouGlish, Jen explained that "You just type the word and you have the chance to hear it in many different Englishes." With Playaling, another source of videos with interactive captions, Cassi noted that "You can choose the level of the students and the dialect and everything. So it's easier to find something that matches your needs."

Focused Listening Resources

- Breaking News English
- EnglishCentral
- EnglishClub
- EnglishForEveryone

When participants wanted resources they could use for focused listening, they utilized several freely available sources. Jen used English Club with her PTLE partner because

Both [my partner] and I are not (native speakers)—we are both learning English. So, when it comes to complicated sounds that we both don't have in our first language, we thought we need to listen to them or hear them. And English Club helped us to—it gives you many minimal pairs.

Practice Opportunities

- Extempore
- Flipgrid

- LyricsTraining
- SpeakPulse
- TikTok
- VoiceThread

Participants used many apps that were capable of recording and listening back. For instance, Jen used Flipgrid as a way for students to practice new vocabulary and speak Arabic, and Bodhi asked his partner to read aloud. Extempore, Flipgrid, TikTok, and VoiceThread allowed for peer feedback from classmates. Advantages of VoiceThread, as Chirru noted, were that it was "useful, powerful, and accessible," accessible in that it comes with the university's LMS. SpeakPulse gave automated feedback based on certain criteria. LyricsTraining was mentioned by Bazey as a way to practice, but she did not elaborate on how she used it.

Visualizing Sound

- Audacity
- Praat
- SketchTogether

Visualizing sound was important, and there were a few apps that visually depicted what learners and teachers were hearing. Audacity and Praat both show time elapsed, sound waves, and amplitude, and Praat goes farther by showing pitch contours and formants. Only one participant used Praat for such purposes. Here's how Bazey used it with a student:

> [students] Focus on saying their name as if they are different members of their family. Like, "say your name as if you were your dad.". . . if it's a female student, she'll like deepen her voice and make it louder. For example, "say your name as if you were angry." And so, it's a repeated phrase that students can play with and it's really low-stakes, and then the next time we work with it, I'll say, "Alright, let's have you give the opening sentence of your presentation, and we'll look at what it looks like. In terms of your wave form, it is close, and all your words run together."

Visualizing letters and characters that represent sounds was also important, and several participants used SketchTogether, a virtual online drawing board. Cassi found it useful as a teacher because she learned from her experience as an Arabic teacher that keyboards can be difficult to use for beginners. She added, "You can analyze everybody's writing at the same time," and her partner, Galen, appreciated being able to "track students' progress," though he noted that a downside was "using the track pad if a stylus was unavailable." This app was particularly useful for remote teaching.

Assessment, Feedback

- Edpuzzle
- ELSA Speak
- Extempore
- Flipgrid
- Kahoot!
- Quizizz
- SpeakPulse

To test perception and comprehension, participants used Edpuzzle, Kahoot!, and Quizizz. Of Kahoot!, Galen explained that "it's fun and engaging. Instead of just me speaking out, like, in a planned way, and then checking, I think it's fun to make it a little competition or game. And it's simple enough to use Kahoot! with minimal pair activity itself was not so complicated." Google Docs and Google Forms were also used for quizzes and needs analyses.

For production assessments, Extempore, Flipgrid, and SpeakPulse were used. The first two are designed for easy teacher feedback on recordings. On the differences between Flipgrid and Extempore, Galen opined that "[Flipgrid] was similar to Extempore but with more focus on design. The website is quite well organized and is very pleasing to the eye. I enjoyed being able to record myself and receive video or written feedback from my teacher."

SpeakPulse, on the other hand, gives users automated feedback. Galen tried SpeakPulse to help him prepare for an upcoming job interview. He described using it like this: "The prompt comes up. After 30 seconds, you record for a minute. And then that's it. You get feedback. It's an excellent tool, but it's not without limitations." ELSA Speak is another AI-powered app that gives feedback on pronunciation, and Chirru chose it for her Tech Show and Tell, but because there is a cost to the app, it was not received with enthusiasm by the class.

RQ 2: Effective Uses of Technology for Teaching

To understand how technology was used effectively, the researchers examined the participants' reflections in the PTLE and the interviews. Following are the hallmarks of effective tech use.

Scaffold Pronunciation Learning

Several participants were clear in their appreciation of technology to support curricular goals. Bazey reflected on her PTLE partner's use of it:

> The lesson was delivered over Zoom and the content was mostly on a slide deck, with a Flipgrid at the beginning. Chirru also had some great videos and several audio samples that we worked on and used in class. We also used a Google Form that was set up as a practical assessment to work on recognition and production of word stress. It was really amazing—I felt that, rather than the technology feeling shoe-horned into the lesson for its own sake, her use of technology was really seamless, and everything worked very well together. The flow was intuitive, and each element supported the objectives.

Tynn shared a similar sentiment: "From my perspective, all the technologies used in [the PTLE] went well and were necessary. The teacher did not use the technology for the sake of using technology, but the technology that he picked really helped me learn."

A key element to the seamless and purposeful use of tech was the quality of teacher instruction regarding how to use it. Many participants mentioned teachers creating or providing tutorials and giving examples. In this way, learners could more easily familiarize themselves with the new tech. Galen credited his teacher's "clear directions with sample videos of herself introducing her own family members" as part of the seamless use in a Swahili lesson, for example.

Another often-mentioned purposeful use of technology was to visualize sound. Visualization took many forms, such as diagrams of what the mouth is doing for certain phonemes or a visual explanation of clapping on the beat for phrasal stress. Some of the more experienced participants worked with Audacity and Praat to make word stress and fillers visible, or to imitate and compare production of stress patterns to a model speaker. For the participants teaching Arabic and Korean pronunciation, sound to written form correspondence was important. Galen explained that his objective, for example, "was for [learners] to produce the vocabulary which contained that consonant," which was written in Korean. He also did this activity with vowel sounds using SketchTogether to help learners to visualize the sounds. Participants appreciated how effective such visual representations were in aiding their understanding and facilitating production.

Engage Students in Collaboration

Participants noted that technology was important for promoting engagement and collaboration. Whether through writing sounds in another language on SketchTogether, playing a Kahoot!, working with interactive videos in Edpuzzle, recording videos in Flipgrid, or creating TikTok duets/stitch ups, participants found ways to make learning enjoyable. Two apps that deserve more explanation are SketchTogether and TikTok.

Regarding SketchTogether—it was well received by the entire class during a teaching demonstration on Korean sounds. Galen, the teacher, would pronounce the sound, and the learners would write it, or the teacher would write the letter and they would say the sound. From his perspective as a teacher, he found the app to be "engaging and very effective because the students could write with me as I guided them through [Korean] character description."

Another use of tech that was engaging was using TikTok. In his teaching reflection, Tynn said that his partner enjoyed it, and both had fun. They used the Duet feature, which is a split screen of the original video that Tynn created on one side and the student's video on the other. As the teacher, Tynn recorded Speaker A and left time for Speaker B's response. His partner recorded the duet, finishing the conversation asynchronously. Tynn described another way he used it—for repetition: "I read, and I leave like three or four seconds and students follow. It['s] really easy." He and his partner chose to make the videos public, and to do well, his partner "realized how many times he needed to practice before shooting the videos—not just for pronunciation but also for timing and lighting, and so on." Afterward, they could read comments from other TikTok users.

Conduct Assessments

Participants relied on technology to assist in many types of assessments and feedback. Following are several effective uses, beginning with needs analyses.

For PTLE, Bazey found a way to conduct a needs analysis through Google Forms:

> The needs analysis that Chirru used to learn about my goals and assess my skills was delivered through Google Forms. It was quite involved, and even asked some questions I hadn't thought about. I appreciated it so much that that was how I decided to deliver my needs analysis.

Of Bazey's use, her partner Chirru wrote: "Bazey used Google Forms to learn about my goals, objectives, and previous knowledge. It was engaging, challenging, and well structured. I enjoyed answering all the questions."

Tech was also used to conduct formative assessments. One notable example comes from Tynn's student reflection:

In the third lesson, Quizizz was added in addition to the technology used in previous lessons. Quizizz was used as an assessment to see if the student can catch the stressed syllable in a sentence.

The importance of self-assessment and how technology can facilitate was often mentioned. With Flipgrid video recordings, for example, Jen explained that "[Learners] know their weak point. Maybe later they'll work on it. So at least they know what is the problem. . . . And they can keep the videos and see how much they could improve or their speaking throughout the semester." Bazey appreciated the video lessons Chirru designed, saying "to be able to have native production that I could hear, so then myself as a student that I could hear, and then immediately respond to, and then have, again, immediate native production come back to me, that was lovely."

Technology also facilitated peer feedback. Jen used Flipgrid in her Arabic class for this purpose, putting students into mixed-speaking ability groups of four for the semester. Each week, the groups had a speaking assignment, and they gave each other feedback. She would comment on the group's work. She found that this way to assess was more comfortable for her as a teacher and for the students. It was also less time-consuming for her since providing individual feedback is time-consuming.

Using TikTok was an innovative way to crowd source feedback from people outside of the course. Tynn's partner agreed to make his videos public on TikTok. While his partner did not participate in this study, Tynn shared:

I feel like the experience I had with [my partner] was pretty successful. Because in our TikTok videos, his pronunciation was so good that some of my Mandarin-speaking friends on TikTok be like, "this is so good. Like he's very talented and the pronunciation was very accurate."

Access Authentic Speech Samples

Finding models of authentic speech was important to several participants, regardless of language taught and whether it was their first language. They felt that these models effectively exposed learners to varieties of speech. Bazey believed that "As language teachers, we are horrible examples of native-like production, because we're . . . aware of all the stuff that we do." Lyra echoed this, explaining that she felt that her production seemed inauthentic when modeling words in isolation as she was asked to do when teaching in Japan. And when teaching Akan, Bodhi had a similar realization, so he helped his partner to notice the target phonemes in a video, to listen for, as he said, "how the sounds actually are articulated in normal speech, because what I was doing with him was . . . kind of artificial." Teachers accessed a variety of speaking models, whether to provide more "authentic" models to address the concerns raised above, an alternative demonstration for teachers who struggled with certain pronunciation features, or simply to provide a variety of samples across multiple dialects. From the student end, these models were used effectively, as in this example that Bazey reported:

> The videos Chirru used as both a demonstrative example of the target language, and as interactive materials allowed me to practice . . . I came to hear the differences between my much more American speech patterns (rhythm and intonation) and the patterns that are more native-like in Spanish . . . Chirru went out of her way to use several different Hispanic-accented examples

Participants also noted that videos were memorable. Jen explained that when using videos, her students had an easier time remembering those they enjoyed, such as videos from famous TV shows and movies. Lyra similarly concluded their usefulness after her engaging teaching demonstration using a clip from a TV show to notice intonation.

RQ3: Challenges with Technology

Accessibility

The participants in this study were fortunate to have access to their own laptops, mobile devices, and reliable wireless internet connection. Nonetheless, they did experience discouraging problems like losing connection in the middle of a Kahoot!, which they pointed out could be unfair if the Kahoot! is for credit and finding that not everything worked on all devices and operating systems. Latency was also an issue, especially when layering multiple items in a remote session, as Bazey and her partner tried doing in their remote sessions. While recording themselves repeating after a YouTube video—the sound became "garbled." Finally, for some apps like ELSA Speak and Speak-Pulse, the free versions were rather inconvenient and limited, making it clear that cost is another potential barrier to accessing tech.

Difficulty with Using Tech

Whether it was Audacity, Praat, or Flipgrid, participants acknowledged the importance of learning how to use it and how to teach students how to use it. For instance, Cassi worried about tech difficulties; nonetheless, she had found a way to reduce her stress:

> I always worried about what if it doesn't work and if students don't enjoy in the beginning, but I am patient and realize that it takes time for me and learners to

learn and become comfortable using it. Always have a Plan B in case it doesn't work and don't feel guilty.

Limitations of Using Tech

While useful, technology was not essential for all pronunciation teaching. For example, Galen rightly explained that "having a tissue in front of you [to demonstrate] aspiration was much more effective than me telling them or using anything else . . . it is quite hard to use technology with that." Videos were not always the answer either. Several participants remarked that despite the massive number of videos available through sites like YouGlish and Edpuzzle, it was difficult to find appropriate videos for their needs, so they ended up demonstrating production themselves. By contrast, Bodhi was teaching Akan and had the opposite problem. He said there was a

> scarcity of resources for learning Akan. . . . Even with the YouTube videos, I have my own problems with them. That's one of the things that we [teachers of less-commonly taught languages] might find—is that the resources to even leverage on are just a few.

Thus, for all of the benefits that technology can provide, technology was not always the answer. Besides, as Bazey concluded, "Ultimately, we use language to interface with humans. So the fact that we use language in technology is great, but it's not the same."

Time was a major factor when tech use was needed; especially regarding remote teaching, time was an issue. It took many participants longer than they would like to train learners in using the technology, and they remarked that the training took away from the valuable teaching and practice time. For example, even with what he thought was a straightforward app, Galen found that he

> needed to let [students] know where they can click to choose the pen type and coloring and everything. So even though it seemed easy to me, sometimes I think it is necessary to teach them how to use it at first.

Despite the engaging nature of how participants used technology, those participants who were language teachers indicated that student reticence was another challenge. One such example was learners' hesitance to show their faces in videos. The teachers explained that in life, it is necessary to interact with others, and encouraged their students to use the practice opportunities to help gain comfort with this. Some participants attributed this reticence to having "shy" or "introverted" learners. Jen and Cassi found that utilizing tech, such as incorporating asynchronous speaking practice, was effective with their Arabic students, helping them participate more comfortably. Chirru, on the other hand, suspected that her Spanish students' reticence was tied to their grades. She observed after trying a few approaches with VoiceThread as a way of rehearsing that she needed to give students credit for their efforts, or they would not do it.

Whether a learner or teacher, part of this reticence could be explained by aversion to embarrassment, as Lyra explained: "[In the teaching demonstrations,] many classmates tried new things and it didn't always go smoothly. I still felt kind of embarrassed, but overall it was a really supportive environment." She recognized that some teachers, including her PTLE partner, wanted to stick with what they found comfortable, and lamented that "it's OK to use what you are comfortable with, but because this was a low-stakes environment, it would have been good to try a few different things!"

RQ4: Skills and Confidence in Teaching Pronunciation with Technology

In their interviews, participants reported on improvements to their pronunciation teaching skills. One participant, Lyra, credited "learning in a safe environment with explicit permission to fail" for her improvement, explaining that fear of failure "is what often stops [teachers] from using it in class—so easy to fail and so embarrassing." For participants whose L1 was not English, they found that technology could support their teaching, especially when they struggled with certain sounds like "back vowels," as Jen pointed out.

This freedom to experiment also increased their comfort level with using technology, as evidenced by a benefit that Bodhi pointed out:

> I wasn't that comfortable [using technology with teaching pronunciation] before the MA program, and I realized that teaching with tech makes teaching very easy and relieves the teachers of a lot of burden. The more you incorporate tech, the more learners can use what you are using—even in your absence, like with YouGlish they can go back and hear the videos on their own, leaving them with something memorable.

Regarding an improvement in using technology for pronunciation teaching, the results were divided into those who felt an improvement and those who were already comfortable with using technology in teaching before the course. For the six whose comfort level improved, they credited experiencing the tools during the in-class teaching demonstrations and Tech Show and Tell, particularly because their peers shared what they enjoyed using themselves. Participants also began to shift their attitudes constructively, like Cassi who said, "I always tell myself not to feel guilty about it [tech not working or students not liking tech] because you can't control everything. You can't." This kind of attitude is both helpful and necessary for risk taking as a teacher. For the two who were already comfortable using technology, both conceded that they learned new ways to use technology and new apps, like Extempore and SpeakPulse.

It seems that this freedom plus explicit instruction in a structured format of pronunciation pedagogy along with opportunities to experience it as both learners and teachers helped participants to improve their confidence in the topic and using the technology to teach it. Here are some of the highlights participants shared:

> "I enjoyed PTLE because one of the most important things was to share with each other—we got triple the technology. As a teacher, I learned how to teach others to use it in the class, and from students' perspective I also got to know what kinds of demonstrations didn't work." —Tynn

> "[PTLE] made me reconsider how I pre-teach. I realize how much pre-teaching is necessary to use the tools." —Lyra

> "Teaching English, the instructor must understand students' needs, struggles, and L1 background to [teach] successfully. . . . The private teaching is really the best thing in pronunciation class. I enjoyed doing this a lot. And I believe [my partner] enjoyed this too." —Jen

IMPLICATIONS FOR TEACHING AND TEACHER TRAINING

The experiences of these Linguistics MA students' technology use for teaching pronunciation as part of the required Pedagogical Phonology course, although not generalizable, certainly give researchers, practitioners, and program developers some compelling points to consider.

The Value of Synthesis: Teaching from a Learner's Perspective

An important takeaway for second language teachers is to consider their lessons from the perspective of a learner. Several of the participants in the current study stated that their experience as a learner was valuable in becoming a more competent pronunciation teacher. After the course, the participants understood which topics were important to teach and how to do so beyond simple modeling. This was made easier because of their fresh experiences as learners. It is with this unique dual perspective of teacher and student that the participants shared their struggles and successes with using technology for pronunciation teaching. For language teachers incorporating new pronunciation and technology into their classrooms, it is highly recommended that they experience instruction not only as a teacher, but also as a student.

Teachers should also consider not only what is effective, but also what is engaging to learners. The field of second language learning has recently started to reflect on the value of everyday technology in language learning (Fouz-González 2017, 650–663). From the student experience, apps like Flipgrid and TikTok provide engaging 24/7 access to practice opportunities that they can do whenever they like, with or without sharing them with others. Having such tasks increases practice opportunities without increasing risk of judgment or non-comprehension from others, different from face-to-face interactions with others (Wallace 2015, 264). While further research is needed to fully understand the value and challenges of these applications in language learning, the current study suggests that they are engaging and motivate students.

The Value of Preparation: Mitigating Risks to Maximize Learning

While the current study suggested that technology is a valuable tool for teaching pronunciation, participants also reported several challenges. Preparation is essential for anticipating the struggles and mitigating the necessary risks of using technology in the classroom:

- *Prepare for access or lack thereof:* Even in a classroom of graduate students experienced in online learning, access to applications and a reliable wireless network were occasional challenges. To prepare for this, teachers should survey their students about access to Wi-Fi and devices. When accessibility is lacking, teachers can offer institutional solutions to these problems such as accessing wireless networks in known locations and finding places where students can check out devices.
- *Prepare to evaluate tech-tools:* As suggested by Fouz-González (2015, 330), not all tech tools are useful in teaching. Discerning when technology is helpful, rather than a hindrance, is essential.
- *Prepare extra time:* Extra time is often necessary when using a tech-tool. Beyond the possibility of unreliable internet and lagging devices, teachers must also familiarize themselves with the tech they wish to use, and help learners understand how to use it. Applying Hubbard's (2004, 64) principles for learner training by sharing and modeling tech use with their students will help.
- *Prepare synchronous and asynchronous practice activities:* The current study supported previous research that suggested tech-tools provide a

valuable chance for students to practice privately (Fouz- González 2015, 316). Through preparing asynchronous activities, instructors can provide all learners with opportunities to practice, especially if they do not participate much in class.

• *Prepare a safe classroom atmosphere:* The current research supported past research that has suggested risk taking is beneficial to language learning (Rubin 1975, 46). To boost risk-taking and class participation, it is crucial that the instructor prioritizes and creates an atmosphere that facilitates trust-building, teamwork, and respectful behavior.

Teacher Training: Taking Risks

The current course was designed to train language teachers in pronunciation instruction through encouraging experimentation and reflection. The trial-and-error nature of the course encouraged the participants to experiment with new technologies and teaching methodologies. Rubin (1975) promoted risk taking as a quality of a good language learner and, in this case, it also encouraged growth in language teachers. Between insecurities about being an authentic speech model, the ephemeral nature of the spoken phrase, and challenge of how to apply theory to practice, teaching pronunciation comes with unique obstacles (Couper 2017, 829–831; Levis et al. 2016, 894–931). Therefore, pronunciation teaching program planners should encourage and reward risk-taking by giving teachers in training opportunities to teach and reflect so that they can learn from their struggles and successes as a group.

CONCLUSION

Certainly, technology can be a powerful ally in providing the tools that both learners and teachers need to understand and implement pronunciation in the classroom. Through their experiences in a pedagogical phonology course where technology was a central tool, interacting as both learners and teachers while learning fundamental concepts, these participants gained the skills and the confidence needed to help learners speak to be understood. They used a wide variety of tech to effectively support their efforts: for assessment and feedback of student needs, to ways to address these needs in practical ways through curated content, authentic speech models, focused listening practice, practice opportunities for listening and speaking, and visualizing sound. Along the way, they experienced struggles and successes that readers can look to as they explore new ways to teach pronunciation using technology.

NOTE

1. Ohio University's Office of Research Compliance granted approval to project number 21-E-16.

REFERENCES

Anderson, Monica, and Andrew Perrin. 2020. "Nearly One-in-Five Teens Can't Always Finish Their Homework Because of the Digital Divide." *Pew Research Center*. Pew Research Center. May 30. https://www.pewresearch.org/fact-tank/2018/10/26/nearly-one-in-five-teens-cant-always-finish-their-homework-because-of-the-digital-divide/.

Carey, Michael David, Arizio Sweeting, and Robert Mannell. 2015. "An L1 Point of Reference Approach to Pronunciation Modification: Learner-Centred Alternatives to 'listen and repeat.'" *Journal of Academic Language and Learning* 9 (1):A18–A30. https://journal.aall.org.au/index.php/jall/article/view/339.

Celce-Murcia, Marianne, Donna M. Brinton, and Janet M. Goodwin. 2010. *Teaching Pronunciation: A Course Book and Reference Guide*. 2nd ed. Cambridge: Cambridge University Press.

Couper, Graeme. 2017. "Teacher Cognition of Pronunciation Teaching: Teachers' Concerns and Issues." *TESOL quarterly* 51, no. 4: 820–843. https://doi.org/10.1002/tesq.354

Derwing, T. M. (2019). Utopian goals for pronunciation research revisited. In J. Levis, C. Nagle, & E. Todey (Eds.), *Proceedings of the 10th Pronunciation in Second Language Learning and Teaching conference*, ISSN 2380-9566, Iowa State University, September 2018 (pp. 27–35). Ames, IA: Iowa State University.

Foote, Jennifer A., and Kim McDonough. 2017. "Using Shadowing with Mobile Technology to Improve L2 Pronunciation." *Journal of Second Language Pronunciation* 3 (1): 34–56. https://doi:10.1075/jslp.3.1.02foo.

Fouz-González Jonás. 2015. "Trends and Directions in Computer-Assisted Pronunciation Training." Essay. In *Investigating English Pronunciation: Trends and Directions*, edited by Jose A. Mompean and Fouz-González Jonás. Basingstoke, Hampshire: Palgrave Macmillan.

Fouz-González, Jonás. 2017. "Pronunciation Instruction through Twitter: The Case of Commonly Mispronounced Words." *Computer Assisted Language Learning* 30 (7): 631–63. https://doi:10.1080/09588221.2017.1340309.

Glesne, Corrine. 2006. *Becoming a Qualitative Researcher: An Introduction*. 3rd ed. Boston, MA: Allyn and Bacon.

Kessler, Greg, and Philip Hubbard. 2017. "Language Teacher Education and Technology." Essay. In *The Handbook of Technology and Second Language Teaching and Learning*, edited by Carol A. Chapelle and Shannon Sauro, 278–92. Hoboken, NJ: John Wiley & Sons, Inc.

Henrichsen, L. 2015. "Video voiceovers for helpful, enjoyable pronunciation prac-
tice." In *Proceedings of the 6th Pronunciation in Second Language Learning and
Teaching Conference* edited by John Levis, R. Mohammed, M. Qian & Z. Zhou
(Eds), (pp. 270–276). Ames, IA: Iowa State University.

Hubbard, Phil. 2004. "Learner Training for Effective Use of CALL." Essay. In *New
Perspectives on Call for Second Language Classrooms*, edited by Sandra Fotos and
Charles Browne, 38–62. Mahwah, NJ: L. Erlbaum Associates.

Hubbard, Philip. 2013. "Making a Case for Learner Training in Technology Enhanced
Language Learning Environments." *CALICO Journal* 30 (2): 163–78. https://
doi:10.11139/cj.30.2.163-178.

Jones, Tamara. 2016. "The Gap Between the Integration of Pronunciation and Real
Teaching Contexts." In *Pronunciation in the Classroom: The Overlooked Essential*,
xi-xii. Alexandria, VA: TESOL Press.

Lee, Junkyu, Juhyun Jang, and Luke Plonsky. 2014. "The Effectiveness of Second
Language Pronunciation Instruction: A Meta-Analysis." *Applied Linguistics* 36, no.
3: 345–66. https://doi.org/10.1093/applin/amu040.

Levis, John. 2007. "Computer Technology in Teaching and Researching Pronunciation." *Annual Review of Applied Linguistics* 27: 184–202. https://doi.org/10.1017
/s0267190508070098.

Levis, John M. 2016. "Research into Practice: How Research Appears in Pronunciation Teaching Materials." *Language Teaching* 49 (3): 423–37. https://doi:10.1017
/s0261444816000045.

Levis, John M, Sinem Sonsaat, Stephanie Link, and Taylor Anne Barriuso. "Native
and Nonnative Teachers of L2 Pronunciation: Effects on Learner Performance."
TESOL quarterly 50, no. 4 (2016): 894–931. https://doi.org/10.1002/tesq.272

Meyers, Colleen. 2018. "Mirroring: A Top-down Approach to Pronunciation Instruction." *Pronunciation for Teachers*. http://www.pronunciationforteachers.com
/teaching-techniques.html.

Murphy, John M. 2014. "Intelligible, Comprehensible, Non-Native Models in ESL/
EFL Pronunciation Teaching." *System* 42: 258–69. https://doi:10.1016/j.system
.2013.12.007.

Murphy, John M. 2018. "Teacher Training in the Teaching of Pronunciation." Essay.
In *The Routledge Handbook of Second Language Pronunciation,* edited by Okim
Kang, Ron I Thomson, and John M Murphy, 1st ed., 298–319. Milton Park, Ox-
fordshire: Routledge.

O'Brien, Mary Grantham, Tracey M. Derwing, Catia Cucchiarini, Debra M. Hardison, Hansjörg Mixdorff, Ron I. Thomson, Helmer Strik, et al. 2018. "Directions for
the Future of Technology in Pronunciation Research and Teaching." Journal of Second Language Pronunciation 4 (2): 182–207. https://doi:10.1075/jslp.17001.obr.

Patton, Michael Quinn. 2002. Qualitative Research and Evaluation Methods. 3rd ed.
Thousand Oaks, CA: SAGE.

Rubin, Joan. 1975. "What the 'Good Language Learner' Can Teach Us." TESOL
Quarterly 9 (1): 41–51. https://doi:10.2307/3586011.

Sardegna, Veronica. "Pronunciation and Good Language Teachers." Essay. In Lessons from Good Language Teachers, edited by Carol Griffiths and Zia Tajeddin, 232–45. Cambridge, MA: Cambridge University Press, 2020.

Stake, Robert. 2005. "Qualitative Case Studies." Essay. In The Sage Handbook of Qualitative *Research*, edited by Norman K. Denzin and Yvonna S. Lincoln, 3rd ed., 443–66. Thousand Oaks, CA: Sage Publications.

Thomson, R. I., and T. M. Derwing. 2015. "The Effectiveness of L2 Pronunciation Instruction: A Narrative Review." *Applied Linguistics* 36 (3): 326–44. https://doi:10.1093/applin/amu076.

Wallace, Lara. 2015. "Reflexive Photography, Attitudes, Behavior, and Call: ITAs [International Teaching Assistants] Improving Spoken English Intelligibility." *CALICO Journal* 32 (3): 449–79. https://doi:10.1558/cj.v32i3.26384.

Chapter Four

Designing and Evaluating an e-Teaching Package of English Phonetics and Pronunciation for Preservice Teachers

Hsueh Chu Chen and Jing Xuan Tian

INTRODUCTION

The role of pronunciation in conducting successful communication in English cannot be disputed, and it is suggested that pronunciation should be considered a key component in English teaching (Bakar and Abdullah 2015). However, the teaching of pronunciation has largely been neglected in English classes (Cox et al. 2019; Foote, Trofimovich et al. 2013; Gilakjani and Ahmadi 2011). Online pronunciation teaching, in particular, has faced problems, with previous studies reporting that online teaching lacks interaction and supervision due to the distance between teachers and students (Dumford and Miller 2018; Hampel 2006).

Given the need to find better ways to teach phonetics and pronunciation courses online, this study aims, firstly, to design an e-teaching package including several digital education tools with different goals for an English phonetics and pronunciation course; secondly, to create a two-way communication environment; and lastly, to evaluate the effectiveness of this online package.

Challenges of Online Teaching

Previous studies have reported a lack of supervision and interaction in online classes (Guichon, Bétrancourt, and Prié 2012; Hampel 2006). Teacher supervision in a normal class has different definitions. According to previous studies (De Pry and Sugai 2002; Haydon and Kroeger 2016), active supervision in class includes 1) moving among students and focusing on the problems that students may have; 2) keeping an eye on students' appropriate and inappropriate behaviours; 3) interacting with students; and 4) providing comments frequently.

Guichon, Bétrancourt, and Prié (2012) reported that giving feedback is the main teacher-student interaction, but it is challenging when teaching through videoconferencing tools because of the distance between teacher and learner. In Guichon et al.'s study, negative written and oral feedback was given to 18 upper-intermediate students after they had received online training. The feedback, however, still required the instructor and the student to have a one-to-one pedagogical interaction in a chatroom. Even though the feedback was shown to be effective, it was not found to be suitable for online subject knowledge courses aimed at enhancing learners' productive skills because the feedback was provided in small groups (one trainee paired with two students or one-to-one interaction). Having a one-to-one or one-to-two interaction is unachievable if there are 20 or more students in an online class. Alzamil (2021) investigated Saudi students' attitudes toward L2 online speaking practice and whether their online speaking learning experiences are effective in mastering English speaking. Results of this study revealed that the majority of participants shared concerns about receiving teachers' feedback in online speaking classes.

Creating an environment that facilitates two-way communication is important for online teaching (Mischel 2019), especially for those classes aiming to teach productive skills such as pronunciation. Previous studies provide teaching tips for creating successful online learning environments. For example, Thompson and Savenye (2007) and Hrastinski (2008) pointed out that boosting learner participation is effective in creating successful online learning environments. Hrastinski (2009) suggested that different types of activities, such as competitions and collaboration, should be included to support learner participation. Peer interaction has also been shown to be a significant aspect of online teaching (Aghaee and Keller 2016; Lai et al. 2019; Robson 2016).

Digital Education Tools in Language Teaching

In the new era of language teaching especially in recent years with the development of new technologies, tools were designed to help build effective online teaching. Digital education tools have been designed to facilitate and encourage collaboration and communication between teachers and learners. Different types of digital education tools (e.g., Padlet, Edpuzzle) have been developed and applied in English teaching. However, they have mainly been applied in teaching vocabulary or writing instead of speaking or pronunciation (e.g., Perevalova, Resenchuk, and Tunyova 2020; Shahriarpour 2014; Zou and Xie 2018).

For example, Zou and Xie (2018) developed a technology-enhanced just-in-time and peer instruction model, using two different types of digital education tools, assessment-centred and cloud-based tools, to cultivate English as a foreign language (EFL) learners' writing skills, motivation and critical thinking ability. The results of their study proved that the model and the application of digital education tools, which can be employed in language classes widely, are effective in enhancing learners' writing skills, motivation, and the tendency toward critical thinking. Perevalova, Resenchuk, and Tunyova (2020) applied digital education tools (i.e., Quizlet) into vocabulary in the English for specific purposes (ESP) context, which aims to help learners enlarge professional English vocabulary, and participants reported that the tools improved their satisfaction in ESP study.

Kahoot has also been used in teaching and learning in previous studies, and researchers suggested that Kahoot should be used in the language classroom. For example, Chiang (2020) examined 65 students' perceptions of using Kahoot in English reading class and discovered that the use of Kahoot can help build a fun learning environment. Both male and female participants enjoyed using this tool. Tao and Zou (2021) investigated 80 students' perceptions of using Kahoot in the EFL context. Results of this study revealed that participants expressed a positive attitude toward the application of Kahoot, and their motivation and learning effectiveness were enhanced. Orcos et al. (2018) proposed and suggested that it is an effective digital education tool that can help teachers to design in-class activities and enhance learners' participation. However, no audio files or video files can be uploaded to Kahoot and used as materials. Kahoot can only be used to help participants consolidate their content knowledge, not cultivate their productive skills.

Li and Suwanthep (2017) investigated the effectiveness of the digital education tool Edpuzzle on vocabulary and grammar in the speech of EFL learners in Thailand. Positive results were reported, and participants had overall better performance in the speaking test after training. Participants also expressed a positive attitude toward the experience they had. However, Edpuzzle in this study was used in a flipped classroom, and the authors reported that the lecturer could not ask immediate questions when learners viewed the materials on the platform. In the current study, Edpuzzle is used as a tool for the recap at the end of each training session. Most importantly, questions related to the topics of the video were embedded, and learners could answer questions while watching the videos.

Fewer studies have been conducted to investigate the application of digital education tools to speaking or pronunciation teaching. Mei, Huang, and Zhao (2021) instructed an e-tool, *Clip*, which can provide automatic feedback, and encouraged language teachers to apply this e-tool in language teaching and learning. However, there were challenges to this e-tool, and inaccurate feed-back was one of the significant challenges. Pourhosein and Rahimy (2020) examined the application of the software Pronunciation Power to help Japa-nese English learners to improve their English pronunciation. Participants in their study showed a positive attitude toward the software and, among those who used it, illustrated significant pronunciation improvement. Automatic speech recognition (ASR) tools have also been applied in pronunciation teaching. The software Talk to Me which provides language learners with automatic feedback was used by Hincks (2005). The results revealed that the feedback on the quality of participants' pronunciation received from the ASR tool was more effective in improving low-level students' pronunciation than the feedback they received from their instructor. Spring and Tabuchi (2021) applied an ASR-based pronunciation tool, NatTos, in the online pronunciation teaching context, with 98 Japanese English learners as participants. NatTos was applied in an online pronunciation teaching context, and intermediate-level participants' intelligibility and articulation rates improved. What is more, participants reported that the digital education tool helped improve the segmental features of pronunciation.

THE CURRENT STUDY

Online language teaching has become common because of the COVID-19 pandemic. In the past two years, the new normal has seen teachers teach-ing from their home office. In the post-pandemic society, using e-tools to strengthen students' learning and improve teaching quality is necessary (Bautista-Vallejo et al. 2020). Teaching via an online video-conferencing platform (e.g., Zoom, Google Meet) has become a daily routine for many language classes (Ying, Siang, and Mohamad 2021). The studies mentioned above show that the pronunciation teaching was mainly conducted in face-to-face classrooms or outside the classroom before the pandemic of COVID-19, and digital education tools were regarded as just one component of the class or as a teaching aid. Very often, only one tool or resource was incorporated into pronunciation teaching. Chen and Tian (2022) introduced several digital education tools with different purposes for online pronunciation teaching.

Few studies have investigated how to use a variety of digital education tools to teach different course topics in phonetics and pronunciation to fit the online teaching context. We also know little about the effectiveness of digital education tools in a subject knowledge course, such as a phonetics and pro-nunciation course, instead of a pure skill-based pronunciation training course. In the former course, the theory and practice of the course content are expected to be integrated. The current study will further develop an e-teaching package and evaluate the digital education tools in such a subject knowledge course. Recap videos on English vowels, consonants and word stress were developed using Edpuzzle. For review purposes, learners answered questions embedded in the recap videos of each topic while watching them after each session. Written feedback was prepared, and participants received written feedback after answering each question. Quizzes on English word stress were developed on Nearpod, and different authentic materials (e.g., video clips) were used to help learners better understand word stress. Participants performed group activities and shared helpful tips and answers to questions proposed by the instructor on Padlet and Mentimeter. In-class quizzes were designed using Kahoot, and learners competed with their classmates, helping to consolidate the knowledge learned in class and to motivate learners. Two additional features were included to enhance teacher supervision: 1) teachers' support in helping learners solve problems and 2) students' completion of assigned tasks. Interactions among students and between teachers and students via digital education tools were also investigated. The use of different digital education tools to boost interactions was analysed. The provision of feedback to students as a group was employed, in addition to one-to-one feedback.

This study aims to address two research questions:

1. To what extent does the e-teaching package help Chinese preservice teachers to improve their English pronunciation and subject knowledge of English phonetics?
2. What are Chinese preservice teachers' attitudes toward the application of the e-teaching package?

METHODS

Participants

Forty preservice teachers in a university in Hong Kong were recruited to participate in a pre-test. These were Chinese EFL learners majoring in English language education. They had been learning English for over ten years and were intermediate-to-advanced level learners. After the pre-test, they were randomly assigned to two groups, the control group (CG) and the experimental group (EG). One participant from the CG dropped out after the pre-test. In total, 19 participants were in the CG and 20 in the EG. All of the 39 participants took the post-test and filled out a questionnaire after the training. Ten participants from each group voluntarily attended the follow-up interviews.

Procedure

Five stages of data collection were conducted in this study: a pre-test, a five-week online course in English phonetics and pronunciation instruction, a post-test, a survey, and follow-up interviews. For the pre-test and post-test, all participants completed a reading aloud task with a word list containing all English consonants and vowels. In order to evaluate English word stress, di- and multi-syllabic words were used in the reading aloud task. Their performances on English vowels, consonants, and word stress were evaluated, and the two groups were compared. Since there were only five training sessions, only one suprasegmental feature was included. Listener judgment is used in the current study. A PhD student majoring in Phonetics and Phonology who had received training in Phonetics and Phonology over four years and has rich experiences in evaluating English pronunciation analysed the reading aloud data of the current study.

In the five-week training session, which included an introduction to the English sound system, the English letter-sound relationship, English vowels, English consonants, and English word stress, both groups received three hours of training per week via Zoom. The teaching content for both groups was the same. Participants in the control group received PowerPoint presentations with Zoom functions (e.g., chat, poll functions). Different functions provided by Zoom were used throughout the training session, with the aim of conducting an interactive online pronunciation teaching class. Participants were encouraged to use the chat function to ask questions and interact with other learners. They were also encouraged to raise their hands to answer questions posed by the instructor. The instructor also used the poll function of Zoom to enhance teacher-student interaction and investigate learners' background knowledge of English phonetics. Learners were also assigned to different rooms randomly to perform group work and to discuss with their peers the questions posted by the instructor. Paper-based tutorial tasks on the topic of each session, which aims to help participants consolidate the knowledge learned in each training session (e.g., fill in the blank: cheap ·tʃ_p·) were used for the CG group participants. For participants in the EG, an e-teaching package was developed and incorporated into the training session. Chat and poll functions were only used in the training session to maintain smooth PowerPoint presentations with Zoom. The teaching content and activities used in both groups are listed in figure 4.1.

Five digital educational tools (e-tools hereafter) with different aims were included in this e-teaching package: Edpuzzle, Nearpod, Padlet, Mentimeter and Kahoot. Screenshots of the tasks designed by these five e-tools can be found online.[1]

Session	Control group	Experimental group
1. Introduction to the English sound system	1. Introduction to the English sound system 2. Paper-based tutorial tasks on the English sound system	1. Introduction to the English sound system 2. Padlet: to share learners' opinions of difficult sounds that they encounter and methods to learn/improve these sounds
2. English letter-sound relationship	1. Introduction to the English letter-sound relationship 2. Paper-based tutorial tasks on the English letter-sound relationship	1. Introduction to the English letter-sound relationship 2. Mentimeter: to share the teaching methods that participants used to learn English pronunciation
3. English vowels	1. English vowel chart 2. Three dimensions of English vowel description 3. Paper-based tutorial tasks on articulatory knowledge of English vowels	1. English vowel chart 2. Three dimensions of English vowel description 3. Kahoot: to help learners consolidate phonetic knowledge of vowels and to enhance learners' participation 4. Edpuzzle: to help receive and review automatic feedback
5. English consonants	1. English consonant chart 2. Articulatory knowledge of English consonants 3. Paper-based tutorial tasks on articulatory knowledge of English consonants	1. English consonant chart 2. Articulatory knowledge of English consonants 3. Kahoot: to help learners consolidate phonetic knowledge of consonants and to enhance learners' participation 4. Edpuzzle: to help receive and review automatous feedback
5. English word stress	1. Introduction to English word stress 2. English word stress rules 3. Paper-based tutorial tasks on English word stress rules	1. Introduction to English word stress 2. English word stress rules 3. Nearpod: to help learners perceive English word stress produced by native speakers 4. Edpuzzle: to help receive and review automatous feedback

Figure 4.1. Teaching content and activities for control and experimental groups.
Source: Hsueh Chu Chen and Jing Xuan Tian

Functions \ Tools	Edpuzzle	Nearpod	Padlet	Mentimeter	Kahoot
Review, strengthen, and consolidate content knowledge received in class with examples	√	√			√
Provide authentic examples		√			
Share opinions with peers or the instructor			√	√	
Conduct competition					√
Conduct collaboration			√		
Active students' in-class participation			√	√	√

Figure 4.2.   Aims of the e-tools used in the e-teaching package.
Source: Hsueh Chu Chen and Jing Xuan Tian

The purposes of the application of these five e-tools in pronunciation class were to achieve six goals. Please find the aims of each e-tool in figure 4.2.

Edpuzzle, Nearpod, and Kahoot were used to help participants review, strengthen, and consolidate content knowledge received in class with examples. Authentic materials (e.g., video clips) were integrated into Nearpod. Padlet and Mentimeter were used to share opinions with peers or the instructor. Competition was conducted using Kahoot, and collaboration was achieved using Padlet. Kahoot, Padlet, and Mentimeter were also used to encourage active students' in-class participation through conducting collaborative and competitive activities.

Edpuzzle

Edpuzzle and self-developed instructional videos were used for course content review. Participants watched five-minute recap videos while answering questions related to the phonetic knowledge introduced in the video (e.g., place and manner of articulation, vowel space). Immediate feedback to the questions was uploaded to the platform between each question and was given after the participants answered each question. Edpuzzle was used to help participants review the key concept of the course content, and second, to provide more phonetic examples to help participants strengthen their content knowledge. Students can get access to the videos of each topic listed on the platform, and students click the video to watch. There is a simultaneous display of the video and the embedded question. Participants need to answer the question before checking the correct answer and reviewing the feedback.

Nearpod

Nearpod was used to design a quiz for English word stress, and various authentic materials were used to create the questions. Participants were asked to produce English and record using the built-in recorder in Nearpod. English word stress has been reported as one of the most challenging features to learn for English language learners (Roach 2009). To provide participants with examples of greater authenticity and to help them acquire this skill, authentic materials provided by native English speakers (i.e., pop songs and short video clips) were embedded in this word stress quiz, along with words with inappropriate English primary stress placement produced by English learners.

Padlet and Mentimeter

The aim of using Padlet and Mentimeter was to collect and share participants' opinions on particular course topics. Learners shared tips on Padlet to help differentiate the difficult sounds for Chinese English learners. Padlet was also used to help enhance group work. Participants discussed with their group members and shared their group work on the platform with other groups. Questions were asked using Mentimeter, and learners' answers were shared with the whole class. Each participant posted a video clip to help solve Chinese EFL learners' pronunciation common errors.

Kahoot

Multiple-choice or true-or-false questions, hosted on Kahoot in a competition-style- format, were used to assess phonetic knowledge taught and help learners consolidate the subject knowledge they received in class. The students' participation was activated by joining the competition and competing with their classmates.

After the training session, a post-test with a different word list from the pre-test was conducted to examine the effectiveness of the e-teaching package. Words in both tests are from BNC-COCA frequency list level 1 to level 21 to make sure that the word lists used in this study have similar difficulty and frequency levels. The accuracy rates on English vowels, consonants and word stress in both tests were examined and compared. Participants were invited to answer a questionnaire and join follow-up interviews to evaluate their attitudes toward the e-teaching package and individual e-tools.

RESULTS

In order to answer the first research question, participants' error rates for English consonants, vowels, and word stress were calculated for the pre-test and post-test and compared. The results of the questionnaire survey and follow-up interviews were summarised to answer the second research question. The results for enhancement of subject knowledge, teacher supervision, teacher-student/peer interaction, teacher feedback, and evaluation of the e-teaching package were analysed.

Error Rates Between the Two Groups in Pre-test and Post-test

All 39 participants in the pre-test made the most errors in English word stress, with 25.67 percent of di- or multi-syllabic words carrying inappropriate word stress. For consonants, the mean error of all 40 participants was 8.70 percent. Participants in the current study made fewer errors in vowels, with a mean error rate of 5.05 percent.

Participants in both groups made the most errors in inappropriate word stress in the pre-test. In the post-test after the five-week training, the error rate produced by the CG declined from 24.54 percent to 21.13 percent while that of the EG increased from 26.82 percent to 30.28 percent. The paired samples T-test results showed that the decline in the error rate of the CG from pre-test to post-test was statistically significant, with $p = 0.034*$. However, the increase in the error rate of the EG of 3.46 percent from pre-test to post-test was not statistically significant.

Participants in both groups displayed lower error rates for English consonants and vowels than for English word stress. The error rates for consonants and vowels produced by CG participants showed an increase from pre-test to post-test (from 6.56 percent to 8.72 percent and from 2.02 percent to 8.33 percent, respectively). The error rate for consonants produced by EG participants declined from 10.52 percent to 8.13 percent, while the error rate for vowels also decreased from 8.08 percent to 4.58 percent. However, paired samples T-results showed that declines were not statistically significant (with $p = .465$ and .174, respectively).

Results of Enhancement of Subject Knowledge

Table 4.1 shows the results of the survey of the CG and EG. Most participants from both groups agreed or strongly agreed that their subject knowledge had been enhanced. For the CG, 87.56 percent said the course had helped them enhance their relevant knowledge; the figure was 96.73 percent for the EG.

Table 4.1.   Results of Survey by Group

	Strongly Agree/ Agree (%)		Neutral (%)		Strongly Disagree/ Disagree (%)	
	CG	EG	CG	EG	CG	EG
1. This course helped to enhance my course-related knowledge or skills.	87.56	96.73	0.00	0.00	12.44	3.27
2. I think I received sufficient support to help me solve the problems I had with the course/I felt that I was supervised.	89.47	60.00	0.00	35.00	10.53	5.00
1. CG: I think the online lectures are as interactive as face-to-face lectures.	89.47		0.00		10.53	
EG: The e-tools allow the online instruction to be interactive.		80.00		10.00		10.00
2. I think appropriate feedback was provided to enhance my learning.	84.67	75.00	0.00	20.00	15.33	5.00

Source: CHEN Hsueh Chu & TIAN Jing Xuan

Enhancement of the subject knowledge can also be supported by the interview data. Participants who attended the follow-up interview self-reported the English phonetics knowledge they had learned in the lectures. Participants in the CG mentioned phonological rules and concepts 55 times while EG members did so 47 times. The times that participants from both groups reported in the interview were compared. If they reported more phonological rules and concepts, they may have a more solid knowledge of the content knowledge. Table 4.2 presents the data for phonological rules and concepts for vowels, consonants and word stress mentioned by participants from both groups. Among the total number of phonological rules and concepts reported by the participants, the phonological rules and concepts for English word stress were mentioned most (CG: 73.12%; EG: 50.50%), followed by phonological rules and concepts for English vowels (CG: 23.37%; EG: 39.17%). The participants demonstrated their acquisition of phonological rules and concepts in the interviews. For example, "For open syllables, the vowel should normally be long."; "ch digraph can usually be pronounced as /tʃ/ or /ʃ/, and sometimes /k/"; "when there is a prefix or suffix, the stress is not on the affix."

Table 4.2. Results for Acquisition of Phonological Rules and Concepts Reported by Participants

Phonological Rules and Concepts for English Vowels (frequency)			
Group	*Mean*	*t*	*p*
Control	23.37%	1.140	0.071
Experimental	39.17%		

Phonological rules and concepts on English consonants (frequency)			
Group	*Mean*	*t*	*p*
Control	3.61%	6.820	0.214
Experimental	10.33%		

Phonological rules and concepts on English word stress (frequency)			
Group	*Mean*	*t*	*p*
Control	73.12%	0.313	0.037*
Experimental	50.50%		

Source: CHEN Hsueh Chu & TIAN Jing Xuan

Results for Teacher Supervision and Teacher-Student Interaction

Table 4.1 shows the survey results that 89.47 percent of participants in the CG agreed that they had received sufficient support when they had problems. However, fewer participants in the EG reported that they felt they had been supervised. Only 60 percent of the participants agreed that they felt adequately supervised.

Table 4.1 also shows that 89.47 percent of participants in the CG agreed that the online lectures on Zoom were as interactive as the face-to-face lectures they had had before and that enough support had been received during the training session.

Table 4.3 shows that participants in the CG enjoyed the Chat function of Zoom the most and felt it to be the most effective. They also reported that they did not like the raising hand function, and it was considered the least interactive function. Since participants in the EG group only used the basic Zoom functions, chat and poll, to maintain smooth PowerPoint presentations, they did not answer these questions. Instead, they answered questions which aimed to investigate their preferences of the e-tools that they used.

Table 4.3. Control Group Participants' Preferences for Zoom Functions

	Chat	Poll	Raising Hand	Breakout Room
1. Which function(s) of Zoom do you like?	50.00%	26.00%	4.00%	20.00%
2. Which function of Zoom do you think is interactive?	36.00%	24.00%	10.00%	30.00%

Source: Chen Hsueh Chu & TIAN Jing Xuan

Participants in the CG showed in the survey that attending online courses via Zoom was not much different than attending face-to-face classes. However, those participants who attended the follow-up interviews said that the interactions among students were less effective, and interactive activities, such as group work, should be further designed and improved. Even though there were group discussions and participants were assigned to different rooms randomly for group discussion tasks, they said that the Breakout Room function provided by Zoom did not help promote peer interaction, and sometimes the team members in a group remained silent during Breakout Room sessions. Four CG participants expressed their concerns and suggested:

CG-2: "More interactive activities should be arranged."

CG-3: "More group activities should be designed."

CG-6: "It would be better if more group work activities could be added."

CG-10: "During Zoom lessons, we had Breakout Rooms for group discussions."

Table 4.1 shows that 80 percent of the participants in the EG agreed that the e-teaching packages were well designed and could make online pronunciation instruction more interactive. Moreover, 75 percent said that they received appropriate feedback when the e-teaching package was used. In the follow-up interview, two participants also suggested that more activities that aimed to increase interactions with peers and provide peer feedback should be added. Even though e-tools were used that enabled participants to post their opinions and share them with their classmates, several participants still felt that the peer interactions were insufficient. Two EG participants expressed their feelings about the lack of peer interaction:

EG-9: "I think the class is interactive, but I think there were some classmates with whom we did not interact. I think more activities in which we can give peer feedback to others could be added."

EG-10: "We received enough feedback from teachers, which is good. But I think we were not interactive with other classmates. We just used the Chat box on Zoom to communicate with other classmates."

Results of Teacher Feedback

Feedback from teachers took two forms: oral and written. Both positive and negative/corrective feedback was provided. Table 4.1 shows that 84.67 percent of the CG agreed/strongly agreed that they had received appropriate feedback, whereas 15.33 percent disagreed/strongly disagreed with this statement. By contrast, 75 percent of the EG agreed that they had received sufficient feedback, and only 5 percent disagreed/strongly disagreed with the opinion.

In the follow-up interviews, EG participants stated that the teacher's oral feedback after the activities was important. Both the oral and written feedback helped them to obtain a better understanding of the knowledge they had learned. Even though e-tools such as Kahoot do not have a written feedback function, the instructor's oral explanations were effective and helpful. Three quotations from the EG support this view:

EG-1: "The feedback provided by the teacher in Edpuzzle (written feedback) is useful. When I make mistakes, I can know the reason why I [made them] by reading the feedback after each question and filling in the gap in my knowledge."

EG-5: "I think I received enough feedback from my teacher. When we played games on Kahoot, the instructor also provided oral feedback after each question."

EG- 7: Our teacher gave us feedback after each activity, and the explanations were very useful.

Preservice Teachers' Attitudes Toward the E-Teaching Package

Results of the evaluation of the e-teaching package by the EG are presented in tables 4.4 and 4.5. They expressed a positive attitude toward the e-learning package. Over 70 percent of the EG participants agreed that the application of the e-teaching package is flexible and user-friendly, helped them to identify their problems better, to improve their English pronunciation, and will use it in their future teaching and recommend this package to other English learners.

Nine of 20 participants (45%) reported that their favourite e-tool was Edpuzzle. In the follow-up interview, participants explained that the reason Edpuzzle was their favourite was that the content knowledge of this course had been reviewed and consolidated and further input for the participants had been provided to help them identify their pronunciation problems. Of

Table 4.4. EG Participants' Attitudes Toward the E-Teaching Package

	Strongly Agree/ Agree	Neutral	Strongly Disagree/ Disagree
1. By doing tasks in the pronunciation e-learning package, I know my pronunciation problem(s) better.	70.00%	25.00%	5.00%
2. The e-learning package is helpful for me to improve my own English pronunciation.	85.00%	5.00%	10.00%
3. I like the flexibility of the e-learning package.	85.00%	5.00%	10.00%
4. I will recommend the pronunciation e-learning package to other English learners.	75.00%	15.00%	10.00%
5. I will use the pronunciation e-learning package in my future English pronunciation teaching.	85.00%	5.00%	10.00%
6. The e-learning package is user-friendly.	75.00%	15.00%	10.00%

Source: CHEN Hsueh Chu & TIAN Jing Xuan

the two e-tools included for the purpose of quizzes, the students tended to be more interested in Kahoot, which is more competitive, than in taking a quiz individually using Nearpod.

Participants in the EG also reported that the e-tools incorporated into the e-teaching package had different aims but were combined effectively. The design of the e-teaching package was effective in helping learners to digest and consolidate the knowledge that they had acquired.

EG-3: "I think the e-tools combine effectively, and different e-tools have different aims. For example, Edpuzzle helps us review the knowledge after each class. I can also receive feedback."

Table 4.5. EG Participants' Preferences for the E-Tools Used in the E-Learning Package

	Edpuzzle	Nearpod	Padlet	Mentimeter	Kahoot
1. I like _____ the best.	45.00%	10.00%	10.00%	10.00%	25.00%
2. I like _____ the least.	10.00%	30.00%	30.00%	30.00%	0.00%
3. I feel that _____ helps me improve my own pronunciation the most effectively.	80.00%	0.00%	0.00%	0.00%	20.00%
4. I feel that _____ helps me to improve my own pronunciation the least effectively.	5.00%	25.00%	40.00%	30.00%	0.00%

Source: CHEN Hsueh Chu & TIAN Jing Xuan

DISCUSSION

In this section, we will discuss five issues raised in this study, namely, pronunciation improvement, subject knowledge enhancement, class interaction, teacher-peer feedback, and teacher supervision.

Pronunciation Improvement

For the English preservice teacher participants, 25.67 percent of the errors in the pre-test were related to word stress while less than 10 percent were related to consonants and vowels. For word stress, the participants in the CG, who focused on more rule-based explicit teaching, made significant improvements from pre-test to post-test; however, no improvements are found for the EG, who received input from authentic audio/video materials via e-tools to enhance their speech perception (using Nearpod, for example). The application of the e-teaching package was not as effective as expected for word stress. A possible reason for this is that only the short-term effectiveness of the e-teaching package was evaluated. According to Chen and Tian (2020), learners who received acoustic-perceptual instruction only improved significantly from pre-test to delayed post-test two months after the training session, rather than improving significantly from pre-test to immediate post-test. Even though various materials were used to help enhance EG participants' perceptual ability of English word stress, they may need some time to digest and transfer the knowledge that they perceived to production.

The error rates for English vowels and consonants produced by both groups were less than 11 percent in the pre-test, and the improvement rates were not statistically significant. The participants in the study were preservice teachers whose English proficiency levels are higher than those of most Chinese English learners. A possible reason for the result may be a ceiling or plateau effect. Most of the participants had already attained high proficiency on segmental features, and it would thus be hard to improve their scores; sometimes, they might even experience a decrease in performance. Another reason may be that language learning is a long-term process (Najeeb 2013), especially for productive skills (i.e., speaking and pronunciation), and subsequent studies should focus on conducting a longitudinal study to investigate the effectiveness of this e-teaching package.

Subject Knowledge Enhancement

Participants in both groups said that their subject knowledge was enhanced. Participants from both groups self-reported English phonetic knowledge in the follow-up interviews. Participants in the CG commented more often on English word stress than did EG participants. The reason may be attributed to the tasks that they performed after receiving the training session on English word stress. CG participants spent more time practicing the word stress rules and concepts using traditional tutorial tasks, such as written or oral practice. EG participants completed quizzes on word stress on Nearpod, and different audio/video materials were used to help cultivate participants' perceptual ability on English word stress. For these preservice teacher participants, it was fun but somewhat time-consuming. The content knowledge that they reported in the interview was less than that reported by CG participants, which means that the knowledge that EG participants gained may need some time to transfer to their production compared to that reported by the CG group.

With regard to vowels, participants in the EG commented more often than CG participants did on the acquisition of subject knowledge. This can also be attributed to the tasks they performed after receiving the training session. Participants in the EG completed quizzes on vowels using Kahoot. The game-based platform helped engage every student, which could be achieved by the paper-based tutorial sessions conducted with the CG group.

Class Interaction

The results indicate that the online training conducted in this study was interactive, consistent with the results of previous studies (Guichon et al. 2012; Hampel 2006). The use of different Zoom functions and the e-learning package contributed to boosting classroom interactions. Previous studies have pointed out that the application of e-tools can help facilitate collaboration and interaction (Canto et al. 2014; Cornillie et al. 2012; Reinhardt 2019). Instead of talking too much, the instructor used different activities to increase classroom interaction. Even though no e-tools were used in the CG, functions provided by Zoom were applied to produce different types of interaction.

However, for peer interaction, which is an important element in an online class (Aghaee and Keller 2016; Lai et al. 2019; Robson 2018), the results were not significant and sufficient in the current study and participants reported that more peer interaction activities should be further designed in the follow-up interviews, even though two functions on Zoom, chat and breakout rooms, were used to boost peer interaction. The chat function was used to send messages and chat, and the breakout room function was used for group work and discussions. The e-tool Padlet was used to help boost peer interaction in the EG. Participants in both groups reported not being engaged in sufficient peer interaction in the current study. It seems that technology like Zoom or e-tools is already designed and applied to support teaching; the problem remains their use by teachers to facilitate peer interaction. Teachers may have to consider how to improve their implementation skills for activities, for example, by giving clear instructions and demonstrations before conducting peer interaction activities.

Teacher-Peer Feedback

Participants from both groups reported that they received feedback during the training session; however, the feedback provided in the current study was not one-to-one as described in Guichon, Bétrancourt, and Prié (2012). EG participants in the current study reported that they received both positive and negative/corrective feedback and that both were effective; this is consistent with previous studies (Guichon, Bétrancourt, and Prié 2012; Long 1996). For future online language lessons, the provision of negative/corrective feedback will also be important.

With regard to peer feedback, participants in both groups reported that they received limited feedback from their peers; this is a limitation to the current study. No activities for giving feedback among peers designed using e-tools were integrated into the training sessions, and the only peer feedback that participants received was through the Zoom Chat box. When participants posted questions in the Chat box, participants who knew the answers would reply and help out. However, peer feedback is significant in language acquisition (Philp and Tognini 2009), and further interactive activities, both in and out of class, should be developed using e-tools. However, the effectiveness of peer feedback when the peers are from different proficiency levels of the target language, and how participants feel about this type of peer feedback can also be further investigated.

Teacher Supervision

Hampel (2006) reported that students found online lessons to be less effective because of the distance between teachers and students and the lack of supervision. In the current study, 60 percent of participants from the EG reported that they received sufficient supervision from their instructor. Teacher support to help learners solve problems and complete assigned tasks were the two types of teacher supervision in the current study. However, participants in the EG said that they had no sense of being supervised when they used e-tools to do online tasks since only the lecturer could access the backend page showing the learners' progress and performance. The participants realised, however, that their performance was being monitored and supervised once the teachers provided feedback based on the data. After explanations were given, all EG participants stated that they received enough teacher supervision.

For future online English phonetics and pronunciation teaching, in order to enhance teacher supervision, after-class supervision should be added. For example, teachers can use online platforms to assign after-class tasks, and feedback on these tasks can be provided to learners. Good use should be made of the functions (i.e., participation or attendance records) provided by the e-tools. By supervising learners' progress and performance in the tasks assigned using e-tools, teacher supervision can be enhanced. Even though there is some distance between the teacher and learners in an online learning context, teacher supervision can be enhanced are used appropriately by supervising the data of learners' progress and performance provided by online platforms.

Participants in the CG reported that the group work conducted in the Breakout Rooms on Zoom was ineffective, and there are limitations to the Breakout Room function. An instructor can only join one room at a time, and there is thus a lack of supervision of other rooms. According to previous studies (De Pry and Sugai 2002; Haydon and Kroeger 2016), keeping an eye on students' appropriate and inappropriate behaviours is one important aspect of teacher supervision in class. It is suggested that student facilitators be assigned when the whole class is divided into groups, and the instructor should take turns to join each group and supervise.

CONCLUSION

This study investigated the effectiveness of an e-package in improving Chinese English preservice teachers' English phonetic knowledge and pronunciation. The results revealed that the e-package was effective in helping these preservice teachers strengthen their subject knowledge of phonetics and slightly improve their pronunciation of English vowels and consonants, but not their English word stress. Through functions provided by different e-tools, class interaction, teacher feedback, and teacher supervision were enhanced.

To make online teaching more effective, e-tools with different purposes should be integrated into online language teaching and learning. For gaming-type e-tools (e.g., Kahoot), questions related to content knowledge should be developed; their use is effective for knowledge consolidation. For video making and sharing platforms (e.g., Edpuzzle), videos and questions can be developed to help learners review the knowledge conveyed in the training session. Written feedback on quizzes should be provided to enhance teacher feedback. The application of quiz-development type platforms (e.g., Nearpod) is helpful for enhancing learners' motivation and perceptual ability because various uploaded authentic materials can provide learners with increased access to real-life speech, allowing them to improve their perception of correct pronunciation. When using the e-tools to conduct quizzes which aim to help consolidate and review learners' knowledge, it is suggested that teachers should also provide oral feedback. Moreover, peer feedback and interaction were insufficient in this study. E-tools, such as Flipgrid[2]: on which students can record their own speech and submit their videos to their instructors and comment on their peers' production, might help to generate peer interaction and peer feedback should be created and integrated. Artificial intelligence products, such as talking robots, also appear to offer some promise for the online teaching of pronunciation and speaking. They could be employed as learners' language partners to practice, or automatic feedback can be provided. Further studies could be conducted to test their effectiveness.

With respect to the limitations in this study, there were only five training sessions, and the e-tools used in the current study were only applied once or twice in the training session. A longitudinal study could be conducted to investigate the long-term effects of the e-teaching package. Another limitation is that participants in the current study were intermediate-to-advanced English learners. Beginners could also be recruited in future studies.

NOTES

1. https://corpus.eduhk.hk/english_pronunciation/index.php/an-e-teaching-pack age-of-english-phonetics-and-pronunciation/.
2. https://info.flipgrid.com/.

REFERENCES

Aghaee, Naghmeh, and Chiristina Keller. 2016. "ICT-supported peer interaction among learners in Bachelor's and Master's thesis courses." *Computers and Education*, no. 94: 276–297. https://doi.org/10.1016/j.compedu.2015.11.006

Alzamil, Abdulrahman. (2021). "Teaching English speaking online versus face-to-face: Saudi students' experience during the COVID-19 pandemic." Arab World English Journal, no. 12: 19–27. http://dx.doi.org/10.2139/ssrn.3826486

Bakar, Zulqarnain Abu, and M. R. Abdullah. 2015. "Importance of correct pronunciation in spoken English: Dimension of second language learners' perspective." *Pertanika Journal of Social Sciences and Humanities* 23, no. 8: 143–158. https://www.researchgate.net/profile/Muhammad-Ridhuan/publication/298091003_Im portance_of_correct_pronunciation_in_spoken_english_Dimension_of_second _language_learners'_perspective/links/5bf61f17299bf1124fe4d96e/Importance

-of-correct-pronunciation-in-spoken-english-Dimension-of-second-language
-learners-perspective.pdf

Bautista-Vallejo, José M., Rafael M. Hernández-Carrera, Ricardo Moreno-Rodriguez, and José Luis Lopez-Bastias. 2020. "Improvement of Memory and Motivation in Language Learning in Primary Education through the Interactive Digital White-board (IDW): The Future in a Post-Pandemic Period." *Sustainability* 12, no. 19: 8109. https://doi.org/10.3390/su12198109

Canto, Silvia, Rick de Graaff, and Kristi Jauregi. 2014. "Collaborative tasks for nego-tiation of intercultural meaning in virtual worlds and video-web communication." In *Technology-mediated TBLT*, edited by Marta González-Lloret and Lourdes Ortega, 183–212. Amsterdam: John Benjamins,

Chen, Hsueh Chu, and Jing Xuan Tian. 2020. "The effects of explicit rule and acoustic-perceptual instructions on Chinese ESL learners' prosodic acquisition of English lexical stress." In *Proc. 10th International Conference on Speech Prosody 2020*, 833–837. https://doi: 10.21437/SpeechProsody.2020-170

Chen, Hsueh Chu, and Jing Xuan Tian. 2022. "Online Lessons for <English Phonetics and Phonology>: My Learning Journey" In *5th Annual e-Resources Roundtable/ Poster Conference.*

Chiang, Hui-Hua. 2020. "Kahoot! in an EFL reading class." *Journal of Language Teaching and Research* 11, no. 1: 33–44. https://doi.org/10.17507/jltr.1101.05

Cornillie, Frederik, Steven L. Thorne, and Piet Desmet. 2012. "ReCALL special is-sue: Digital games for language learning: challenges and opportunities: Editorial Digital games for language learning: From hype to insight?." *ReCALL* 24, no. 3: 243–256. https://doi:10.1017/S0958344012000134

Cox, Jenelle L., Lynn E. Henrichsen, Mark W. Tanner, and Benjamin L. McMurry. 2019. "The needs analysis, design, development, and evaluation of the English pro-nunciation guide: An ESL teachers' guide to pronunciation teaching using online resources." *TESL-EJ* 22, no. 4: 1–24. https://eric.ed.gov/?id=EJ1204566

De Pry, Randall L., and George Sugai. 2002. "The effect of active supervision and pre-correction on minor behavioral incidents in a sixth grade general educa-tion classroom." *Journal of Behavioral Education* 11, no. 4: 255–267. https://doi.org/10.1023/A:1021162906622 11, no. 4: 255–267. https://doi.org/10.1023/A:1021162906622

Dumford, Amber D., and Angie L. Miller. 2018. "Online learning in higher education: exploring advantages and disadvantages for engagement." *Journal of Computing in Higher Education* 30, no. 3: 452–465. https://doi.org/10.1007/s12528-018-9179-z

Foote, Jennifer Ann, Pavel Trofimovich, Laura Collins, and Fernanda Soler Urzúa. 2016. "Pronunciation teaching practices in communicative second language classes." *The Language Learning Journal* 44, no. 2: 181–196. https://doi.org/10.1080/09571736.2013.784345

Gilakjani, Abbas Pourhossein, and Mohammad Reza Ahmadi. 2011. "Why Is Pronun-ciation So Difficult to Learn?." *English language teaching* 4, no. 3: 74–83. https://doi:10.5539/elt.v4n3p74

Guichon, Nicolas, Mireille Bétrancourt, and Yannick Prié. 2012. "Managing written and oral negative feedback in a synchronous online teaching situation." *Computer assisted language learning* 25, no. 2: 181–197. https://doi.org/10.1080/09588221.2011.636054

Hampel, Regina. 2006. "Rethinking task design for the digital age: A framework for language teaching and learning in a synchronous online environment." *ReCALL* 18, no. 1: 105–121. https://doi.org/10.1017/S0958344006000711

Haydon, Todd, and Stephen D. Kroeger. 2016. "Active supervision, precorrection, and explicit timing: A high school case study on classroom behavior." *Preventing School Failure: Alternative Education for Children and Youth* 60, no. 1: 70–78. https://doi.org/10.1080/1045988X.2014.977213

Hincks, Rebecca. 2005. "Computer support for learners of spoken English." PhD diss., KTH, 2005. https://www.diva-portal.org/smash/get/diva2:13348/FULLTEXT01.pdf

Hrastinski, Stefan. 2008. "What is online learner participation? A literature review." *Computers & Education* 51, no. 4: 1755–1765. https://doi.org/10.1016/j.compedu.2008.05.005

Hrastinski, Stefan. 2009. "A theory of online learning as online participation." *Computers & Education* 52, no. 1: 78–82. https://doi.org/10.1016/j.compedu.2008.06.009

Lai, Chih-Hung, Hung-Wei Lin, Rong-Mu Lin, and Pham Duc Tho. 2019. "Effect of peer interaction among online learning community on learning engagement and achievement." *International Journal of Distance Education Technologies (IJDET)* 17, no. 1: 66–77. https://doi: 10.4018/IJDET.2019010105

Li, Shuangjiang, and Jitpanat Suwanthep. 2017. "Integration of flipped classroom model for EFL speaking." *International Journal of Learning and Teaching* 3, no. 2: 118–123. https://doi: 10.18178/ijlt.3.2.118-123

Long, Michael. 1996. "The role of the linguistic environment in second language acquisition." In *Handbook of second language acquisition*, edited by Ritchie, William C., and Tej K. Bhatia, 1–8. Academic Press.

Mei, Bing, Shuo Huang, and Qian Zhao. 2021."Using Clips in the Language Classroom." *RELC Journal*. https://doi.org/10.1177/00336882211026168.

Mischel, Leann J. 2019. "Watch and learn? Using EDpuzzle to enhance the use of online videos." *Management Teaching Review* 4, no. 3: 283–289. https://doi.org/10.1177/2379298118773418

Najeeb, Sabitha SR. 2013. "Learner autonomy in language learning." *Procedia-Social and Behavioral Sciences* 70: 1238–1242. https://doi.org/10.1016/j.sbspro.2013.01.183

Palma, Lara Orcos, Pedro J. Blázquez Tobías, Marta Curto Prieto, Francisco Javier Molina León, and Ángel Alberto Magreñán Ruiz. 2018. "Use of kahoot and EdPuzzle by smartphone in the classroom: the design of a methodological proposal." In *International Workshop on Learning Technology for Education in Cloud*, 37–47. Springer.

Perevalova, Alena, Anna Resenchuk, and Nina Tunyova. 2020. "Teaching Professional Vocabulary to the Students in Coal Region Universities through Digital Educational Tools." In *E3S Web of Conferences*, vol. 174, p. 1–8. https://doi.org/10.1051/e3sconf/202017404051

Philp, Jenefer, and Rita Tognini. 2009. "Language acquisition in foreign language contexts and the differential benefits of interaction." *International Review of Applied Linguistics in Language Teaching, IRAL*, no. 47: 245–266. https://doi.org/10.1515/iral.2009.011

Pourhosein Gilakjani, Abbas, and Rahimy Ramin. 2020. "Using computer-assisted pronunciation teaching (CAPT) in English pronunciation instruction: A study on the impact and the Teacher's role. " *Educ Inf Technol,* no. 25, 1129–1159. https://doi.org/10.1007/s10639-019-10009-1

Reinhardt, Jonathon. 2019. "Social media in second and foreign language teaching and learning: Blogs, wikis, and social networking." *Language Teaching* 52, no. 1: 1–39. https:// doi:10.1017/S0261444818000356

Roach, Peter. 2009. *English phonetics and phonology: A practical course.* 4th ed. New York: Cambridge University Press.

Robson, James. 2018. "Performance, structure and ideal identity: Reconceptualising teachers' engagement in online social spaces." *British Journal of Educational Technology* 49, no. 3: 439–450. https://doi.org/10.1111/bjet.12551

Shahriarpour, Nahid. 2014. "On the effect of playing digital games on Iranian intermediate EFL learners' motivation toward learning English vocabularies." *Procedia-Social and Behavioral Sciences* 98: 1738–1743. https://doi.org/10.1016/j.sbspro.2014.03.601

Spring, Ryan, and Ryuji Tabuchi. 2021. "Assessing the Practicality of Using an Automatic Speech Recognition Tool to Teach English Pronunciation Online." *Journal of English Teaching through Movies and Media* 22, no. 2: 93–104. https://doi.org/10.16875/stem.2021.22.2.93

Tao, Yingxu, and Bin Zou. 2007. "Students' perceptions of the use of Kahoot! in English as a foreign language classroom learning context." *Computer Assisted Language Learning*: 1–20. https://doi.org/10.1080/09588221.2021.2011323

Thompson, Emily W., and Wilhelmina C. Savenye. 2007. "Adult Learner Participation in an Online Degree Program: A program-level study of voluntary computer-mediated communication." *Distance Education* 28, no. 3: 299–312. https://doi.org/10.1080/01587910701611336

Ying, Yong Hua, Winson Eng Wei Siang, and Maslawati Mohamad. 2021."The Challenges of Learning English Skills and the Integration of Social Media and Video Conferencing Tools to Help ESL Learners Coping with the Challenges during COVID-19 Pandemic: A Literature Review." *Creative Education* 12, no. 7: 1503–1516. https://doi.org/10.4236/ce.2021.127115

Zou, Di, and Haoran Xie.2019. "Flipping an English writing class with technology-enhanced just-in-time teaching and peer instruction." *Interactive Learning Environments* 27, no. 8: 1127–1142. https://doi.org/10.1080/10494820.2018.1495654

Chapter Five

Developing Portuguese Oral Skills Via Instructional Technology Tools

Students' Views and Recommended Practices

Vivian Flanzer and Veronica G. Sardegna

INTRODUCTION

The Open Educational Resource *ClicaBrasil* (Flanzer 2010, 2019) was designed to help learners improve their Portuguese language skills and increase their intercultural competence and knowledge of the Brazilian culture. Because *ClicaBrasil* depicts a diversity of Brazilians spontaneously speaking about their lives and country, it exposes users to sociolinguistic variation, showing that language use is not homogeneous, and is influenced by social factors, such as region, class, age, and gender, and the context of the interaction. In addition, *ClicaBrasil*'s audiovisual materials and accompanying activities prompt students to understand and produce the Portuguese language while they reflect upon and deepen their knowledge of Brazilian society (Flanzer in Press). Due to its rich cultural content, high instructional quality, and focus on exposing students to a wide range of Brazilian accents and walks of life, *ClicaBrasil* is the main instructional resource for teaching Intermediate level Portuguese as a foreign language (PFL) at the University of Texas (UT) at Austin. Other foreign language (FL) programs and language centers teaching PFL around the world use some (selective use) or all of its materials for instruction.

In this chapter, we explore the value of using *ClicaBrasil* as a technology and language resource for a university-level PFL course and examine, in particular, to what extent it provides opportunities for PFL students to develop their oral and pronunciation skills. The chapter consists of three parts. The first part describes *ClicaBrasil*'s contents and provides an overview of prior research and technology resources that can support pronunciation learning. The second part reports on a study that explored PFL students' opinions

79

of *ClicaBrasil* and analyzed evidence of students' increased awareness of Portuguese pronunciation features and accents after using *ClicaBrasil* as a resource for language development and practice. The final part provides suggestions for classroom implementation based on the study. The main goal of this chapter is to show how pronunciation development can be integrated into a classroom activity using *ClicaBrasil's* resources.

ClicaBrasil

ClicaBrasil (Flanzer 2010) is an Open Educational Resource developed to teach the Portuguese language and Brazilian culture to intermediate and advanced language learners of Portuguese. It consists of a free-access website[1] and a textbook (Flanzer 2019) that can be purchased at cost price or downloaded for free. Through *ClicaBrasil's* homepage, users can find an introduction with tips, the downloadable textbook, a Who's Who section with the speakers introducing themselves, a grammar bank with 104 pages of grammatical explanations, a video index, a unit index, and a bibliography. They can also access the following instructional units by clicking on *Units* at the top of the page:

1. *Todos os dias* ("Everyday life")—Work, study routines, and life styles in Brazil.
2. *Fim de semana* ("Weekends")—Weekend leisure options for different Brazilians.
3. *Trajetórias* ("Trajectories")—Personal and professional trajectories that led to migration.
4. *Rio, de norte a sul* ("Rio, from North to South")—Discussions about the city of Rio de Janeiro.
5. *Na internet* ("On the Internet")—Brazilians using the Internet and social media.
6. *Festas, compras, encontros e desencontros* ("Parties, shopping, and gatherings")—Brazilians organizing parties and social gatherings, and shopping in person or online.
7. *Salvador da Bahia* ("The city of Salvador da Bahia")—Testimonies about the city of Salvador.

Each unit has four integrated sections with a wide range of grammatical and cultural topics and activities. The four sections are as follows:

1. *Pano de fundo* (Backdrop) activates and builds background knowledge by providing context and filling in some cultural gaps prior to reading a text or viewing a video.

2. *Leitura* (Reading) presents an authentic reading that exposes students to new vocabulary and structures, and different aspects of the Brazilian culture and society.
3. *Gramática* (Grammar) reviews or introduces challenging grammar topics featured in the readings and/or videos, prompting students to analyze language in context.
4. *Aproximando o foco* (Zooming in) offers critical thinking activities that explore the sociocultural aspects embedded in the readings and the videos.

The units feature culturally rich and authentic texts (e.g., song lyrics, magazine articles, and short stories) and videos (157 total) in which 28 Brazilians from different regions and sectors of society (professions, social classes, ethnicity and age group) speak spontaneously about their lives, Brazil, and topics that arise from the readings. Thus, students are able to both experience the language as "lived" by native speakers in Brazil and grasp the sociocultural context of the readings through their testimonies. Glossaries accompany the readings, and Portuguese transcriptions and English translations accompany the videos. Learners can choose to show or hide the transcription and/or the translation. The units also include 335 activities (available through Google-Docs) based on the readings and videos. The goal of these activities is to help students develop their language skills—reading, grammar, vocabulary, writing, listening and reading comprehension, and oral competence—and cross-cultural knowledge and competence. Guiding written questions prompt discussions and reflections on the Brazilian culture and language. An Answer Key is available for all the activities.

Research Support

To achieve the five goal areas of the *World-Readiness Standards for Learning Languages* (National Standards Collaborative Board 2015)—communication, cultures, connections, comparisons, communities—FL teachers need to find ways to expose students to a range of native speakers and up-to-date examples of how the language is currently used (Sardegna and Hughes 2022). Texts written or spoken by native speakers for a native speaker audience (e.g., newspaper articles, literary texts, TV shows, and videos with testimonies) "convey a real message of some sort" (Gilmore 2007, 98). These authentic materials can be used to teach culture through perspectives, products, and practices within the five goal areas. Technology can bring these authentic materials into the FL classroom (Sardegna and Hughes 2022). As culture and language are closely interrelated, it is through these same authentic materials that students can develop their oral comprehensibility and intelligibility.

Comprehensibility refers to how difficult it is for the learner to understand a spoken message, and intelligibility pertains to what extent a learner's spoken message is understood by others (Derwing and Munro 2015; Levis 2018).

Improving students' second language (L2) intelligibility involves a process that starts with raising students' awareness of what they need to improve (Sardegna 2021). Most research on awareness-raising activities has focused on the oral production benefits of prosodic feature awareness training through explicit instruction of rules and strategies (Luchini 2017; Sardegna 2009, 2012, 2020, 2021; Sardegna and McGregor 2013). Other critical instructional components that maximize students' chances of improving their oral and pronunciation skills include goal prioritization, guided focus-on-form practice activities, ongoing feedback, and opportunities for reflection on progress (Sardegna 2021). Yet, despite the increasing evidence indicating the benefits of explicit pronunciation instruction and corrective feedback (Lee, Jang and Plonsky 2015; Sardegna and McGregor 2022; Spada and Lightbown 1993; Thomson and Derwing 2015), the effects of raising awareness of speech features and accents using authentic technology resources have been largely unexplored.

Of the few Open Educational Resources available for teaching and learning Brazilian Portuguese pronunciation, three stand out: *ClicaBrasil* (Flanzer 2010), *Fonética e Fonologia* (Cristófaro Silva, n.d.), and *Tá Falado* (Kelm 2006). *Fonética e Fonologia* includes an introduction to the studies of phonetics and phonology (targeting Brazilian Portuguese), and sections on articulatory phonetics, acoustic phonetics, and phonology, and exercises with answer keys. It provides comprehensive information about Brazilian Portuguese phonetics and phonology; yet, it can be a bit overwhelming for Intermediate PFL learners not familiarized with linguistics. In addition, the exercises target a native-Portuguese audience or advanced-high PFL learners, and thus are not appropriate for the Intermediate level unless learning is scaffolded by the instructor. *Tá falado* is a series of podcasts about Brazilian Portuguese pronunciation. Each podcast includes a lesson built around a dialogue that illustrates a specific sound, and/or sound differences (Portuguese regional variation and/or differences with Spanish). The podcasts are easily accessible, fun to listen to, and a useful learning tool for PFL learners at all levels of proficiency. Yet, because the lessons' discussions are in English and the dialogues are written and recorded by the podcast's hosts to illustrate the lessons, *Tá Falado* does not expose students to authentic audio materials. Finally, this resource does not include any activities, leaving it up to the instructor to design them around the podcasts. In sum, of the three technology resources, *ClicaBrasil* offers the most comprehensive and learner-friendly coverage of information, authentic materials, practice exercises, and supporting language resources (e.g., vocabulary and grammatical information) for PFL learning. Hence, we decided to conduct a classroom-based study to examine its value as a supporting resource for advancing the development of PFL students' oral and pronunciation skills.

THE STUDY

Specifically, the goal of this study was to explore the value of using *ClicaBrasil* for providing opportunities for PFL students to develop their pronunciation and oral skills. The following research questions guided the study:

1. What was PFL students' opinion of the value of using *ClicaBrasil* for Portuguese language and culture learning, and especially for providing opportunities for the development of Portuguese oral skills?
2. To what extent did *ClicaBrasil* contribute to PFL students' increased awareness of Portuguese pronunciation features and accents?

Participants

Sixteen undergraduate students (F = 10; M = 6) taking an intermediate course on *Portuguese Conversation and Culture for Spanish Speakers* at an American university participated in this study. They were pursuing degrees in STEM (4), Fine Arts (2), and Humanities (10). Of the 10 students in Humanities, seven were in the program of International Relations and Global Studies. Fourteen of the students were Spanish speakers, and two were Portuguese heritage speakers. Among the Spanish speakers, seven were native speakers from different Spanish-speaking countries (Mexico, Chile, Spain, Cuba and Peru), three were heritage speakers, and four were language learners.

The Course

The course met for one hour three times a week for 15 weeks via *Zoom*—a web-based video conferencing tool. Its main objectives were to increase fluency and intelligibility, improve speaking and listening skills, expand vocabulary, and learn to express opinions while discussing sociocultural issues in the Portuguese-speaking world and in connection to Brazil. Canvas was the course management system used to post and organize multimedia course content, assign and grade homework, and facilitate communication with peers and the teacher. *ClicaBrasil* (Flanzer 2010) was used as the main instructional technology tool. Table 5.1 describes the course assignments using *ClicaBrasil* resources.

Table 5.1.   Course Assignments using *ClicaBrasil* Resources

Assignments	Purpose	Grade (%)	Times	Weeks
Oral Presentations	• Develop pronunciation, fluency, and presentation skills. • Learn about the target culture and society.	30	3	3, 8, 12
Language and Cultural Discussions	• Increase cultural and language awareness. • Promote discussion. • Analyze language use in a social context.	25	4	2, 5, 10, 14
Role-Plays	• Increase oral fluency, turn-taking, and negotiation skills. • Practice new vocabulary and grammar structures in context.	0	5	4, 7, 9, 10, 11
Group Work	• Develop conversational skills. • Express opinions. • Agree and disagree.	0	42	Every class
Homework	• Listen to different accents and registers. • Provide authentic language/cultural input. • Practice new vocabulary and grammatical structures in controlled activities.	30	34	3x/week
Multiple-Choice Tests	• Assess language learning.	15	3	5,10, 15

Source: Flanzer & Sardegna.

Oral Presentations

Each of the three oral presentations had a different purpose and focus. The purpose of Presentation 1 was to raise students' awareness about different regional accents in Brazil, and similarities and differences between Portuguese and Spanish, and to practice pronunciation by mimicking native speakers. It consisted in reading aloud for the class the transcription of a one-minute video from *ClicaBrasil*. The reading was chosen by the student and expected to be as close as possible to the original, including pronunciation, intonation, pauses, contractions, and hesitations, which are characteristics of spontaneous speech. The purpose of Presentation 2 was to enhance students' pronunciation, fluency and presentation skills while deepening their knowledge of Brazilian history and society. After finishing Unit 3, *Trajetórias* ("Trajectories"), the students were asked to choose a group, a family, or an individual who moved within, to, or from Brazil, and present their trajectories in Portuguese to the class. They were not allowed to read from a script, but they were encouraged to prepare their presentations ahead of time. These student presentations were followed by a Q&A and conversation. The purpose of Presentation 3 was to enhance students' listening comprehension skills, transcription skills, take-turning, fluency, pronunciation, and intonation, and develop their ability to display emotions and use body language during a presentation. It consisted of a three-minute pair reenactment of a scene (of choice) of a TV show, series or movie from a Portuguese-speaking country, followed by (a) the watching of the original scene as a class, and (b) a class discussion in Portuguese about the linguistic and cultural topics that were depicted in the scenes. After each of the three presentations, the instructor gave detailed individualized feedback in Portuguese via Canvas.

Language and Cultural Discussions

The purpose of the four oral discussions was to guide the students to analyze the Portuguese language in specific sociocultural contexts and to think criti-cally about language use and its relation to society. Each discussion lasted one class period (50 minutes). It involved a short presentation in Portuguese from each student about their observations regarding the language and the culture depicted in *ClicaBrasil* videos, followed by a whole class discussion in Portuguese. As this was a complex assignment that involved critical think-ing, discussion, and oral and cross-cultural skills, it was worth 25 percent of the final grade.

Roleplays

The purpose of the five roleplays was to increase students' fluency in free speech. They had three parts. In part one, the instructor divided the class into two groups with each group receiving a script describing a situation and a point of view. The groups then met in a breakout room in Zoom to read their scripts, clarify vocabulary, and brainstorm ideas for negotiating their point of view with the other group. In part two, the instructor assigned breakout rooms with pairs made up by one member of each of the original groups. The pairs roleplayed their scenarios in Portuguese while the instructor visited the break-out rooms without interrupting or interfering with their interactions. In part three, the class reunited for a whole-class discussion in Portuguese. When time allowed, some pairs reenacted their conversation to the whole group. The roleplay situations were related to the themes/characters in the unit, but they always had an absurd or nonsense spin to make the situation humorous.

Group Work

ClicaBrasil contains 335 activities based on authentic videos and readings with guiding questions that prompt discussions and reflections on cross-cultural knowledge and competence. Many of these activities were performed in class in pairs, small groups, or as a whole class discussion. The course was designed in a way that students had many opportunities to speak in Portuguese and listen to Portuguese speech in every class meeting.

Homework and Tests

In line with the belief that feedback is a process that empowers learners to take an active role (Chong 2018) in order to obtain, understand and incorporate feedback information (Winstone et al. 2022), all homework assignments had an Answer Key that the students could use after completing the homework. To reinforce their importance, daily homework assignments were worth a higher percentage of the grade (30%) than the exams (15%). The three tests consisted of multiple-choice questions administered online via Canvas.

Data Collection and Analysis

Participants' opinions regarding *ClicaBrasil* and other aspects of the online course were gathered through an online anonymous questionnaire via the Qualtrics Survey platform. The questionnaire included open-ended questions and 60 5-point Likert scale items. The students received a link to the survey through Canvas and were told that their participation was voluntary. This chapter only provides a descriptive report of the survey items that elicited information relevant to answer research question #1 (i.e., What was PFL students' opinion of the value of using *ClicaBrasil* for Portuguese language and culture learning, and especially for providing opportunities for the development of Portuguese oral skills). Descriptive statistics were computed on the Likert scale items. The open-ended responses were analyzed using procedures adapted from a general inductive approach to coding qualitative data (Thomas 2006). Two researchers reviewed the responses independently to identify salient themes in relation to creating opportunities for the development of Portuguese oral skills. Intercoder agreement was obtained by consulting a third researcher when disagreements in data coding occurred between the two primary researchers (Creswell 2016; Creswell and Creswell 2018). In other words, at least two researchers had to agree on a code for it to be considered in the analysis. Based on the identified themes, a set of categories was developed and then these categories were triangulated with the information obtained from students' Likert scale responses. To answer research question

#2 (i.e., To what extent did *ClicaBrasil* contribute to PFL students' increased awareness of Portuguese pronunciation features and accents), students' oral presentations from the activity Language and Cultural Discussions were recorded, transcribed, and coded according to language-related and pronunciation-related comments, and then the pronunciation-related comments were further analyzed in terms of comment types. The procedures followed for data coding and intercoder agreement were the same as those followed for research question #1.

Results

Students' Opinions about ClicaBrasil

The anonymous survey revealed that the students appreciated the resources and activities that *ClicaBrasil* offered in support of developing their Portuguese language and cultural knowledge. Fifteen out of the 16 students reported enjoying working with *ClicaBrasil* (one student was neutral), and when asked about what they enjoyed the most about the course, many students highly complimented *ClicaBrasil*, as shown in the following comments:

> *ClicaBrasil is amazing, I will continue to use it after this semester. It is a wonderful method to hear, read, and talk about real life Brazilian culture and Portuguese language.*

> *I really liked it [ClicaBrasil], there were no drawbacks.*

> *ClicaBrasil was engaging, very genuine.*

> *ClicaBrasil is a great website-the best class resource I've used so far.*

One thing that most students highlighted about *ClicaBrasil* was the accessibility of the materials and its clear organization and navigation:

> *It is quick to log on to, and activities are readily available, WHEREVER (without needing Canvas); I like the organization of it; personal stories that help learn Portuguese.*

> *I thought using ClicaBrasil was great because it made the learning material very accessible (provided one has access to technology) and also fun and interactive.*

> *The information there is very organized, and it has a variety of topics that are very interesting to learn.*

> *Very easy to navigate*

> *It was beneficial to have everything searchable and in one place.*

Most importantly, 81 percent of the students strongly agreed that *ClicaBrasil* facilitated their learning of the Portuguese language and culture, and 94 percent agreed or strongly agreed that completing the activities in *ClicaBrasil* was a good use of their time.

When asked whether they saw any drawbacks to using *ClicaBrasil*, the majority said that they could not think of any. One student mentioned information overload and another said that some videos did not have good audio. The latter could be related to a technical issue. The class was online via Zoom, and two students (12.50%) commented that they experienced some technical problems that hindered their learning (e.g., "*video quality always affected, lots of crashes, video/student computer quality also affects how we are heard.*"). A few others also had some connectivity issues from time to time; yet, that did not seem to affect the learning experience given that 14 students reported having had a good time in class.

An exploration of students' views regarding the value of the specific resources and activities provided via *ClicaBrasil* revealed that they appreciated the videos the most, as the following comments illustrate:

> *I loved the videos from ClicaBrasil.*
>
> *I enjoyed watching Brazilian culture such as tv shows, interviews and commercials.*
>
> *I enjoyed watching the videos and talking about Brazilian culture.*

In fact, all 16 students strongly agreed (81%) or agreed (19%) with the statement "I enjoyed listening to *ClicaBrasil* videos" and gave a variety of reasons for this sentiment, such as the following:

> *I loved that they* [the videos] *provided key vocabulary and a transcription so we could read what they were actually saying, and instantly correct yourself.*
>
> *It was also really fun to watch the videos of local Brazilians from different areas of Brazil.*
>
> *Seeing actual Brazilians speak Portuguese was very helpful! It gave us an idea of how to actually speak the language with slangs and accents.*
>
> *ClicaBrasil allowed us to see and hear how normal people speak the language.*

The videos were used as a springboard for the four Language and Cultural Discussions, and many of the Group Work activities that took place in the breakout rooms via Zoom. These activities aimed at creating opportunities for reflection, exploration, discussion, and language and cultural awareness development in connection to different Brazilian accents and speech features.

Students' comments suggested that they enjoyed these activities and perceived them as useful for developing their oral skills and exposing them to different accents and colloquial language:

I enjoyed discussions about readings and films.

I also liked going into breakout rooms to do work and getting together to share afterward.

It was nice to orally present them [written journals based on videos] *in a cultural discussion.*

The cultural discussions were a great and natural way to get us to work on our speaking and thinking in Portuguese [smiley face]

I liked when we did breakout rooms with 3–4 people where we could all brainstorm and work with each other on an activity. I enjoyed giving personal opinions about everyday tasks Brazilians do in relation to my life.

Utilizing Brazilian culture helped us learn colloquial Portuguese.

High participation was an important goal in the course as it is the best way to develop oral fluency and pronunciation skills. Additional opportunities for oral practice and cultural discussions were offered through two other course activities that were implemented using *ClicaBrasil* videos and readings: roleplays and oral presentations. One of the students said that the "*roleplays were scary—I wish we maybe had more time to prepare sometimes (let us know in a previous lecture)?*" Yet, 12 of the students answered that they strongly agreed (56%) or agreed (18%) with the statement "I enjoyed doing roleplays." One thing that students appreciated was the humorous atmosphere in the class (75 percent strongly agreed), which was largely accomplished through the roleplays, as these students noted:

I enjoyed the activities in which we had to create dialogues, or imitate other dialogue. I found that a very funny way to learn and to delve into the Brazilian culture.

I enjoyed the most when we were partnered up and recited a 3-minute dialogue!

Presenting a show was really fun and insightful.

The teacher's attitude also encouraged participation: "*The Professor really made me feel comfortable to speak in class.*" Still, despite the welcoming atmosphere (strongly agreed by 94 percent of the class), nine students reported experiencing some kind of language anxiety (fear of making errors or losing face in front of the class) during the course, especially during the activities that required active oral participation, such as during oral presentations (37%) and talking in class (26%). This feeling may be unavoidable in a language class, but also not necessarily a bad thing, as the following comment illustrates:

> *This class made me speak in front of class and talk in breakout rooms. I struggle with speaking up and this class helped me open up a bit more.*

Additionally, 12 students indicated that they strongly agreed (50%) or somewhat agreed (25%) that they enjoyed the oral presentations that they prepared based on the information provided in the *ClicaBrasil* videos. In fact, four chose them as their favorite activity because they found the presentations "helpful" despite the fact that nine of the 16 students also found them "challenging," with one going as far as saying that "everything that had to do with talking in Portuguese" was challenging.

In sum, *ClicaBrasil*'s resources successfully supported and organized students' learning, and made the experience enjoyable for all through a wide range of activities. At times, the course activities that made use of *ClicaBrasil*'s resources were perceived as challenging because they prompted students to share their perspectives, express their creativity, and interact with classmates in Portuguese—to which 80 percent, 94 percent, 100 percent of the students agreed or strongly agreed, respectively. As a result, some of these challenging activities created some sort of anxiety in some of the students. However, when it came to reporting the value of *ClicaBrasil* for developing their language and cultural skills, many students strongly believed they had improved these skills (see table 5.2).

Evidence of Increased Pronunciation Awareness

The students participated in four Language and Cultural Discussions in which they orally presented their observations about the language and culture they perceived while interacting with *ClicaBrasil*. To determine whether this activity increased their awareness of the Portuguese language and its pronunciation features, we examined the topics that emerged during the language and cultural discussions regarding their observations about language. As table 5.3 shows, students made 87 comments about language, with 54 percent of them focused on pronunciation features. The number of pronunciation-related comments decreased throughout the semester. As the semester progressed, students commented more about lexical choices and grammar topics but also continued to comment on pronunciation.

Table 5.2. Students' Perceptions of Improvement

I believe I have improved my . . .	Strongly Disagree	Somewhat Disagree	Neutral	N	Somewhat Agree	N	Strongly Agree	N	Total
language skills	0.00%	0.00%	0.00%		31.25%	5	68.75%	11	16
listening skills	0.00%	0.00%	12.50%	2	12.50%	2	75.00%	12	16
oral skills	0.00%	0.00%	6.25%	1	25.00%	4	68.75%	11	16
reading skills	0.00%	0.00%	12.50%	2	25.00%	4	62.50%	10	16
writing skills	0.00%	0.00%	12.50%	2	12.50%	2	75.00%	12	16
cultural knowledge	0.00%	0.00%	0.00%	2	12.50%	2	87.50%	14	16

Source: Flanzer & Sardegna.

Table 5.3.   Number and Percentage of Comments per Discussion

Discussion #	N of Comments on language*	N of Comments on Pronunciation	% of Pronunciation Comments of all Language-Related Comments
1	26	24	92%
2	23	10	43%
3	22	10	45%
4	16	3	19%
TOTAL	87	47	54%

*As many students made more than one comment, the number of comments is larger than the number of students.

Source: Flanzer & Sardegna.

Table 5.4 illustrates the different types of comments that emerged in the analysis with respect to pronunciation issues. The examples shown in the table were made in Portuguese and translated into English to make them more accessible to readers. Most comments (34%) were related to the different accents and sounds produced by the Brazilians on *ClicaBrasil*,

Table 5.4.   Types, Number, Percentage, and Sample Comments on Pronunciation Features

Types of Comments on Pronunciation	N of Comments	%	Example
differences in accents and sounds	16	34	. . . *people from Rio pronounce the "s" like a "sh" but in São Paulo they don't do that.*
rhythm and pitch range	10	21	*While listening to ClicaBrasil's videos, I noticed that Brazilians speak with a rhythm. Because I am a novice, I speak Portuguese very monotonously. I need to practice speaking with rhythm.*
shortenings/ reductions in oral speech	9	19	*ClicaBrasil shows how people cut words when they speak fast. Glória and Lúcia said "cê" instead of "você."*
contractions	5	11	*Diana says "pros" instead of "para os." I think that this is because they are speaking informally.*
filler words	4	9	*I noticed filler words like "né" and "hã." . . . These are important and interesting, but I don't think I could learn it from a book.*
different ways of speaking due to profession/social status	3	6	*I noticed that the teachers are more articulate . . . I think that this is because they are more used to pronounce the words well. . . . This happens everywhere.*
TOTAL	47	100	

Source: Flanzer & Sardegna.

followed by comments regarding the rhythm and pitch range in their informal oral speech (21%). Students also noticed the use of reductions (19%), contractions (11%) and filler words (9%). This awareness, especially at the beginning of the semester, is crucial to building students' knowledge about register. During the course, they were exposed to formal and informal written and audiovisual texts, and they made a habit of noticing the specific characteristics of each genre of communication.

Discussion

The goal of this study was to explore the value of using *ClicaBrasil* as the main instructional material for providing opportunities for PFL students to develop their pronunciation and oral skills. Students' opinions revealed high satisfaction with *ClicaBrasil*'s content, organization, interactivity, and accessibility. Above all, they praised the authenticity of the materials (videos and texts) and the opportunities they had for cultural and language growth through exposure to different accents, people of different social backgrounds and occupations, and personal stories regarding life in Brazil. The students also noticed and appreciated the carefully designed curriculum around *ClicaBrasil*. They reported learning gains with respect to language, listening, oral, reading, writing, and cultural knowledge and skills after engaging in the course activities that used *ClicaBrasil*'s resources. This finding provided strong evidence for the value of using *ClicaBrasil* as a technology resource that can effectively support the Portuguese classroom.

Students' comments also indicated that they were constantly encouraged to think critically, share their perspectives, and actively participate in discussions in Portuguese, which some found challenging and anxiety-inducing. Yet, they also reported experiencing positive emotions—e.g., success, high enjoyment, welcoming atmosphere—which facilitated their learning and led them to conclude that the activities were well worth their time (94 percent agreement). This finding supports the view that anxiety contributes to learning effort (Papi 2010), especially when students associate language anxiety with positive emotions (MacIntyre and Vincze 2017) and recognize the cognitive value of their efforts (Sardegna, Lee and Kusey 2018).

The analysis of the topics that emerged during the Language and Cultural Discussions activity suggested that, when exposed to the authentic and unscripted *ClicaBrasil* videos, students noticed the speech of different Brazilians regarding pronunciation. It seems that some pronunciation features were salient in the videos as it was the most immediate thing the students noticed (92 percent of the comments in the first discussion were about pronunciation features). Perhaps this is related to the fact that there was a class about pronunciation in the first week, or maybe it is because it was the first time that they listened to the authentic, spontaneous speech of diverse native Brazilians. Regardless, this finding provides evidence that the explicit pronunciation instruction and/or the watching of the authentic videos helped raise students' awareness of different speech accents and the pronunciation features that made them different (e.g., rhythm and articulation speed). Given that learning cannot take place without the learner consciously noticing the target form (Schmidt 1990), this is an important finding. The students' increased pronunciation awareness could make it possible for them to start working on improving the accuracy of the target features they noticed in the input (Sardegna 2009, 2021; Sardegna and McGregor 2013, 2017). Furthermore, the students also noticed differences in linguistic forms and pronunciation based on professions, social status, and context characteristics (formal/informal). Through this process, they began to acquire not only linguistic skills and cultural competence, but also a better understanding and appreciation of other peoples and cultures.

The fact that students' first comments were mostly on pronunciation features and differences in accents deserves some discussion as it shows it is the first thing people notice when listening to an authentic language speech sample. As the semester progressed, students' comments during the Language and Cultural Discussions progressively focused more on specific grammar forms and lexical items, perhaps in an effort to present on something different given that new grammar and lexical forms appeared in every video, but the pronunciation features of each speaker remain relatively the same as students viewed multiple videos of each speaker. Also, a decrease in pronunciation comments does not necessarily mean that the students were not paying attention to pronunciation issues anymore. It is highly probable that a presentation made on an aspect of pronunciation during the first oral presentations motivated other students to pay attention to that aspect in successive video recordings even if they were not choosing to discuss the same topic in their future presentations. Future research might want to investigate the effects of class presentations on other students' attention focus in future lessons. Future research might also want to look at whether single pronunciation-focused lessons spaced throughout the semester reignite focus on pronunciation in subsequent discussions.

Implication for Teaching

Students' opinions and the linguistic analysis of what they noticed in the videos underscored four aspects that enhanced students' opportunities for oral skills development via *ClicaBrasil*:

- *Authentic video materials*
  The students praised the videos in *ClicaBrasil* for their richness in terms of the variety of topics, speech accents, and people of different social backgrounds and professions. As their oral presentations demonstrated, the authenticity of these videos prompted cross-cultural comparisons and reflections that ultimately raised their awareness of different speech features and accents, including the use of colloquial language and slang. Hence, with these resources, *ClicaBrasil* appeared to support three critical instructional components in L2 pronunciation and oral skills development: Exposure to different speech accents, reflection (Sardegna 2021; Sardegna and McGregor 2013, 2022), and awareness-raising (Sardegna 2021; Sardegna and McGregor 2017, 2022).

- *Clear guidelines and useful, organized and accessible materials and activities*
  Many students highlighted how much they valued the accessibility of the materials, and the easy navigation and careful organization of *ClicaBrasil*. They also appreciated the clarity of the instructions and the supporting materials (e.g., transcriptions, glossaries with key vocabulary). This aspect of *ClicaBrasil* seemed to ensure that the students had an enjoyable experience when using the embedded materials and activities, which undoubtedly also facilitated their learning. Students' comments also indicated that the website promoted self-exploration and willingness to continue using the materials autonomously after the course ended. This is an important finding given the increasing evidence suggesting the need for frequent, self-regulated, and long-term oral practice to achieve lasting L2 pronunciation gains (Sardegna 2009, 2012, 2021). Hence, with its supporting and organized structure, *ClicaBrasil* seemed to feature another crucial instructional component for improving oral skills: teaching and practice scaffolds for autonomous learning (Sardegna 2021; Sardegna and McGregor 2022).

- *Thought-provoking topics and personal stories*
  The uniqueness of the resources in *ClicaBrasil* resides in that they are all based on authentic readings and videos. Students' comments stressed that they liked preparing their oral presentations and then sharing their perspectives orally in class because their discussions were based on personal stories and real people (the people featured on the website). To be successful at expressing their opinions in Portuguese, the students prepared their presentations ahead of time. Oral practice in covert rehearsal (e.g., in preparation for oral presentations) helps students focus on form, change their pronunciations to match speech models, and improve the accuracy and fluency of their speech (Sardegna 2009, 2012, 2020, 2021). Also,

authentic interaction helps turn declarative knowledge (e.g., knowledge of a speech feature) into procedural knowledge (e.g., accurate pronunciation of the speech feature in free speech) and, as such, it is essential for oral skills development (DeKeyser 2015). Hence, with the inclusion of thought-provoking and engaging topics, *ClicaBrasil* seemed to encourage not only rich and critical group and whole-class discussions, but also oral practice in controlled and free speech—two other important instructional components for developing L2 pronunciation and fluency (Sardegna 2021).

• *Classroom structure and teacher feedback*
  ClicaBrasil offers feedback on grammar and reading comprehension activities through Answer Keys—which the students found useful for autonomous learning. However, it does not include feedback on oral/pronunciation skills. Also, while the materials promote discussion and elaboration of topics, there needs to be a classroom structure for that interaction to actually take place. Thus, the findings showed that the resources in *ClicaBrasil* are optimized when used as a complement to classroom instruction. In other words, *ClicaBrasil* seemed to effectively promote exposure to different accents, reflection, awareness-raising, and controlled focus-on-form oral practice (through mimicry of speech models). Yet, it was through their participation in the course that the students were able to share perspectives, express thoughts, and interact orally with others, and receive teacher feedback on their oral production. Focus-on-Form through corrective feedback has been found to maximize students' learning opportunities (Saito and Saito 2017), and thus should also be incorporated into the language class. Also, the scaffolded nature of the activities and resources available through *ClicaBrasil* helped students be successful at learning and, ultimately, recognize that, even if they experienced some sort of language anxiety in the process, it did not hinder them from learning.

USING CLICABRASIL FOR LANGUAGE AND CULTURAL DISCUSSIONS

Language and Cultural Discussions is an excellent example of a classroom activity to teach/learn an FL within a social context using authentic materials via technology (in this case, via *ClicaBrasil*). This activity was designed to raise awareness of different speech accents and cultural perspectives, and scaffold the development of students' pronunciation and oral skills. Based on the findings and the pedagogical implications of our research, we recommend its use in any language classroom. Next, we describe tips for teaching this activity to learners of Portuguese using *ClicaBrasil*.

Tips for Teaching Using ClicaBrasil

Based on the findings, we recommend the following five instructional steps for implementing the activity Language and Cultural Discussions using the resources available through *ClicaBrasil*:

1. *Cultural and Language Awareness-Raising Through ClicaBrasil Videos.*

   - Purpose: Scaffold students into building awareness of diverse pronunciation features, linguistic expressions, and cultural perspectives within the different Brazilians portrayed in *ClicaBrasil* while relating to their own cultural experiences.
   - Tips: Watch a unit video in *ClicaBrasil* as a whole class. During and after watching the video, ask questions that prompt reflection, endorse and add to students' comments, engage students in class discussions that respect different opinions, and make comments about language and cultural issues using examples from the videos. Then assign other videos from *ClicaBrasil* with corresponding activities for homework. Ask students to choose topics featured in the videos for a critical language and cultural analysis that they will orally present to the class in Portuguese.

2. *Scaffolding Through Teaching, Modeling, and Detailed Instructions.*

   - Purpose: Guide students into becoming acute observers who use critical thinking to analyze language use in a social context.
   - Tips: Give detailed oral and written instructions on how to prepare for their oral presentation (and discussion) of their critical language and cultural analysis. Post the written instructions in the course learning management system for future reference. The instructions should provide explicit explanations and modeling of expectations, and stress the importance of listing the sources and note-taking—i.e., who says what and under which circumstances. Ask students to connect their observations with concrete examples from the authentic materials.

3. *Individual Reflection and Preparation Practice via a Written Homework*

   - Purpose: Scaffold students into organizing thoughts, synthetizing and connecting main points, critically reflecting on their observations, and ensuring they know the language they will need to express their opinions. Stress the importance of thinking ahead, preparing, and practicing for a presentation.
   - Tips: As part of the preparation for the oral presentation, include a written homework assignment, due minutes before the presentation time, in which students write their critical language and cultural analysis in

250–300 words. Students are expected to practice their oral presentation (focus on form), use this written assignment as a support/memory/
organizational aid during the oral presentation, and not read from the
assignment while presenting.

4. *Oral Presentation and Reflection on Learning*

- Purpose: Offer students opportunities to (a) practice their pronunciation,
  fluency, and presentation skills; (b) express their opinions; (c) gain a
  deeper understanding of diverse linguistic and cultural perspectives
  among Brazilians; and (d) engage in an active process of cross-cultural
  and self-awareness.
- Tips: On the day of the presentation, instruct each student to present
  their language and cultural observations to the class, and then engage the
  whole class in a discussion of what was presented. Encourage students
  to monitor their language as they present, agree/disagree, ask questions,
  and add their own insights/experiences to their classmates' comments.
  Guide the class to discuss the diversity of linguistic expressions and cultural perspectives they found in the materials and compare them to their
  own experiences. Prompt reflection about how different/similar cultural
  norms inform the worldviews of the peoples they are studying and their
  own. Encourage understanding and acceptance of others. Build a sense
  of community through respectful and open conversation. Provide general feedback and/or summary comments regarding what was learned/
  discussed so that everyone can benefit from teacher feedback.

5. *Individualized Feedback on Pronunciation and Oral Skills.*

- Purpose: Provide positive reinforcement, speech models to follow/imi-
  tate, and redirect students' language learning as needed.
- Tips: After the class discussion, provide a grade with a written comment regarding the student's oral skills and ability to communicate
  and exchange ideas in Portuguese. Also, offer individualized oral
  feedback via voice recording. Voice recordings allow you to make
  suggestions, provide explanations, model pronunciations, notice areas
  in need of improvement, praise students for their efforts and progress,
  and answer questions.

ClicaBrasil has a myriad of authentic videos that can be used to implement
this activity in the Portuguese language class. We strongly recommend doing
this activity multiple times, and assigning the first discussion early in the se-

mester so that students can start developing their pronunciation, fluency, and presentation skills from the beginning of the course.

This multi-step activity can be done with any authentic audio-visual materials in any L1 and teachers may be able to find similar repositories of materials available online. Two examples of open educational resources (OER) with videos and activities (as in *ClicaBrasil*) in other languages are the following:

- Français Interactif[2]—It includes over 320 videos featuring students of French completing a summer program in Lyon, France, and a wide range of resources for learning French, including vocabulary and phonetics audio, self-correcting exercises, and audio dialogues.
- Rockin Russian[3]—It exposes students to the Russian language and culture through music. It is supplemented with exercise materials focusing on pronunciation, vocabulary development, grammar, and cultural features.

CONCLUSION

ClicaBrasil is an excellent language and technology resource for the Portuguese language classroom due to its supporting structure, richness of resources and activities, and focus on teaching the Portuguese language and Brazilian culture simultaneously. Moreover, as this chapter has shown, *ClicaBrasil* is particularly powerful with respect to supporting the development of oral and pronunciation skills in an integrated curriculum. It features a variety of speech accents and topics with authentic videos, readings, and accompanying activities that foster exploration, reflection, critical thinking, cross-cultural and language awareness, and collaboration in addition to language growth. PFL students' opinions of *ClicaBrasil* and the linguistic analysis of what they noticed in *ClicaBrasil*'s videos highlighted three aspects of this instructional technology tool that enhanced their opportunities for oral skills development: (a) authentic video materials; (b) clear guidelines, and useful, organized and accessible materials and activities; and (c) thought-provoking topics and personal stories. A further aspect that contributed to learning was the classroom structure and teacher feedback. Based on the findings, the chapter offered tips for implementing an activity using the resources embedded in *ClicaBrasil*. We call for future research on *ClicaBrasil* investigating students' pronunciation improvement through pre-/post-test designs and with Portuguese language learners of different L1 backgrounds and ages.

NOTES

1. https://laits.utexas.edu/clicabrasil/.
2. https://www.laits.utexas.edu/fi/home.
3. https://rr.coerll.utexas.edu/.

REFERENCES

Chong, Ivan. 2018. "Interplay Among Technical, Socio-Emotional and Personal Factors in Written Feedback Research." *Assessment & Evaluation in Higher Education* 43, no. 2: 185–196. https://doi.org/10.1080/02602938.2017.1317712

Creswell, John W., and J. David Creswell. 2016. *30 Essential Skills for the Qualitative Researcher*. Thousand Oaks, CA: Sage.

Creswell, John W., and J. David Creswell. 2018. *Research Design: Qualitative, Quantitative, and Mixed Methods Approaches*. 5th ed. Thousand Oaks, CA: Sage.

Cristófaro Silva, Thaïs. n.d. *"Fonética e Fonologia."* Accessed February 24, 2022. www.fonologia.org

DeKeyser, Robert M. 2015. "Skill Acquisition Theory." In *Theories in Second Language Acquisition: An Introduction* (2nd ed.), edited by Jessica Williams and Bill VanPatten, 95–112. Mahwah, NJ: Erlbaum.

Derwing, Tracey M., and Murray J. Munro. 2015. *Pronunciation Fundamentals: Evidence-Based Perspectives for L2 Teaching and Research.* Amsterdam/Philadelphia: John Benjamins. https://benjamins.com/catalog/lllt.42

Flanzer, Vivian. 2010. *"ClicaBrasil: Portuguese Language and Culture for Intermediate Students."* [Website] Austin, TX: LAITS and COERLL. Accessed February 24, 2022. https://laits.utexas.edu/clicabrasil/

Flanzer, Vivian. 2019. *"ClicaBrasil: Portuguese Language and Culture for Intermediate Students."* [Textbook] Austin, TX: COERLL. Accessed February 24, 2022. https://www.laits.utexas.edu/clicabrasil/sites/laits.utexas.edu.clicabrasil/files/cb_textbook.pdf

Flanzer, Vivian. In Press. *"Integrando Literatura, Cultura e Tecnologia na Sala de Aula de PLE: O Uso de Crônicas em ClicaBrasil."* In *O Ensino e a Aprendizagem de Português em Universidades nos Estados Unidos,* edited by E. V. Da Silva and K Silva. Campinas, SP: Mercado de Letras.

Gilmore, Alex. 2007. "Authentic Materials and Authenticity in Foreign Language Learning." *Language Learning* 40, no. 2: 97–118. https://doi.org/10.1017/S0261444807004144

Kelm, Orlando. 2006. *"Tá Falado."* Accessed February 24, 2022. https://www.coerll.utexas.edu/brazilpod/tafalado/

Lee, Junkyu, Junkyu Jang, and Luke Plonsky. 2015. "The Effectiveness of Second Language Pronunciation Instruction: A Meta-Analysis." *Applied Linguistics* 36, no. 3: 345–66. https://doi.org/10.1093/applin/amu040

Levis, John. 2018. *Intelligibility: Oral Communication, and the Teaching of Pronunciation*. Cambridge: Cambridge University Press.

Luchini, Pedro. 2017. "Measurements for Accentedness, Pause and Nuclear Stress Placement in the EFL Context." *Ilha do Desterro* 70, No. 3: 185–200. https://doi .org/10.5007/2175-8026.2017v70n3p185

MacIntyre, Peter D., and Laszlo Vincze. 2017. "Positive and Negative Emotions Underlie Motivation for L2 Learning." *Studies in Second Language Learning and Teaching* 7, no. 1: 61–88. https://doi.org/10.14746/ssllt.2017.7.1.4

The National Standards Collaborative Board. 2015. *"World-Readiness Standards for Learning Languages."* 4th ed. Alexandria, VA: Author. Accessed January 3, 2022. https://www.actfl.org/resources/world-readiness-standards-learning-languages

Papi, Mostafa. 2010. "The L2 Motivational Self-System, L2 Anxiety, and Motivated Behavior: A Structural Equation Modeling Approach." *System* 38, no. 3: 467–479. https://doi.org/10.1016/j.system.2010.06.011

Saito, Yukie, and Kazuya Saito. 2017. "Differential Effects of Instruction on the Development of Second Language Comprehensibility, Word Stress, Rhythm, and Intonation: The Case of Inexperienced Japanese EFL Learners." *Language Teaching Research* 21, no. 5: 589–608. https://doi.org/10.1177/1362168816643111

Sardegna, Veronica G. 2009. "Improving English Stress Through Pronunciation Learning Strategies." PhD diss, University of Illinois at Urbana-Champaign.

Sardegna, Veronica G. 2012. "Learner Differences in Strategy Use, Self-Efficacy Beliefs, and Pronunciation Improvement." In *Proceedings of the 3rd Pronunciation in Second Language Learning and Teaching Conference,* edited by John Levis and Kimberly LeVelle, 39–53. Ames: Iowa State University.

Sardegna, Veronica G. 2020. "Pronunciation and Good Language Teachers." In *Lessons from Good Language Teachers,* edited by Carol Griffiths and Zia Tajeddin, 232–245. Cambridge: Cambridge University Press. https://doi.org/10.1017 /9781108774390.021

Sardegna, Veronica G. 2021. "Evidence in Favor of a Strategy-Based Model for English Pronunciation Instruction." *Language Teaching.* 1–16. First View. https://doi .org/10.1017/S0261444821000380

Sardegna, Veronica G., and Joan E. Hughes. 2022. "Teaching and Learning Languages with Technology." In *Integrating Educational Technology into Teaching* (9th Ed), edited by M. D. Roblyer and Joan E. Hughes, 332–362. New York: Pearson.

Sardegna, Veronica G., Juhee Lee, and Crystal Kusey. 2018. "Self-Efficacy, Attitudes, and Choice of Strategies for English Pronunciation Learning." *Language Learning* 68, no. 1: 83–114. https://doi.org/10.1111/lang.12263

Sardegna, Veronica G., and Alison L. McGregor. 2013. "Scaffolding Students' Self-Regulated Efforts for Effective Pronunciation Practice." In *Proceedings of the 4th Pronunciation in Second Language Learning and Teaching Conference,* edited by John Levis and Kimberly LeVelle, 182–193. Ames: Iowa State University.

Sardegna, Veronica G., and Alison L. McGregor. 2017. "Oral Communication for International Graduate Students and Teaching Assistants." In *Teaching the Pronunciation of English: Focus on Whole Courses,* edited by John Murphy, 130–154. Ann Arbor: University of Michigan Press.

Sardegna, Veronica G., and Alison L. McGregor . 2022. "Classroom Research for Pronunciation." In *Bridging the Gap Between Pronunciation Research and Teaching,* edited by John M. Levis, Tracey M. Derwing, and Sinem Sonsaat-Hegelheimer, 107–128. Hoboken, NJ: Wiley.

Schmidt, Richard, W. 1990. "The Role of Consciousness in Second Language Learning." *Applied Linguistics* 11, no. 2: 129–158. https://doi.org/10.1093/applin/11.2.129

Spada, Nina, and Patsy M. Lightbown. 1993. "Instruction and the Development of Questions in L2 Classrooms." *Studies in Second Language Acquisition* 15, no. 2: 205–224. http://www.jstor.org/stable/44487618

Thomas, David R. 2006. "A General Inductive Approach for Analyzing Qualitative Evaluation Data." *American Journal of Evaluation* 27, no. 2: 237–246. https://doi.org/10.1177/1098214005283748

Thomson, Ron I., and Tracey M. Derwing. 2015. "The Effectiveness of L2 Pronunciation Instruction: A Narrative Review." *Applied Linguistics* 36, no. 3: 326–344. https://doi.org/10.1093/applin/amu076

Winstone, Noami, David Boud, Phillip Dawson, and Marion Heron. 2022. "From Feedback-as-Information to Feedback-as-Process: A Linguistic Analysis of the Feedback Literature." *Assessment & Evaluation in Higher Education* 47, no.2: 213–230. https://doi.org/10.1080/02602938.2021.1902467

Chapter Six

Performance-based Test

A Technology-based Achievement Assessment in Introductory Japanese Courses

Mariko M. Wei, Mayu Miyamoto, Namiko Uchida, Atsushi Fukada, and Jessica L. Sturm

INTRODUCTION

This article introduces the *Performance-Based Test* (PBT), a new technology-based achievement assessment that utilizes an online platform, *Speak Everywhere* (Fukada 2009). In many language programs today, large portions of periodic assessments utilize the traditional pencil-and-paper format, ignoring pronunciation and other oral aspects. These tests typically emphasize grammar and written language, and multiple-choice and cloze test items are often used. These tests do not reflect the actual pedagogical focus of communicative language classrooms, and as such, they are not appropriate indicators of a learner's ability to use their target language in real-life situations.

Assessment methods have not enjoyed the innovations that have been made in teaching methods, both in Japanese language education specifically, as well as in foreign language education in general. To put it concretely, there are many institutions that rely on conventional written examinations for evaluation, even though they have adopted class content and curricula that emphasize oral skills at least at the elementary and intermediate levels. Such a situation existed at the North American university where the authors work (our institution) until we developed and implemented the PBT. While written tests were administered about six times per semester, including chapter tests, mid-term, and final exams, oral tests could only be administered once or twice a semester due to time constraints, making oral assessment, which should be a continuous process, quite sporadic. When the course goal is to foster oral proficiency, but only written tests are used to test knowledge of grammar and kanji, the logographic Japanese writing system, the lack of consistency between the content of teaching and the evaluation method would be justifiably criticized.

Brown (2007) and Hughes (1989) argue that achievement tests should cover the content, purpose, and scope of the textbook, reflect the class activities, and serve as a basis for the learning objectives of the entire course. In light of this, we set out to develop a method that would allow for continuous assessment of oral skills throughout the semester. By implementing such an assessment, we thought it would be possible to promote learners' oral practice and have a washback effect on their acquisition of oral skills.

Furthermore, considering the recent remarkable development of technology and online/remote and/or hybrid learning, the availability of well-developed, user-friendly platforms for oral testing outside of the classroom is crucial. This both frees up class time for practice and communicative activities and makes the assessments usable in any course delivery format, from fully in-person to asynchronous online.

In order to meet this requirement and to remedy the assessment situation discussed above, the PBT has been developed on *Speak Everywhere*, a web-based oral practice/assessment platform (Fukada 2009, 2013). *Speak Everywhere* focuses on promoting the speaking skills of learners of Japanese, including pronunciation and fluency. The PBT tasks include monologue, read aloud, read and answer, Q&A, and guided conversation. As a performance test, the tasks for a particular chapter are made available as soon as the chapter begins, and the students are allowed and encouraged to keep practicing the tasks as many times as they want. At the end of the chapter, they are to submit their best performance.

A survey study was conducted to elicit students' and instructors' perceptions of both the PBT and the traditional written test, and how each testing format related to their learning goals. Thirty-four students enrolled in Japanese Level 2 (JPNS 102) and four instructors participated in the study. The results indicated that the students preferred the PBT over the traditional written test; they felt motivated to prepare for it and felt a sense of accomplishment upon completion. The instructors commented that the students had become more used to speaking Japanese, and that showed in their more active engagement in class activities. Thus, we conclude that our implementation of the PBT was a viable and promising alternative to conventional written tests that do not address students' oral skills.

PREVIOUS RESEARCH

Task-Based Language Teaching/Assessment

Task-based language teaching (TBLT) is "a pedagogical approach to language instruction with the central aim of preparing students to accomplish real-world tasks that are directly relevant to their needs" (González-Lloret and Nielson 2015, p. 526). TBLT is based on the concept of achieving tasks in the L2 as a means of learning, rather than organizing courses around linguistic or functional units. According to González-Lloret and Nielson (2015), "teaching methods based on traditional textbooks and methods are unlikely to meet the real-world needs of current students" (p. 525). TBLT is an answer to that dilemma; by re-framing a new language as a skill that one practices while learning it, learners and teachers can focus on what learners can do with the language. Further, this re-framing emphasizes the difference between learning a new language and learning other academic subjects: to reiterate, a language is a skill that you practice while learning it.

A major component of any methodological approach is assessment. Task-based language assessment (TBLA) is "an alternative form of assessment to replace discrete-skills assessment" (Noroozi and Taheri 2021, p. 688). Even beyond the scope of TBLT, Puppin (2007) noticed a "mismatch" between communicative language teaching and traditional paper-and-pencil tests. According to Norris (2016), "Fundamentally, a primary motivation for incorporating TBLA into language education has to do with the need to align assessment, curriculum, and instruction such that they complement each other in supporting effective language learning." Norris (2016) notes (pp. 240–241) several advantages to TBLA, among those, "Task-based performances can reveal multiple aspects of language ability and/or development within a single instance (e.g., accuracy, complexity, and fluency; content knowledge; procedural knowledge; expertise; and pragmatic sensibility)" (p. 241). When assessing oral language, accuracy, complexity, and fluency are all crucial dimensions for evaluation.

Performance-Based Tests

Performance-based tests (PBTs) are a subset of task-based language assessments; learners complete a specific task or tasks and are evaluated on their performance of said task(s). According to Puppin (2007), "performance tests that are designed around authentic tasks are a more valid way to assess the students' language learning progress" (p. 10). Stiggins (2005) notes that "Performance assessments involve students in activities that require them actually to demonstrate performance of certain skills. . . . In this case, we directly observe and judge their performance while it happens." Norris (2016) notes that "Not only have language performance tasks continued to play important roles in classroom-based testing, but their use—often in combination with emerging technological affordances—has expanded within this and other assessment contexts in order to accommodate the real-world needs of test users" (p. 232).

Sturm (2020) noted that "PBTs fit the general category of Task-Based Language Assessments (TBLA), as described by Norris (2016): 'From portfolios to performance assessments, new approaches to testing [are] a way of reorienting teaching and learning to meaningful goals (p. 231)'" (Sturm 2020, p. 183). Espinosa (2015) reminds us that pen-and-paper assessments do not always reveal what students know. Sturm (2020) believes that "PBTs allow students to construct their own responses rather than choosing from a list of options, which is a more real-life, communicative activity" (p. 184).

Sturm (2020) used PBTs in an advanced-level French pronunciation class, along with traditional paper-and-pen quizzes, and surveyed students on their preferences, experiences, and preparation for the two types of assessment. She found that students slightly preferred PBTs; they felt that PBTs were fairer, better aligned with their learning goals, and better reflected what they can do in French. Sturm's (2020) students felt more anxiety and a higher sense of accomplishment from traditional quizzes, which they believed were more challenging.

Speak Everywhere as a platform for PBT

Speak Everywhere (SE) (Fukada 2009, 2013) is an online platform for oral practice and assessment in general, and it was used to develop, administer, and assess PBTs in L2 classes. There are five task types available in our implementation of PBT: monologue; reading aloud; read and answer; question and answer; and role-play. These tasks can be assigned as homework or as tests/ quizzes. The instructor can determine how long each task is available to students, affording students the opportunity to practice tasks before submitting a final performance. SE uses video prompts as well as written prompts to give students direction and stimuli to which they can respond. Sturm (2020) used monologue, read and answer, and question and answer on the SE platform in her French pronunciation class. Yoshida and Fukada (2014) used repeat-after-the-model vocabulary exercises on the SE platform in the beginning-level Japanese classes. They confirmed that the SE exercises had a significant effect on the acquisition of Japanese word accentuation, a notoriously complex pitch-accent system. Furthermore, Ikeda and Fukada (2012) found that beginning-level Japanese learners felt less anxious when engaging in the speaking exercises via SE than teacher-student and student-student interactions in a classroom.

Characteristics of the PBT

PBTs were devised as an alternative to the conventional achievement tests given at the end of each lesson, but they differ greatly from our conventional written tests (which are closed-book, timed, and proctored) in the following five aspects (see table 6.1 below for what we mean by "conventional written tests").

- Validity
  Suppose an English learner responds to this English test question "How do you think it is appropriate to greet people you meet for the first time? (a) Good-bye. (b) Nice to meet you. (c) Thank you." by correctly choosing (b) in a written test. This does not ensure that the learner would be able to say "Nice to meet you" in a first encounter context and that the learner would be able to pronounce the phrase reasonably correctly. With PBT, it is possible to set up a video or text of a situation where learners meet someone for the first time and see if they can say "Nice to meet you" in a natural intelligible fashion. In this way, the PBT has greater face validity than a written test in terms of measuring oral proficiency.

- Disclosure of test content
  The content of the test is disclosed to the students at the start of each chapter. Learners will know what tasks they need to do and how well they need to do them by the end of the chapter and can set goals. Clarifying the goal of each chapter and allowing learners to practice the test tasks freely and as many times as they want will encourage practice, which is one of the aims of the PBT.

- Scoring criteria
  Since the tasks are disclosed in advance, the scoring is not only based on whether the learner can do the tasks or not, but also on how accurately and fluently the learner can perform them. This point is clearly communicated to learners, and the scoring rubrics are shown to them as well.

- Oral focus
  Unlike the traditional written test, 90 percent of the test items are oral items. This assessment method is closer to the learners' language learning goal of "I want to be able to speak Japanese," and is considered to be more in line with their needs than traditional written tests.

- Take-home method
  Dictation is done together in the classroom (in the case of online courses, it is done during a synchronous session), but all other tasks are done on SE as a take-home test, with deadlines set within half a day or a day. This allows students to take the test in a relaxed and private environment at a time of their choosing. The tasks can be repeated as many times as necessary within the deadline until a satisfactory performance is recorded. In

addition, since class time is not sacrificed, the class time can be used more effectively. Finally, as course delivery formats develop and change with technology and global crises, the tasks can be implemented in any type of course, from traditional in-person to asynchronous online.

Next, we describe the details of each PBT task. As this is an achievement test, it goes without saying that the tasks will be based on the content of the chapter studied.

- Timed dictation
  This task is designed to develop accuracy and fluency in writing. First, an audio recording of about 15 sentences containing important grammatical items and new vocabulary of the chapter is prepared. Each sentence is read out twice, followed by a pause of about 1.5 times the time it takes a native speaker to write the sentence on a piece of paper. (The length of the pause should be adjusted according to the learners' writing ability.) This recording is for student practice and is disclosed at the beginning of a chapter. In the actual test, 10 sentences, chosen randomly out of the 15 that students have heard and practiced, are used for dictation. This activity has two fairly significant side benefits. First, since the sentences they write repeatedly are key sentences of each chapter, this activity reinforces their vocabulary and grammar learning. Second, it also enhances their listening accuracy.

- Monologue
  In this task, we set up as natural a situation as possible for the students to produce a discourse of a reasonable length by themselves. Examples include real-life activities such as introducing yourself to a group you've just joined or leaving a voicemail for a friend. As in the other tasks, students may record as many times as they like until they are satisfied with their performance. Length of activity will vary according to students' level; for example, for the first-year students in the present study, they were expected to record a 10–15 second monologue.

- Reading aloud
  In this task, students are presented with a paragraph or two of text to read aloud. A model voice is provided so that the students can practice following it. The students must read aloud accurately and fluently, paying attention to pronunciation, such as accent and intonation, and expression, including the placement of pauses in consideration of sentence structure and meaning. There will be a time limit as the course progresses. Since the learners must

read the given passage within the time limit, they have to practice it many times, which should help them to improve their fluency.

- Read and answer
This task integrates the three skills of reading, listening, and speaking by having students read a short passage and answer questions about the content orally. The order of the questions in this task changes randomly each time, in order to deter them from memorizing the answers and reciting them.

- Q&A
In this task, students are asked a variety of questions in a set context using charts, pictures, photos, videos, audio, etc., and are required to give appropriate answers both in terms of content and pragmatics. The order of questions in this task also changes randomly.

- Role-play
This task is usually created using model conversations from the chapter. First, the complete model conversation is made available for reference at any time. If the conversation is between A and B, a video of A's speech part is played and learners are asked to play the role of B. Then a video of B's speech part will be played to allow learners to practice A's skills. If the model conversation in the chapter is not suitable as material for such a role-play, a role-play called Guided Conversation was created. This is not a scripted role-play as explained above, but rather a conversation students carry on using their own words following the instructions of the cue. In the following example, A is the video and B is an example of the learner's speech. (The cue is written in the learner's native language.)

A: I'm looking forward to the trip to Okinawa tomorrow.

(Cue: Express that you are also looking forward to it and ask what the weather will be like.)

B: Yes, I'm looking forward to it. Will the weather be good?

A: Well, I'll check the weather forecast.

(Cue: TV weather forecast says "Tomorrow's weather in Okinawa will be sunny with occasional cloudiness. The temperature will be high and humid.")

A: Cloudy, huh? I wonder if it will rain.

(Cue: Tell A that because it might rain, they might need an umbrella.)

B: It might rain. We might need an umbrella.

A: That's right. Then let's take an umbrella with us.

THE CURRENT STUDY

Research Questions

In order to verify the effectiveness of our implementation of the PBT, the following research questions were formulated in this study. Note that we are assessing not PBT in general but our technology-enabled implementation of it.

[RQ1] Does the replacement of the written test with the PBT reduce writing and grammar skills?

[RQ2] Does the introduction of the PBT contribute to the improvement of global oral proficiency as measured by an Elicited Imitation Task (EIT)?

[RQ3] Which of the two assessment methods (the traditional written test and the PBT) do learners think is more aligned with their own learning goals?

[RQ4] Which test do learners prefer, the traditional written test or the PBT?

[RQ5] How do learners perceive the two assessment methods? (For example, in terms of anxiety, motivation, fairness, etc.)

[RQ6] Do students report changes in learning behaviors in preparing for PBT?

RQ 1, 3, 4, 5, and 6 were examined using data collected in 2015, and RQ 2 was examined using data collected in 2016.

Time Period and Subjects

Subjects from 2015 Data Collection

The subjects were students (34 students in total) enrolled in three sections of a face-to-face course in elementary Japanese (JPNS102) at our institution during the spring semester of 2015. The course consisted of five 50-minute classes per week, using the elementary Japanese textbook *Nakama 1* (Hatasa, Hatasa, and Makino 2014), and students were expected to complete chapters 7 through 12 as a continuation of chapters 1 through 6 of JPNS101.

For chapters 7, 8, 10, and 11, the written test group took written tests, while the PBT group took PBT tests on SE. At chapter 9 (mid-term) and chapter 12 (final exam) both groups took a written exam.

There were 158 learners (11 sections) who took JPNS102 that semester, and in the three sections where 34 subjects were enrolled, a PBT chapter test was given after each chapter (except for chapter 9). Only for chapter 9, a written test was given as a mid-term exam, not by PBT, and the final exam consisted of a written test and a face-to-face interview to comprehensively evaluate what the students had learned in this course. As mentioned earlier, the chapter test consisted of two parts: a timed dictation and a PBT. The dictation was given in class using 10 minutes of class time, and the online PBT test was made available to the students for 24 hours on the test date so that they could take it from home.

For the 124 learners enrolled in the remaining eight sections, chapter tests, midterm, and final exams were all written exams administered simultaneously in class, with no opportunity to take the PBT. These sections were each taught by instructors trained in the use of PBT. The final exam aimed to comprehensively evaluate the content learned in JPNS 102 and consisted of six components: vocabulary, grammar, fill-in-the-blank conversations, short essays, reading comprehension, and listening comprehension. The details of the exam are provided below. In the 2015 study, the PBT group ($N = 34$) included 25 men and nine women, with a mean age of 20.5 years. Their native languages were English ($N = 20$), Chinese ($N = 13$), and Korean (N = 1). In the Written Test group ($N = 124$) there were 67 men and 57 women, mean age 19.57 years. Their native languages were Chinese ($N = 79$), English ($N = 39$), Korean ($N = 4$), Arabic ($N = 1$), and Thai ($N = 1$). In addition, four instructors participated by filling out the instructor survey. They were native-speaking female instructors in their 20s and 30s with two to four years of teaching experience.

In 2016, data were collected only to examine RQ 2. The subjects were students enrolled in a year of Elementary Japanese (JPNS 101 and 102) at our institution in 2016. The textbook, number of class hours, and the pace of instruction were the same as in the previous year. The PBT group ($N = 33$) included 22 men and 11 women, mean age 19.97 years. Their native languages were English ($N = 15$), Chinese ($N = 16$), Burmese ($N = 1$), and Cantonese ($N = 1$). In the Written Test group ($N = 44$), there were 25 men, and 19 women, mean age 19.95 years. Their native languages were Chinese ($N = 26$), English ($N = 16$), and Korean ($N = 2$).

Survey

After the final exam, a survey was used to evaluate the PBT by learners and Japanese language instructors. It consisted of three sections: (1) learners' learning goals, (2) comparison between the PBT and the conventional written test, and (3) changes in study habits. For (2) and (3), for example, when asked which type of test they preferred, PBT or written test, respondents were asked to choose from five options: "overwhelmingly PBT," "somewhat PBT," "both," "somewhat written," and "overwhelmingly written." In the analysis of these survey items, a z-test (two-tailed) was used to determine whether there was a statistically significant difference between the number of 1s and 2s and the number of 4s and 5s on the five-point scale.

In addition, four Japanese language instructors who implemented the PBT were asked to complete an instructor survey. In this survey, the instructors were asked about their views on the introduction of the PBT, changes in their students, and changes in their teaching methods. Content analysis was performed on the responses, by classifying them, summarizing them, and tabulating them.

Comparison of the Final Exam

As mentioned earlier, both the three sections that took the PBT chapter tests and the remaining eight sections that took the written test took the exact same written test for the final exam. We used a *t*-test to examine the difference in the mean scores of the two groups on the final exam. (Because there was no pre-test at the beginning of the semester, the comparison is not ideal.)

Table 6.1.   Components of the Written Exam

Task	Number of Items	Points per Item	Points for Section
Fill in the blanks in sentences with grammatical particles	18	0.5	9
Write out in syllabaries the underlined kanji (logograms) in sentences	12	0.5	6
Fill in the blanks in sentences with Japanese words appropriately conjugated based on English cues	13	2	26
Fill in the blanks in clozed dialogues with words or short phrases	7	1	7
Choose an appropriate response to a question (multiple choice)	5	1	5
Conjugate underlined verbs in a passage	4	1	4
Read a passage and answer multiple-choice comprehension questions	4	1	4
Answer in English comprehension questions about a passage written in English	4	1	4
Underline the relative clause that modifies a designated noun in a passage	2	1	2
Translate an underlined sentence in a passage	1	2	2
Short composition	1	6	6
Listening portion with three dialogues each with multiple-choice comprehension questions	10	1.5	15

Source: Wei, M., Miyamoto, M., Uchida, N., Fukada, A., & Sturm, J.

Comparison of Verbal Ability

In order to address RQ2, we collected data in 2016 with only the comparison of oral proficiency in mind. The written group took only the written test, while the PBT group took only the PBT without any written test. For the comparison of verbal skills, both groups were administered an Elicited Imitation Test (EIT). The EIT is a task in which participants listen to recorded sentences one at a time, pause for two seconds, and then reproduce the sentence orally as accurately as possible, and is said to measure overall oral proficiency (see Wu & Ortega 2013; Yan, Maeda, Lv, & Ginther 2015). The oral test was administered face-to-face with an instructor who did not teach that student's class, and the instructor in charge listened to and scored the audio recordings. The EIT was scored by counting the number of morae that were repeated recognizably. The scoring was done by two people, and the inter-rater reliability was 0.98.

The scores obtained were aggregated, and the two groups were compared using *t*-test.

RESULTS

Comparison Results of the Written Final Exam (RQ1)

To dispel the concern that the learners' writing ability and grammatical knowledge may decrease when the test format is switched to PBT, we compared the scores of the PBT group and the written test group on the final exam (written format). The mean, standard deviation, lowest score, and highest score of the two groups are summarized below:

- N = Written 124; PBT 34
- Mean score: Written, 65.65; PBT 63.48
- SD Written 12.95; PBT 11.92
- Lowest score: Written 30.87; PBT 39.2
- Highest score: Written 88.38; PBT 84.8

The results of the *t*-test showed that there was no statistically significant difference in the mean scores of the two groups ($t=0.36$, n.s.), indicating that the subjects who had taken chapter tests using the PBT had acquired the same level of proficiency in writing and grammatical knowledge as those who had always taken the test using the written method.

Evidence from this comparison can be strengthened by having a pre-test at the beginning of a semester. We plan to compare the two groups using a pre-test in the coming years.

Comparison Results of Oral Proficiency (RQ2)

In order to compare the oral performance of the PBT group and the written test group, an oral test consisting of an Elicited Imitation Test (EIT) was conducted. The mean, standard deviation, lowest score, and highest score of the two groups are summarized below:

- N = Written 40; PBT 33
- Mean: Written 163.93; PBT 187.94
- SD: Written 26.20; PBT 21.48
- Lowest score: Written 91; PBT 135
- Highest score: Written 210; PBT 209

The scores of both groups, upon meeting the assumption of homogeneity of variances, were subjected to an independent-samples t-test, and the results show that the PBT group significantly outperformed the written test group (2-tailed, $t=4.355$; $p <.000$). It would be ideal if there were a pre-test for this oral test as well, but for that, we must overcome the difficulty of measuring the oral ability of complete beginners, and relatedly, the difficulty that the same test cannot be used for pre-test and post-test.

Results of the Survey

Learning Goals (RQ 3)

Table 6.2 summarizes the results of the survey regarding the learning goals of the learners. For "1. Purpose of taking Japanese," the most common answers were "I want to learn Japanese" and "I want to know about Japanese culture," in addition to "It is a required course." Next, to the question "2. Why did you choose Japanese instead of other languages?" half of the respondents answered that they were interested in the culture, including anime and music. When asked which of the four skills (speaking, listening, writing, and reading) they wanted to improve, 52.9 percent of the students chose speaking. The lowest percentage was for writing. Furthermore, for "4. Goals to achieve in one semester," the majority of the responses focused on oral skills, such as "to become fluent in speaking" and "to be able to

Table 6.2.   Results of the Survey: Learning Goals

Question	Response
1. Purpose of taking Japanese	I want to learn Japanese. (29%) I am interested in Japanese culture. (23.5%) Because it is a required course. (23.5%)
2. Why did you choose Japanese instead of other languages?	I like Japanese culture and am interested in it. (55.8%) I think the Japanese language is interesting. (23.5%)
3. Which of the four skills (speaking, listening, writing, and reading) do you want to improve? (One student chose more than one.)	Speaking (%)	Listening (%)	Writing (%)	Reading (%)
	52.9	32.4	5.8	11.8
4. Goal to be achieved in one semester	I want to be able to speak fluently. (41%) I want to be able to have basic conversations. (35%)

Source: Uchida, N

have basic conversations." Here, a strong interest in Japanese culture seems to be the trigger for taking Japanese language courses, but in terms of learning, it became clear that the majority of the students' goal was to improve their speaking ability, including conversation.

Comparison between the Written Test and the PBT (RQ4 and 5)

In response to the question "1. Which do you prefer, written test or PBT?" 70.6 percent of the total students chose the PBT, while 23.8 percent chose the written test, a statistically significant difference. The most common reason was that it would help them practice and improve their speaking and listening skills. This is in line with the speaking-focused responses we saw in the last row of table 6.3. In response to the question "2. Which test did you feel more anxious about?" 52.9 percent of the students chose the written test and 20.6 percent chose the PBT, indicating that the written test significantly exceeded the PBT in terms of anxiety. The reasons given were that "the test questions are difficult," "there is a lot to memorize," and "accuracy in writing is required." When asked which test they felt more accomplished on, half of the students chose the PBT, while less than 20 percent of the students chose the written test. There was a statistically significant difference in the sense of accomplishment between the two tests, and the reasons given by the learners who chose the PBT were "I can feel the improvement in my speaking" and "I can feel what I have learned." Although there was no significant difference

Table 6.3. Survey Results: Comparison between the Written Test and the PBT

Question	Overwhelmingly PBT (%)	Somewhat PBT (%)	Both (%)	Somewhat Written (%)	Overwhelmingly Written (%)	No Response (%)	z value
1. Which do you prefer, written test or PBT?	38.2	32.4	5.9	20.6	2.9	0.0	(3.2344)*
2. Which test did you feel more anxious about?	11.8	8.8	26.5	29.4	23.5	0.0	(2.3756)*
3. Which test gave you a greater sense of accomplishment?	29.4	20.6	32.4	11.8	5.9	0.0	(2.4948)*
4. Which test was more difficult?	14.7	11.8	26.5	38.2	8.8	0.0	(1.4422)
5. Which test motivated you more to learn?	35.3	11.8	23.5	8.8	20.6	0.0	(1.2014)
6. Which test did you feel was fairer?	5.9	20.6	41.2	14.7	17.6	0.0	(1.5828)

*$p<0.05$

Source: Uchida, N.

in "4. Which test was more difficult," nearly half of the students chose the written test, while only about a quarter of the students chose the PBT. The reasons given for choosing the written test were that "the grading criteria are strict," "it is not possible to redo (as with the PBT)," and "I have to study harder." There was no statistically significant difference in "5. Which test motivated you to learn more": learners who chose the PBT mainly mentioned that it helped them improve their speaking and listening skills, and that it gave them more retention and confidence. However, students who answered that the written test motivated them more said, "In the PBT, you can redo the test as many times as you want, but in the written test, you don't have that, so you have to study hard," and "In the written test, there is a sense of urgency because you take it in a classroom (so it motivates you)." In other words, these students felt that the PBT was not enough for them. It is necessary to take measures to address this issue, such as devising a task that encourages students to learn. Regarding the question "6. Which test was fairer?" there was no significant difference between the groups; the largest number of students felt that both tests were fair.

Relatively speaking, based on the fact that students preferred the PBT over the written test and they felt a greater sense of accomplishment from the PBT than the written test, we conclude that the PBT was better received than the written test.

Change in Study Habits (RQ6)

In this section, we compared the PBT and the written test and focused on the differences in the students' (self-reported) study habits (see table 6.4). First, in "1. Preparation for the written test," the majority of students memorized grammar and vocabulary and read textbooks and other materials. Second, 73.5 percent of the students agreed that their learning methods had changed as a result of the PBT. Specifically, the majority of the students answered, "I have become more focused on speaking" and "I have more opportunities to speak." Based on this question, in response to "Which test preparation is more consistent with the objectives you stated in Section 1-1?" 64.7 percent of the students chose the PBT, and a significant difference between the PBT and the written test was confirmed. As in the previous answer, the reason given was that it gave them more opportunities to practice speaking and listening. Third, some students said that they practiced outside of class, that it was practical, and that it measured their fluency and accuracy. Finally, in response to the question "Which test better reflects what you have learned and become able to do in the Japanese language course?" 44.1 percent of the students answered the PBT, while 20.6 percent of the students answered the written test. In addition to "Being able to speak is the best evidence," other

Table 6.4. Survey Results: Changes in Study Habits

Question	Responses					
Preparation for the written test	Reviewed materials (44.1%) Memorized vocabulary and grammar (35.2%) Read the textbook (29.4%)					
Preparation for the PBT	Practiced speaking (29.4%) Reviewed grammar (23.5%) Others (47.1%)					
Did the PBT change your study habits?	Yes (%) 73.5			No (%) 26.5		No response (%) 0.0

Question	Definitely PBT (%)	Somewhat PBT (%)	Both (%)	Somewhat Written (%)	Definitely Written (%)	No Response (%)	z-value
Which test preparation is more consistent with the objectives you stated in Section 1-1?	41.2	23.5	11.8	8.8	11.8	2.9	(3.1849)*
Which test better reflects what you have learned and become able to do in the Japanese language course?	26.5	17.6	35.3	8.8	11.8	0.0	(1.7836)

*$p<0.05$

Source: Uchida, N.

comments included "It's a more natural way of learning" and "I can't pretend to be able to speak," suggesting that students allotted more time for oral practice outside of class.

Summary of Student Survey Results

From the above results, we can say that the PBT was generally positively evaluated. It was found that the priority goal of many students was speaking ability. Many students preferred the PBT and felt a greater sense of accomplishment with it than the written test. Students were motivated to practice speaking and listening skills, and they perceived that such learning methods met their learning goals. These results suggest that the PBT, with its emphasis on speaking and listening, may be an assessment method that meets the needs of learners. However, in the free responses, there were some comments such as "PBT was easy" and "I did not do any preparation." These remarks caution that the subjects might prefer the PBT because it was easier and less monitored. This concern could be addressed by tightening the grading criteria, such as not being too lenient in grading, deducting points for submissions that seem to have been put together hurriedly, and giving detailed feedback on why points were deducted.

Evaluation by Instructors

The overall evaluation of the PBT by the four Japanese language instructors was divided into "good" and "not good." To summarize their opinions, the good points were that the students became less hesitant to speak Japanese and became more active in class activities, that they were able to check the students' speech, and that they were able to rate the students' pronunciation and fluency. On the other hand, although this course was focused on oral proficiency, there were some instructors who were concerned about students' writing ability and recommended that the PBT be used together with the written test. They could not readily accept the idea of going 90 percent oral with all assessments. It took them a couple of semesters to appreciate the value of PBT. Moreover, the instructors also pointed out that students did not seem to look at the tasks in advance even though they were made public. This may refer to the students who reported not preparing for the test as mentioned above. By reviewing the grading method and giving detailed feedback from the practice stage, it may be possible to encourage those who do not practice. As for the changes in teaching methods, instructors mentioned having students practice in such a way as to broaden their range of expression. This may be a reflection of our PBT often asking students to produce a discourse as in a monologue task or to respond to rather open-ended questions in the Q&A section.

DISCUSSION

To summarize the results of the present research following the research questions, a significant number of learners preferred the tech-based PBT assessment method and perceived it to be in line with their learning goals. The tech-based PBT also gave learners a sense of accomplishment and made them feel less anxious. In addition, the PBT allowed learners to do more speaking practice than before. In addition, the PBT group did not perform worse on the written test compared to the written test group. Finally, the PBT group showed a greater improvement in oral proficiency as measured by EIT than the written test group.

The PBT is a take-home test designed to assess not only whether learners can perform the tasks on the test, but also how accurately and fluently they can perform the tasks. Since about 90 percent of the test questions are computer-based tests consisting of oral tasks using the SE online oral training system, it does not take as long as a face-to-face interview even with a large number of learners. In addition, the PBT can measure true mastery rather than one-time performance because the questions are open to the students from the beginning and the tasks can be repeated as many times as necessary within the time limit until a satisfactory performance is recorded. Furthermore, the results of the implementation at our institution showed that the learners' evaluation of the PBT was very high, and they perceived it as a good fit for their learning objectives and as an opportunity to increase their oral practice outside of class. Therefore, we can say that the PBT is a viable and promising alternative to conventional written tests that do not address students' oral skills.

Let us compare these results with those of Sturm (2020). Sturm's French students slightly preferred PBTs over traditional written assessments, while a significantly greater number of students (70.6%) in the present study preferred PBTs over written tests (23.8%). In terms of difficulty and anxiety, in both studies the students found traditional assessments to be more difficult and anxiety-producing. The two studies, however, had differing results with respect to the sense of accomplishment. Sturm's students had a higher sense of accomplishment from written tests, while the present study found that from PBTs. Although Sturm (2020) and the present study used the same technology platform, Sturm's study was about an advanced-level French pronunciation course, whereas the present study examined an elementary-level Japanese course; the contexts were vastly different. This may suggest that beginners are more likely to feel a greater sense of accomplishment from completing oral PBT tasks, but the PBT tasks themselves were undoubtedly quite different as well, making straight comparison very difficult. In the future, we will continue to use the PBT in both face-to-face and online courses in a variety of language courses at varying levels to see its effectiveness. We need to examine in detail the learning effects of using the PBT with more participants with pre-tests and post-tests.

Although the learner surveys were positive, PBT is not perfect. For example, PBT includes interactive tasks such as Q&A and role-plays, but these are qualitatively different from speaking face-to-face with Japanese speakers, and it is important to know whether the skills acquired through PBT practice can be demonstrated when facing Japanese speakers. Therefore, we are now starting an experiment in which the PBT is conducted consistently throughout the semester and a face-to-face oral test is given only once at the end of the semester. In addition, performance assessment is more difficult to grade than written tests because it is subjective. In this regard, we are currently working on building an evaluation system that follows the best practices of language testing and incorporating it into the PBT platform, SE.

In this study, we wanted to compare the assessment methods, so we changed only the assessment methods between the two groups and tried to keep the other course elements the same. However, in order to maximize the effect of the PBT, it will be necessary not only to introduce the PBT, but also to seek the best teaching method suitable for the evaluation method.

PEDAGOGICAL IMPLICATIONS

Speak Everywhere[1] (SE) has a multitude of uses at any institution, in any language. SE can be used for language, linguistics, or culture courses. For example, at the university where this research was conducted, five out of 14 world language programs, including Japanese, French, German, Chinese, and Korean, use SE. In German classes, SE is used for oral presentations and final projects; in French classes, SE is primarily used for assessment in pronunciation and culture courses. Sturm (2020) compared SE and written quizzes in an advanced French pronunciation course. Beginning in fall 2021, all quizzes for this course will be completed via SE, using Question and Answer tasks to test students' knowledge of phonetic rules and sound/spelling correspondences; Monologue to give students a chance to practice longer oral discourse; and Read and Answer to allow them to react to a written text with an oral response. Students also completed SE-based quizzes in a French food culture course. They engaged in Role-Play tasks to practice discussing food, ordering in a restaurant or café, and making dining plans with friends. This type of Role-Play activity can also be used to familiarize students with speech acts they may routinely perform while studying abroad. Chinese, Japanese, and Korean classes (both face-to-face and online) have used SE extensively for asynchronous speaking practice and assessment.

Language coordinators and instructors were asked to comment on how SE affected their teaching. Overall, the responses were positive. One major benefit of SE, according to all the instructors, was that it significantly increased students' opportunities to produce comprehensive output outside the classroom. After implementing SE, the instructors started assigning speaking practice as homework and requiring students to do oral exercises in preparation for class discussions. A Korean instructor said she has added a speaking component to every exam, while previous tests consisted only of listening, grammar, reading, and writing. Limited opportunities for students to speak and engage in meaningful interactions in a crowded classroom has been a problem, but SE can increase the students' opportunities to produce comprehensible output.

Speak Everywhere also provides students with a relaxed environment for self-paced L2 study. Students have the flexibility to log in and practice a target language at any time, from anywhere. They can watch model video clips as many times as they want; after practicing, they can submit their best performance. More flexibility and less pressure promote student engagement in language learning.

Students using SE can receive more specific individual feedback on their oral performance, compared to in the classroom. Since students' oral productions are saved on a server, teachers can review them carefully and give detailed feedback on student performance in audio and text modes. By giving frequent feedback via SE, instructors can see what students struggle with, assess their progress and learning status, and optimize lesson plans. They do not have to wait for test results to obtain this information. Other aspects of the course (e.g., reading comprehension, listening, and grammar) are graded automatically using learner platforms; as a result, instructors actually spend less time grading overall.

Not least, SE can be a vital tool for teaching pronunciation. SE supports various formats, such as the repeat-after-the model, oral flashcards, and oral reading. Students can watch model videos repeatedly and observe the instructor's lip, jaw, and tongue movements to improve pronunciation. During the pandemic, when instructors had to wear face masks, SE became even more crucial for teaching pronunciation. By implementing PBT, we've been able to correct the misalignment between instruction and evaluation. The assessments presented here can be easily adapted to other languages. We have implemented PBTs in 101 through 202 as well as an advanced linguistics course. By the time students complete 202, they will have produced a large number of recordings. These can be used for research on pronunciation development, for instance, as well as program evaluation and assessment.

NOTE

1. Speak Everywhere is commercially available to any language instructors. No special technology knowledge is required to use it. For details and sign-up information, visit: http://speak-everywhere.com/.

REFERENCES

Brown, Henry Douglas. 2007. *Teaching by Principles: An Interactive Approach to Language Pedagogy (3rdedition)*. White Plains, NY: Pearson Education.

Espinosa, Ligia. 2015. Effective Use of Performance-Based Assessments to Identify English Knowledge of Skills of EFL Students in Ecuador. *Theory and Practice in Language Studies* 5, no. 12: 2441–2447.

Fukada, Atsushi. 2009. *Speak Everywhere,* licensed to and operated by e-Language Learning LLC.

Fukada, Atsushi. 2013. "An Online Oral Practice/Assessment Platform: Speak Everywhere." *The IALLT Journal* 43, no. 1: 64–77.

González-Lloret, Marta, and Katharine Nielson. 2015. "Evaluating TBLT: The Case of a Task-Based Spanish Program." *Language Teaching Research* 19, no. 5: 525–549.

Hatasa, Yukiko, Hatasa, Kazumi and Seiichi Makino. 2014. *Nakama 1: Communication, Culture, Context. Third edition.* Stamford, CT: Cengage Learning.

Hughes, Arthur. 1989. *Testing for Language Teachers.* Cambridge, UK: Cambridge University Press.

Ikeda, Junko, and Atsushi Fukada. 2012. "Speak Everywhere o Tōgō Shita Speaking Jyūshi no Course Sekkei to Jissen [Design and Implementation of a Speaking-Focused Course that integrates Speak Everywhere]. *Nihongo Kyōiku* 152: 46–60.

Noroozi, Majeed, and Seyyed Meisam Taheri. 2021. "The Distinguishing Characteristic of Task-Based Language Assessment." *Journal of Language Teaching and Research* 12, no. 5: 688–695.

Norris, John. 2016. "Current Uses for Task-Based Language Assessment." *Annual Review of Applied Linguistics* 36: 230–244.

Puppin, Leni. 2007. "A Paradigm Shift: From Paper-and-Pencil Tests to Performance-Based Assessment." *English Teaching Forum* 45, no. 4: 10–17.

Stiggins, Rick. 2005. "From Formative Assessment to Assessment for Learning: A Path to Success in Standards-Based Schools. *Phi Delta Kappan* 87: 324–328.

Sturm, Jessica. 2020. "Performance-Based Testing in a French Pronunciation Course Using Speak Everywhere." *The French Review* 94, no. 2: 207–218.

Wu, Shu-Ling, and Lourdes Ortega. 2013. "Measuring Global Oral Proficiency in SLA Research: A New Elicited Imitation Test of L2 Chinese." *Foreign Language Annals* 46, no. 4: 680–704.

Yan, Xun, Maeda, Yukiko, Lv, Jing, and April Ginther. 2015. "Elicited Imitation as a Measure of Second Language Proficiency: A Narrative Review and Meta-Analysis." *Language Testing* 33, no. 4: 497–528. https://doi.org/10.1177/0265532215594643

Yoshida, Kayo, and Atsushi Fukada. 2014. "Effects of Oral Repetition on Learners' Word Accentuation." *The IALLT Journal* 44, no. 1: 17–37.

Part 3

AUTOMATIC SPEECH
RECOGNITION

Chapter Seven

Transparent Language

Learners' Perceptions, Successes, and Challenges of Using a Speech Recognition Tool for Molding Beginner Spanish Pronunciation in Online Courses

Karen Acosta and Michelle Ocasio

INTRODUCTION

Current research in learners' preferences in second language (L2) pronunciation suggests students are largely in favor of corrective feedback (Tian and Li 2018, Saribas 2020, Zielinski and Yates 2014). Learning a language takes time not only because it takes time for learners to acquire a new language, but also for the teachers to effectively guide students on the right path to second language competency and mutual intelligibility. In school classrooms, tolerable pronunciation that could be understood by a sympathetic native speaker is often acceptable in favor of near-perfect grammar and memorization of vocabulary lists, a vestige of second language acquisition's history of neglect in pronunciation practice (Bajorek 2017, Hincks 2003). Students with previous experience in the target language (such as regular contact with target-language speaking relatives, time spent in the country of the target language, or former formal study), may unintentionally cause beginners to feel insecure and embarrassed to participate in classroom oral activities. In addition, many teachers are professionally unprepared or have received little training in how to explicitly teach pronunciation (Derwing 2008).

The mid-twentieth century saw the debut of new technology for language learning, where an entire classroom in a language lab or the individual armchair learner listened to vinyl records and passively decided for oneself whether to repeat a word or phrase aloud. Later, cumbersome bundles of CD-ROMS installed on one's home computer and web-based software programs provided learners with a more interactive experience. Presently, a growing number of mobile applications and virtual reality applications for language learning are just around the corner.

This chapter discusses current trends in technology that utilize feedback based on the learner's speech output using Automated Speech Recognition (ASR) technology for pronunciation practice, with a focus on the classroom or at-home learner. A brief exploration of the latest and most popular software and web-based programs, mobile applications, and virtual reality experiences are taken into consideration. Transparent Language Online, a web and mobile application that offers study in over one-hundred languages, is at the center of this study, due to its innovative use of ASR and versatile ability to be tailored to almost any existing curriculum or home-study program. For this study, students who utilized Transparent Language as mandatory assignments in their beginning Spanish courses were invited at the end of the term to share perspectives on their experience about using Transparent Language as a tool for pronunciation practice.

LITERATURE REVIEW

ASR Technology and the WER Algorithm

If modern technology is to play a role in supporting or becoming the sole source of pronunciation improvement and prevention of fossilization for learners, then ASR must be able to recognize unintelligible pronunciation and deliver instant and engaging feedback. Often used interchangeably with *automatic* speech recognition, and also known as Speech-To-Text, ASR largely works to convert raw audio into a sequence of words. There are a variety of ASR tools on the market, and they function in largely the same way: an audio sample is captured, digitized into a wave-length type code, and the code is converted into a word or phrase.

Though they may work in the same way, the rate for errors within different brands of ASR tools differs greatly. If you have ever said, *"representative"* into your phone for automated service and were connected to the shipping department, you already have an understanding that not all ASR tools are built equally. A popular metric called the Word Error Rate (WER) can be used to determine the ASR tool's efficacy; it is calculated using an algorithm that captures a transcript and determines how many words the ASR computed incorrectly. The ultimate WER goal is "0" (zero); understandably, companies and organizations hold their WER as a closely guarded secret. Nevertheless, Microsoft's Speech-To-Text feature claims to have a WER of 5.1 percent, and Google boasts a WER of 4 percent. As a comparison, human transcribers have a rate of 4 percent (Chen 2021). Filippidou and Moussiades (2020) posit three common errors in ASR applications, including substitution (a word is replaced, such as fine is transcribed instead of vine); insertion (a word is inserted, such as voice is being transcribed instead of voices); and deletion (a word is left out, such as to library being transcribed instead of to the library).

When considering accuracy, however, there is a question as to whose pronunciation level beginning students are expected to aspire. Over 15 years ago, Levis (2005) identified two opposing approaches to teaching pronunciation: the intelligibility principle, in which learners are expected to reach a basic level to which they can be understood by native speakers, and the nativeness principle, where students ought to aim to achieve native-like fluency which includes target accent acquisition. These terms became part of the regular conversation in SLA (Momenian 2011, Thomson 2017, Munro and Derwing 2015). Revisiting this distinction, Levis (2020) argues that there is "no justification to demand near-native fluency in any context of language teaching." Nevertheless, most learners do not feel that they are learning a language unless they can pronounce it better than at a basic level, and the goal of many second language students continues to be near-native fluency (Bogach et al. 2021, Levis 2020, Saribas 2020).

CALL (Computer Assisted Language Learning) Technologies for Pronunciation Practice

Mobile apps for language learning that employ the ASR tool for pronunciation practice often manipulate the desire of the L2 learner to emulate the target language accent. For example, Mango Languages advertise, ". . . tweak your accent to standards that would impress the locals (Mango Languages n.d.)," and Rosetta Stone promises that you will ". . . get the accent juuuuust right with instant feedback on your pronunciation (Rosetta Stone n.d.)." It is critical for apps to strike the ideal balance in attracting, engaging, retaining, and teaching the mobile language learner. The speech recognition tool, when used as an enticing promise of native-like pronunciation is undoubtedly a way to appeal to the learner who longs to be conversational, but this type of guarantee comes with the possibility of compromising the credibility of a language learning app.

None of the language learning mobile apps piloted for this study have a "sensitivity" option, in which the student may choose if they want to achieve a level of pronunciation equal to that of a native speaker or to a level that is "passable," to be somewhat understood in the local pub, for example. Rather, the developers of the app have chosen the sensitivity level for the learner. On one end of the scale there are mobile apps such as the Mondly app created for mobile devices such as phones and tablets, Duolingo and Babbel, which the authors tested and found to allow greater leniency in one's pronunciation. In self-guided tests, the authors—native and near-native speakers of Spanish—

were permitted to move forward through the lessons with deliberately slow and stilted pronunciation, and even with vowel sounds that did not match the word or phrase given. On the other end of the scale, Rosetta Stone and Transparent Language required that the authors utter a word or phrase closely resembling the target, displaying an assessment gauge for how closely the pronunciation matched that of the model speaker.

Allowing the speech recognition tool—no matter how attractive and popular a language app—to give too wide a berth to pronunciation varieties can have adverse effects; there is a danger in producing learners who complete a language course with unintelligible articulation. On the other hand, if the ASR tool is too rigid, the program runs the risk of demotivating the student, thus discouraging them from continuing their program of study (Dillon and Wells 2021). Transparent Language is an example of a mobile language learning platform that attempts to appeal to students and produce learners with intelligible pronunciation ability in the target language.

TRANSPARENT LANGUAGE

Transparent Language Inc. is a language learning technology company with platforms available on the web and for mobile applications. Of the three programs Transparent Language offers, Transparent Language Online, the CL-150 Platform (targeted for government agencies) and Transparent Connect (live language instruction directed to individual learners), this research study focuses on Transparent Language Online (Transparent Language). A fee-based program, Transparent Language is purchased by institutions through a campus-wide (entire campus) or seat license (specific number of students), or through individual bookstore purchases. If an individual wishes to study with Transparent Language on their own, they can choose a package that includes either one language or access to all languages, monthly or per year. Transparent Language offers over one hundred languages from which to choose, including, for example, English courses to those who speak Arabic or Spanish, Korean for Spanish speakers, and Swahili for Turkish speakers. Not all languages have a complete program of study; for example, while Spanish, Arabic, Dakota (and others) offer full courses with dozens of general and specialized assignments based on different regional accents, other languages such as Mongolian, Yoruba, and Nahuatl offer fewer lessons. In addition, eight languages offer a choice of dialects to study, for example, within Spanish one can choose between Latin American, Castilian or Colombian Spanish, Arabic offers Modern Standard, Egyptian, Iraqi and Levantine Arabic, and Chinese offers the Mandarin and Cantonese dialects.

Individuals who are not a part of a language class but have institutional, campus-wide access to Transparent Language (such as administrative, maintenance, or physical plant staff) are free to use one of the many pre-designed paths that begin with greetings and progress to advanced thematic topics from inviting someone for coffee to going through customs at an airport. Learners may also choose targeted learning that includes practice in well-known topics such as ordering in a restaurant or answering the phone, and more specific topics such as credit and loans, marketing strategy and tax regulations. When used as part of a class, instructors can use the online lessons as graded, required material, and match the exercises from the platform to what is being currently taught in the textbook or offer a handful of exercises as extra credit.

Transparent Language's linear layout mimics that of a traditional classroom; the first lesson on the Learning Path is "Welcome," followed by Lesson 2, Lesson 3, Lesson 4, an assessment, and so on with further lessons and assessments. Whatever one's language selection may be, four areas are covered in each lesson: listening, speaking, reading, and writing.

All lessons comprise eight activities with one assessment at the end of each lesson:

1. Preview It: familiarize the student with the words, phrases, sounds and written forms of the target language
2. Recognize & Say It: practice receptive skills by seeing and hearing the words and guessing their meanings
3. Pronunciation: use the automated speech recognition tool to speak a word or phrase in the target language
4. Multiple Choice: use the ASR to read a word or phrase from the target language and speak the correct word or phrase from a selection of four
5. Matching: drag each word or phrase from one side of the screen to its meaning on the other side of the screen
6. Produce & Say It: read a word or phrase in the native language and say the corresponding word aloud in the target language
7. Dictation: listen to the word in the target language, then write the word
8. Produce & Write It: read a word or phrase in the native language and write the target language word
9. Assessment: take an assessment to determine the learner's mastery of the material. It employs a variety of types of questions from listening, reading, and speaking.

Transparent Language places great emphasis on providing the student with meaningful feedback in grammar, reading, dictation and speaking. The

Transparent Language developers have created a proprietary ASR tool called EveryVoice™, in which the student listens to a native speaker and repeats utterances into a microphone. Within a few seconds, the student's utterance is processed through the EveryVoice™ sound analysis program, and the app responds with a rating and areas to review. Displayed for the learner are three images: the first two are soundwave bars, one represents the soundwave of the native speaker and the other shows a soundwave of the learner's repetition. If there are noticeable differences in pronunciation between the two samples, the area of the learner's soundwave that demonstrates the most variation is highlighted in yellow and is clickable for review. In addition to the soundwaves, a gauge similar to a color-coded speedometer with a needle displays a rating ranging from red/orange (needs work), orange/yellow (average), and yellow/green (well done).

PURPOSE OF THE STUDY AND RESEARCH QUESTIONS

The purpose of the study was to have beginning Spanish learners explore a range of pronunciation activities on the Transparent Language platform that encourage focused pronunciation practice and reflect on their experience using these activities. In addition, this study aimed to identify which pronunciation activities students found to be the most (and least) effective and helpful.

The specific questions that guided this research were:

RQ1: How did students describe their overall experience using Transparent Language?
RQ2: What types of activities did the students find to be the most and least useful for pronunciation improvement?
RQ3: What is students' self-perception of their Spanish pronunciation after using Transparent Language?

METHODS

Context

The participants in the study were English-speaking college students enrolled in beginning Spanish language classes at a mid-size public university in the southeastern United States. Five sections of a fully online, first-level beginning Spanish course whose instructors incorporated the Transparent Language platform in their online Spanish courses were selected for this study. Throughout the course of the term, students were required to complete roughly 30 lessons as mandatory homework, where they were presented with pronunciation practice assignments on Transparent Language, each assignment paired with vocabulary content that had been covered in the course that week. Students were invited to complete the survey at the end of the term.

Participants

Out of 113 students enrolled in the five fully online sections of the first semester Spanish course, 91 students volunteered to complete the survey at the end of the course, a response rate of 80.5 percent. Seventy-seven surveys were retained for analysis after removing surveys from students who preferred to not have their data included in the study, surveys from dual enrollment students younger than 18 years of age, and incomplete surveys.

The participants of this study were enrolled in the beginning Spanish course, intended for students without previous Spanish learning experience, to fulfill a foreign language requirement of their study program or college, as an elective course, or as part of their Spanish major requirement. Only six out of the 77 participants listed Spanish as their major; the other 71 listed various other majors, such as business, dental hygiene, psychology, criminal justice, engineering, biology, among others.

Nineteen percent of the participants identified as male and 81 percent identified as female. Twenty-two percent were in their freshman year of studies, 33 percent were sophomores, 26 percent were juniors, 18 percent were seniors, and 1 percent other. With regards to age, 78 percent of participants were in the 18–24 range, 12 percent were between 25–34 years old, 6 percent between 35–44, 1 percent between 45–54, and 2 percent were between 55–64 years of age.

Data Collection

The researchers distributed the survey during the last two weeks of the course, so that students had enough time to use and get acquainted with Transparent Language before being asked to reflect on it. The participants completed the survey online, hosted on Qualtrics. The survey included demographic questions to gain background information on the respondents as well as nine questions about the students' experience using the Transparent Language platform for Spanish pronunciation practice. There were both close-ended and open-ended questions, some requiring Likert-scale answers, some questions with options for comments, and some open-ended questions that required text comments.

The survey questions were intended to elicit comments about students' experience using Transparent Language, their perception of the effectiveness of the platform for pronunciation practice and learning, as well as any challenges they encountered with the tool. The open-ended questions allowed students to express opinions on their experience, as well as to make any additional comments not covered by the close-ended questions.

Data Analysis

The survey yielded two sets of data: quantitative data from the close-ended questions and qualitative data from the open-ended questions. The researchers conducted a data analysis following the data transformation approach as described by Creswell (2003). According to Creswell (2003), this approach involves "creating codes and themes qualitatively, then counting the number of times they occur in the text data" (221). Creswell (2003) argues that this quantification of qualitative data "enables a researcher to compare quantitative results with the qualitative data" (221).

The researchers used frequency counts to analyze the data from the close-ended survey questions, and the patterns that emerged became the preliminary themes. Then, the data from the open-ended survey questions were analyzed through a comparative method, coding the participants' responses to these open-ended questions for themes, then comparing and defining the main themes. The researchers ensured reliability in their coding through a process of (1) negotiation of codes, (2) separate coding of the data, and (3) comparison of the coded data. When needed, themes and codes were defined and renegotiated.

The main themes that emerged were related to the students' overall experience with Transparent Language, perceived benefits of using the platform, specific activities they found helpful, challenges and limitations of the instructional tool, and suggestions for improvement. Several of the main themes that emerged from the two data sets help answer the study's research questions.

RESULTS

The data analysis indicates that, overall, participants had a positive experience using the Transparent Language platform to practice and improve pronunciation. Students were able to identify which Transparent Language activities they perceived to be the most and least helpful, as well as reflect on the benefits and limitations of their use of the tool throughout the term. This section presents results related to each of the research questions.

RQ1: Students' Overall Experience Using Transparent Language

To answer the first research question, two open-ended survey questions specifically asked participants to share their overall experience using Transparent Language and to identify any challenges they faced using the tool, asking them to explain or provide examples whenever possible. Out of the 71 participants who answered this survey question, 68 (95.77%) reported having an overall positive experience using Transparent Language, one (1.41%) participant reported having an overall neutral experience with the platform, and two (2.82%) participants reported having an overall negative experience. All three students who reported having a neutral or negative experience with Transparent Language mentioned problems with the audio or voice enabling, specifically citing microphone issues.

While microphone and audio issues were also mentioned by several of the students who reported having an overall positive experience, the most common themes in the written responses were related to pronunciation, helpful practice activities, platform features, the website and app layout, and the students' overall satisfaction with the platform.

Sample comments from participants to this question were:

- Overall positive: "It was amazing. I enjoyed being able to compare my voice to native speakers. This tool allowed me to make adjustments to my pronunciations."
- Overall neutral: "My experience was more positive than negative. I liked the layout and the length of the lessons. I did not like the speaking portions because it doesn't reliably hear you."
- Overall negative: "There was a lot of problems with enable microphones. The program starts out using the microphones then stops."

Participants were also specifically asked about any problems they encountered with Transparent Language. Out of the 75 students who answered this survey question, 48 (64%) did not experience any problems using the platform, while 27 (36%) students reported experiencing technical problems or other challenges. Of the students who experienced problems, microphone/audio issues was the most frequently recurring theme in the responses, sometimes related to the students' unstable Internet connection and sometimes related to the voice recognition tool not picking up the student's voice. Other problems included account setup, getting logged out of the lesson, mobile app crashes, and other technical problems, with at least eight of the respondents reporting the issue being on their end.

Sample comments from participants who experienced problems were:

- "Sometimes the voice meter would not grade my pronunciation."
- "Yes, I sometimes had microphone problems."
- "Yes, there were a few times where I had to turn off my internet in order to complete the 'say it' phase."

Sample comments from participants who did not experience problems were:

- "I did not experience any technical problems or other challenges with transparent language."
- "No I did not. I was very satisfied with this program."
- "Not even once."

RQ2: Most and Least Useful Activities

To answer the second research question, participants were asked to rank the nine types of practice exercises available on the Transparent Language platform in their order of usefulness to them, with 1 being the most useful and 9 being the least useful. The researchers then used frequency counts to determine which practice activities were the three most useful (most frequently ranked by participants with 1, 2, or 3) and which practice activities were the three least useful (most frequently ranked by participants with 7, 8, or 9). In addition, participants also discussed specific practice activities in their responses to the open-ended questions. Table 7.1 shows which types of activities students found to be the most useful.

Table 7.1. Most and Least Useful Practice Activities as Reported by Participants (*n* = 69)

Activities Ranked as Most Useful	Type of Activity	Mean Score	S.D.	Frequency Ranked Among Most Useful	Percentage Ranked Among Most Useful
	Pronunciation	3.75	2.15	39	56.52
	Preview It	3.95	2.99	38	55.07
	Recognize & Say It	3.75	1.89	36	52.17
Activities Ranked as Least Useful	Type of Activity	Mean Score	S.D.	Frequency Ranked Among Least Useful	Percentage Ranked Among Least Useful
	Assessment	6.49	2.94	39	56.52
	Dictation	6.04	1.97	35	50.72
	Produce & Write It	5.34	1.95	33	47.82

Source: Acosta, K. and Ocasio, M.

Table 7.1 shows the three activities most frequently ranked as useful by the students: Pronunciation, Preview It, and Recognize & Say It. Out of 69 participants who responded to this survey question, 39 (56.52%) of them ranked Pronunciation, 38 (55.07%) of them ranked the Preview It activity, and 36 (52.17%) students ranked the Recognize & Say It exercise to be among the top three most useful activities on the platform.

Because this was a close-ended survey question, not every respondent offered comments about each type of activity, but the most frequently recurring theme that emerged from the open-ended comments about activities was the usefulness of the Pronunciation tool, some samples of which are shared below.

- "I enjoyed repeating after the voice recorder and seeing how accurate my pronunciation is."
- "I really liked how the pronunciation activity worked. A native speaker would say the word or phrase and then I would repeat. I was assessed using a visual implement that told me how close I was to the native speaker. I am a visual learner, so that was very helpful to see."
- "Well I have a Southern accent. It was hard to say the words. I found that hearing it then practicing it till I got it right helped greatly."
- "Even though I had issues with the recording feature, I think that hearing and attempting to repeat the vocabulary helps a lot."
- "Its voice recognition and the repetition throughout has immensely helped."

In addition to identifying the most useful practice activities, participants also identified the exercises that they considered to be the least useful. Table 7.1 shows which types of Transparent Language activities were ranked by students to be the least useful. As shown in table 7.1, students considered the Assessment, Dictation, and Produce & Write It activities to be the least useful. Out of 69 participants who answered this survey question, 39 (56.52%) of them ranked the Assessment at the end of the lesson, 35 (50.72%) of them ranked the Dictation, and 33 (47.82%) of them ranked the Produce & Write It exercise to be among the three least useful to them out of the activities available on Transparent Language.

As was the case with the most useful activities, not all respondents discussed all types of activities in their comments, but some of them did specifically mention the Assessment and Dictation while discussing activities in their open-ended responses. Although these activities were not among the most recurring themes, it is worth noting that outside of two respondents who specifically mentioned disliking the Assessment activity, there were no negative comments about the activities that were ranked as least useful.

RQ3: Students' Self-Perception of their Spanish Pronunciation

While the first research question focused on the students' overall experience with the platform, the third research question centered on the use of Transparent Language specifically for pronunciation practice and learning. To answer the third research question, three survey questions asked participants about (1) their self-perception of improvement in pronunciation after using the platform, (2) their level of satisfaction with Transparent Language to improve their pronunciation, and (3) whether they would in turn recommend its use to others for pronunciation improvement.

First, participants were asked whether they perceived their Spanish pronunciation to have improved, remained the same, or gotten worse after using the tool throughout the term. Out of the 71 participants who responded to this question, 69 (97.19%) perceived an improvement in their Spanish pronunciation after their use of the tool, two (2.81%) participants considered their pronunciation to have remained the same, while no participants perceived a deterioration in their Spanish pronunciation after using Transparent Language.

Next, a survey question asked participants to rate their overall experience using Transparent Language for the purpose of improving Spanish pronunciation. Finally, another question asked participants whether they would recommend Transparent Language to other language learners for pronunciation improvement based on their experience. Both questions gave participants an option to elaborate on their responses through written comments.

Table 7.2 shows how all 77 participants rated their experience using Transparent Language specifically for improving Spanish pronunciation, as well as whether they would recommend it to others for that purpose. In addition, table 7.2 shows sample responses from some of the participants who offered written comments explaining their responses.

As shown in table 7.2, the majority of students indicated satisfaction with the use of Transparent Language to improve their Spanish pronunciation, with 73 (94.80%) of them being either moderately or very satisfied. Two (2.60%) students reported being neither satisfied nor dissatisfied, and two (2.60%) students expressed dissatisfaction with their experience, citing technical problems as the reason for their rating.

Out of the 77 participants, 73 (94.80%) said they would either definitely or probably recommend using Transparent Language for pronunciation improvement, while four (5.20%) participants said they would probably or definitely not recommend its use.

A recurring theme that emerged from the written comments among the students who would recommend Transparent Language was that the pronunciation practice activities had helped them improve throughout the term, with several students mentioning that they consider it to be especially helpful for

Table 7.2. Students' (n = 77) Overall Experience Using Transparent Language to Improve Spanish

	Level of Satisfaction	Frequency	Percentage	Sample Response
Overall Satisfaction with Transparent Language to Improve Pronunciation	Very satisfied	48	62.33	"I have seen a difference in my pronunciation across the semester with the use of Transparent Language. I have also noticed that when I am speaking Spanish to others I have increased self-corrections prior to being corrected. I believe this is because of the continued use of the website/app."
	Moderately satisfied	25	32.47	"I felt like it helped my pronunciation more than sitting in a class because i could listen to the recordings over."
	Neither satisfied nor dissatisfied	2	2.60	"It did not cause me any stress so I would not take away any points, but it did not change my life so not a 10."
	Moderately dissatisfied	1	1.30	"The microphones enabling was a huge problem for me."
	Very dissatisfied	1	1.30	"Because the software is unreliable and frustrating to use."
	Recommendation	**Frequency**	**Percentage**	**Sample Response**
Would/Would Not Recommend Transparent Language for Pronunciation Improvement	Definitely would recommend	54	70.13	"I think it is a great tool to help anyone wanting to speak in a more natural way. It allows you the opportunity to compare how you speak to a native speaker and that's invaluable when trying to learn and speak a new language."
	Probably would recommend	19	24.67	"It genuinely helps you pronounce things correctly and the app is easy to use."
	Probably wouldn't recommend	2	2.60	"I would recommend Transparent Language for learning the terms and how to use them, but relying on it to grade my speech so I can 'improve' it is not something I'd do. It only frustrates me to say the same word three or four different times (with the same, correct pronunciation) before it will grade my speech as correct."
	Definitely wouldn't recommend	2	2.60	"You can get more usability on the free version of other software."

Source: Acosta, K. and Ocasio, M.

beginner learners. Other themes were related to specific practice activities, the platform itself, and the importance of repetition and review in language learning. Of the four students who said they would not recommend the platform, only one of the "definitely wouldn't" and one of the "probably wouldn't" respondents wrote comments expanding on their decision, both of which can be seen in table 7.2.

Additional Findings

In response to an open-ended survey question that asked participants what would have made their experience with Transparent Language better, 34 students wrote comments offering suggestions for improvement. Table 7.3 shows some of the recurring themes as well as sample comments from participants who responded to this question.

Table 7.3. Students' (*n* = 34) Suggestions for Improvement

Suggestions for Improvement	Sample Response
More updates/bug fixes	"I think regular maintenance and updates to its server is the only thing that I can really think of to improve it. I didn't really have any issues at all with the platform." "Work on bug fixes." "The app just needs to be tweaked just a tad." "More modern UI to match current apps and website could make the experience better. Also, encouragement throughout the use of using the website/app could make people more engaged in learning."
Improvement to speech recognition tool	"In my opinion, If it could block out the sounds around us and focus on our voice only, that would make the experience better." "Easier microphone recordings."
More available content	"Incorporating a video clip with a conversation using the new vocabulary would be awesome." "I personally have no big recommendations, however, I would like to see words implemented into sentences in the practice and even assessment. I think we could benefit from having to translate sentences with the words in them or pick sentences that the words work with." "Maybe instead of just vocab the program could go over the conjugation of verbs too." "Give more writing prompts. Writing the words out helps me with memorization."
No suggestions for improvement	"None that I can think of." "I can't think of any recommendations to make my experience better. I found everything to work really well." "Nothing. The system worked great to me. I don't have any recommendations."

Source: Acosta, K. and Ocasio, M.

Some of the respondents mentioned the need for updates and bug fixes to the app, while others focused specifically on suggestions related to the type of content that they would like to see available on the platform, such as the incorporation of video clips, sentence-level practice, and the addition of more writing prompts. Another recurring theme was the improvement of the speech recognition tool. Finally, some of the participants who answered this open-ended question did not offer suggestions for improvement, but rather reiterated that the platform worked well for them and did not need improvement.

DISCUSSION

This study found that a majority (95.77%) of participants had an overall positive experience using the Transparent Language platform in their beginning Spanish course. The learners in this study found the platform to be helpful to review, practice, and learn the pronunciation of the vocabulary that was covered in the course.

While these findings demonstrate an overwhelming satisfaction with Transparent Language, students did note some concerns with the tool. Thirty-six percent of the participants reported experiencing problems or challenges with the platform, most of which were technical issues involving the microphone/audio enabling, the speech recognition tool sensitivity, or an unstable Internet connection while completing the assignments. Students' difficulties with the computer program should indeed be taken seriously. In fact, Freud (1912) argued that frustration is a very real obstacle to achieving one's goal, and researchers have found that hard to find/missing items in digital applications are the second highest source of frustration, preceded by operating system crashes (Lazar, Jones, and Shneiderman 2006). Interestingly, technological problems did not seem to impact the participants' perception of their experience as an overall positive one.

Over half of the learners ranked the Pronunciation, Preview It, and Recognize & Say It exercises to be the most useful activities on the platform. Two of the activities ranked as most useful, Pronunciation and Recognize & Say It, are speaking practice activities, and the third one, Preview It, is an activity that combines flashcards with audio of the pronunciation of words or phrases. Conversely, over half of the learners ranked the Assessment, Dictation, and Produce & Write It exercises to be the least useful activities on the platform. Two of the activities ranked as least useful, Dictation and Produce & Write It, are writing practice activities, and the third one is the Assessment activity that wraps up each lesson. It is worth considering whether students ranked Dictation and Produce & Write It among the least useful activities because they did not see them as particularly relevant to their pronunciation. Further, in the case of the Dictation activity, they may not have considered the link between listening and pronunciation improvement. Regarding the Assessment, it is possible that participants did not view it strictly as a "practice" activity, since it is an activity that provides them with a score. Overall, these findings suggest that learners in this study perceive pronunciation practice and learning to be a particularly important aspect of their Spanish learning experience, although they may not always see how practice with related skills may benefit their pronunciation development.

Further, an overwhelming majority of participants (97.19%) perceived an improvement in their pronunciation of the target language, and no students perceived a deterioration in their Spanish pronunciation after using Transparent Language. Similarly, a majority of students (94.80%) was satisfied with their use of the platform for pronunciation improvement and most (94.80%) said they would recommend it to others for pronunciation improvement based on their experience with the tool. In addition, 60 out of 77 (77.92%) participants indicated that they would continue to use Transparent Language on their own to improve their pronunciation if their next Spanish course did not require its use. Overall, these findings indicate that in online learning situations, students found the use of the online platform to be crucial to their Spanish pronunciation improvement.

Limitations and Suggestions for Future Research

One limitation of this study is the scope of the sample. The findings are based on data collected from five sections of the same undergraduate Spanish course from a single university over a single academic term. Surveying additional groups of students, from different proficiency levels, across several terms, would be helpful in further research.

Another limitation is that the data the study is based on is self-reported data from student surveys, which although valuable and valid to explore and identify students' experiences and opinions, offer an incomplete picture of the issue. Future research could include other data points, such as measures of pronunciation improvement, oral assessments, or reports of student progress. Currently, the Transparent Language platform offers very limited reporting on students' work. With improved reporting tools and more instructor resources, following and measuring students' progress in the platform and the practice activities offered would be possible and could be useful in future studies.

Because the students' use of the Transparent Language tool for practice throughout the course did not directly feed into the students' oral assessments, it was not possible to see whether their use of the platform correlated with their grades for the present study. Furthermore, because participants completed the survey during the last two weeks of the term when most course grades were already known to them, students' attitudes about their grades may have guided their perception and their overall positivity or negativity in responses. It would be interesting to survey other groups of students at different points of the term, as well as to look at other measures of student success in the course in conjunction with their use of the pronunciation practice tool in the future.

IMPLICATIONS FOR IMPLEMENTATION AND INSTRUCTION

The successes that arise from students' use of Transparent Language in the online and face-to-face classroom significantly outweigh the challenges. In the beginning language classroom setting, the presence of heritage speakers and those who have previous experience with the target language unintentionally increase self-deprecating worries of L2 learners (Dewaele and Al-Saraj 2015, Sevinç and Backus 2017) and exacerbate already stressed affective filters with communication apprehension, an issue that affects nearly 20 percent of college students (Du 2009). This, in turn, may result in less proficiency in the foreign accent (MacIntyre and Mercer 2014). Timid L2 students (though they may have a strong desire and ability to participate) silently pray that they are invisible, sometimes compelling the instructor to demote pronunciation practice into a peripheral component in favor of other activities that are easily suitable for the large class setting such as silent reading, writing exercises, and listening comprehension. In the online classroom, it can be impossible to truly know if students are engaged in the speaking activities at home or in the institution's language lab, uttering the words and phrases aloud. A language learning application, rich in pronunciation activities that offer useful and comprehensive feedback to the students and reporting to the instructor, serves as an effective and practical supplement to an already-established program of study.

The numerous topics available for study in Transparent Language are a reliable guarantee that, especially for beginning language students, there are more than enough themes that correspond to material being taught in the classroom. Fortunately, most language learning mobile applications offer numerous topics and would be readily adaptable to a pre-existing language curriculum. For example, Duolingo begins with "greetings" and offers a wide range of topics from directions and weather to job preparation and renovating a home. Mondly offers an expansive thematic range as well, from romance to sports to preparing for a vacation. Especially when the individual mobile app lessons are short, students may not feel overwhelmed by the mobile app activities in addition to the regular classroom coursework assigned by the instructor. Transparent Language allows instructors to author lessons so that they precisely match classroom topics. The lesson authoring tool enables course designers to create their own content and add their own voice as model speakers. The list of lexical items that the instructor has added is then applied to the Transparent Language pronunciation tools.

Although the mobile applications surveyed for this study are intuitive and require only basic technical capabilities, there is the tedious task of choosing activities that correspond as closely as possible to the classroom material. This takes a bit of time and effort on the part of the instructor, ensuring that there is just the right amount of overlap (lexical items and grammatical content not yet introduced in the current lesson). Taking the time to select the most appropriate exercises that demonstrate a seamless match to the current lesson contributes significantly to the academic breadth of the class. Nevertheless, it is time well spent once it is completed; there is little risk in assigning the same activities year after year. Notwithstanding online course pressures such as the discipline needed to adhere to strict deadlines and navigate what may be a new mobile app or learning management system (Russell 2020), the online platform that allows students to practice pronunciation in a safe environment with reliable target speech feedback may serve to reinforce learners' confidence and empower them against language anxiety in the classroom (Direnzo and Dustin 2018). Daily homework given to students should include pronunciation practice with a platform that the instructor has vetted for trustworthy feedback. Pronunciation practice should not be optional for extra credit, but rather treated as importantly as reading, writing, or listening comprehension.

The instructor should be familiar enough with the technology to be prepared to answer students' questions about navigating the platform. The instructor needs to set aside time to learn the technology well, even enrolling themselves as a learner on the same Transparent Language roster as their students. Registering as a student allows the instructor access to the student view of the assignments, which is often different from the instructor view. This tactic is often very helpful when students have difficulties navigating a new platform. Additionally, the instructor can use a free screen recorder (such as screencast-o-matic.com) to create a brief video that demonstrates exactly how to register for the accompanying mobile app. Using Transparent Language, the process of assigning exercises to a class is straightforward and registration for learners includes a dedicated link. This link registers the student directly into the Transparent Language class that the instructor has created, with easy access to the activities the instructor may have already assigned.

On the other hand, we recommend that platforms such as Transparent Language not be relied upon solely for an assessment of target language pronunciation ability, in other words, trusting an acceptable grade from the reporting section of the app without having heard the student speak. While the reporting tools offer a good idea of how the student is progressing, they are not a substitute for an oral examination. Potentially deceptive loopholes such as asking a friend or family member with superior skills in the target language to quickly complete their assignments are a real possibility, since none of the mobile apps reviewed for pronunciation practice offer voice or webcam recordings for the instructor. An oral exam is highly recommended to complement the pronunciation practice, either through face-to-face interviews, webcam conversations or speech recording technology that records the student speaking (such as VoiceThread, a collaborative app in which learners can record their voice through both audio and video options).

With the assistance of technology that uses the automated speech recognition tool with helpful feedback, the practice of pronunciation at the beginning level does not have to be a sporadic component monopolized by the small group of students with previous language experience, but rather an attainable objective by all learners.

REFERENCES

Bajorek, Joan Palmiter. 2017. "L2 Pronunciation in CALL: The Unrealized Potential of Rosetta Stone, Duolingo, Babbel, and Mango Languages." Issues and Trends in Learning Technologies 5, no. 1. https://doi.org/10.2458/azu_itet_v5i1_bajorek

Bogach, Natalia, Elena Boitsova, Sergey Chernonog, Anton Lamtev, Maria Lesnichaya, Iurii Lezhenin, Andrey Novopashenny, Roman Svechnikov, Daria Tsikach, Konstantin Vasiliev, Evgeny Pyshkin, and John Blake. 2021. "Speech Processing for Language Learning: A Practical Approach to Computer-Assisted Pronunciation Teaching" Electronics 10, no. 3: 235. https://doi.org/10.3390/electronics10030235

Chen, Helena. 2021. "Does Word Error Rate Matter?" January 20, 2021. https://www.smartaction.ai/blog/does-word-error-rate-matter/.

Creswell, John W. 2003. Research Design: Qualitative, Quantitative, and Mixed Approaches Thousand Oaks: Sage Publications.

Derwing, Tracey M. 2008. "Curriculum Issues in Teaching Pronunciation to Second Language Learners." Phonology and Second Language Acquisition 36: 347–369.

Dewaele, J.-M., and Al-Saraj, T. M. 2015. "Foreign Language Classroom Anxiety of Arab Learners of English: The Effect of Personality, Linguistic and Sociobiographical Variables." Studies in Second Language Learning and Teaching 5: 205–228. https://doi.org/10.14746/ssllt.2015.5.2.2.

Direnzo, Elida Raquel, and Hayley Dustin. 2018. "Learning Online: A Safe and Engaging Place." Teaching and Learning Together in Higher Education 1, no. 25: 6.

Du, Xiaoyan. "The Affective Filter in Second Language Teaching." 2009. Asian Social Science 5, no. 8: 162–165. http://files.onthewebquest.webnode.com/200000022-762bb77278/krashen%20hypothesis.pdf.

Freud, S. 1912. "Types of Onset and Neurosis." In The Standard Edition of the Complete Psychological Works of Sigmund Freud, by J. Strachey, 227–230. London: Hogarth Press.

Hincks, Rebecca. 2003. "Speech Technologies for pronunciation feedback and evaluation." ReCALL no.15: 3–20. https://doi.org/10.1017/S095834400300021.

Lazar, Jonathan, Adam Jones, and Ben Shneiderman. 2006. "Workplace User Frustration With Computers: An Exploratory Investigation of the Causes and Severity." Behaviour & Information Technology 25, no. 03: 239–251. https://doi.org/10.1080/01449290500196963.

Levis, John M. 2005. "Changing Contexts and Shifting Paradigms in Pronunciation Teaching." TESOL Quarterly 39, no. 3: 369–377. https://doi.org/10.2307/3588485.

Levis, John M. 2020. "Revisiting the Intelligibility and Nativeness Principles." Journal of Second Language Pronunciation 6, no. 3: 310–328. https://lib.dr.iastate.edu/engl_pubs/283/.

MacIntyre, Peter D., and Sarah Mercer. 2014. "Introducing Positive Psychology to SLA." Studies in Second Language Learning and Teaching 4, no. 2: 153–172

Mango Languages. n.d. "How It Works." https://mangolanguages.com/how-it-works/.

Momenian, Mohammad. 2011. "The Identity and L2 Accent From an EIL Angle." Journal of Languages and Culture 2, no.1: 1–5. http://www.academicjournals.org/app/webroot/article/article1379495047_Momenian.pdf

Munro, Murray J., and Tracey M. Derwing. 2005. "Intelligibility in Research and Practice: Teaching Priorities." In The handbook of English pronunciation, edited by Marnie Reed and John M. Levis, 377–396. John Wiley & Sons, Inc.https://doi.org/10.1002/9781118346952.ch21.

Rosetta Stone. n.d. "Buy English." https://www.rosettastone.com/buy-english-british/.

Russell, Victoria. 2020. "Language Anxiety and The Online Learner." Foreign Language Annals 53, no. 2: 338–352.

Saribas, Elif. 2020. "Corrective Feedback in L2 Pronunciation: The Learner Lens." Masters thesis, University of Central Florida. https://purls.library.ucf.edu/go/DP0024203.

Sevinç, Yeşim, and Ad Backus. 2019. "Anxiety, Language Use and Linguistic Competence in An Immigrant Context: A Vicious Circle?" International Journal of Bilingual Education and Bilingualism 22, no. 6: 706–724. https://doi.org/10.1080/13670050.2017.1306021.

Thomson, Ron. 2017. "Measurement of Accentedness, Intelligibility, and Comprehensibility." In Assessment in Second Language Pronunciation, edited by Okim Kang and April Ginther, 11–29. London: Routledge.

Tian, Lili, and Li Li. 2008. "Chinese EFL Learners' Perception of Peer Oral and Written Feedback as Providers, Receivers and Observers." Language Awareness 27, no. 4: 312–330. https://doi.org/10.1080/09658416.2018.1535602.

Zielinski, Beth, and Lynda Yates. 2014. "Pronunciation Instruction is Not Appropriate for Beginning-level Learners." in Pronunciation Myths: Applying Second Language Research to Classroom Teaching, 56–79. University of Michigan Press

Chapter Eight

Integrating Mobile-based Text-To-Speech (TTS) and Speech-To-Text (STT) to Advance Proficiency and Intelligibility in French

Aurore Mroz

INTRODUCTION

With the inequality gap and the digital divide widening (Gonzalez and St Louis 2014; Tate and Warschauer 2017), educators have sought open educational resources (OER), that is, public domain resources that are free tools for language learning (Blyth 2017; Gleason and Suvorov 2019). Speech-technology, openly available on smartphones, may be one promising OER to support a more equitable approach to Mobile-Assisted Language Learning (MALL). Indeed, in 2020, smartphones were the most owned piece of technology worldwide—and, in 20 percent of cases, the only internet-connected technology at home (Pew Research Center 2021; O'Dea 2021). Smartphones have also often been the only reliable technological solution in low-tech classrooms (Gonzalez and St Louis 2014). Yet, with only 2.7 percent of research publications on MALL (Gillepsie 2020), more research is urgently needed.

Moreover, as Mercer explained, "as opportunities for self-directed learning proliferate given the advancements in various technologies (. . .), it has become increasingly important for learners to feel a sense of agency in order to make the most of the learning opportunities they [encounter]" (2011, 427). More specifically, with speech-technology on smartphones, the opportunity for L2 practitioners to advance their L2 learners' oral skills is at their fingertips. Indeed, Speech-To-Text (STT) and Text-To-Speech (TTS) have undergone remarkable technical growth, with the ability to handle the type of continuous, spontaneous, non-native speech that language learners produce (Moussalli and Cardoso 2019; Van Moere and Suzuki 2018; Vu et al. 2014).

The current study investigated whether and how speech technology used in *Gmail* on smartphones differentially benefited learners of French enrolled in two distinct forms of instruction targeting advanced proficiency and intelligibility.

LITERATURE REVIEW

Speech-Technology and Google

Born from the technological breakthrough of deep neural networks, modern-day speech-technology refers to the processing of speech by intelligent machines. On the one hand, Text-To-Speech (TTS) synthesizes intelligible human speech *from* text. TTS thus consists in transforming written text into spoken output, uttered by a synthetic voice, the quality and naturalness of which has improved drastically in the past few years, making it "a mature technology (. . .) ripe for deployment in educational settings" (Chiaráin and Chasaide 2020, 155). On the other hand, Speech-To-Text (STT) recognizes spoken utterances and transforms them *into* text. STT has more commonly been associated with *Siri*, *Alexa*, or *OK Google*. When it comes to using speech-technology for language learning, García et al. pointed out that "one of [its] great promises is [its] ability to provide individualized, automated, and impactful feedback (. . .) [as] no phonological expertise is required by either the learner or instructor [since] the feedback provided (. . .) is eminently interpretable as text and audio" (2020, 216–218). Indeed, knowing that L2 learners have a hard time hearing their own pronunciation errors (Mitterer, Eger, and Reinisch 2020), even after playing back their own recording (Foote 2010), this study built off Mroz's (2018) study and hypothesized that STT alone, or STT combined with TTS, could help learners adjust their pronunciation by "seeing how people hear them" and "how things are supposed to sound" (p. 627).

Speech-technology is progressively replacing typing, with 20 percent of *Google* queries on smartphones inputted by voice in 2016 (Meeker 2017). Publicizing a 4.9 percent word-error rate (WER), *Google* offers the most accurate speech-technology currently available (Meeker 2017; Tatman and Kasten 2017). However, this WER is based on U.S. native English speakers only, and studies about sociolinguistic biases in *Google*'s WER related to accents or gender have been inconclusive (Tatman 2017; Tatman and Kasten 2017), triggering questions about whether such biases could skew the use of speech-technology for language learning or whether other individual factors may also be at play.

Proficiency in Computer-Assisted Language Learning (CALL)

Proficiency is defined as the extent to which a language learner can function globally and systematically "in real-world situations in spontaneous, non-rehearsed [interpersonal interactions in the language]" (ACTFL 2012, 3). Proficiency can be assessed via Oral Proficiency Interviews (OPIs), considered as a "valid and reliable testing method [anchored in] a standardized procedure [that] measures language production holistically" (4). Advanced speakers are defined as being able

> to engage in conversation in a clearly participatory manner (. . .) to communicate information on [and beyond] autobiographical topics (. . .) by means of narration and description in the major time frames (. . .), [while also] deal[ing] with unexpected complication[s]. (. . .) Advanced-level speakers' [language] is abundant (. . .) [– at the scale of a paragraph –] and [they] have sufficient control of basic structures (. . .) *to be understood by native speakers of the language, including those unaccustomed to non-native speech* (ACTFL 2012, 5; emphasis added).

Most of CALL research has considered proficiency as a tangential, explanatory covariate but rarely ever as a central, dependent variable (Chapelle and Sauro 2017; Leclercq, Edmonds, and Hilton 2014; Thorne and May 2017). In the last ten years, only Bibauw, François, and Desmet's (2017) meta-analysis investigated the impact on proficiency of dialoguing with an automated agent (*Alexa*) and found a significant effect of dialogue-based CALL on low proficiency levels but no mention was made of advanced levels—a void representative of the fact that only in 9 percent of cases has CALL research focused on *advanced* levels (Burston and Arispe 2018). This study thus set to determine whether using mobile speech-technology interpretatively via Text-To-Speech—that is, with the goal to understand an oral utterance rendered from a text—and/or presentationally via Speech-To-Text—that is, with the goal to have one's oral utterance be understood and thus rendered accurately as textual output—could foster the development of advanced interpersonal proficiency skills.

Intelligibility in Speech-Technology

Intelligibility is defined as "the extent to which a speaker's message is actually understood by a listener" (Munro and Derwing 1995, 76), and can be operationalized as the degree to which its verbatim transcription corresponds to the originally intended text at the word level (Moussalli and Cardoso 2019; Munro and Derwing 2015; Thomson 2018).

Intelligibility is at play in Advanced proficiency as the latter entails being understood by a listener *unaccustomed* to language learners, making it challenging to measure. Indeed, while reliability in assessing intelligibility requires highly trained listeners, ecological validity in assessing Advanced proficiency requires lay listeners. Moreover, Munro and Derwing cautioned that human ratings "can be contaminated by listener bias" (2015, 33; see also Thomson 2018). This study addressed this validity/reliability paradox by combining human-based and speech-technology-generated ratings of intelligibility.

Five series of publications focused on TTS/STT for L2 pronunciation informed this study, putting the emphasis on a variety of key aspects of interest. First, in her three-weeklong study on 84 ESL university students focused on questions of autonomy, growth, and outcomes, McCrocklin (2016) compared a control group (instruction only), a comparison group (instruction + strategy training), and a treatment group (instruction + strategy training + use of *Windows Speech Recognition* (*WSR*) once weekly during 30-minute in-class sessions). Students who used speech-technology displayed significantly more autonomy than other students (1.96 hours of voluntary use of speech-technology outside of class) (McCrocklin 2019a). Performance was compared in the 27 students from the control and treatment groups. Although both improved significantly, no significant differences in outcomes emerged. McCrocklin (2019b) reported that students considered that STT provided useful feedback. However, three limitations arose: (1) the sometimes-unsatisfying level of recognition by *WSR*, (2) its lack of portability, and (3) the absence of audio-model, all of which the current study attempted to address. Moreover, an important recommendation was made by the author to combine mandated task with autonomous practice sustained over a longer period, which was fully integrated into this study.

Similar results of significant differences in learning growth but not in learning outcomes emerged from the second series of publications. Indeed, in their seven-weeklong study on 42 Novice French learners who completed five 20-minute read-aloud tasks weekly, Liakin et al. (2015) compared instruction without feedback, with teacher-based feedback, or with STT-based feedback using *Nuance Dragon Dictation*. Only the STT group improved significantly. However, no significant differences emerged between groups. Liakin et al. (2017) replicated this procedure on 27 Novice French learners to compare instruction without audio-model, with teacher-pronounced audio-model, or with TTS-generated audio-model using *NaturalReader*. Although students with audio-models improved significantly, no significant differences emerged between groups.

Also aiming to evaluate learning growth, García, Nicholai, and Jones' (2020) fifteen-week-long classroom study on 76 second-semester Spanish learners compared levels of comprehensibility, nativeness, fluency, and confidence in a control group (with instructor-led explicit phonetic sessions) versus a treatment group (with STT-based pronunciation training in *iSpraak*). The experiment relied on six 20-minute pronunciation modules in the form of read-aloud tasks. Results showed significant semester-long benefits of STT for fluency, as well as short-term benefits for all characteristics except nativeness when working specifically on vowels, and for all characteristics when working on letters "g," "j," and "h."

Questioning whether understanding through speech-technology could be comparable to human understanding, Moussalli and Cardoso's (2019) study on 11 ESL university students with varying L1s and proficiency levels aimed to determine whether *Alexa* could reliably understand and be understood by accented learners who asked 30 prescribed questions for 30–45 minutes. By comparing human-based verbatim transcriptions of learners' questions with *Alexa*'s speech-technology-generated transcripts, the authors established that "*Alexa* can understand accented L2 speech and be understood by the same accented L2 learners with a performance relatively similar to that of two human judges" (2019, 20), at above 80 percent. Based on these results, the current study set to combine human-based ratings with speech-technology-generated ratings.

Similarly interested in whether *learners* would consider that being understood by speech-technology could credibly be equivalent to the experience of attempting to be understood by a human listener, Mroz's (2018) sixteen-week-long study on 16 Intermediate French learners qualitatively explored how students experienced intelligibility using STT in *Gmail* for read-aloud and semi-spontaneous speaking tasks. She determined that speech-technology's multisensory properties served as a form of visual feedback of oral output that students had agentively manipulated to adjust their pronunciation. She also found that students had developed an outward awareness of what is at stake in intelligible communication with others, as most learners found that STT could credibly simulate a lay listener's understanding.

Ecological Paradigm: Agency and Affordances

This study answered Blin's (2016) call for a shift in research paradigm in CALL, following an ecological approach à la van Lier (2004), where CALL is conceived as an ecosystem of "interacting components including language learners, (. . .) other users of the target language, technological devices, applications and platforms, and multimodal (. . .) resources, all of which participate in language learning" (Blin 2016, 39).

A key ecological construct framed the study: agency. *Agency* is an individual's will and capacity to act. According to van Lier (2008), "learning depends on the activity and initiative of the learner, more so than any 'inputs' that are transmitted to the learner" (163). It starts with learners' initiative, that is, their self-determined choice of a learning goal and their self-regulated, autonomous, motivated willingness to pursue that goal through actions. As goal-oriented actions are produced, learners control them by assigning relevance and significance to them, as well as to the social cultural context within which they are situated and within which they interact. When an actual learning outcome emerges, it is evaluated against the initial goals, with the purpose to take responsibility for the way in which the actions undertaken affected their selves, as well as others and the environment. Future actions are then revised accordingly.

RESEARCH QUESTIONS

Three research questions (RQ) structured this study:

RQ1) Was there a *relationship* between proficiency and intelligibility (a) at the onset and (b) at the end of the study?

RQ2) Were there any differences in *proficiency* between the six groups formed based on type of instruction and technology in terms of (a) outcome and (b) growth?

RQ3) Were there any differences in *intelligibility* between the six groups in terms of (a) outcome and (b) growth?

METHODS

Participants

Thirty-five French learners enrolled in a U.S. institution of higher education participated in this 16-week-long study. Participants were 22.23 years old on average (*SD* = 3.068), 21 females and 14 males. Their average Age of Onset Learning (AOL) of French was 13.57 years old (*SD* = 4.152). Twenty-seven were L1 English speakers and 8 were L1 speakers of other languages (4 Spanish, 2 Mandarin, 1 Basque, 1 Arabic). Twelve were L2 French learners, whereas 23 were L3+ French learners. The non-native languages represented included French, English, Spanish, Mandarin, Japanese, Czech, Polish, Greek,

Hebrew, German, Latin, and Russian. Finally, 10 had had an immersive experience of 6 months or longer in French (study abroad or immersion school).

Instructional Setting and Groups

Participants were recruited from two 16-week-long courses (ORAL: $n = 18$; PRON: $n = 17$), taught at the same level of instruction by native or Superior speakers of French, with identical weekly frequency (50 minutes three times weekly), and with syllabi that targeted Advanced oral skills (ACTFL 2012). They differed in their approaches to integrated instruction (Darcy 2018; Ranta and Lyster 2018). ORAL primarily aimed at the development of proficiency with the integration of some sporadic activities related to the development of intelligibility, while PRON's primary goal was to develop intelligibility with the integration of some sporadic activities related to proficiency.

For instance, at week 9, Advanced proficiency in ORAL was targeted by discussing graphic novels, comparing and contrasting characters from several *bandes-dessinées* (e.g., *Tintin*, *Astérix et Obélix*, *Lucky Luke*, *Les Bidochons*) with specific rather than generic vocabulary, and narrating sequences of events, while a sporadic pronunciation activity on nasal vowels was integrated (adapted from Violin-Wigent, Miller, and Grim (2013). Conversely, Advanced intelligibility in PRON was targeted by working on nasal vowels' spelling-to-sound and grammar-to-sound patterns, followed by laboratory practice to perceive, transcribe, predict, and produce contrastive oral and nasal vowels, while a sporadic proficiency activity was integrated through discussing *Astérix et Obélix*.

Each course had three sections, randomly assigned as either a control group (*Control*, with no speech-technology), a first treatment group (*Single*, with the use of Speech-To-Text only), or a second treatment group (*Mix*, with the use of both Text-To-Speech and Speech-To-Text), resulting in six research groups: Oral*Control* ($n = 4$), Oral*Single* ($n = 10$), Oral*Mix* ($n = 4$), Pron*Control* ($n = 6$), Pron*Single* ($n = 6$), and Pron*Mix* ($n = 5$).

Data Collection

Data collection lasted 16 weeks and entailed three phases.

Pre- and Post-tests

Pre-tests happened at week 1. No speech-technology was used. They entailed (1) an online background questionnaire to elicit individual factors, (2) an unrehearsed, audio-recorded read-aloud task of a 110-word-long text to establish onset intelligibility, and (3) an audio-recorded 10- to 15-minute face-to-face modified Oral Proficiency Interview (OPI) administered by a certified tester to establish onset proficiency (ACTFL 2012).

Post-tests happened at week 16 and replicated the pre-tests' read-aloud and OPI. They also entailed a semi-structured interview conducted in English to elicit participants' experience with the technology, notably to determine, following McCrocklin (2016), whether participants had agentively used the speech-technology introduced during the experiment to work on their French of their own volition beyond the phases of experiment.

Experiment

The experiment started at week 4 with a 20-minute training of participants exposed to speech-technology, with the installation of a *Google* language package and learning how to generate Speech-To-Text and/or Text-To Speech in *Gmail* on their smartphones.

The intervention started at week 5 and was repeated at week 9 and 13. Each time, the 30-minute in-class intervention comprised two 15-minute tasks in French: a read-aloud task and a semi-spontaneous oral task. Read-aloud tasks relied on 60- to 100-word-long text focused on specific phonetic features (e.g., liaisons). Semi-spontaneous oral tasks were based on the OPI protocol (ACTFL 2012) and entailed a series of probes at the Advanced level (e.g., Tell me about your best friend. How did you meet? Why are you best friends? What does s/he look like? What's his/her personality like? How does it compare to yours? What does s/he do for a living? Where does s/he live? Tell us about the best memory you have of something you two did together?).

Each task comprised a 10-minute Practice activity followed by a 5-minute Perform activity. While practicing the read-aloud task, all participants were given the printed text. *Mix* students were also emailed the text in *Gmail*. No audio-model was provided to *Control* and *Single* students. *Mix* students, however, could utilize Text-To-Speech in *Gmail* to hear a synthetic aural rendition of the text. All students were instructed to practice as many times as possible for 10 minutes. They could all use a voice-recorder to record and playback their oral production. *Single* and *Mix* students were also instructed to use Speech-To-Text in *Gmail* to generate a text rendition of their oral production, to track discrepancies between intended and actual output, and pinpoint areas in need of improvement (see Mroz (2018)). Then, students had 5 minutes to perform a final audio-recorded read-aloud. The same Practice-then-Perform procedure was used for semi-spontaneous tasks. Students were instructed they could rehearse but could not script their answers to produce a one- to two-minute-long final response to the probe.

Use of speech-technology between each of the three intervention sessions by students in *Single* and *Mix* was neither mandated nor discouraged, following McCrocklin (2016). Post-tests semi-structured interviews revealed that 44.00 percent of participants exposed to speech-technology (11 out of 25) had agentively used the technology to work on their French of their own volition beyond the three rounds of intervention—more specifically, 31.25 percent of *Single* participants (5 out of 16) and 66.67 percent of *Mix* participants (6 out of 9). Some examples of autonomous uses of speech-technology beyond the experiment comprised attempts at simply practicing French at length in the absence of native speakers outside of the classroom, but also training to be intelligible for a French presentation, starting a paper in French when no writing device was otherwise available, or interacting with speakers of French through other applications such as *Snapchat*.

Analyses

Proficiency

Participants' proficiency was blindly, randomly, and independently assessed by two certified OPI testers using participants' pre- and post-OPI audio-recordings. Scores were attributed as Intermediate-Low (IL) = 1, Intermediate-Mid (IM) = 2, Intermediate-High (IH) = 3, Advanced-Low (AL) = 4, and Advanced-Mid (AM) = 5 (ACTFL 2012). Inter-rater reliability, assessed through two-way random interclass correlations of absolute agreement (ICC), was strong ($M_{ICCProficiency}$ = .754, p < .001 on all correlations).

Intelligibility

Participants' intelligibility rate was established using their pre- and post-read-aloud audio-recordings, which underwent two complementary ratings: human-based ratings, averaged with speech-technology-generated ratings.

Human-based ratings served as the primary analysis, since intelligibility is primarily a "listener-based phenomenon" (Munro and Derwing 2015, 45). They were established by two native speakers of French: one expert, highly trained, and accustomed to L2 learners; the other naïve, trained for one hour, and unaccustomed to L2 learners. Both blindly, randomly, and independently rated all and re-rated 10 percent of the recordings. As recordings were all based on the same 110-word-long text, asking raters to provide a verbatim transcription of each recording was an invalid procedure, as raters would have quickly become accustomed to the text, leading to a repeated task-effect. Instead, a procedure of confirmatory verbatim transcription was chosen by which raters were presented with a copy of the text and instructed to only listen to each recording once and follow the prompt: "If you had had to provide a verbatim transcription of what you are hearing, would your transcription have matched the words you are seeing in this text? If not, please circle all parts where you find a discrepancy." Intelligibility rate was established at the word-level. Intra- and inter-coder reliability, assessed via ICC, were strong (intra-rater rate: $ICC_{minimally\text{-}trained\,rater}$ = .898, p = .003, and $ICC_{highly\text{-}trained\,rater}$ = .955, p < .001; inter-rater rate: $M_{ICCIntelligibility}$ = .891, p < .001 on all correlations).

Next, speech-technology-generated ratings were conducted. All recordings were played to the researcher's smartphone's microphone to obtain a verbatim transcription via Speech-To-Text in *Gmail*. Transcriptions were then inspected and corrected when cases of undue discrepancy related to homophones appeared (e.g., *Gmail* transcribing "et moi" (and me) instead of "émoi" (commotion), both pronounced [emwa]). An intelligibility rate was established with Ukkonen's (1985) string similarity test to determine the level of similarity between the intended text and the speech-technology-generated text.

Finally, human-based and speech-technology-generated ratings were compared using a Pearson correlation test, which showed a strong, positive correlation (M_r = .841, p < .05 on all correlations). A final intelligibility rate was then attributed to each read-aloud recording by averaging human-based and speech-technology-generated ratings.

Robust Statistics

Larson-Hall (2016) and Plonsky (2015), among others, have been arguing for a methodological reform to advance quantitative studies in applied linguistics, and to switch from "classical parametric" to "robust" statistics. Three components of robust statistics were selected, namely, bootstrapping, effect sizes, and confidence intervals (CIs).

Tested since the 1960s, bootstrapping has only recently been adopted in SLA research (e.g., Hessel 2015; McLean et al. 2020; Nikitina et al. 2019; Zhang 2017). According to LaFlair et al.,

the sample sizes typical of L2 research provide the most compelling reason to employ bootstrapping [with average sample sizes found from meta-analyses to be 19]. (. . .) By resampling from the observed data, bootstrapping enables researchers to obtain a data set that simulates a sample much larger than what is typically found, simulating Ns in the thousands (. . .) to overcome the lack of statistical power and Type II error resulting from analyses based on small samples [and violation of assumptions, notably of normality] (2015, 47)

Bootstrapping allows to do with a computer what researchers wish they could do in the field, that is, replicate the experiment multiple times, resulting in thousands of proxy samples generated *without* regards to the original groupings, from which it creates an empirically generated distribution that estimates the population distribution. In this study, bootstrapping was set at $N = 1000$, following Larson-Hall and Herrington (2010). With that said, it is important to emphasize that bootstrapping is not a substitute to collecting large samples but "simply that, when ideal sampling conditions cannot be met, [it] may assist researchers in making the most of their data" (Plonsky et al. 2015, 607). Limitations related to small sample sizes, as is the case in this study, remain, notably when it comes to generalization of results.

Furthermore, to counter the weaknesses found in null-hypothesis significance testing, significance was determined based on effect sizes and confidence intervals (CIs) or bias corrected accelerated 95 percent confidence intervals (BCa 95% CIs) rather than p-values—although p-values are also reported (Plonksy 2015). The method consists of ensuring that "the mean of one group falls (. . .) outside the CI for the other group's mean (. . .) [or that] the CI around the mean difference does not cross 0" (40–42). Finally, using Norouzian and Plonsky (2018), partial eta-squared (η_p^2) were computed as effect sizes and interpreted using Cohen (1988), with $\eta_p^2 = .01$ considered a small effect, $\eta_p^2 = .06$ a medium effect, and $\eta_p^2 = .14$ a large effect.

Initial Differences

Preemptive analyses were conducted to assess potential differences in group formation in terms of age and AOL through bootstrapped one-way analyses of variance (ANOVAs), as well as gender, L1, language background, and immersive experience through Pearson chi-square tests of homogeneity. Then, for each oral skill (proficiency and intelligibility), a bootstrapped multiple regression was run to predict pre-scores from all other factors—namely, group and all individual factors. Estimated means and BCa 95% CIs provided descriptive statistics to compare groups. Finally, for each skill, a bootstrapped one-way ANOVA served to determine whether any differences existed between groups in initial oral performance.

Relationship Between Proficiency and Intelligibility (RQ1)

Two bootstrapped Pearson correlation tests were run to establish whether proficiency scores and intelligibility scores were correlated, at the onset and at the end of the study.

Proficiency (RQ2)

First, to determine if any differences existed between the six groups in terms of proficiency *outcome*, a bootstrapped one-way analysis of covariance (AN-COVA) was conducted on proficiency post-scores controlling for pre-scores, followed by post-hoc analyses. Second, to determine differences in proficiency *growth*, a two-way mixed ANOVA was run in search for Group x Time interactions, followed by post-hoc analyses using a Bonferroni adjustment.

Intelligibility (RQ3)

The same procedures used to analyze proficiency scores was adopted to analyze intelligibility scores.

RESULTS

Descriptive statistics of pre- and post-performances are reported in table 8.1.

Initial Differences

No significant differences were found between groups for age, AOL, gender, L1, language background, and immersive experience at the onset of the study. The two multiple regressions conducted to respectively predict proficiency pre-scores and intelligibility pre-scores from groups and individual factors yielded non-significant results (Proficiency: F (7, 27) = 1.834, p = .121, adj R^2 = .147; Intelligibility: F (7, 27) = 1.506, p = .207, adj R^2 = −.094).

For proficiency, although the one-way ANOVA did not reveal any significant differences based on p-value ($F(5,29)$ = 2.063, p = .099), the large effect size (η_p^2 = .262) warranted further pairwise comparisons based on estimated marginal means and BCa 95% CIs. These showed that groups initially ranged from Oral*Control* as the most proficient group, followed by Pron*Mix*, Pron*Single*, Oral*Single*, Pron*Control*, and Oral*Mix*. Oral*Mix* had significantly *lower* proficiency pre-scores than Oral*Control* (p = .018, CI = [.300, 3.330], $M_{Est.Diff.}$ = 1.875), than Pron*Mix* (p = .003, CI = [.500, 2.210], $M_{Est.Diff.}$ = 1.400), than Pron*Single* (p = .042, CI = [.043, 1.931], $M_{Est.Diff.}$ = 1.000), and than Oral*Single* (p = .110, CI = [.211, 2.000], $M_{Est.Diff.}$ = .950). Finally, Pron*Control* also had significantly *lower* proficiency pre-scores than Oral*Control* (p = .042, CI = [.028, 3.130], $M_{Est.Diff.}$ = 1.542), and than Pron*Mix* (p = .017, CI = [.186, 1.973], $M_{Est.Diff.}$ = 1.067).

For intelligibility, the one-way ANOVA yielded significant results ($F(5,29)$ = 2.800, p = .035, η_p^2 = .326 (large effect)) and post-hoc analyses

Table 8.1. Descriptive Statistics for Proficiency and Intelligibility Pre- and Post-Scores, and Post-Hoc Results on Growth per Group

Proficiency	Pre-Proficiency		BCa 95% CI		Post-Proficiency		BCa 95% CI		Post-Hoc Results of Two-Way Mixed ANOVA (Growth)		95% CI	
	Est. Mean	SD	Lower Bound	Upper Bound	Est. Mean	SD	Lower Bound	Upper Bound	Est. Marginal Mean Diff.	p-value	Lower Bound	Upper Bound
OralControl	3.875	1.315	2.500	5.000	2.422	1.658	1.087	3.639	-.625	.099	-1.375	.125
OralSingle	2.950	1.235	2.282	3.656	3.669	1.358	3.091	4.233	.750*	.003	.276	1.224
OralMix	2.000	.817	1.000	2.859	3.788	.817	3.344	4.213	1.000*	.011	.250	1.750
PronControl	2.333	.983	1.500	3.250	3.084	.917	2.629	3.566	.250	.411	-.362	.862
PronSingle	3.000	.707	2.500	3.500	3.343	.917	2.727	4.039	.417	.175	-.196	1.029
PronMix	3.400	.418	3.000	3.750	3.881	.570	3.251	4.409	.900*	.010	.229	1.571

Intelligibility	Pre-Intelligibility		BCa 95% CI		Post-Intelligibility		BCa 95% CI		Post-Hoc Results of Two-Way Mixed ANOVA (Growth)		95% CI	
	Est. Mean	SD	Lower Bound	Upper Bound	Est. Mean	SD	Lower Bound	Upper Bound	Est. Marginal Mean Diff.	p-value	Lower Bound	Upper Bound
OralControl	80.908	2.793	74.120	87.950	80.907	3.875	77.196	84.560	.070	.972	-3.958	4.098
OralSingle	80.308	2.713	78.438	82.058	84.138	2.950	82.031	86.559	3.537*	<.001	1.736	5.338
OralMix	75.790	1.670	73.300	76.880	87.382	2.000	85.412	91.934	8.250*	<.001	5.402	11.098
PronControl	81.397	2.815	79.810	84.135	81.570	2.333	78.452	84.040	.615	.592	-1.710	2.940
PronSingle	82.713	3.174	79.808	84.230	84.406	3.000	80.898	86.516	3.023*	.013	.698	5.349
PronMix	82.302	3.533	80.467	84.188	84.519	3.400	82.408	86.297	3.270*	.014	.723	5.817

SD: standard deviation; BCa 95% CI: bias corrected accelerated 95% confidence interval; *: significant, as based on CI.
Source: Mroz 2022

based on estimated marginal means and BCa 95% CIs revealed that groups initially ranged from Pron*Single* as the most intelligible group, followed by Pron*Mix*, Pron*Control*, Oral*Control*, Oral*Single*, and Oral*Mix*. Oral*Mix* had significantly *lower* intelligibility pre-scores than all other groups except Oral*Control* (with Pron *Single*: $p = .002$, $CI = [3.387, 9.982]$, $M_{Est.Diff.} = 6.923$; with Pron*Mix*: $p = .001$, $CI = [4.048, 9.095]$, $M_{Est.Diff.} = 6.512$; with Pron*Control*: $p = .001$, $CI = [3.424, 8.287]$, $M_{Est.Diff.} = 5.607$; with Oral*Control*: $p = .103$, $CI = [.961, 11.745]$, $M_{Est.Diff.} = 5.117$; with Oral*Single*: $p = .003$, $CI = [2.395, 6.998]$, $M_{Est.Diff.} = 4.518$).

Relationship Between Intelligibility and Proficiency (RQ1)

A significant correlation was found between intelligibility and proficiency pre-scores ($r = .491$ (moderate), $p = .003$, $CI = [.256, .704]$), and post-scores ($r = .512$ (moderate), $p = .002$, $CI = [.271, .715]$).

Differences in Proficiency (RQ2)

Although the one-way ANCOVA on proficiency post-scores, controlling for pre-scores, did not yield significant results based on p-value ($F(5,28) = 2.501$, $p = .054$), the large effect size ($\eta_p^2 = .309$) warranted further pairwise comparisons based on estimated marginal means and BCa 95% CIs. These showed that groups ranged from Pron*Mix* as the most proficient group, followed by Oral*Mix*, Oral*Single*, Pron*Single*, Pron*Control*, and Oral*Control*. Moreover, Pron*Mix*, Oral*Mix*, and Oral*Single* were found to have significantly outperformed Oral*Control* and Pron*Control* respectively (Pron*Mix* with Oral*Control*: $p = .137$, $CI = [.209, 3.674]$, $M_{Est.Diff.} = 1.460$; Pron*Mix* with Pron*Control*: $p = .046$, $CI = [.253, 1.294]$, $M_{Est.Diff.} = .797$; Oral*Mix* with Oral*Control*: $p = .108$, $CI = [-3.716, -.222]$, $M_{Est.Diff.} = 1.367$; Oral*Mix* with Pron*Control*: $p = .002$, $CI = [-.990, -.406]$, $M_{Est.Diff.} = .704$; Oral*Single* with Oral*Control*: $p = .168$, $CI = [.017, 3.574]$, $M_{Est.Diff.} = 1.248$; Oral*Single* with Pron*Control*: $p = .069$, $CI = [.157, 1.049]$, $M_{Est.Diff.} = .585$).

The two-way mixed ANOVA conducted to determine whether there was a significant difference in proficiency between the six groups from pre-test to post-test yielded a significant two-way interaction ($F(5, 29) = 2.940, p = .029$, $\eta_p^2 = .336$ (large effect)). Post-hoc pairwise comparisons (table 8.1) indicated that three groups had undergone significant growth in proficiency, namely, Oral*Mix*, Pron*Mix*, and Oral*Single* (figure 8.1).

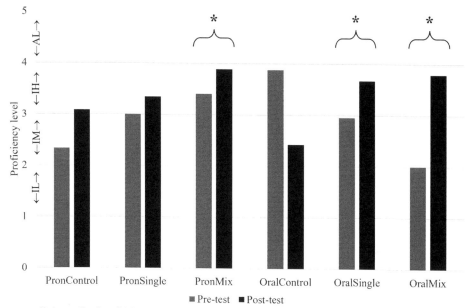

IL: Intermediate-Low; IM: Intermediate-Mid; IH: Intermediate-High; AL: Advanced-Low
*: significant at $p < .05$

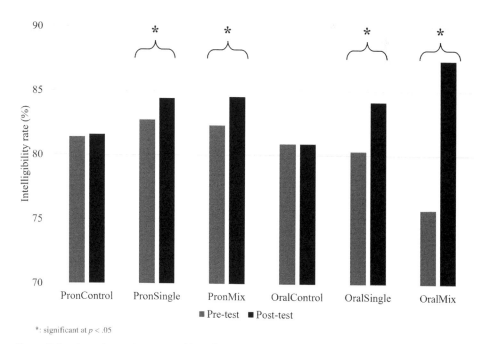

*: significant at $p < .05$

Figure 8.1. Learning outcomes and learning growth in proficiency and intelligibility.
Credit: Mroz 2022

Differences in Intelligibility (RQ3)

The one-way ANCOVA on intelligibility post-scores, controlling for pre-scores, yielded significant results ($F(5,26) = 2.656$, $p = .046$, $\eta_p^2 = .338$ (large)). Estimated marginal means and BCa 95% CIs showed that groups ranged from Oral*Mix* as the most intelligible group, followed by Pron*Mix*, Pron*Single*, Oral*Single*, Pron*Control*, and Oral*Control*. Oral*Mix* significantly outperformed all other groups (with Oral*Control*: $p = .008$, $CI = [-12.535, -3.979]$, $M_{Est.Diff.} = 6.475$; with Pron*Control*: $p = .009$, $CI = [2.398, 11.770]$, $M_{Est.Diff.} = 5.813$; with Oral*Single*: $p = .020$, $CI = [-5.264, -1.703]$, $M_{Est.Diff.} = 3.245$; with Pron *Single*: $p = .156$, $CI = [-7.849, -.645]$, $M_{Est.Diff.} = 2.977$; with Pron*Mix*: $p = .096$, $CI = [-5.869, -.865]$, $M_{Est.Diff.} = 2.864$). Pron*Mix* also significantly outperformed Pron*Control* ($p = .061$, $CI = [.130, 5.860]$, $M_{Est.Diff.} = 2.949$).

The two-way mixed ANOVA conducted to determine whether there was a significant difference in intelligibility between the six groups from pre-test to post-test yielded a significant two-way Group x Time interaction ($F(5, 27) = 4.231$, $p = .006$, $\eta_p^2 = .439$ (large effect)). Post-hoc pairwise comparisons (table 8.1) indicated that four groups had undergone significant growth in intelligibility, namely, Oral*Mix*, Oral*Single*, Pron*Mix*, and Pron*Single* (figure 8.1).

DISCUSSION

Summary of Results

The use of Text-to-Speech with Speech-to-Text was found to be the most beneficial type of speech-technology, leading to both significant outcomes *and* growth in proficiency *and* intelligibility, compared to an absence of speech-technology. The two-way process afforded by the combined use of Text-to-Speech with Speech-to-Text seems to have both reinforced the primary oral skill emphasized by each type of instruction, while also rendering students more capable of individually and agentively attending to the skill that was only sporadically integrated into their course, with ORAL students gaining valuable feedback through speech-technology on both spelling-to-sound and sound-to-spelling pronunciation patterns, while PRON students gained feedback on both interpretive and presentational aspects of proficiency.

Implications and Tips for Teaching and Learning

Although speech-technology should by no means be considered a substitute for real, spontaneous, human-to-human interactions in the target language, it has nonetheless proven to be a very promising tool to promote the independent and individual development of oral skills (both proficiency and intelligibility) at the advanced level. More specifically, this study unveiled that nearly half of the students exposed to speech-technology during the controlled experiment also decided to use it of their own volition outside of any mandated tasks for their own idiosyncratic needs in the target language, which might have contributed to the significant learning outcomes and learning growth witnessed here. Beyond these results, a wide array of learning possibilities is indeed at the students' fingertips at different levels in the learning process. To use speech-technology in *Gmail*, the first step is to ensure that the target language has been installed on the phone from the *Google Input Tools*. To launch Text-To-Speech, make sure the function has been activated in the phone's Accessibility settings and then simply press the Accessibility icon to get to the control bar allowing to play the synthetic voice that reads the text as words get highlighted (figure 8.2). To launch Speech-To-Text, simply

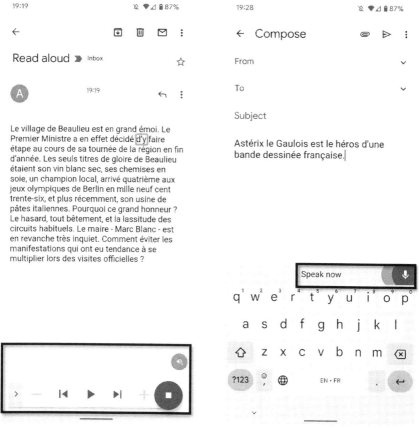

Figure 8.2. Example of the Text-To-Speech and Speech-To-Text functions in Gmail.
Credit: Mroz 2022

start a new email by choosing Compose, then select the microphone icon and start talking. You will see the transcription of your speech appear almost instantaneously in the body of the email (figure 8.2). These functions work on both *iPhones* and *Android* phones alike. For general pedagogical purposes, it is recommended that the Practice-then-Perform structure employed in this study's experiment be used to plan for learning activities where speech-technology is used, to give learners ample time and opportunities to become familiar with the technology to use it more optimally.

On the one hand, the most beneficial aspect of Text-To-Speech is that it allows learners to transform any textual content into an oral one. As such, it offers instructors with an infinite range of possibilities as to the type of materials they can present to their students, freed from their dependence on pre-recorded resources or on native or superior speakers of the language to model how things sound (Chiaráin and Chasaide 2020). This is particularly interesting when presenting learners with linguistic content they have never encountered before, as it thus removes the impression of not being able to gain access to the material unless a speaker of the language is present to introduce it, by providing a key to autonomously decipher it. Moreover, Text-To-Speech allows modeling to be done at the word-, the sentence-, or even the paragraph-level. Although, admittedly, synthetic voices in Text-To-Speech still sound somewhat unnatural and lack some important human-like features of oral discourse (e.g., lack of natural imperfection in speech, monotonous intonations), Text-To-Speech nevertheless is accurate enough at this point in time to allow different areas of focus in listening, including for pronunciation purposes, and catering to different learning levels—is it a particular sound, a particular word, or the flow linking several elements in the sentence that I am interested in working on? Any text-based in-class or homework activity can thus be augmented to feature an oral component to serve the broad development of listening comprehension in conjunction with more traditional activity, including grammar or writing. Because access to oral content becomes infinite, automatic, and instantaneous, learners are offered readily accessible opportunities for more creative or more interactional tasks in the target language, that, in turn, can foster engagement, motivation, as well as agentive and independent learning.

On the other hand, the most beneficial aspect of Speech-To-Text is that it renders the fleeting and intangible nature of oral discourse visible and manageable by generating a textual transcript of speech (Mroz 2018). As such, it allows learners to have the time to pause to compare what they actually said—the generated transcript—with what they had intended to say. This comparative task serves for learners as comprehensive feedback received in the type of real time and highly individualized manner that is simply impossible to get from a listener or an instructor due to human limitations and to general classroom constraints. This feedback is particularly impactful as it provides confirmation as to when pronunciation was intelligible enough to be accurately transcribed as intended—admittedly, a motivation booster—but also readily pinpoints specific areas of the utterance when the transcript deviates from what was intended, thus requiring attention and correction. It is this clinical ability to pinpoint when speech is understood versus when it fails to be understood that makes Text-To-Speech particularly promising for the advancement of oral skills. As shown in Mroz (2018) and confirmed here, this technological feature is even more fruitful when it is paired with the explicit teaching and learning of pronunciation, since learners can use the declarative knowledge they acquire on spelling-to-sound patterns to guide the correction of their speech. Here too, any text-based in-class or homework activity can be augmented to feature an oral component by asking students to read aloud or produce speech spontaneously, and to then verify the intelligibility of their output. Learners who used Speech-To-Text in Mroz (2018) further noted that it credibly simulated the understanding a native speaker would have of their speech but without the more anxiety-driven component that one usually gets when interacting spontaneously with a speaker of the language. However, two main limitations of importance in the use of Speech-To-Text need to be noted. First, some confusion between certain homophones can happen (e.g., "au temps" = at the time of, vs. "autant" = as much as, both pronounced [o tã]). Second, the longer and the more complex the text inputted, the more likely some grammatical inaccuracies related to homophony will appear (e.g., lack of pluralization of the verbs "chanter" and manger" in the sentence "Les membres du village gaulois chante* et mange* des sangliers" (instead of "chant<u>ent</u>" and "mang<u>ent</u>" = members of the Gallic village sing and eat boars). Moreover, based on how old the technology is, as the text inputted becomes too long, the phone might just stop transcribing altogether.

CONCLUSION

This study contributed to advance research on CALL and MALL by establishing that integrating mobile-based speech-technology to instruction could benefit French learners' advancement of oral skills (both intelligibility and proficiency), by providing an audio-model of "how things are supposed to sound" via Text-To-Speech and an opportunity "to see how people hear you" via Speech-To-Text (Mroz 2018, 367).

Although limited in its ability to generalize results due to its small sample size, the study nevertheless enhanced the field of quantitative L2 research by relying on robust statistical procedures, including bootstrapping, effects sizes, and confidence intervals. It also advanced the field of L2 pronunciation research by linking intelligibility to proficiency and by offering an innovative model of triangulation between human- and machine-generated measures of intelligibility. It also contributes to supporting language teachers and learners by providing concrete guidance on why and how to use speech-technology in *Gmail* for the advancement of oral skills inside and outside the classroom.

Future research should examine the role of language background, immersive experiences, and gender in MALL. It should also try to determine which specific features of intelligibility (e.g., segmental vs. suprasegmental) and of proficiency (e.g., narrating vs. describing) are most impacted by speech-technology.

REFERENCES

ACTFL. 2012. "Oral proficiency interview. Familiarization manual." Accessed February 3, 2020, https://www.languagetesting.com/wp/wp-content/uploads/2013/05/ACTFL-OPI-Familiarization-Manual1.pdf

Bibauw, Serge, Thomas François, and Piet Desmet. 2017. "Effectiveness of dialogue-based CALL on L2 proficiency development: A meta-analysis." Presentation at the CALICO conference, Flagstaff, AZ, USA, May 16–18, 2017.

Blin, Françoise. 2016. "Toward and 'ecological' CALL theory. Theoretical perspectives and their instantiation in CALL research and practice." In *The Routledge Handbook of Language Learning and Technology*, edited by Fiona Farr and Liam Murray, 39–54. Routledge.

Blyth, Carl. 2017. "Open Educational Resources (OERs) for language learning." In *Language, education, and technology*, edited by Steven Thorne and Stephen May, 1–11. Springer. https://doi.org/10.1007/978-3-319-02328-1_14-2

Burston, Jack, and Kelly Arispe. 2018. "Looking for a needle in a haystack: CALL and advanced language proficiency." *CALICO Journal 35*, no. 1: 77–102. https://doi.org/10.1558/cj.31594

Chapelle, Carol, and Shannon Sauro. 2017. *Handbook of technology and second language teaching and learning.* Wiley Blackwell.

Chiaráin, Neasa Ní, and Ailbhe Ní Chasaide. 2020. "The Potential of Text-to-Speech Synthesis in Computer-Assisted Language Learning: A Minority Language Perspective." In *Recent Tools for Computer- and Mobile-Assisted Foreign Language Learning*, edited by Alberto Andujar, 149–169. IGI Global. http://doi:10.4018/978-1-7998-1097-1.ch007

Cohen, Jacob. 1988. *Statistical power analysis for the behavioral sciences (2nd ed.).* Lawrence Erlbaum Associates.

Darcy, Isabelle. 2018. "Powerful and effective pronunciation instruction: How can we achieve it?" *The CATESOL Journal* 30, no. 1: 13–45. Retrieved from https://files.eric.ed.gov/fulltext/EJ1174218.pdf

Foote, Jennifer. 2010. "Second language learners' perceptions of their own recorded speech." *PMC Working Papers Series W P10-02*: 3–27. Retrieved from https://sites.ualberta.ca/~pcerii/WorkingPapers/WP1002.pdf

García, Christina, Dan Nickolai, and Lillian Jones. 2020. "Traditional versus ASR-based pronunciation instruction: An empirical study." *CALICO Journal* 37, no. 3: 213–232. https://doi/org/10.1558/cj.40379

Gillepsie, John. 2020. "CALL research: Where are we now?" *ReCALL* 32, no. 2: 127–144. https://doi.org/10.1017/S0958344020000051

Gleason, Jesse, and Ruslan Suvorov. 2019. "Promoting social justice with CALL." *CALICO Journal* 36, no. 1: i—vii. https://doi.org/10.1558/cj.37162

Gonzalez, Dafne, and Rubena St. Louis. 2014. "CALL in low-tech contexts." In *Contemporary Computer-Assisted Language Learning*, edited by Michael Thomas, Hayo Reinders, and Mark Warschauer, 217–242. Bloomsbury.

Hessel, Gianna. 2015. "From vision to action: Inquiring into the conditions for the motivational capacity of ideal second language selves." *System* 52: 103–114. https://dx.doi.org/10.1016/j.system2015.05.008

LaFlair, Geoffrey, Jesse Egbert, and Luke Plonksy. 2015. "A practical guide to boot-strapping descriptive statistics, correlations, *t* tests, and ANOVAs." In *Advancing quantitative methods in second language research*, edited by Luke Plonsky, 46–77. Routledge.

Larson-Hall, Jenifer. 2016. *A guide to doing statistics in second language research using SPSS and R.* Routledge.

Larson-Hall, Jenifer, and Robert Herrington. 2010. "Improving data analysis in second language acquisition by utilizing modern developments in applied statistics." *Applied Linguistics* 31, no. 3: 368–390. https://doi.org/10.1093/applin/amp038

Leclerq, Pascale, Amanda Edmonds, and Heather Hilton. 2014. *Measuring L2 proficiency. Perspectives from SLA.* Multilingual Matters.

Liakin, Denis, Walcir Cardoso, and Natallia Liakina. 2015. "Learning L2 pronunciation with a mobile speech recognizer: French /y/." *CALICO Journal* 32 no. 1: 1–25. https://doi.org/10.1558/cj.v32i1.25962

Liakin, Denis, Walcir Cardoso, and Natallia Liakina. 2017. "The pedagogical use of mobile speech synthesis (TTS): Focus on French liaison." *Computer Assisted Language Learning* 30, no. 3–4: 325–342. https://doi.org/10.1080/09588221.2017.1312463

McCrocklin, Shannon. 2016. "Pronunciation learner autonomy: The potential of automatic speech recognition." *System* 57: 25–42. https://doi.org/10.1016/j.system.2015.12.013

McCrocklin, Shannon. 2019a. "ASR-based dictation practice for second language pronunciation improvement." *Journal of Second Language Pronunciation* 5, no. 1: 98–118. https://doi.org/10.1075/jslp.16034.mcc

McCrocklin, Shannon. 2019b. "Leaners' feedback regarding ASR-based dictation practice for pronunciation learning." *CALICO Journal* 36, no. 2: 119–137. https://doi.org/10.1558/cj.34738

McLean, Stuart, Jeffrey Stewart, and Aaron Olaf Batty. 2020. "Predicting L2 reading proficiency with modalities of vocabulary knowledge: A bootstrapping approach." *Language Testing, Online First*: 1–23. https://doi-org/10.1177/0265532219898380

Meeker, Mary. 2017. "Internet trends report." Last modified June 2, 2017. https://youtu.be/UC8GwG6srqs

Mercer, Sarah. 2011. "Understanding learner agency as a complex dynamic system." *System* 39: 427–436. https://doi.org/10.1016/j.system.2011.08.001

Mitterer, Holger, Nikola Anna Eger, and Eva Reinisch. 2020. "My English sounds better than yours: Second language learners perceive their own accent as better than that of their peers." *PLOS ONE* 15, no. 2: 1–12. https://doi.org/10.1371/journal.pone.0227643

Moussalli, Souheila, and Walcir Cardoso. 2019. "Intelligent personal assistants: Can they understand and be understood by accented L2 learners?" *Computer Assisted Language Learning*: 1–26. https://doi.org/10.1080/09588221.2019.1595664

Mroz, Aurore. 2018. "Seeing how people hear you: French learners experiencing intelligibility through automatic speech recognition." *Foreign Language Annals*, no. 51: 617–637. https://doi.org/10.1111/flan.12348

Munro, Murray J., and Tracey M. Derwing. 1995. "Foreign accent, comprehensibility, and accentedness of L2 speech: The role of listener experience and semantic context." *Language Learning* 45, no. 1: 73–97. https://doi.org/10.1111/j.1467-1770.1995.tb00963.x

Munro, Murray J., and Tracey M. Derwing. 2015. "A prospectus for pronunciation research in the 21st century. A point of view." *Journal of Second Language Pronunciation* 1, no. 1: 11–42. https://doi.org/10.1075/jslp.1.1.01mun

Nikitina, Larisa, Rohayati Paidi, and Fumitaka Furuoka. 2019. "Using bootstrapped quantile regression analysis for small sample research in applied linguistics: Some methodological considerations." *PLOS One* 14, no. 1, e0210668. https://doi.org/10.1371/journal.pone.0210668

Norouzian, Reza, and Luke Plonsky. 2018. "Eta- and partial eta-squared in L2 research: A cautionary review and guide to more appropriate usage." *Second Language Research* 34, no. 2: 257–271. https://doi.org/10.1177/0267658316684904

O'Dea. 2021. "Forecast number of mobile users worldwide from 2020 to 2025." Last modified July 12, 2021. https://www.statista.com/statistics/218984/number-of-global-mobile-users-since-2010/

Pew Research Center. 2021. "Mobile fact sheet." Last modified April 7, 2021. https://www.pewresearch.org/internet/fact-sheet/mobile/

Plonsky, Luke. 2015. *Advancing quantitative methods in second language research.* Routledge.

Plonsky, Luke, Jesse Egbert, and Geoffrey Laflair. 2015. "Bootstrapping in applied linguistics: Assessing its potential using shared data." *Applied Linguistics* 36, no. 5: 591–610. https://doi.org/10.1093/applin/amu001

Ranta, Leila, and Roy Lyster. 2018. "Form-focused instruction." In *The Routledge handbook of language awareness*, edited by Peter Garrett and Jopsep Vots, 40–56. Routledge.

Tate, Tamara, and Mark Warschauer. 2017. "The digital divide in language and literacy education." In *Language, education, and technology*, edited by Steven Thorne and Stephen May, 1–12. Springer. https://doi-org./10.1007/978-3-319-02328-1_5-2

Tatman, Rachael. 2017. "Gender and dialect bias in YouTube's automatic captions." In *Proceedings of the First Workshop on Ethics in Natural Language Processing*, 53–59. https://www.aclweb.org/anthology/W17-16.pdf

Tatman, Rachael, and Conner Kasten. 2017. "Effects of talker dialect, gender, and race on accuracy of Bing Speech and YouTube automatic captions." In *INTERSPEECH 2017*, 934–938. https://dx.doi.org/10.21437/Interspeech.2017-1746

Thomson, Ron. 2018. "Measurement of accentedness, intelligibility, and comprehensibility." In *Assessment in Second Language Pronunciation*, edited by Okim Kang and April Ginther, 11–29. Routledge.

Thorne, Steven, and Stephen May. 2017. *Language, education and technology* (3rd edition). Springer.

Ukkonen, Esko. 1985. "Algorithms for approximate string matching." *Information and Control* 64, no. 1–3: 100–118. https://doi.org/10.1016/S0019-9958(85)80046-2

van Lier, Leo. 2004. *The ecology and semiotics of language learning. A sociocultural perspective*. Kluwer Academic Publishers.

van Lier, Leo. 2008. "Agency in the classroom." In *Sociocultural theory and the teaching of second languages*, edited by James Lantolf and Matthew Poehner, 163–186. Equinox.

Van Moere, Alistair, and Masanori Suzuki. 2018. "Using speech processing technology in assessing pronunciation." *Assessment in Second Language Pronunciation*, edited by Okim Kang and April Ginther, 137–152. Routledge.

Violin-Wigent, Anne, Jessica Miller, and Frédérique Grim. 2013. *Sons et sens. La prononciation du français en contexte*. Georgetown University Press.

Vu, Ngoc Thang, Yuanfan Wang, Marten Klose, Zlatka Mihaylova, and Tanja Schultz. 2014. "Improving ASR performance on non-native speech using multilingual and crosslingual information." In *Fifteenth Annual Conference of the International Speech Communication Association.* Singapore.

Zhang, Dongbo. 2017. "Derivational morphology in reading comprehension of Chinese-speaking learners of English: A longitudinal structural equation modeling study." *Applied Linguistics* 38, no. 6: 871–895. https://doi.org/10.1093/applin/amv072

Chapter Nine

Developing Pronunciation Learner Autonomy with Automatic Speech Recognition and Shadowing

Solène Inceoglu

INTRODUCTION

Learner autonomy, the capacity to learn independently, is widely regarded as a crucial aspect of second language (L2) learning and has, therefore, attracted a great deal of interest from L2 researchers and practitioners. In one of the earliest definitions, Holec (1981, 3) described learner autonomy as "the ability to take charge of one's own learning" and since then teaching methodologies have emphasized the benefits of learners assuming responsibility for their learning (Benson and Voller 1997; Lee 1998), especially outside the classroom (Benson 2011). Indeed, because of the limited number of hours students spend in classrooms, it is crucial for learners to develop learning strategies and autonomous practice. As noted by Pawlak and Szyszka (2018, 294), this is particularly important for pronunciation learning and it requires that learners "choose appropriate ways of learning, engage in constant monitoring and conduct valid self-evaluation." Over the past decades, technology has led to changes in how we teach and learn, and has enabled learners to exercise more autonomy (Reinders and White 2016) and become more aware of their pronunciation (Hardison 2004; Liakin, Cardoso, and Liakina 2017). The COVID-19 pandemic and the consequent move to online teaching have also raised the importance of incorporating technological resources in language courses to support learner autonomy. In this context, the present chapter focuses on how shadowing and automatic speech recognition (ASR) were used for technology-mediated autonomous practice in a French pronunciation online course. The goal of the study was twofold: to examine learners' fluency during autonomous practice, and to report on learners' perceptions of the two types of activities.

AUTOMATIC SPEECH RECOGNITION IN L2 RESEARCH

ASR is "an independent, machine-based process of decoding and transcribing oral speech (. . .) usually in the form of a text" (Levis and Suvorov 2020, 149) and its potential for computer-assisted language learning (CALL) has been an area of interest for several decades. As Neri et al. (2002, 447) noted, ASR provides a "private, stress-free environment in which students can access virtually unlimited input, practice at their own pace and (. . .) receive individualized, instantaneous feedback." Yet, early studies also pointed out the unreliability of ASR to recognize L2 speech (Derwing, Munro, and Carbonaro 2000) due to the fact that ASR had been developed to recognize speech produced by native speakers (Neri, Cucchiarini, and Strik 2003).

Recent advancement in speech technology has led to greater improvement in how ASR-based dictation systems recognize L2 speech, with recognition patterns approaching those of native (L1) listeners (McCrocklin and Edalatishams 2020)—although this may depend on the L2 speaker and the speaking task (Inceoglu, Chen, and Lim forthcoming). Consequently, researchers have started to explore whether ASR-based dictation tools can contribute to the development of L2 language pronunciation, especially segmentals, both when ASR training is part of the classroom activities and when used outside of class for autonomous practice. For instance, Liakin et al. (2015) found that a group who completed pronunciation activities with ASR improved significantly in their production (but not perception) of the French /y-u/ contrast, whereas two other groups (i.e., same activities but with teacher feedback, and conversation practice with no feedback) did not. Similarly, McCrocklin (2019) compared an ESL group who received 50 percent pronunciation instruction face-to-face and 50 percent of pronunciation practice on a computer equipped with ASR with a group who had all their instruction face-to-face. Results from native listener ratings indicated that the pronunciation of the two groups improved equally, thus suggesting that ASR can be a useful tool for pronunciation practice. Yet, differences in the results of studies targeting L2 English vowels (Chen, Inceoglu, and Lim 2020; Guskaroska 2019; Inceoglu, Lim, and Chen 2020; McCrocklin 2019) show that ASR training may also depend on the learners' L1, their proficiency, and the targeted sounds. There is also initial evidence that ASR can contribute to the development of intelligibility in L2 French (Mroz 2020). However, a recent semester-long classroom study revealed that although L2 Spanish learners who received ASR pronunciation practice improved more on certain phonemes than their peers who were taught by the teachers, they did not experience as much gain in comprehensibility as their peers (García, Nickolai, and Jones 2020).

What is also important is how language learners perceive and interact with ASR. Studies have reported that ASR speaking and pronunciation activities enable learners to develop a greater sense of their own intelligibility (Mroz 2018), increase their learning autonomy (McCrocklin 2016), and enhance learners' motivation and enjoyment (Ahn and Lee 2016; Guskaroska 2019; McCrocklin 2016). However, despite noted benefits, studies also report learner frustration and distrust toward ASR for pronunciation practice (Chen, Inceoglu, and Lim 2020; Inceoglu, Lim, and Chen 2020; McCrocklin 2016). For instance, 78 percent of the Taiwanese EFL learners in Chen et al. (2020) responded that they would not continue using ASR to practice their pronunciation either because it did not recognize their speech, they did not see the value of practicing with ASR or believed that the technology is not advanced enough to recognize accented speech, and/or felt self-conscious using ASR for speaking. Yet another drawback of ASR that has been pointed to is the lack of modeling (Guskaroska 2019; Inceoglu, Lim, and Chen 2020); that is, the purpose of ASR-based dictation practice is to encourage the production of sentences or words, but in some cases, learners do not know how these words are pronounced. This brings us to the second focus of the current study, shadowing activities.

SHADOWING IN L2 RESEARCH

Shadowing has been defined as "a paced, auditory tracking task which involves the immediate vocalization of auditorily presented stimuli, that is, word-for-word repetition, in the same language, parrot-style, of a message" (Lambert 1992), but other definitions also specify that the repetition of the model can be nearly simultaneous or with a small delay (Goldinger 1998). Originally, used to train simultaneous interpreters, shadowing is a popular and effective technique to teach listening in the Asian EFL context, particularly in Japan (Hamada 2016; Kadota 2019). Nonetheless, the scope of shadowing extends beyond listening comprehension. Using shadowing on a mobile application to practice speaking can enhance linguistic self-confidence, attitudes toward communicating in English, and interest in English (Teeter 2017). In addition, an increasing number of studies have explored the effectiveness of shadowing on L2 pronunciation, suggesting that shadowing contributes to the development of L2 English intonation (Hsieh, Dong, and Wang 2013; Mori 2011) and fluency (Foote and McDonough 2017; Hsieh, Dong, and Wang 2013), Japanese pitch accent (Rongna and Hayashi 2012), and overall pronunciation quality as rated by native listeners (Bovee and Stewart 2009). In their study, Foote and McDonough (2017) had learners of English shadow dialogues from popular sitcoms for eight weeks, a minimum of four times a week. Native listeners rated learners' productions of a shadowing and an extemporaneous task for comprehensibility, fluency, and accentedness at pre-, mid-, and post-test. In addition, learners were interviewed about their perception and use of shadowing. Results revealed significant improvements on comprehensibility and fluency (but not accentedness) and positive opinions of the activities. In another study (Martinsen, Montgomery, and Willardson 2017), high school learners of French spent a semester shadowing video segments as a whole class and in self-directed computer-lab exercises. In addition to shadowing native speakers' speech on a variety of topics, learners could choose to track sentences with English subtitles or French captions. During the self-directed sessions, they were also given leeway to pause and repeat videos. Pronunciation ratings of pre and post reading and picture description tasks were performed by three (near) native listeners. Although not clearly defined by the authors, these ratings combined a measure of comprehensibility, accentedness, suprasegmental and segmental features of speech. Results revealed that learners' productions significantly improved in the reading task, but not in the picture description task. Martinsen et al. (2007) also reported on learners' perception of shadowing, noting that they appreciated the authenticity of the task, the technological affordances, and how it "offered them control over the process, the practice, and the pacing" (p. 674).

CURRENT STUDY

The current study aimed to compare L2 French learners' use and perception of ASR-based dictation and shadowing activities as ways to promote autonomous pronunciation learning. In particular, the study focused on the learners' speed of speech delivery during these autonomous pronunciation activities. The research questions that guided this study were:

1. How fluently do learners speak when practicing pronunciation with ASR-based dictation and shadowing activities?
2. What perceptions and attitudes do learners of French have of ASR-based dictation and shadowing practice for the autonomous development of French pronunciation?

METHOD

Setting

The study was carried out in French pronunciation and phonetics courses at a large Australian university. The goal of this 12-week course was to help learners develop the skills to improve both their pronunciation and their understanding of spoken French, improve their phonological awareness of how French sounds are produced and how they differ from their L1s, and engage with technology to record and analyze speech. The course explored the perception and production of segmental and suprasegmental features of French and emphasized the rules of correspondence between sounds and spelling, as well as the rules governing phenomena, such as liaisons and when to drop the schwa. A specific topic (e.g., intonation, nasal vowels) was introduced each week, along with exercises in oral practice, sound discrimination, and phonetic transcription from IPA to French and vice versa.

Pre-COVID, groups in the course met twice a week in a classroom for a total of three hours. However, because of issues associated with the pandemic (e.g., online teaching and large groups due to budgetary concerns), one contact hour was converted to one hour of autonomous asynchronous activities (from the start of the semester) to allow the instructor to work synchronously with smaller groups of students on Zoom. In practice, learners had one hour of phonetics class in a large group, one hour of speaking practice with the instructor in smaller groups, and one hour of autonomous ASR-based or shadowing practice. The prerequisite to enroll in the course was the completion of five semesters of French. The instructor, also the researcher, is a native speaker of Parisian French with extensive experience teaching French pronunciation.

Participants

A total of 53 students were enrolled in the course for the whole semester and 43 of them, aged between 18 to 38, consented to participate and completed all the tasks appropriately. They all reported English as (one of) their native language(s). Four were bilingual English/language other than French, and 26 had past or current experience with a third or fourth language. Responses from the background questionnaire highlighted the heterogeneity of the group in terms of when they had started learning French and how long they had been learning French (see table 9.1). This wide range of experiences was also evident in learners' self-assessments—on a scale from 1 (poor) to 7 (excellent)—of their comprehensibility, accentedness, and fluency, defined to them as:

- *comprehensibility*: "the degree of effort required by a listener to understand what you say."
- *accentedness*: "how your oral productions vary from standard French," and
- *fluency*: "the flow and smoothness of your speech, that is, how fast you speak, whether you pause (and how natural and frequent the pauses are), and how much you hesitate."

Table 9.1. Learners' Language Background Information

	M (SD)	Range	Mdn
Age started learning French	12.85 (4.95)	2–30	13
Years of French instruction	8.43 (4.01)	3–20	7
Self-rating accentedness Week 1	5.32 (1.58)	2–9	5
Self-rating comprehensibility Week 1	6.57 (1.21)	3–9	7
Self-rating fluency Week 1	4.96 (1.64)	1–8	5
Self-rating accentedness Week 12	5.27 (1.78)	2–8	6
Self-rating comprehensibility Week 12	6.77 (1.88)	2–9	7
Self-rating fluency Week 12	5.80 (1.52)	2–9	6

Source: Inceoglu 2022

Autonomous Oral Tasks: ASR and Shadowing

Over the course of the semester, learners completed a total of four sessions of shadowing activities and four sessions of ASR practice. Group 1 completed the ASR activities during the first half of the semester (i.e., Weeks 2–5) and the shadowing activities during the second half (i.e., Weeks 7–10), and Group 2 did the opposite. Both the ASR and the shadowing activities consisted of the same two types of exercises (and a third extemporaneous speaking task not discussed here). In the first exercise, half the students shadowed a news report by imitating the journalist's production with a slight delay, while the other half read the transcript of that same report using the ASR-based dictation tool accessible on a Google Doc by clicking on "tools" > "voice typing" > and selecting French.[1] The news report excerpts were taken from "Le Journal en Français Facile" broadcast every day by Radio France Internationale.[2] The length of the news reports was edited and resulted in an average of 192 words per week. In the second exercise, learners either used the audio software program Audacity[3] to shadow short sentences targeting the pronunciation focus of the week (e.g., French nasal vowels) or practiced the same sentences using ASR on a Google Doc. Each week, learners practiced 15 to 20 sentences carefully selected and piloted on the ASR program with native speakers, but were given autonomy in how much they practiced.

During these autonomous production activities, learners were encouraged to reflect on their pronunciation by listening to their recordings, comparing their pronunciation to the models shadowed, or paying attention to the ASR output. To ensure that learners completed the tasks appropriately, they were asked to submit their audio recordings (for the shadowing activities) and video recordings of their screens (for the ASR activities). For an illustration of a sentence practice with Audacity, see figure 9.1.

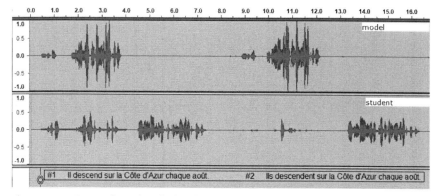

Figure 9.1. Screenshot of Audacity showing the top track with the native model and the lower track with the native model followed by one learner's production. When playing track 2 only, learners were able to hear the model directly followed by their own production, facilitating comparison and analysis of their pronunciation.
Source: Solène Inceoglu

Reflective Journals

Over the course of the semester, learners submitted four reflective journals either in French or in English. For each journal, learners were prompted to reflect on novel learning and on errors they were not previously aware of in order to help them notice the gap between their explicit knowledge and their actual pronunciation. In the last journal, learners were invited to reflect on their experiences using ASR and shadowing activities and share their opinion by answering the question: *This semester, during the autonomous hour of class, you worked on your pronunciation with 1) an ASR program, and 2) shadowing type of "listen and repeat" exercises. According to you, were these activities useful? What type of activity did you prefer, and why?*

Analysis

The analysis of learners' fluency and practice behavior using ASR and shadowing focused on the news report segments of Weeks 4 and 9 only. The rationale is that by that time, learners were familiar with the activities and the technology, having already completed two weeks of similar activities. The news reports were similar in type and were, therefore, better suited for a comparison analysis than the sentences targeting specific weekly pronunciation features. Learners were presented with the transcript of the news reports already divided into intonational phrases. In this study, fluency was defined as the speed of delivery of intonational phrases, each measured manually on Praat and reported as total sentence duration per learner. A second coder measured a subset (25%) of the data, with 100 percent agreement (± 1 second) for each learner. In addition, the total practice time, that is the time spent Week 4 and Week 9 with the particular tool (as measured from the screen capture and audio recordings), was reported to compare learners' general use of ASR and shadowing activities. Unlike the total sentence duration, the total practice time captures learners' attempts to repeat words and sentences.

RESULTS AND DISCUSSION

Fluency and Practice Time

The total sentence duration of the native speakers in the news reports was 56.38 seconds (Week 4) and 60.62 seconds (Week 9). In comparison, students' practice with ASR led to much slower averages: 88.66 seconds (Week 4) and 97.21 seconds (Week 9), whereas shadowing practice led to slightly faster delivery, 71.02 seconds (Week 4) and 81.49 seconds (Week 9). Two independent sample t tests confirmed that the difference in fluency between the two groups was statistically significant at Week 4: $t(41) = -4.31, p < .001$, and Week 9: $t(41) = -2.59, p = .015$. Furthermore, as reported in table 9.2, large individual differences were observed, with some learners producing the sentences almost twice as slowly as the native speakers in the two ASR groups (but not in the shadowing groups). Conversely, shadowing led to faster speech delivery, with some learners approaching native speed.

The results of the total practice time show that ASR practice took on average 1.5 times and twice longer than shadowing, for Weeks 4 and 9, respectively. This was due not only to a slower speech delivery, but also to more instances of repetition in the ASR practice. Again, individual differences were strong. Some learners spent a total of eight to nine minutes doing ASR, about three times longer than the longest practice with shadowing. To gain a better understanding of learners' use of the activities, future studies should also investigate when and how often learners repeat sentences and whether the repetition is more accurate/fluent.

The current data did not involve extemporaneous speech production and was not analyzed in terms of accuracy. Nevertheless, it is useful to briefly note that L2 performance and L2 proficiency are multi-dimensional constructs that can be described in terms of complexity, accuracy, and fluency. Although there is an ongoing debate on this issue, some researchers (e.g., Ellis 2005; Skehan 1998) posit that limited processing capacity forces flu-

Table 9.2. Fluency and Total Duration of Practice (in Seconds) for the ASR and Shadowing New Reports Activities Week 4 and Week 9

| | Total Sentence Duration | | | | Total Practice Time (in Seconds) | | | |
	M (SD)	Min	Max	Mdn	M (SD)	Min	Max	Mdn
Week 4								
G1: ASR	88.66 (17.65)	63.59	128.05	88.09	178.47 (127.82)	81	568	136
G2: Shadow	71.02 (7.89)	58.25	87.62	70.12	112.61 (35.25)	66	166	125
Week 9								
G2: ASR	*97.21* (23.55)	73.11	162.5	95.14	224.73 (107.06)	135	515	196
G1: Shadow	81.49 (10.32)	63.95	105.52	82.01	105.35 (34.41)	67	197	93

Source: Inceoglu 2022

ency to compete with accuracy (and complexity) for attentional resources. Consequently, increases in accuracy may occur at the expense of fluency. In the context of the current study, the strong focus on segmental accuracy that guided ASR practices appears to be a reason why fluency was hindered. This does not suggest that ASR is an inappropriate tool for autonomous pronunciation practice; on the contrary, practice with ASR showed that learners paid very close attention to segmental features, albeit at the expense of fluency, thus potentially becoming more aware of pronunciation problems.

Learners' Perception of ASR and Shadowing Activities

In their last journal, learners were encouraged to reflect on the ASR and shadowing activities they completed during their one-hour of autonomous learning throughout the semester. The journal entries were analyzed and coded for learners' stated preference (ASR, shadowing, or both) and for mentions of positive and negative aspects for each activity. In general, almost half the learners (46.5%) reported a preference for the shadowing activities, 32.6 percent were not partial for one type of activity over the other, stating for example that *"I don't think you could pick one over the other—they served different functions and both were helpful,"* and only one-fifth of the learners (20.9%) stated a preference for ASR-based dictation activities. Taken from another perspective, almost 80 percent of the learners had a positive impression of the shadowing activities, but only half the participants felt positively about ASR. More specifically, the same number of learners (55.8 percent of the participants) provided positive and negative comments about ASR. These findings echo the occasional negative experiences with ASR-based pronunciation practice that have been observed in previous studies (Chen, Inceoglu, and Lim 2020; McCrocklin 2016). On the other hand, shadowing seems to be highly valued by learners, which is aligned with previous studies looking at learners' perceptions of shadowing (Foote and McDonough 2017; Martinsen, Montgomery, and Willardson 2017). In the current study, 74.4 percent of the learners shared positive comments about shadowing and only 11.2 percent reported negative aspects of the activity.

The learners' journal entries provide more details on their perceptions and attitudes toward ASR and shadowing. The list below summarizes the principal pros and cons of ASR emerging from learners' journal entries:

- Pros: Feedback; indication of intelligibility; pronunciation awareness; engagement/fun; autonomy
- Cons: Frustration; technical problems (microphone; ASR turning off; ASR slow); errors not understood/lack of explanation; false positive

Likewise, learners reported the following pros and cons for the shadowing activities:

- Pros: Comparison with models; intonation and rhythm; speed; connecting spelling and pronunciation
- Cons: Technical difficulties; comparison with models

The next sections further explore these themes, starting with the pros and the cons of ASR, before illustrating the pros and the cons of shadowing activities. Each theme is illustrated with quotes from learners' journals (note: the quotes in brackets are directly translated from French).

Pros of ASR

ASR-based dictation activities enable learners to monitor their speech for pronunciation errors by examining the written output provided by ASR. The match or mismatch between the original sentence and the written text transcribed by ASR can serve as an evaluation of whether one's pronunciation is accurate. For an example of how ASR correctly transcribed sentences of a learner with correct pronunciation, whereas another learners' incorrect production led to multiple ASR transcriptions, see figure 9.2.

The most important aspect of ASR is its potential to provide immediate feedback that may raise learners' awareness of pronunciation errors (Mc-

Figure 9.2. Screenshot of two learners' ASR practice, with correct pronunciation of "chaque août" /ʃa·kut/ (and ASR output) on the left and incorrect pronunciation (and ASR confusion) on the right.

Source: Solène Inceoglu

Crocklin 2019; Neri et al. 2008). In the current study, ten learners either commented explicitly on the fact that ASR can provide feedback or alluded to the role that ASR can play in helping them identify pronunciation errors:

> *[What is missing when I'm at home is to have the teacher tell me, oh that it's not correct, but with ASR it's like I had a teacher at home (. . .) it wasn't time consuming and it gave me immediate feedback]*
>
> *I really liked using automatic speech recognition, as if I pronounced a word incorrectly, google docs would produce a different French word to the one that I had intended to say and I was then able to understand the nuanced differences between the word that I had tried to pronounce and the word that I had actually pronounced.*

Figure 9.3 illustrates how a learner who mispronounced "initiative" [i.ni.sja.tiv] as [ɛ̃.ni.sja.tiv]—recognized as "indicative" [ɛ̃.di.ka.tif]—self-corrected herself upon examining the ASR transcription. Interestingly, 40 percent of the learners doing shadowing mispronounced this word and none corrected themselves (at least while doing the practice), whereas 42 percent

Figure 9.3. Learner's ASR practice (in red), with original text (in blue), incorrect pronunciation of "initiative," negative feedback from ASR, and self-correction (underlined here for salience).

Credit: Inceoglu 2022

of the ASR group mispronounced the word and 16 percent immediately self-corrected themselves. In fact, an examination of the recordings of all autonomous activities showed that most instances of self-correction occurred during ASR practices.

In line with previous research highlighting how ASR enables L2 learners to develop an awareness of their intelligibility (Mroz 2018, 2020), four learners in this study expressed trust that their speech can be understood by ASR the same way it would be by a native speaker of French. There is no study on L2 French comparing judgment of native listeners and ASR, but recent studies in L2 English have shown that ASR approaches L1 listeners at recognizing accented speech (McCrocklin and Edalatishams 2020) although it may also depend on the speakers and the task (Inceoglu, Chen, and Lim forthcoming). In particular, learners noted that ASR was *"beneficial as it gave me an awareness of how my pronunciation is perceived by an outsider," "[helps us to know whether what we say would be understood]," and "[was useful for me because I do not know how others perceive me when I speak, and this activity showed me their perception]."*

Similarly, three additional learners also indicated that ASR helped them notice error patterns they were previously not aware of, noting that the activity was *"really helpful. Once I'd spent enough time using it (. . .), it helped me pick up mispronunciations that I wasn't aware of"* and that it was *"super interesting. It did help me see where I was possibly getting lazy with pronunciation and not annunciating correctly. Accidentally saying the wrong <e> vowel for example stuffed up a whole sentence. Which helped me realise I needed to be a bit more careful."*

Furthermore, motivation and engagement are of paramount importance in second language acquisition (Ushioda 2011), and research has shown that mobile technology can enhance learners' engagement in pronunciation learning (Cho and Castañeda 2019; Liakin, Cardoso, and Liakina 2017). Importantly in the current study, learners did report frustration or difficulty in using ASR, but two learners also mentioned the entertaining or fun aspect of the activity: *"I liked both activities, I'd say that I prefer the speech to text recognition activity because it was more entertaining, despite it being quite frustrating at times"* and *"it was easier to use and a little bit more fun (even though it was harder)."*

Finally, although one of the main goals of ASR-based dictation practice is to promote learner autonomy (McCrocklin 2016), only one learner commented on that potential: *"For me, using a google doc was like a revelation. The ability to see my oral production has immediately changed my perception of how I speak (. . .) Moreover, it gave me a tool that I can use on my own as much as I want."* This does not necessarily mean that the other learners who enjoyed ASR do not see its value as a way to practice autonomously; however, the absence of further comments, coupled with only half the class commenting positively on ASR, may indicate that most learners did not consider the possibility of using ASR outside the context of the class as a way to continue practicing their pronunciation autonomously.

Cons of ASR

As it has been reported in previous studies (Chen, Inceoglu, and Lim 2020; Inceoglu, Lim, and Chen 2020; McCrocklin 2016), learners sometimes report frustration when using ASR. In the current study, nine participants directly commented on feeling frustrated, or even discouraged, when they were doing the ASR activities. In the voice of a learner, ASR was *"quite frustrating because I wasn't sure in what way I was pronouncing the word wrong when it was picking up a different word, I'm not sure how helpful this dimension of the exercises was."* The same feeling was echoed in a classmate's comment: *"I often had a lot of trouble correcting these errors. In general, I found these activities to be frustrating and discouraging, since they took me a long time to complete, but were still full of mistakes that I couldn't seem to fix (. . .) I didn't learn much from my errors, as there were too many for me to gain a clear idea of what I was doing wrong, and my patience in re-recording myself would run out after three or four attempts."*

It therefore appears that for some of the learners, the ASR activities were not constructive and while some learners recognized the usefulness of being able to visualize their speech, they still reported frustration, such as a learner who noted that *"Using the google doc tool was helpful to visualise, but sometimes it was frustrating if it wasn't working properly."* Yet, compared to reports of EFL learners feeling frustrated with ASR due to a mistrust in the technology, that is, believing that ASR is not advanced enough to accurately recognize (accented) speech (Chen, Inceoglu, and Lim 2020), none of the participants in the current study doubted the ability of ASR to transcribe what they said. This is probably because the instructor used ASR several times during class, thus demonstrating its efficiency. Nevertheless, learners highlighted several problems that impeded their ASR practice. One type of problem has to do with technical hindrances. For instance, three learners wrote that their microphones failed to capture their speech, and one learner reported that Google's ASR *"seemed to randomly stop transcribing in the middle of me talking, or just couldn't cope with certain words,"* something that has been pointed out in previous studies (McCrocklin, Humaidan, and Edalatishams 2019).

In a similar vein, two learners commented that Google was slow to transcribe from speech to text, one of them stating that *"Sometimes I found it tedious to constantly wait for the Google Doc to register my voice, check the correct response, re-record etc. but I know that this is necessary if I want my French to improve.*" For both learners though, the slowness of ASR was not a deterrent (i.e., they both also listed positive aspects and fell into the "ASR" and "both" preference categories), yet, ideally ASR should transcribe what speakers say with very little delay. In addition, it may be useful to encourage learners not to wait for ASR to transcribe individual words, but rather to produce an entire sentence with appropriate fluency before checking the ASR output.

More negatively, four learners noted a tendency for ASR to work better when they enunciated slowly or overarticulated, and as the analysis of learners' production showed, ASR practice led to significantly slower speech delivery than shadowing. This can have counterproductive effects when it comes to practicing not only fluency, but also connected speech features such as enchaînements and liaisons in French. For instance, a learner commented that "*[s]ometimes it felt like I had to exaggerate completely for the program to understand what I was saying or speak very slowly, so it didn't feel natural at all.*" This issue echoes the discussion on the trade-off between accuracy and fluency and emphasizes the importance for learners to distinguish between fluency-oriented activities, which foster faster delivery, and accuracy-oriented activities more focused on forms. While the ASR and shadowing activities completed by the learners in the current study both targeted accuracy, focusing on fluency was only likely during shadowing. Furthermore, evidence that proficient speakers (e.g., the teacher, peers) could effectively use ASR without significantly slowing down their speech or overarticulating may point to pronunciation problems for those who reported needing to exaggerate their productions. From this perspective, ASR may actually be a useful tool to highlight such issues, but additional guidance from the teacher is recommended.

One aspect of the autonomous ASR practice that some learners struggled with is the lack of explanations regarding their pronunciation errors. As one noted, "*[s]ometimes the Google doc would think I said a completely different word to what I actually said, and I didn't quite understand where I went wrong.*" Likewise, four learners reported pronouncing words and sentences accurately, but still getting incorrect ASR output. For instance, one learner noted: "*I just remember the exercise with 'les héros' and 'les zéros' and it couldn't pick up the difference even though I didn't do the liaison in the first one! I just had to let it go after a few attempts*" (watching the ASR video confirmed that the learner correctly pronounced the sentences). Receiving negative feedback despite accurate pronunciation is, perhaps, the biggest drawback of ASR technology as the activity can be viewed pointless or inefficient or, worse, misleading and discouraging. In that particular example, the student disregarded the feedback and moved on. However, others tended to get stuck on some sounds. For instance, one learner shared that they *"had trouble with the voice to speech activities especially, as [they] would try to reproduce a sound over and over and would not make progress. So it was easy to get stuck on one sound, which made speaking naturally difficult."* Others also spent much more than the allocated time on the activity; a learner who spent close to 8 minutes—when the group's average was close to 3 minutes— commented that: *"I quickly became frustrated each time I did the activity without succeeding in correctly transcribing the sentences, and, therefore, I often spent more than two hours during the off-zoom activity."*

Conversely, a learner commented that ASR may sometimes provide positive feedback even when an error was produced: *"there were a couple of issues, with the AI being able to correctly transcribe what you'd said even if you hadn't pronounced a word correctly, and as such possibly may have reinforced incorrect pronunciation."* This was, indeed, apparent from the observations of the screen-capture recordings of the ASR practice. For example—among many others, in the sentence ". . . à tous /tu/ les examens," the "s" of the predeterminant "tous" is silent; however, learners who produced /tus/ still received a good transcription from ASR, therefore, given them the false impression that their pronunciation was accurate. To date, however, no study has explored the feedback ASR provides learners, and this needs to be addressed in future studies.

Pros of Shadowing

As previously reported, learners viewed shadowing practice as extremely favorable. The main reason is that they found the possibility to listen to and repeat after a native model very useful. Fifteen learners directly commented on the advantage of being able to compare their production to the model, which enabled them to notice differences clearly. According to a learner, shadowing provided *"a model to copy, and also to compare myself to, to know if I had good pronunciation or not."* This was echoed by several others, including one writing that *"if I am pronouncing a word differently to how it should be pronounced, I gain a direct comparison by hearing myself after the recording, which allows me to understand how I need to change my pronunciation,"* and another noting that the activities were *"really good because you could listen to both your voice and ours afterward, and the difference was very very clear."*

Some of these learners also specified that comparing native models to their own pronunciation allowed them to identify pronunciation errors. One learner wrote that *"[t]he shadowing exercises were the most useful as [they] could directly see where mistake in pronunciation were,"* while another one felt like the activity provided *"a tangible point of reference and allow [them] to identify [their] errors more easily."*

Previous studies had demonstrated that shadowing can lead to improvement in intonation (Hsieh, Dong, and Wang 2013; Mori 2011). Likewise, six of the learners in the current study reflected on the usefulness of shadowing for the development of French intonation and speech rhythm, commenting that it was *"more useful in terms of learning how native French speakers speak because I tried to follow their rhythm and intonation pattern too"* or that they *"saw it as more of an intonation exercise than one of pronunciation, but it definitely helps with both."*

Similarly, while ASR practice was criticized for preventing fluent natural speech, three learners highlighted that shadowing helped them work on their *"speed"* or *"pace"* to become *"more natural,"* echoing the results from the fluency analysis. A learner mentioned that shadowing was *"more useful"* because they *"could adjust the pace to how a native speaker would say the words,"* while another one also commented that the activities *"were useful to hear where native speakers pause/speed up."* Again, as previously mentioned, ASR and shadowing do not necessarily serve the same purposes. Keeping in mind that learners completed these activities autonomously and without specific guidelines on what to pay attention to, it appears that shadowing was successful in directing the attention of some of the learners to aspects of utterance fluency such as speed and pauses.

Finally, three learners commented that shadowing practice enabled them to better connect spelling and pronunciation. For instance, one shared that the activities *"were very helpful as they made us more consciously listen to the sounds and pronunciation but also to make the association with the written words or sounds in front of us."* This is particularly relevant for languages, such as French, which have an opaque orthography. For instance, learners of French often erroneously produce silent final consonants, fail to produce features of connected speech, or mispronounce vowels (Inceoglu 2019). Clearly, shadowing offers learners the important benefit of not only connecting the oral input to their production, but also connecting it to the written input, thus strengthening lexical and phonological representations of the words.

Cons of Shadowing

The learners' positive attitude toward and perception of shadowing activities is also apparent from the small number of learners (11.2%) who provided negative comments. Contrary to Bovee and Stewart (2009) and Li-Chi (2009), none of the participants reported finding the activities boring. Instead, the principal issue concerned the technical difficulties that learners encountered when recording themselves or attempting to compare their pronunciation with those of the models, which 30 percent of the participants in Bovee and Stewart (2009) also commented on. One learner wrote that "*the negative would be that sometimes it was hard to find where you were in the audio—so you had to keep relistening to certain parts, but this was only a minor downside.*" Two additional learners commented on minor difficulties they encountered when using Audacity, saying that they found it "*a bit fiddly but other than that it was a great exercise*" and that it was a "*particularly difficult program to use at times (however that could just be my ill familiarity with the program).*"

As the learners' comments show, they still found value in the activities and the technical difficulties they encountered were minor, especially compared with ASR. The other type of issue that was raised by two learners was that they either struggled to compare their pronunciation with the models provided: "*Negative: hearing yourself you sometimes don't hear/realise your own faults even comparing to the model*" or they had difficulties to keep up with the pace of the native speakers: "*The shadowing was tricky sometimes with the speed and pronunciation to know if you were right, because I never sounded like the speaker!*"

CONCLUSION AND RECOMMENDATIONS

At first sight, findings from this study may point to a superiority of shadowing over ASR, both in terms of overall learners' perception and means to develop fluency. However, the results also highlighted that the two activities had numerous clear advantages (e.g., feedback and awareness (ASR) vs. model and prosody (shadowing)) that the other activity cannot offer. ASR and shadowing might instead be better considered as complementary as they enable the practice of different pronunciation foci, or, in the words of one learner, "*both exercises were useful in their own ways: (. . .) ASR forced you to pronounce and create sounds well in order to be understood. The shadowing was good because it was helpful to hear and then mimic natural speech patterns.*" Over the course of a semester, learners in the current study practiced their pronunciation autonomously with ASR or shadowing; yet, combining the two activities together, that is, shadowing *while* using ASR may enhance the practice. This would enable learners to receive more input and work on their prosody—therefore offsetting some insufficiencies of ASR—*while* receiving feedback and developing an awareness of their intelligibility, which shadowing cannot do.

Although the current study was conducted in an upper-intermediate French pronunciation and phonetics course, learners of all proficiency levels can benefit from practice with ASR and shadowing as long as the materials (i.e., models' speed of speech, targeted pronunciation features) are adapted to their level. Below are some additional recommendations for instructors and learners:

1. Demonstrate and clarify purpose:

   • Provide practical and technical how-tos for practicing pronunciation with ASR and shadowing, ideally in the form of short video tutorials that learners can watch anytime (e.g., how to use Audacity for shadowing).
   • Demonstrate that ASR works by modeling, therefore increasing learners' confidence in the technology.
   • Emphasize that fluency is not the primary focus of the practice with ASR; rather, ASR is to be viewed as a tool to receive feedback on the production of segmentals.

2. Minimize difficulties, frustration, and technical issues:

   • When preparing shadowing activities involving long sentences, segment them into manageable phrases appropriate to the learners' levels (e.g., no more than 10 words for intermediate learners; less if some words are challenging) to avoid working memory and processing difficulties. In addition, leave silences long enough (i.e., twice as long as the segment) between phrases to give learners ample time for repetitions.
   • Audacity enables users to play an audio recording in one track and use a second track to record themselves (click "track" > "add new" > "mono track") (see figure 9.1). This makes it easy to compare one's pronunciation with a model. Some learners reported technical issues with recording when using EarPods on Mac computers; these can be avoided by using the computer's internal speakers.
   • Speaking close to the microphone can make a difference with ASR recognizing a word or not.
   • When Google's ASR is not available (e.g., Google not popular in a country, Internet connection problem), use alternative options such as Windows Speech Recognition or Siri.
   • Learners should be encouraged to move on after X number of repetitions regardless of ASR output to avoid frustration.

3. Orientate learners to online resources so they can become more self-directed and autonomous:

- Many podcasts and videos are accompanied with transcriptions (beware of flawed auto-generated transcripts on YouTube)
- YouGlish (available for all commonly taught languages) enables learners to shadow, adjust down the speed of delivery, and follow along (or not) with a simultaneous written transcript.

To conclude, the goal of instruction is to help learners produce language that is both accurate and produced in a fluent manner. Focusing on activities that promote these two dimensions is essential, but one tool does not necessarily need to address the two constructs. To reiterate what was said in the introduction, learner autonomy is a crucial aspect of L2 acquisition; thus, familiarizing learners with tools that offer different affordances when it comes to practicing pronunciation can help them become better in charge of their own learning in and outside the classroom.

NOTES

1. For more directions on how to use ASR on a Google doc, see https://support .google.com/docs/answer/4492226?hl=en.
2. https://savoirs.rfi.fr/fr/apprendre-enseigner/langue-fracaise/journal-en-français -facile.
3. www.audacityteam.org.

REFERENCES

Ahn, Taeyoun, and Sangmin Michelle Lee. 2016. "User Experience of a Mobile Speaking Application with Automatic Speech Recognition for EFL Learning." *British Journal of Educational Technology* 47, no. 4: 778–86.

Benson, Phil. 2011. "Language Learning and Teaching beyond the Classroom: An Introduction to the Field." In *Beyond the Language Classroom*, edited by Phil Benson and Hayo Reinders. London, UK: Palgrave Macmillan.

Benson, Phil, and Peter Voller. 1997. "Introduction: Autonomy and Independence in Language Learning." In *Autonomy and Independence in Language Learning*, edited by Phil Benson and Peter Voller, 1–12. New York: Routledge.

Bovee, Nicholas, and Jeff Stewart. 2009. "The Utility of Shadowing." In *JALT 2008 Conference Proceedings*, edited by A. M Stoke, 888–900. Tokyo: JALT.

Chen, Wen-Hsin, Solène Inceoglu, and Hyojung Lim. 2020. "Using ASR to Improve Taiwanese EFL Learners' Pronunciation: Learning Outcomes and Learners' Perceptions." In *Proceedings of the 11th Pronunciation in Second Language Learning and Teaching Conference*, edited by Okim Kang, Shelley Staples, Kate Yaw, and Kevin Hirschi, 37–48. Flagstaff: Northern Arizona University.

Cho, Moon-Heum, and Daniel Castañeda. 2019. "Motivational and Affective Engagement in Learning Spanish with a Mobile Application." *System* 81: 90–99.

Derwing, Tracey M, Murray J Munro, and Michael Carbonaro. 2000. "Does Popular Speech Recognition Software Work with ESL Speech?" *TESOL Quarterly* 34, no. 3: 592–603.

Ellis, Rod. 2005. *Planning and Task Performance in a Second Language*. Philadelphia: John Benjamins.

Foote, Jennifer, and Kim McDonough. 2017. "Using Shadowing with Mobile Technology to Improve L2 Pronunciation." *Journal of Second Language Pronunciation* 3, no. 1: 34–56.

García, Christina, Dan Nickolai, and Lillian Jones. 2020. "Traditional versus ASR-Based Pronunciation Instruction: An Empirical Study." *CALICO Journal* 37, no. 3: 213–32.

Goldinger, Stephen D. 1998. "Echoes of Echoes? An Episodic Theory of Lexical Access." *Psychological Review* 105, no. 2: 251–79.

Guskaroska, Agata. 2019. *ASR as a Tool for Providing Feedback for Vowel Pronunciation Practice*. Unpublished master thesis. Iowa State University.

Hamada, Yo. 2016. "Shadowing: Who Benefits and How? Uncovering a Booming EFL Teaching Technique for Listening Comprehension." *Language Teaching Research* 20, no. 1: 53–74.

Hardison, Debra M. 2004. "Generalization of Computer-Assisted Prosody Training: Quantitative and Qualitative Findings." *Language Learning & Technology* 8, no. 1: 34–52.

Holec, Henri. 1981. *Autonomy in Foreign Language Learning*. Oxford, UK: Pergamon.

Hsieh, Kun Ting, Da Hui Dong, and Li Yi Wang. 2013. "A Preliminary Study of Applying Shadowing Technique to English Intonation Instruction." *Taiwan Journal of Linguistics* 11, no. 2: 43–66.

Inceoglu, Solène. 2019. "Exploring the Effects of Instruction on L2 French Learner Pronunciation, Accentedness, Comprehensibility, and Fluency: An Online Classroom Study." *Journal of Second Language Pronunciation* 5, no. 2: 224–47.

Inceoglu, Solène, Wen-Hsin Chen, and Hyojung Lim. Forthcoming. "Assessment of L2 Intelligibility: Comparing L1 Listeners and Automatic Speech Recognition." *ReCALL*.

Inceoglu, Solène, Hyojung Lim, and Wen-Hsin Chen. 2020. "ASR for EFL Pronunciation Practice: Segmental Development and Learners' Beliefs." *Journal of Asia TEFL* 17, no. 3: 824–40.

Kadota, Shuhei. 2019. *Shadowing as a Practice in Second Language Acquisition: Connecting Inputs and Outputs*. New York: Routledge.

Lambert, Sylvie. 1992. "Shadowing." *Meta* 37, no. 2: 263–73.

Lee, Icy. 1998. "Supporting Greater Autonomy in Language Learning." *ELT Journal* 52, no. 4: 282–90.

Levis, John, and Ruslan Suvorov. 2020. "Automatic Speech Recognition." In *The Concise Encyclopedia of Applied Linguistics.*, edited by Carol A Chapelle, 149–156. Hoboken, NJ: Wiley-Blackwell.

Liakin, Denis, Walcir Cardoso, and Natallia Liakina. 2015. "Learning L2 Pronunciation with a Mobile Speech Recognizer: French /Y/." *CALICO Journal* 32, no. 1: 1–25.

———. 2017. "Mobilizing Instruction in a Second-Language Context: Learners' Perceptions of Two Speech Technologies." *Languages* 2, no. 3: 11.

Lin, Li-Chi. 2009. *A Study of Using "Shadowing" as a Task in Junior High School EFL Program in Taiwan.* Taipei, Taiwan: Unpublished master's thesis, National Taiwan University of Science and Technology.

Martinsen, Rob A, Cherice Montgomery, and Véronique Willardson. 2017. "The Effectiveness of Video-Based Shadowing and Tracking Pronunciation Exercises for Foreign Language Learners." *Foreign Language Annals* 50, no. 4: 661–80.

McCrocklin, Shannon. 2016. "Pronunciation Learner Autonomy: The Potential of Automatic Speech Recognition." *System* 57: 25–42.

———. 2019. "ASR-Based Dictation Practice for Second Language Pronunciation Improvement." *Journal of Second Language Pronunciation* 5, no. 1: 98–118.

McCrocklin, Shannon, and Idée Edalatishams. 2020. "Revisiting Popular Speech Recognition Software for ESL Speech." *TESOL Quarterly* 54, no. 4: 1086–97.

McCrocklin, Shannon, Abdulsamad Humaidan, and Idée Edalatishams. 2019. "ASR Dictation Program Accuracy: Have Current Programs Improved?" In *Proceedings of the 10th Pronunciation in Second Language Learning and Teaching Conference,* 191–200. Ames: Iowa State University.

Mori, Yoko. 2011. "Shadowing with Oral Reading: Effects of Combined Training on the Improvement of Japanese EFL Learners' Prosody." *The Japan Association for Language Education & Technology* 48: 1–22.

Mroz, Aurore. 2018. "Seeing How People Hear You: French Learners Experiencing Intelligibility through Automatic Speech Recognition." *Foreign Language Annals* 51, no. 3: 617–37.

———. 2020. "Aiming for Advanced Intelligibility and Proficiency Using Mobile ASR." *Journal of Second Language Pronunciation* 6, no. 1: 12–38.

Neri, Ambra, Catia Cucchiarini, and Helmer Strik. 2003. "Automatic Speech Recognition for Second Language Learning: How and Why It Actually Works." *Proc. ICPhS*, no. January: 1157–1160.

Neri, Ambra, Catia Cucchiarini, Helmer Strik, and Louis Boves. 2002. "The Pedagogy-Technology Interface in Computer Assisted Pronunciation Training." *Computer Assisted Language Learning* 15 (November 2014): 441–67.

Neri, Ambra, Ornella Mich, Matteo Gerosa, and Diego Giuliani. 2008. "The Effectiveness of Computer Assisted Pronunciation Training for Foreign Language Learning by Children." *Computer Assisted Language Learning* 21, no. 5: 393–408.

Pawlak, Mirosław, and Magdalena Szyszka. 2018. "Researching Pronunciation Learning Strategies: An Overview and a Critical Look." *Studies in Second Language Learning and Teaching* 8, no. 2: 293–323.

Reinders, Hayo, and Cynthia White. 2016. "20 Years of Autonomy and Technology: How Far Have We Come and Where to Next?" *Language Learning & Technology* 20, 2: 143–54.

Rongna, A., and Ryoko Hayashi. 2012. "Accuracy of Japanese Pitch Accent Rises during and after Shadowing Training." *Proceedings of the 6th International Conference on Speech Prosody, SP 2012* 1: 214–17.

Skehan, Peter. 1998. *A Cognitive Approach to Language Learning.* Oxford, UK: Oxford University Press.

Teeter, Jennifer. 2017. "Improving Motivation to Learn English in Japan with a Self-Study Shadowing Application." *Languages* 2, no. 4: 1–27.

Ushioda, Ema. 2011. "Language Learning Motivation, Self and Identity: Current Theoretical Perspectives." *Computer Assisted Language Learning* 24, no. 3: 199–210.

Chapter Ten

Exploring Pronunciation Learning in Simulated Immersive Language Learning Experiences in Virtual Reality

Shannon McCrocklin, Rachel Stuckel,
and Eugenie Mainake

INTRODUCTION

Virtual reality (VR) is a relatively new technology. Researchers and educators are becoming increasingly interested in its potential for language learning both inside and outside the classroom. VR technologies provide users with immersive sensations engaging sight, hearing, and touch in a digital environment (Pinto et al. 2019). This chapter explores the potential for pronunciation learning in an application, Mondly VR, available for use on Gear VR and Oculus devices. The research study explores how learners practice with Mondly VR, including their general perceptions of the tool, level of attention to pronunciation, use of supportive tools, and pronunciation improvement following negative feedback. After discussing the research study, the chapter considers issues or concerns in implementing VR in the classroom and provides ideas for getting started with VR.

LITERATURE REVIEW

In order to provide an understanding of Mondly VR, the following sections describe technologies that predate Mondly VR and serve as the foundation for the current technology, explore the history and development of VR technologies, and summarize the current Mondly VR application. In each section, research related to the second language (L2) learning potential of each technology is introduced.

Precursors to Mondly VR

Although VR is a newer technology, many of the precursor technologies to Mondly VR, including 3D virtual spaces, gamified LLEs, spoken dialog systems, and Automatic Speech Recognition (ASR) have been available for many years and are more heavily researched. Simulated language learning environments (LLEs), graphical or technological settings in which language learning is encouraged or enabled, were precursors to VR's immersive environments and provide a reference point for measuring the effectiveness and usefulness of VR. Virtual worlds, such as Second Life, which allow users to navigate a user-generated 3D space as avatars on a computer screen, have been one area of interest for researchers in second language (L2) learning (Sadler and Dooley 2012). These 3D worlds accessed on a computer are considered non-immersive systems as they do not envelop users' senses in a virtual environment (Boas 2013). Because of Second Life's widespread appeal and large number of users, learners could access the platform to engage with native or proficient speakers of their L2 or engage in cooperative tasks with other learners (Lan et al. 2013). Sadler and Dooley (2012) note that one of the advantages of virtual practice is lowered learner anxiety, which can be attributed to increased time for responding and the anonymity provided by the avatar.

Another common, non-immersive format for LLEs is programmed software games on the computer. A meta-analysis of studies on digital games for L2 English learning revealed that many games focus on improving both learner communication abilities and learner cognition (Xu et al. 2020). Although the only element present across all games was the presence of goals, common elements included ongoing feedback, sensory stimuli, and interactive problem solving. These were not uniform in their integration or form in the games, however (Xu et al. 2020). Structure has been found to be a determining factor in how well learners are able to progress through a game's language learning goals (Li and Topolewski 2002). Zip and Terry, a popular LLE computer game for children, relies on structure and attainable goals to encourage the user to complete the particular goals. While users have some control over what their character does, the experience is structured to ensure that the learner continues to work toward language goals (Li and Topolewski 2002). If the learner does not complete a goal, or progresses too slowly toward the goal, their virtual character is locked in a cage as punishment (Li and Topolewski 2002).

While there may not be a one size fits all, ideal LLE for all language learners (Sydorenko et al. 2019), Tsai and Tsai (2018) found digital game-based learning of vocabulary to be superior to traditional, in-class vocabulary instruction. Thus far, research has shown that other aspects of language that can be learned with simulated LLEs including pragmatics, grammar, writing, and speaking (Xu et al. 2020). Reinhardt and Thorne (2020) note that a major affordance of simulated LLEs is that they provide low-stakes, sheltered learning environments as learners can practice without being forced to interact with a native speaker (NS), potentially lowering anxiety and leading to greater willingness to practice.

One way that LLEs might be used as structured tools for pronunciation learning is through the integration of an automated spoken dialog system which allows learners to provide responses to conversation prompts (Sydorenko et al. 2019). Dialog systems are built around scenarios (e.g., making an appointment) and prompts that can be either branched (dialog) or unbranched (pseudo-dialog). An unbranched pseudo-dialog, or single-order, fixed prompt system means that the user's response has no bearing on the order of the program prompts (Evanini et al. 2015). In a scenario where the user speaks to an automated interlocutor to schedule an appointment, once the user replies with an acceptable response, the program's unbranched responses continue in a linear, automated fashion. In contrast, a program with a branched dialog can choose which prompt to give the learner next based on the learner's utterance. Not surprisingly, reports have shown that branching dialogues raise the authenticity of the learner experience as well as the perceived naturalness of the interaction (Timpe-Laughlin et al. 2017). Research has shown that spoken dialog LLEs are particularly useful for new L2 vocabulary learning (Jensen 2017; Sydorenko et al. 2019; Xu et al. 2020).

One of the major differences between dialog systems is the method for deciding acceptability of a learner response. Frequently, systems look for a correct response among pre-determined options or assess the pronunciation of a particular response. Recently, more attention has been given to scoring appropriateness of free, uncontrolled responses more holistically which may include grammar and vocabulary choices along with issues in delivery and social appropriateness of specific content (Evanini et al. 2015). However, many systems still rely on a fixed set of possible responses. For pronunciation learning, a crucial development is the use of Automatic Speech Recognition (ASR) in order to determine the acceptability of the learner's pronunciation of a particular response. ASR is "an independent, machine-based process of decoding and transcribing oral speech. A typical ASR system receives acoustic input from the speaker through a microphone, analyzes it using some pattern, model or algorithm, and produces an output, usually in the form of a text" (Levis and Suvorov 2020, 1). Spoken dialog systems that incorporate ASR provide a prompt (and often provide options for acceptable responses), record the learner's response, and assess whether the speaker accurately produced the sounds of an acceptable response.

Although ASR was met with heavy criticism in its early development due to low levels of accuracy, computer-assisted pronunciation training programs using ASR have improved in accuracy thanks to enhanced acoustic analysis (Truong et al. 2005), greater incorporation of data from non-native speakers (Bouselmi, Fohr, and Illina 2012; Moustroufas and Digilakis 2007), and increased attention to changes in pronunciation when words are used as part of phrases and larger discourse (Saraçlar 2000). Today, many ASR technologies have improved to the point that they behave similarly to human raters of speech (Cincarek et al. 2008; Cucchiarini, Strik, and Boves 2000; McCrocklin and Edalatishams 2020).

ASR can provide learners with a sense of where their pronunciation is successful and where they may lack intelligibility, a useful tool for both learners and instructors to identify learner areas needing improvement (Mroz 2018). Further, numerous studies have shown that ASR is able to support pronunciation learning and lead to learner improvement in segmental accuracy (Hincks 2003; Liakin, Cardoso, and Liakina 2014; McCrocklin 2019; Neri et al. 2008). The use of ASR to evaluate speech in language learning practices has proven beneficial for lowering learner anxiety and fear of mistakes (Bashori et al. 2021; Junining, Alif, and Setiarini 2020) and may increase willingness to practice (Junining, Alif, and Setiarini 2020).

Many of the precursor technologies to Mondly VR (3D virtual spaces, gamified LLEs, spoken dialog systems, and ASR) not only still exist today in non-immersive forms, but form the foundation of current VR technologies. VR technologies seek to take user experience further, however, with the integration and immersion of the senses.

Virtual Reality Technology

Although VR is typically considered a relatively new technology, it is important to note that many of the central elements to modern VR have existed since the 1960s. For example, the Telesphere Mask, patented by Morton Heilig, was the first head mounted display, although it lacked any motion tracking or integration of computer processing (BBC Research Editorial 2018; Virtual Reality Society 2020). Real time motion tracking was debuted in Headsight in 1961 (Poetker 2019). A crucial development that hinted at how complex VR systems would become was the integration of computer graphics and processing in 1965, when Ivan Sutherland, a Harvard professor, was the first to integrate computer hardware into a head mounted VR system (Poetker 2019). Although there have been continued developments and variations of VR, the base components, head mounting, motion tracking, and computer processing have existed for decades.

VR did not take off commercially, however, until much more recently. Credit for the revitalization of the VR market is often pointed to Palmer Luckey who improved VR with his debut of the Oculus Rift system in 2012 (Clark 2014; Schnipper n.d.). Soon, impressive devices from both Oculus Rift and HTC Vive were creating a stir and reigniting interest in VR. Interest has only grown as inventors have integrated more powerful processing into the headsets (facilitating the removal of cumbersome wires that originally connected the headset to a computer providing the processing power for the graphics) and companies have introduced increasingly affordable options. At the time of writing, the Oculus Quest 2, a wireless headset with internal movement sensors and touch controllers, is available for $299 from the Oculus Store[1]. The market for VR is expected to increase from less than 5 billion U.S. dollars in 2021 to more than 12 billion dollars by 2024, with the greatest growth expected in North America and China (Alsop 2021).

VR may be effective for learning because of the high sense of presence (SOP) it offers users, which allows for the feeling of real immersion in the digital space to the point that the computer world feels as if it's the user's world (Pinto et al. 2019). Although it could be hypothesized that high SOP would lead to higher learner engagement and, thus, greater learning, Makransky, Lilleholt, and Aaby (2017) raised some alarms noting that in a study of medical student learning, students reported higher SOP when using VR, but had lower learning retention scores. Looking specifically at language learning, a study comparing L2 learning in a VR environment versus an audio-training format showed that learners felt more satisfaction and SOP in the VR format, but that the amount of learning did not differ between the two formats (Pinto et al. 2019).

Additional concerns regarding the integration of VR in learning are lack of resources, the technological learning curve associated with VR use, the cognitive demand it places on users, and lack of VR pedagogy. Because each VR system can only be used by one learner at a time, schools may need to invest in multiple devices for them to be useful in the classroom (Craddock 2018). Further, because the VR technology can take a while to get used to, the technology presents a steep learning curve that may result in learners feeling overwhelmed. Some learners may thus feel resistant to the incorporation of new technologies in the classroom. Notably, this resistance can be diminished through careful exposure to, practice with, and integration of the VR system (Xie, Ryder, and Chen 2019). Another source of concern is the cognitive demand that VR programs place on the user. As the immersive experience engages user senses, learners may be pushed to extraneous cognitive processing not focused on learning (Lege and Bonner 2020). Finally, teachers looking to incorporate VR into language learning will be confronted with the stark lack of VR language learning pedagogy (Lege and Bonner 2020). As more research on VR emerges, further information about sound pedagogical practices with VR will become available, but, for now, there are no firm directions or advice specifically regarding the integration of VR in language learning.

Yet, despite these concerns and the need for more research regarding the efficacy of language learning with VR in comparison to other formats (computer, traditional in class, etc.), several studies report that VR can be effective for language learning (Chen 2016; Huang et al. 2021; Lai and Chen 2021). For example, learners put in a VR environment and tasked with solving a problem with others in a target language experienced both language improvement and critical thinking skills (Mroz 2015). Learners can also use VR to increase exposure to new cultures and improve their cultural learning through immersing themselves in a VR setting that displays another place or allows interaction with users from another culture (Shih 2015). Incorporating VR into language learning may also improve learners' self-efficacy and sense of autonomy (Yeh and Lan 2018).

Although there are not sufficient studies yet to claim that learners can improve all aspects of language through VR, Vázquez et al. (2018) documented that learners can acquire new vocabulary through VR practice. A major advantage of the use of VR is the tangibility of previously abstract concepts for language learners. As an example, Craddock (2018) points to a common definition of mitochondria as the "powerhouse of the cell" but notes that language learners may struggle to understand not only the words of the definition, but also the use of metaphor (p. 8). When using VR, however, learners are given a direct visual of an object that the learner can virtually turn and manipulate in order to learn parts and functions (Craddock 2018; Lege and Bonner 2020). With additional spatial awareness brought on by VR and no written language to decipher, the language barrier is lessened and content knowledge is more accessible (Craddock 2018; Lege and Bonner 2020).

More research is needed to explore learning in VR in general, but specifically pronunciation learning in VR. For our study, we focused on pronunciation learning as part of an application built specifically for language learning in VR, Mondly VR.

Mondly VR

Mondly VR can be run on Gear VR (on smartphones adapted into headsets) and on Oculus devices. It offers 30 different languages for study, including English, Chinese, Arabic, and Spanish. When Mondly VR first debuted, it offered five language learning scenarios (e.g., checking into a hotel), but has since expanded to not only offer additional scenarios, but also new types of activities including vocabulary learning and is beta-testing multi-player live conversation practice.

Mondly VR provides learners with a high-immersion language learning experience built through unbranching pseudo-dialogs. Learners select a language-learning scenario based on a situation or context of language use (e.g., at a hotel) and interact with a digital interlocutor to progress through a conversation and accomplish their goal (e.g., checking into the hotel). Learners can access translations of the phrases they are learning and are prompted to respond orally using one of several pre-determined utterances. Learners can access audio files to hear the correct pronunciation of each possible response.

The promotional materials for Mondly VR advertise it as a complement to the larger language learning website, Mondly, and emphasize that learners get instant feedback on their pronunciation (Mondly 2021). The application uses ASR to monitor learners' production accuracy and provides feedback in the form of visual symbols (e.g., smiley faces for well-recognized answers) as well as feedback from the digital interlocutor if the speech could not be understood or background audio interfered with the ASR. Although the program does not score pronunciation, it prevents learners from moving on unless the learner meets a certain threshold of recognition for an acceptable answer. The other main tool provided by Mondly VR to support pronunciation learning is the audio recordings, both of the interlocutor's prompt and the possible responses.

Given its relatively recent launch in 2017, studies of Mondly VR are limited, but one study, Kaplan-Rakowski & Wojdynski (2018) examined learner perceptions of the application. The study found that learners report that using Mondly VR to practice both learned and unknown languages is engaging and provides benefits for learning including SOP and sense immersion (Kaplan-Rakowski & Wojdynski 2018). Given Mondly VR advertises its pronunciation feedback, it is important to examine users' actual pronunciation learning practice and improvement in the application.

RESEARCH QUESTIONS

This exploratory research study examined participant experiences using Mondly VR for practicing both new, unknown languages and previously learned, studied languages. It explores the potential of Mondly VR for pronunciation learning by examining the following questions:

1. What are learners' perceptions of Mondly VR as a language-learning tool?
2. Which language skills (reading, writing, listening, speaking, grammar, or pronunciation) do learners report attending to during practice with Mondly VR?

3. To what degree do learners make use of language-learning support tools within Mondly VR during practice?
4. Are language learners able to make improvements to their pronunciation following negative feedback from Mondly VR?

THE RESEARCH STUDY

Methods

Participants

The participants ($n=37$) in this study were a mixture of undergraduate and graduate students with diverse cultural and linguistic backgrounds enrolled at a medium-sized, diverse, state-funded university located in the United States Midwest region. Participants were selected using random sampling techniques via campus recruitment flyers requesting participation and on campus classroom introductions where fellow instructors incentivized participation with classroom extra credit. Participants ranged in age from 18 to 39 ($M=22.70$) and were split evenly between males and females (with one participant reporting "prefer not to answer" for gender). More than half (62.5%) had used a VR headset before, mostly to play games, but also as part of a class for a couple of participants.

Participants reported a variety of native languages. The most common native languages reported were English ($n=17$), Chinese ($n=8$), and Arabic ($n=4$), but additional native languages reported included French, German, Japanese, Russian, Spanish, and Wolof. All participants had experience learning a second language. The languages they had learned varied and included English, Japanese, French, and Spanish. The average age that participants began learning their L2 was 12.70 years.

Data Collection and Procedure

The study took place in a virtual reality lab on campus. All participants physically attended the face-to-face session. After providing informed consent, participants answered demographic questions about themselves and their language learning. The demographic questions were built into a Google Forms survey. The survey also had several different sections and participants completed different sections at different points during the study, which are described in more detail below.

Participants then completed three of the Mondly VR scenarios each in a different language, one in their native language, one in a learned/studied language, and one in a completely unknown language. Each simulation in Mondly VR consists of a major task aimed at giving the participant an opportunity to experience hands-on language learning and practice. All experiences include Mondly VR real-time voice communication and vivid 3D graphics. More information about each scenario is provided below:

a. Native Language (NL) Simulation:

To give participants a chance to familiarize themselves with Mondly VR, the first scenario that all participants experienced was in their native language (NL). The Mondly VR simulation titled "Appointment" asked participants to make a doctor's appointment with a simulated interlocutor. The time it took to complete the simulation varied between four and 10 minutes. In the one case in which Mondly VR did not have one of a participant's native languages, Wolof, the participant was bilingual and simply used their other bilingual language, French.

b. Learned/Studied Language (LSL) Simulation:

The second scenario that all participants experienced was titled "Hello" and required that the participant have a conversation with a stranger (the simulated interlocutor) on a train and address questions from the simulated train conductor checking tickets. Participants were asked to select a language they had previously learned and/or studied other than their native language. The majority of participants spent five to 10 minutes on this interaction.

c. Unknown Language (UL) Simulation:

For the third and final simulation, participants completed an interaction in a language they were unfamiliar with (i.e., had not studied the language and had no substantial contact with the language as part of their lives). The scenario in the simulation was called, "Reception" and users checked into a hotel front desk. This simulation took the longest on average with times ranging from seven to 15 minutes. This was a challenging task for participants, but they could access translations of both the digital interlocutor's questions and the possible responses, along with audio files to hear how each response should be pronounced.

Data during each simulated encounter was collected during the practice with audio and screen-captured video recording. After each scenario, participants returned to the survey and completed a section including questions about their perceptions of the experience, including the skills they focused on during the encounter, reactions to Likert-scale statements about the experience, and open-ended questions about their perceptions of the experience. The entire research session took less than an hour for each participant.

Analysis and Results

General Perceptions of Mondly VR as a Language Learning Tool

Using Likert scales ranging from 1 "strongly disagree" to 4 "strongly agree," participants noted their agreement to various statements regarding practice with Mondly VR. Not all statements were used for all three experiences (see table 10.1 below). Participants agreed that the language used for their native language was realistic (*M*=3.30) and found Mondly VR overall easy to use (*M*=3.47). Interestingly, however, when examining ease of use across the three different scenarios and language backgrounds, participants did find Mondly VR harder to use (shown as decreasing agreement) as they progressed from their native language (NL) (*M*=3.57) to their learned/studied language (LSL) (*M*=3.43) to their unknown language (UL) (*M*=3.41) despite the increasing familiarity with the application. When participants used the program for their language learning specifically, there was general agreement that the program was useful for learning a language (*M*=3.46) and many felt that they improved their language skills by using Mondly VR for language practice (*M*=3.10). The lowest scored item was "I received helpful feedback to help me improve" (*M*=2.80) showing that participants may have struggled to identify or use the feedback provided. As noted previously, learners were provided a smiley face if their response was well-understood and the interaction was allowed to continue. If the program could not identify an acceptable answer, the learner was asked to try again through the digital interlocutor stating that they didn't understand or was provided with feedback suggesting background noise may have interfered with recognition. Comparing across uses, however, the participants seem to have recognized or appreciated the

Table 10.1. Average Participant Agreement to Likert Statements after each Language Learning Experience

Likert Scale Statement	NL M	NL SD	LSL M	LSL SD	UL M	UL SD
I thought the language used was realistic	3.30	0.85				
I found the program easy to use	3.57	0.80	3.43	0.80	3.41	0.83
I think (imagine) that the program is useful for language learning	3.51	0.80	3.46	0.73	3.46	0.73
I feel like I improved my language skills by practicing with Mondly			3.16	0.93	3.03	0.99
I received helpful feedback to improve			2.70	1.05	2.89	1.05

Note. Empty cells in this table indicate that this statement was not evaluated by the participant for the particular language experience indicated. Also, acronyms used include Native Language (NL), Learned/Studied Language (LSL), Unknown Language (UL).

Source: McCrocklin Stuckel Mainake 2022

feedback more in the UL (*M*=2.89) versus the LSL (*M*=2.70). Differences across experiences were checked for statistical significance using the non-parametric Wilcoxon Ranks test. Only the statement regarding helpful feedback was found to be marginally significant (*p*=.07).

When asked what they most enjoyed about Mondly VR, participants indicated aspects such as SOP and immersion: "I like that it is a real-life situation and that I am in there," authentic language use: "Real situation and really practical," reduced anxiety: "It's fun, and it's okay to make mistakes and make the digital characters repeat," and getting to practice new vocabulary: "Gaining a small understanding of some greetings and agreement words."

Language Skills Participants Reported Focusing on During Practice

For the language skills that participants focused on during the LSL and UL simulations, participants were asked to select any skills they felt they focused on from a list of six skills: reading, writing, listening, speaking, grammar, and pronunciation after their LSL and UL experiences. Participants reported focusing on an average of 3.52 language skills during the LSL and UL experiences. The majority of participants reported focusing on speaking, pronunciation, and listening (See figure 10.1).

In explaining their primary focus in response to the question, "What skill did you feel you were focusing on the MOST in Mondly for this practice?

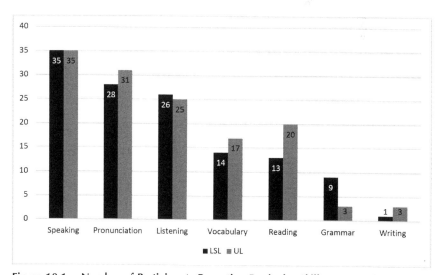

Figure 10.1. Number of Participants Reporting Particular Skill Focus During Practice by Language Experience (Learned/Studied Language [LSL] vs Unknown Language [UL]).
Credit: McCrocklin, Stuckel, and Mainake 2022

WHY?" many participants focused on speaking and pronunciation. Examples of participant explanations are included below:

- "Pronunciation, there was no real "wrong" answer. You were just choosing from options and saying them correctly."
- "Speaking. For the rest of the skills, in the case of listening, I wouldn't say I was practicing it, as everything the characters were saying were on screen, as well as the things I was expected to say."
- "Pronunciation, because some of my responses had to be repeated several times."
- "Pronunciation and speaking. There were so many new phrases, and it was hard to say all of them properly. I had to listen to them several times."

To compare the reported foci across the LSL and UL experiences, a McNemar test, which allows paired tests of categorical data (Larson-Hall 2010), in this case yes/no decisions, was used. The results showed that no skills showed a statistically significant difference in focus across experiences, although differences in grammar ($p=.07$) were marginally significant with participants reporting a slightly greater focus on grammar during the LSL experience.

Use of Tools within Mondly VR to Support Pronunciation Learning

Researchers used the audio recordings and screen-captured video recordings to analyze learners' use of tools within Mondly VR that support pronunciation learning. Researchers counted tips provided about how to more effectively use the VR application (e.g., that audio files and translations were provided, that learners could skip a turn if they got stuck) as well as the number of participants that made use of a particular feature or tool during their practice, which was visible in the screen-captured video when students clicked on the tool.

A surprising finding was that to get started using the program, almost all of the participants (97.37%) had to be told how to use the controller and that they needed to hold down a button to respond to the first prompt despite directions also being provided within Mondly VR. Less surprising was the use of the skip function. If a participant received negative feedback from the application and was not allowed to immediately move on in the pseudo-dialog, Mondly VR provides the option to skip this part of the interaction and move on to the next prompt. Participants were provided with a tip that the option existed if they expressed frustration with not being able to move forward following multiple attempts. Almost half of the participants (48.65%) received this tip. Notably, though, only six participants utilized the skip option while practicing with their LSL, while 15 participants used it during the UL. On a positive note, participants were willing to try more times before using the skip option during the UL simulated encounter. While participants tried an item an average of 1.67 times before skipping in the LSL, they tried an item 2.68 times before skipping in the UL.

Mondly VR provided two major tools to support language learning, audio recordings, both of the interlocutor's prompt and the possible responses, and translations, again both for the interlocutor and responses. These audio recordings and translations are meant to be a form of support that the user could access or replay as many times as desired. The research tracked how many participants needed to receive tips to become aware of these tools (often prompted by the participant voicing frustration that they did not know how to accomplish a particular part of the task) and then also how many participants used the tools (see table 10.2). For the LSL and the UL experiences, use of the tools was divided by whether they accessed support for the interlocutor's turns or the responses.

The analysis showed substantial differences among the use of tools, particularly the use of audio files for the responses, between the LSL and UL experiences. The amount of times that participants were provided a tip about listening to the audio files increased from the NL to the LSL and from the LSL to the UL. Note that participants, once provided a tip, would then also know how to access that resource in any following experiences. There was also a large increase in use of the audio recordings of responses in the UL as learners worked to figure out how to produce an acceptable utterance. In contrast, very few learners needed tips to access the translations and these saw rather wide use during both the LSL and UL.

Table 10.2. Number of Participants Receiving Tool Tips and Using Tools in Their Practice

	NL		LSL		UL	
	Tips	Used	Tips	Used	Tips	Used
Listen to Audio Files	2	11	3		11	
• *Interlocutor*				6		13
• *Responses*				5		28
Accessing Translations	1	14	1		1	
• *Interlocutor*				22		27
• *Responses*				23		30

Note. Native Language (NL), Learned/Studied Language (LSL), Unknown Language (UL)
Source: McCrocklin, Stuckel, Mainake 2022

Pronunciation Improvement Following Negative Feedback
from Mondly VR

To explore pronunciation improvement, the audio recordings of the LSL experience for those using English were analyzed. This analysis included only a sub-set of the larger participant group (*n*=10) as the researchers only analyzed the simulated language learning experiences for LSLs conducted in English. The analysis began by identifying response attempts that were not successful (i.e., the application did not accept the utterance and did not allow the pseudo-dialog to move forward). The researchers then identified what, if any, segmental errors were present in that utterance (categorized as sound additions, deletions, or substitutions), the participants' course of action following the negative feedback (options included trying the response again, trying a different response, or skipping the response entirely), and, if the participant tried the response again, whether they were able to improve their pronunciation of the utterance. The tracking of segmental errors and subsequent improvement was determined through simple auditory rating (no acoustic analysis was used). The errors in the recordings were coded by one of the researchers and then checked for accuracy by a second member of the research team, who found no errors in the coding.

Only five participants received negative feedback during their LSL experience, and, across the five participants, there were six responses that received negative feedback and triggered a chain of further attempts. Through analysis of the errors that led to negative feedback (i.e., non-acceptance of turn), Mondly VR seemed to be most sensitive to sound substitutions. Examining the errors that may have caused the negative feedback, 66.67 percent of turns with negative feedback featured substitution errors compared to 16.67 percent for deletions. An example of a substitution error came from the word "south" /sauθ/ in which the learner substituted an /s/, pronouncing /saus/. An example deletion error came from the word, "nine" /naɪn/, in which the learner did not clearly articulate a final "n" so that it sounded very much like /naɪ/. Only one participant utterance received negative feedback on the first try, but had no identifiable error.

The analysis then tracked participants' choices across subsequent attempts. At the identification of an error, all of the participants initially tried the same utterance again. Notably, however, two participants who chose to repeat the utterance, "I'm from _____" tried changing the location provided, which was the likely source of mis-recognition given that they provided rather specific international locations with a first-language pronunciation. Both of these participants actually introduced a new error in the second location (addition of /s/ in Illinois and deletion of /i/ in Saudi [Arabia]) provided in their second attempt and had their responses rejected again. While one participant was able to improve their pronunciation of the location in the third attempt, which was accepted, the other moved on to another response option, which was also accepted. For the errors in which participants tried the exact same utterance again (n=4), there was no pronunciation improvement in subsequent attempts. Notably, one of these included the negative feedback in which there was no identifiable pronunciation error in the first attempt. These participants continued to try the attempt with the same errors or, eventually, tried another response until the turn was accepted.

Summary of Findings

In brief, the results showed that participants' perceptions of the tool were generally positive and they thought it could be useful for language learning. Participants reported being focused on speaking, pronunciation, and listening, although many reported attention to reading and vocabulary as well. Participants' primary hesitation centered on whether the tool provided sufficient feedback for learning and improvement. This is a reasonable concern; although learners could potentially receive both positive feedback in the form of a smiley face and negative feedback in the form of interlocutor requests to try again, the feedback boiled down to whether learners met an unspecified threshold of accuracy and were allowed to progress through the interaction. Learners did not receive specific feedback on segmental or suprasegmental errors within the speech or any tips on how to improve pronunciation on a subsequent attempt if their speech was deemed unacceptable by the system.

As participants practiced, they frequently needed tips to successfully navigate the features of Mondly VR. In particular, participants needed to be told how to provide responses to the prompts and that they could access audio files of both the interlocutor's turns (for replay) or of the possible responses. It seems that Mondly VR may have since noticed this issue as their newest version of Mondly VR for Quest offers an introductory demo to help users get started that may help them notice useful features of the application. However, participants made limited use of the response audio files, especially in the LSL, suggesting that knowledge of the tools may be insufficient to prompt learners to take full advantage of the resource.

The audio analysis of pronunciation errors and improvement showed that while some participants did elect to retry their original utterance, there was only one instance of the participant improving their pronunciation through the repetition. Instead, participants were likely to repeat their errors during repetition of an utterance until it was accepted or switched to a new response option. Thus, while participants felt focused on speaking, listening and pronunciation, it does not seem they were able to make use of the limited pronunciation feedback to make improvements to their pronunciation in sub-sequent attempts. Although Mondly VR may provide chances for learners to gain access to linguistic input and try producing output, teachers should be aware that learners may not be successful at using this application to monitor or improve the accuracy of the pronunciation.

Despite concerns raised through the research regarding pronunciation learning in Mondly VR, learners did feel that they could practice their speaking, listening, and pronunciation through the application and research has suggested that, as a spoken dialog LLE, it is likely to be particularly useful as part of new vocabulary learning (Jensen 2017; Sydorenko et al. 2019; Xu et al. 2020). Further, given the provision of audio files in Mondly VR, learners may be able to use mimicking or implicit learning to improve pronunciation over time, even though they were unable to immediately improve pronunciation following negative feedback. Finally, given that repetition can help foster greater fluency (Nation and Newton 2008), Mondly VR may be able to support greater fluency as students could potentially practice each interaction multiple times. Additional discussion of the pedagogical implications of these findings are included in the next section, along with other tips for getting started with VR.

TIPS FOR GETTING STARTED WITH VR AND PEDAGOGICAL IMPLICATIONS

Given the wide-range of applications available for VR, including resources specifically designed for language learning, instructors may be interested in employing VR in the classroom. For instructors interested in getting started with VR, one of the first decisions will need to be the device(s) to be used. Primary considerations should include price, capabilities, and applications available. Many VR devices are commercially available across a range of prices. Currently, high end headsets can cost upward of $1,000 while the cheapest options make use of a smartphone inserted into a headset (Gear VR) that allows the learner to experience 3D visuals. Be aware, however, that we have found it can be a challenge to get the view (focal length) set appropriately with Gear VR, which can lead to blurry or double vision, and the applications available for Gear VR may be limited. As part of the consideration of price, instructors (or schools) also need to consider the number of VR headsets that are needed for successful implementation in their situation. One VR headset probably cannot service 35 students in an hour-long class, but buying a headset per student may not be an option. Price point will most likely be a major consideration that limits which VR devices that can be purchased and how many.

While price will likely be a major factor, instructors should also carefully review the capabilities and applications available for each. Device capability will differ across the brands and models. Some of the most expensive VR headsets are tethered, meaning they are attached by a long cord that feeds into a computer. The processing power of the computer allows the device to handle complex games and impressive graphics. Sensors may also need to be placed around the physical space for the VR device to read and sense the room space and user movement. Currently, it is actually the cheaper options that often stand alone. They are one headset that handles all of the game graphics, processing, and sensing. Many games designed for the more afford-able headsets alter (simplify) their graphics to relieve strain on the processors but provide a similar overall experience. Most headsets will have applications that support conversation/chatting (e.g., VR Chat), community or group ac-tivities (e.g., Rec Room), virtual exploration of spaces (e.g., Google Expedi-tions), artistic creation (e.g., Tiltbrush), and games. Some games and applica-tions, however, may not be available across all headsets. Because language learning applications are currently less common among VR applications, instructors should carefully review the applications available on a particular device to ensure desired access.

No matter what device is selected, the ability of the device, or the pro-grams on the device, the language learning objective(s) of the class or lesson should always be at the forefront of educational VR use. Because of both the lack of language-learning VR applications and the lack of testing and vetting of existing language-learning applications, it can be a challenge to incorpo-rate VR in the classroom. Studies on the handful of available language learn-ing VR applications (e.g., Mondly VR, ImmerseMe) have yielded mixed results. For example, although learners like ImmerseMe, a conversation simulator, they also report wanting more feedback, more support, more cost-free experiences, and better voice recognition software (Meri-Yilan 2019). Our study has also raised concerns that learners may not notice or effectively use language learning tools within such applications. Further, not only did our participants have some hesitation about the feedback provided, we were unable to see clear evidence that learners were able to use the broad (utter-ance accepted or not-accepted) feedback in order to improve in subsequent attempts. Only one participant was able to improve their pronunciation in a repeated attempt. Teachers should spend time examining what their language goal is and if the program is able to help students meet the goal. Teachers may be able to use pseudo-dialog simulators, such as Mondly VR, to in-crease student comfort and familiarity with vocabulary and phrases used in particular interactions, but, currently, should not rely on such programs for substantial pronunciation feedback.

Teachers may be able to utilize additional applications and games that are not specifically designed for language learning to support learning goals. Using Rec Room, a VR application, learners can seek out real, meaningful conversation with other users while engaging in fun games and activities. An interesting game option in Rec Room for language learning might be its 3D charades. Tiltbrush is another VR application which provides a space for 3D painting. Learners could work to craft drawings of new vocabulary items, perhaps including a picture element that represents pronunciation features. Finally, with Google Expeditions, learners are able to explore different parts of the world through VR. An instructor could scaffold an activity where learners visit a place with Google Expeditions and have to give a short presentation of everything they saw or encountered. Many of the non-language focused VR applications are able to support some form of language practice, whether just by providing language input or supporting meaningful communication with other users. No matter what applications and tasks are used, instructors should have open communication with learners about what the task is, how it will help their language learning, and what learners should focus on or try to accomplish.

Once teachers have chosen headsets and applications for use in the classroom, a final practical consideration is how to help learners get started with VR. One way teachers might introduce the applications is to show screen-captured video recordings to highlight how to use the application. Many programs offer video recordings as part of their advertisements and teachers are likely to find specific tutorials on YouTube. The various headsets may also have applications to help users get used to the hand controls, such as First Steps for Oculus, which guides users in learning the hand controls by leading them through mini-tasks that utilize the various controller functions and buttons. Because many of our participants needed tips to get started with support tools, our research indicates that teachers may also provide vital support by highlighting language-learning tools available to learners within specific applications. Finally, in addition to technological difficulties in getting started, teachers may want to prepare for the possibility that learners may become motion sick while using VR, a relatively common issue. Teachers can limit early uses of the application to short time limits, such as 10 minutes, encourage students to stop use if they begin to feel unwell, and consider having ginger candies or drinks available to help settle stomachs. Applications that limit movement through the VR 3D space, such as Mondly VR which can be completed while sitting in a chair, may be less likely to trigger motion sickness than games encouraging substantial movement, such as dodgeball in Rec Room.

In conclusion, language-learning VR programs can provide learners with useful language experience, but the programs have yet to reach maturity or their final form and may not adequately support pronunciation learning at this time. Instructors looking to incorporate VR in their classroom(s) will want to weigh the benefits and disadvantages of VR models, prices, and learning goals. If teachers choose to move forward with VR, they should consider the ways they can help pronunciation learners make the practice more successful by showing helpful tools within the application or guiding learner focus during the activity.

NOTE

1. https://www.oculus.com/compare.

REFERENCES

Alsop, Thomas. 2021. "Virtual Reality (VR)- Statistics and facts." *Statista.* https://www.statista.com/topics/2532/virtual-reality-vr/.

Bashori, Muzakki, Roeland Van Hout, Helmer Strik, and Catia Cucchiarini. 2021. "Effects of ASR-based websites on EFL learners' vocabulary, speaking anxiety, and language enjoyment." *System 99*, 1–16. https://doi.org/10.1016/j.system.2021.102496.

BCC Research Editorial. 2018. "The history and evolution of virtual reality technology." *BBC Research.* https://blog.bccresearch.com/the-history-and-evolution-of-virtual-reality-technology.

Boas, Yuri Antonio Gonçalves Vilas. 2013. "Overview of virtual reality technologies." *Interactive Multimedia Conference*, 1–6.

Bouselmi, G., D. Fohr, and I. Illina. 2012. "Multilingual recognition of non-native speech using acoustic model transformation and pronunciation modeling." *International Journal of Speech Technology* 15, 203–213. https://doi.org/10.1007/s10772-012-9134-8.

Chen, Yu-Li. 2016. "The effects of virtual reality learning environment on student cognitive and linguistic development." *The Asia-Pacific Education Researcher*, 25, no. 4, 637–646. https://doi.org/10.1007/s40299-016-0293-2

Cincarek, Tobias, Rainer Gruhn, Christian Hacker, Elmar Nöth, and Satoshi Nakamura. 2008. "Automatic pronunciation scoring of words and sentences independent from the non-native's first language." *Computer Speech and Language* 23, 65–88. https://doi.org/10.1016/j.csl.2008.03.001.

Clark, Taylor. 2014. "How Palmer Luckey created Oculus Rift." *Smithsonian Magazine.* https://www.smithsonianmag.com/innovation/how-palmer-luckey-created-oculus-rift-180953049/.

Craddock, Ida Mae. 2018. "Immersive virtual reality, Google Expeditions, and English language learning." *Library Technology Reports* 54, no. 4, 7–9.

Cucchiarini, Catia and Helmer Strik, and Lou Boves. 2000. "Different aspects of expert pronunciation quality ratings and their relation to scores produced by speech recognition algorithms." *Speech Communication* 30, 109–119. https://doi .org/10.1016/S0167-6393(99)00040-0.

Evanini, Keelan, Sandeep Singh, Anastassia Loukina, Xinhao Wang, and Chong Min Lee. 2015. "Content-based automated assessment of non-native spoken language proficiency in a simulated conversation." In *NIPS Workshop on Machine Learning for Spoken Language Understanding and Interaction.*

Hincks, Rebecca. 2003. "Speech technologies for pronunciation feedback and evaluation." *ReCALL* 15, no. 1, 3–20. https://doi.org/10.1017/S095834400300021.

Huang, Xinyi, Di Zou, Gary Cheng, and Haoran Xie. 2021. "A systematic review of AR and VR enhanced language learning." *Sustainability* 13, no. 9, 1–28. https:// doi.org/10.3390/su13094639.

Jensen, Signe Hannibal. 2017. "Gaming as an English language learning resource among young children in Denmark." *CALICO Journal*, 34, no. 1, 1–19.

Junining, Esti, Sony Alif, and Nuria Setiarini. 2020. "Automatic speech recognition in computer-assisted language learning for individual learning in speaking." *Journal of English Educators Society 5*, no. 2, 219–223.

Kaplan-Rakowski, Regina and Thomasz Wojdynski. 2018. "Students' attitudes toward high-immersion virtual reality assisted language learning." *Future-Proof CALL: language learning as exploration and encounters—short.* Papers from EUROCALL, 124–129.

Lai, Kuo-Wei and Hao-Jan Howard Chen. 2021. "A comparative study on the effects of a VR and PC visual novel game on vocabulary learning." *Computer Assisted Language Learning*, 1–34. https://doi.org/10.1080/09588221.2021.1928226

Lan, Yu-Ju, Yu-Hsuan Kan, Indy Y. T. Hsiao, Stephen J. H. Yang, and Kuo-En Chang. 2013. "Designing interaction tasks in Second Life for Chinese as a foreign language learners: A preliminary exploration." *Australasian Journal of Educational Technology* 29, no 2, 184–202.

Lege, Ryan and Euan Bonner. 2020. "Virtual reality in education: The promise, progress, and challenge." *The JALT CALL Journal* 16, no. 3, 167–180. https://doi .org/10.29140/jaltcall.v16n3.388.

Levis, John and Ruslan Suvorov. 2020. "Automated speech recognition." In The Encyclopedia of Applied Linguistics, edited by Carol Chapelle, 1–8. https://doi .org/10.1002/9781405198431.wbeal0066.pub2

Li, Rong-Chang and David Topolewski. 2002. "ZIP & TERRY: A new attempt at designing language learning simulation." *Simulation & Gaming* 33, no. 2, 181–186.

Liakin, Denis, Walcir Cardoso, and Natallia Liakina. 2014. "Learning L2 pronunciation with a mobile speech recognizer: French /y/." *CALICO Journal* 32, no. 1, 1–25. https://doi.org/10.1558/cj.v32i1.25962.

Makransky, Guido, Lau Lilleholt, and Anders Aaby. 2017. "Development and validation of the multimodal presence scale for virtual reality environments: A confirmatory factor analysis and item response theory approach." *Computers in Human Behavior, 72*, 276–285. https://doi.org/10.1016/j.chb.2017.02.066.

McCrocklin, Shannon. 2019. "ASR-based dictation practice for second language pronunciation improvement." *Journal of Second Language Pronunciation* 5, no. 1, 98–118. https://doi.org/10.1075/jslp.16034.mcc.

McCrocklin, Shannon and Idée Edalatishams. 2020. "Revisiting popular speech recognition software for ESL speech." *TESOL Quarterly* 54, no. 4, 1086–1097. https://doi.org/10.1002/tesq.3006.

Meri-Yilan, Serpil. 2019. "A study on technology-based speech assistants." In *New educational landscapes: Innovative perspectives in language learning and technology*, edited by Alessia Plutino, Kate Borthwick, and Erika Corradini, 11–17. Research-publishing.net. https://doi.org/10.14705/rpnet.2019.36.950.

Mondly. 2021. "Mondly VR: Practice languages in virtual reality." https://www.mondly.com/vr.

Moustroufas, N., and Y. Digalakis. 2007. "Automatic pronunciation evaluation of foreign speakers using unknown text." *Computer Speech and Language*, 21, 219–230. https://doi.org/10.1016/j.csl.2006.04.001.

Mroz, Aurore. 2015. "The development of second language critical thinking in a virtual language learning environment: A process-oriented mixed-method study." *CALICO Journal* 32, no. 3, 528–553.

Mroz, Aurore. 2018. "Seeing how people hear you: French learners experiencing intelligibility through automatic speech recognition." *Foreign Language Annals* 51, no. 3, 1–21. https://doi.org/10.1111/flan.12348.

Nation, I. S. P. and Jonathan Newton. 2008. *Teaching ESL/EFL Listening and Speaking*. New York: Routledge.

Neri, Ambra, Ornella Mich, Matteo Gerosa, and Diego Giuliani. 2008. "The effectiveness of computer assisted pronunciation training for foreign language learning by children." *Computer Assisted Language Learning* 21, no. 5, 393–408. https://doi.org/10.1080/09588220802447651.

Pinto Darque, Bruno Peixoto, Aliane Krassmann, Miguel Melo, Luciana Cabral, and Maximino Bessa. 2019. "Virtual reality in education: Learning a foreign language." In *New Knowledge in Information Systems and Technologies*, edited by Álvaro Rocha, Hojjat Adeli, Luís Paulo Reis, and Sandra Costanzo, 589–597. Springer. https://doi.org/10.1007/978-3-030-16187-3_57.

Poetker, Bridget. 2019. "The very real history of virtual reality (+a look ahead)." *G2*. https://www.g2.com/articles/history-of-virtual-reality.

Reinhardt, Jonathon and Steven L. Thorne. 2020. "Digital Games as Language-Learning Environments." In the *Handbook of Game-Based Learning* edited by Jan L. Plass, Richard E. Mayer, and Bruce D. Homer, 409–435. MIT Press.

Sadler, Randall and Melinda Dooley. 2012. "Language learning in *virtual worlds: Research and practice*." In *Contemporary Computer-Assisted Language Learning*, edited by Michael Thomas, Hayo Reinders, and Mark Warschauer, 159–182. Bloomsbury.

Saraçlar, Murat. 2000. "*Pronunciation modeling for conversational speech recognition*." PhD diss., The John Hopkins University.

Schnipper, Matthew. n.d. "Seeing is believing: The state of virtual reality." *The Verge*. https://www.theverge.com/a/virtual-reality/intro.

Shih, Ya-Chun. 2015. "A virtual walk through London: Culture learning through a cultural immersion experience." *Computer Assisted Language Learning* 28, no. 5, 407–428.

Sydorenko, Tetyana, John Hellermann, Steven L. Thorne, and Vanessa Howe. 2019. "Mobile augmented reality and language-related episodes." *TESOL Quarterly* 53, no. 3, 712–740.

Timpe-Laughlin, Veronika, Keelan Evanini, Ashley Green, Ian Blood, Judit Dombi, and Vikram Ramanarayanan. 2017. "Designing interactive, automated dialogues for L2 pragmatics learning." In the *Proceedings of the 21st Workshop on the Semantics and Pragmatics of Dialogue*, 143–152. SEMDIAL.

Truong, Khiet, Ambra Neri, Febe de Wet, Catia Cucchiarini, and Helmer Strik. 2005. "Automatic detection of frequent pronunciation errors made by L2-learners." In the *Proceedings from InterSpeech 2005 (IS2005)*, Lisbon, Portugal, 1345–1348.

Tsai, Yu-Ling and Chin-Chung Tsai. 2018. "Digital game-based second-language vocabulary learning and conditions of research designs: A meta-analysis study." *Computers & Education*, 125, 345–357.

Vázquez, Christian, Lei Xia, Takako Aikawa, and Pattie Maes. 2018. "Words in motion: Kinesthetic language learning in virtual reality." In the *2018 IEEE 18th International Conference on advanced learning technologies*, 272–276. IEEE.

Virtual Reality Society. 2020. "History of virtual reality." https://www.vrs.org.uk/virtual-reality/history.html.

Xie, Ying, Lanhui Ryder, and Yan Chen. 2019. "Using interactive Virtual Reality tools in an advanced Chinese language class: a case study." *TechTrends: Linking Research & Practice to Improve Learning* 63, no. 3, 251–259. https://doi.org/10.1007/s11528-019-00389-z.

Xu, Zhihong, Zhuo Chen, Lauren Eutsler, Zihan Geng, and Ashlynn Kogut. 2020. "A scoping review of digital game-based technology on English language learning." *Educational Technology Research and Development* 68, no. 3, 877–904.

Yeh, Yi-Lien and Yu-Ju Lan. 2018. "Fostering student autonomy in English learning through creations in a 3D virtual world." *Educational Technology Research Development* 66, 693–708. https://doi.org/10.1007/s11423-017-9566-6

Part 4

SPEECH VISUALIZATION

Chapter Eleven

L2 Japanese Vowel Production

A Closer Look at Transfer Effects from Perception Training with Waveforms

Debra M. Hardison and Tomoko Okuno

INTRODUCTION

About 30 years have passed since Pisoni and colleagues (e.g., Lively, Logan, and Pisoni 1993) demonstrated that the adult perceptual system could be modified to improve the auditory perceptual identification accuracy of non-native sounds. The focus of that research was the perceptual learning of American English /r/ and /l/ as a second language (L2) by individuals whose first language (L1) was Japanese. Based on the results of a series of studies, the hallmarks of successful training emerged and included the use of (a) multiple exemplars of the target sound(s) in a range of phonetic environments, (b) natural versus synthesized speech, (c) multiple talkers (i.e., different voices), (d) compatible approaches in testing and training, and (e) feedback during training. These criteria clearly pointed to a key element underlying the success: training stimuli need to reflect the variable nature of the input found in the natural language environment. This training model came to be known as High Variability Phonetic Training (HVPT). From the learners' perspective, successful training results in generalization of improved perceptual abilities to novel stimuli and unfamiliar talkers, with transfer to production improvement even in the absence of explicit production training. From a theoretical perspective, findings that demonstrate significant effects of phonetic context and talker characteristics on perception are compatible with exemplar-based theories of speech perception, which posit that attended details of perceptual events are preserved in long-term memory traces and facilitate later processing (Hardison 2012; Lively et al. 1993). Incorporating (vs. discarding) sources of variability in the speech signal during training promotes the development of perceptual categories robust to the variability in natural speech.

This chapter delves more deeply into one of the characteristics of successful perception training, specifically production improvement, by taking multiple approaches to analyzing speech samples produced by L2 learners of Japanese before and after perception training to increase identification accuracy of vowel duration in Japanese. Their perception training, discussed in detail in Okuno and Hardison (2016), compared the effectiveness of auditory-only (A-only) and auditory-visual (AV) input; the AV input included waveform displays to highlight the durational difference between short and long vowels in Japanese. Waveforms are two-dimensional images of changes in intensity over time that represent a measure of the variations in air pressure that we perceive as sound (see figure 11.1). The ability to perceive and produce long and short vowels accurately in Japanese is important because this distinction can contrast meaning between words; however, despite its importance, many beginning-level textbooks, such as *GENKI* (Banno et al. 2020), explain the topic very briefly when Japanese orthography is introduced. Therefore, teachers need to create their own practice opportunities to help learners correctly identify the duration contrast. Practice can include waveform displays of minimal pairs such as *obaasan* "grandmother" (long vowel) versus *obasan* "aunt" (short vowel), and *hakko* "eight small objects" (geminate consonant) versus *hako* "a box" (singleton consonant). Waveform training resulted in significant improvement of learners' perception and production of the distinction between singleton consonants and their longer geminate counterparts in Japanese (Motohashi-Saigo and Hardison 2009). The question arises as to whether the use of waveforms in perception training might also contribute to learners' improved production of vowel duration in Japanese. In this chapter, we begin with a brief overview of studies involving AV and A-only perception training and the perception-production link. In L2 perception training, visual input has involved cues from talkers' faces and gestures as well as electronic displays (see Hardison 2021 for a research timeline).

PERCEPTION TRAINING AND
PRODUCTION IMPROVEMENT

Facial and Gestural Cues in L2 Speech Training

Following the HVPT model established for successful auditory perception training, subsequent auditory training studies continued to show success for Japanese speakers learning American English /r/ and /l/ with generalization to novel stimuli and unfamiliar voices as well as transfer to improved production (e.g., Bradlow et al. 1999). Other studies expanded the investigation to additional English sounds and a comparison of AV and A-only training for

Japanese and Korean speakers where visual cues came from talkers' faces (e.g., Hardison 2003). This training also demonstrated generalization to novel stimuli and unfamiliar talkers, and transfer to production improvement in addition to earlier identification of words beginning with the target sounds when presented in isolation and in sentence context (Hardison 2005, 2018).

Among other target languages, both AV and A-only approaches in HVPT studies resulted in significant improvement in accuracy for English speakers perceiving French nasal vowels (Inceoglu 2016); however, in that study, AV training, which involved input from the faces of talkers, resulted in greater production improvement. Hirata and Kelly (2010) explored whether a Japanese speaker's mouth and/or hand movements would aid perception of Japanese vowel length contrasts by speakers whose L1 was English with no prior exposure to Japanese. Only the participants who saw the speaker's mouth movements showed significantly better identification accuracy of short and long vowels. In a subsequent study, L1 English participants observed a native speaker (NS) of Japanese using different hand gestures corresponding to short or long vowels (Hirata et al. 2014). Perception of vowel length improved the most for participants assigned to the group that observed the speaker's small downward hand movement following or preceding a short vowel.

Computer-based Visual Feedback in L2 Speech Training

Advances in speech technology offer several sources of visual input for perception and production training; for example, Praat (Boersma and Weenink 2014), a free software package for speech analysis, can display the speech signal's acoustic components. Pitch displays are perhaps the most user-friendly for L2 learners and have facilitated production of intonation in French (Hardison 2004) and tone in Chinese (Chun et al. 2015; Wang 2012). Fewer studies have used waveforms and spectrograms. Spectrograms show the formants in the speech wave represented by horizontal dark bands of energy at various frequencies.

With instruction on the use of Praat and the interpretation of spectrograms, intermediate-low proficiency learners of L2 Spanish (L1 English) improved their understanding and production of the intervocalic variants of stop consonants /b, d, g/ (Olson 2014). In a later study using spectrograms and waveforms, Offerman and Olson (2016) trained L1 English learners to produce voice-onset time (VOT) that was more characteristic of L2 Spanish voiceless stops /p, t, k/ in word-initial position. VOT is the temporal lag between the release of a stop consonant and the onset of voicing for the following vowel. Spanish has a shorter lag VOT compared to English. Offerman and Olson stated that misarticulations by learners involving VOT can be the source of perceived foreign accent. Importantly, they may also result in miscommunication. Learners recorded stimuli using Praat and were guided in the analysis of the spectrograms and waveforms. Results indicated significant VOT improvement (i.e., toward more native-like targets) in both the relatively controlled stimuli (e.g., read-aloud sentences) and less controlled stimuli (picture-naming task).

In a follow-up study, Olson and Offerman (2021) compared different methods for using visual feedback in VOT training involving the stop consonants /p, t, k/ for English-speaking learners of Spanish. Methods differed according to the number of interventions: one (referred to as "short") versus three (referred to as "long"), and the approach to presenting the target stimuli within the longer intervention (i.e., simultaneous or sequential presentation of the stops). In the short intervention method, each learner worked with a specific voiceless stop. In the longer simultaneous approach, in which three interventions were conducted over 4 weeks, all learners worked with all three voiceless stops in words produced in isolation and connected discourse. In the longer sequential intervention, each training focused on one stop (/p/, /t/, or /k/) at a time and sessions were separated by 2–3 weeks. In these approaches, learners used Praat to produce and print waveforms and spectrograms of words in isolation. They answered a series of guiding questions about the images of their productions and segmented the component sounds. They were then given waveform and spectrographic images of the same words produced by an NS of Spanish and answered similar questions about how they determined boundaries in those images, and the relative duration of the consonant and following vowel. Findings indicated that all approaches resulted in a reduction in VOT, which was the ultimate goal, but the longer sequential approach outperformed the others. The advantage of the sequential versus simultaneous focus on target sounds (Olson and Offerman 2021) could reflect the value of focused attention on one versus multiple targets and/or the ability of training on one phonetic feature to generalize to other instances (de Jong, Hao, and Park 2009), in this case, other stop consonants sharing the same feature. All methodologies were conducted with an intact class and some of the analysis work was assigned as homework. Given the success of this training approach, teachers could consider incorporating this technology in their curriculum.

Waveforms, which are well suited for visualizing segmental duration, were used to help learners identify duration differences that distinguish singleton and geminate Japanese consonants (Motohashi Saigo and Hardison 2009). A pretest-posttest design compared AV (using waveforms) and A-only web-based training. Findings revealed improvement in geminate identification accuracy following 10 sessions of training, with a significant advantage for the AV group, and a significant effect of geminate type; scores were lower for the fricative /s/ versus the stops /t/ and /k/. Most errors were misperceptions of geminates as long vowels. Based on rater judgments, geminate production accuracy also improved, again with a significant advantage for the AV group, with improvement greatest for /k/ and smallest for /s/. Most production errors involved substitution of a singleton for a geminate. In post-study interviews, all participants provided very positive comments about the training, and those in the AV group reported that the use of waveforms increased their awareness of durational differences.

In dealing with segmental duration, raising L2 learners' awareness involves an understanding of the mora, a unit of timing important for both perception and production (e.g., Kubozono 1999; Tsujimura 2013), which is often a challenge for learners. Special morae include the second half of a long vowel; for example, figure 11.1 provides the waveform produced by a native speaker of Japanese of the short vowel /u/[1] taken from the first syllable in *kuku* (a), which has two morae /ku-ku/ and two syllables /ku.ku/, and the long vowel /u/ from the first syllable in *kuukuu* (b), which has four morae /ku-u-ku-u/ and two syllables /kuu.kuu/. Research has suggested that the position of a long vowel in a word (i.e., in the first or second syllable) may also be a factor in learners' perceptual accuracy. Long vowels in word-final versus word-initial position were more difficult for learners to perceive accurately (Koguma 2000).

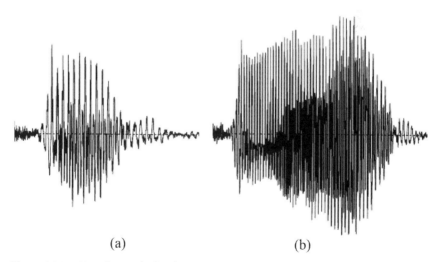

(a)   (b)

Figure 11.1.   Waveform Display for (a) Short /u/ Taken from the First Syllable of kuku and (b) Long /u/ from the First Syllable of kuukuu.
Source: Hardison and Okuno

An additional challenge for L2 Japanese learners is the pitch-accent system, which can also serve a contrastive role. In the Tokyo dialect, accent is realized as a high (H) pitch followed by a low (L) pitch (e.g., Haraguchi 1999; Tsujimura 2013). The location of the accent corresponds to the mora before the pitch drop. For example, when *kuku* is produced with a H.L pitch pattern with the accent on the first syllable, it means "randomness"; however, with a L.H pattern, it would mean "cane." In the case of long vowels, as in *saasaa* (figure 11.2) produced with a HL.LL pattern, the first accented mora carries the H pitch and the HL pitch contour occurs within the first long vowel.

Native listeners appear to use pitch cues to differentiate long and short vowels when duration cues become ambiguous (Kinoshita, Behne, and Arai 2002). L2 learners of Japanese have also demonstrated some sensitivity to pitch pattern differences and their association with duration cues (Minagawa 1997). In Minagawa's study, learners from a range of L1s (e.g., Korean, Chinese, English) showed greater perceptual accuracy of long vowels in the HH pattern, and a tendency to misperceive a long vowel as a short vowel in the LL pattern. More recently, Hui and Arai (2020) explored how duration and pitch were used by learners of Japanese (multiple L1s) to differentiate *obaasan* (long vowel) "grandmother" and *obasan* (short vowel) "aunt" pro-

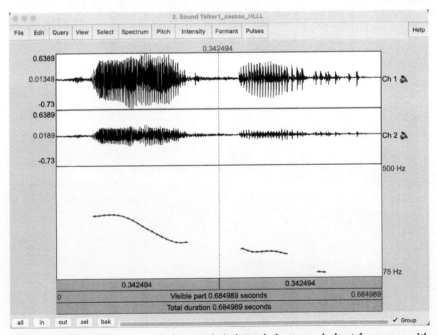

Figure 11.2. Waveform (top window) and Pitch Track (bottom window) for saasaa with a HL.LL Pitch Pattern.

Source: Hardison and Okuno

duced in a sentence by a native speaker. Praat was used to modify the duration, pitch, or both features of the stimuli. Findings demonstrated a pattern in which learners may have used pitch cues when stimuli had ambiguous duration cues. There was no effect on perception of variables such as length of stay in Japan, length of Japanese study, learner's L1, or Japanese proficiency. Some of the learners had an explicit knowledge of pitch but others did not; therefore, such metalinguistic knowledge may not be necessary in order for pitch cues to be beneficial in perception.

To investigate the role played by pitch in the L1 on L2 pitch discrimination ability, Wiener and Goss (2019) conducted a discrimination task with L2 listeners grouped according to their L1 and language learning backgrounds: a) L1 Mandarin + L2 English + L3 Japanese, b) L1 Japanese + L2 English, and c) L1 English + L2 Mandarin or L2 Japanese. The languages were classified according to the information value of their pitch cues, which placed Japanese between English (lowest) and Mandarin (highest). Findings revealed that L1 Mandarin listeners with no experience learning Japanese discriminated pitch accent with nativelike ability. L1 Mandarin listeners who had studied both English and Japanese discriminated pitch accent more accurately than L1 Japanese listeners, suggesting that discrimination ability was not language specific. The authors proposed that the increases in sensitivity were additive.

The effects of pitch-accent pattern and segmental duration as well as vowel type, preceding consonant, and training talker's voice were explored in a training study involving L2 learners of Japanese in the United States (Okuno and Hardison 2016) to improve their ability to perceive vowel duration accurately. Using a pretest, training, posttest design, 48 L1 English speakers were assigned to one of three groups: AV training using waveform displays, A-only, or no training (control). Results indicated significant improvement for both training groups who were also able to generalize improved abilities to the perception of novel stimuli, and stimuli produced by a new voice. Although the difference in the amount of improvement demonstrated by the two training groups did not reach statistical significance, the AV group, which saw the waveforms, showed a greater rate of improvement over the course of training as shown in figure 11.3. Vowel type (/a/ or /u/), preceding consonant (/k/ or /s/), and pitch pattern significantly affected perception in testing and training as did the training talker's voice. Perceptual accuracy was greater with /a/ versus /u/, which represent the longest and shortest vowels respectively in the Tokyo dialect (Yoshida 2006). Accuracy was also greater when the preceding consonant was /k/ versus /s/. The easiest pitch pattern for learners was Low–High in the first syllable, perhaps reflecting English prosodic preference, and High–High in the second, which may be a more salient pattern. Perception was facilitated by talkers who produced greater pitch movement. Participants reported finding the waveform displays very helpful.

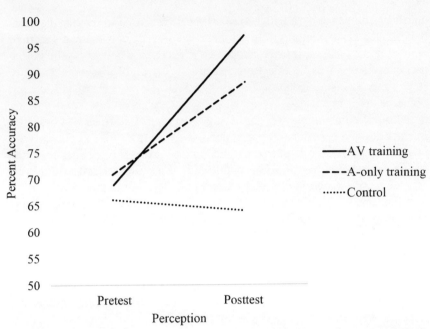

Figure 11.3.   Mean Percent Accuracy by Group for Perception at Pretest and Posttest.
Source: Hardison and Okuno

CURRENT STUDY

The current study investigated the effects of the aforementioned perception training on learner production accuracy of Japanese vowel duration. The between-groups variable was training type: AV using waveform displays, A-only, and control (no training). Within-group variables were vowel type (/a/, /u/), preceding consonant (/k/, /s/), stimulus condition (token presented in isolation or in a carrier sentence), and token type to address both vowel length and position in the first or second syllable. In the following token types, c denotes a consonant, v represents a short vowel, and vv a long vowel. Upper case (i.e., V or VV) denotes the target vowel. For short vowels, token types were: cV.cvv, cvv.cV, cV.cv, and cv.cV; for long vowels, token types were: cVV.cvv, cvv.cVV, cVV.cv, and cv.cVV.

Participants

Participants were 48 L2 learners of Japanese (aged 18–22; 36 female, 28 male) at a university in the United States. Their first language was American English. There were no heritage speakers of Japanese or students who had studied abroad in Japan. All reported normal hearing and vision. Neither segmental duration nor pitch accent was an explicit focus in their courses although their instructors corrected inaccurate pronunciation during oral exercises and communicative activities.

Materials

Materials for production testing included four practice tokens (e.g., *noono)* and 16 bisyllabic tokens contrasting long and short vowels in a range of syllable structure types: CVV.CVV, CVV.CV, CV.CVV, and CV.CV. The consonants /k/ and /s/ were combined with vowels /a/ and /u/ to construct pseudowords (e.g., kaakaa, saasa, kukuu, susu) to avoid the effects of word frequency and learner knowledge (e.g., Bundgaard-Nielsen, Best, and Tyler 2011).

Procedure

Production data were collected as part of a larger study in which data collection followed this sequence: pretests (production and perception), two weeks (8 sessions) of perception training with feedback, and posttests (production and perception) the day following the end of training. Participants were divided into three groups: AV training (*n* = 16), A-only training (*n* = 16), and no training (control) (*n* = 16). Each group included a similar range of pretest perceptual identification accuracy scores. This chapter is limited to a discussion of the production tests and findings (see Okuno and Hardison 2016 for a discussion of the perception findings).

A computer-based test was created using the E-Prime software (Psychology Software Tools) and administered to learners individually. Participants were instructed to produce the target that appeared on the computer screen in two conditions: isolated (token presented alone) and carrier sentence. In the carrier sentence condition, they saw the full sentence prompt on the screen with a blank where the target word was to be produced: Tanaka-san wa ____ to iimashita ("Tanaka said ____."). All tokens were written in *romaji* (the Roman alphabet representation of Japanese sounds), which makes the vowel duration distinction clearer compared to *hiragana* (the Japanese syllabary). Learner productions were digitally recorded and saved for analysis.

RESULTS

Statistical analyses were performed with SPSS v. 27. The alpha level was set at .05. Effect sizes are reported as partial eta-squared (η^2) and may be interpreted as follows following Field (2018): $\eta^2 = .01$ (small effect); $\eta^2 = .06$

(medium effect); $\eta^2 = .14$ (large effect). Evaluation of improvement in learner productions was approached from different perspectives. First, NSs of Japanese listened to the recorded speech samples and were asked to identify what they heard each participant say from a list of options (referred to below as Assessment of Accuracy). Second, ratings were provided by a separate group of NSs for the native-likeness of the learners' vowel durations. Third, durations of the vowels produced by the learners were measured and a correlation analysis was conducted between the duration measurements and the native-likeness ratings. Finally, a comparison was made between the durations of the learners' vowels and the durations of the vowels produced by the NSs who had provided their perception training input. Each of these approaches to the assessment of production improvement is addressed in turn.

Assessment of Accuracy

Mean pretest and posttest production accuracy ratings were provided by three NSs of Japanese from the Tokyo area who had a background in linguistics and experience teaching Japanese. Raters identified what they heard a participant say from a list of options which varied according to the duration and syllable position of the vowel. Based on earlier pilot testing, options included a geminate consonant. For example, for the target *kaakaa*, response options were (a) kaakaa, (b) kaaka, (c) kakka, (d) kaka, and (e) other. If raters chose option (e), they were asked to write what they had heard. Data were analyzed per vowel.

The predominant production error patterns in the pretest were generally comparable for both /a/ and /u/, especially in terms of the short vowels. Learners produced the target short vowels with an exaggerated duration, whether the vowel was in the first or second syllable; for example, the predominant error pattern for the target token CVV.CVV (i.e., with a long vowel in each syllable) involved shortening the vowel in the second syllable, especially when the vowel was /u/.

As indicated by the pretest pattern of results, learners needed to shorten all of their vowels. Analysis of the posttest data revealed that mean production accuracy showed significant improvement from .66 ($SD = .20$) to .91 ($SD = .08$) for the AV perception training group and .69 ($SD = .14$) to .90 ($SD = .09$) for the A-only group. ANOVA results revealed a significant effect of time, $F(1, 30) = 67.148$, $p < .001$, partial $\eta^2 = .691$, with no significant difference between the two training groups, $F(1, 30) = 1.600$, $p = .216$. There was also a significant effect of token type, $F(3, 90) = 5.392$, $p = .002$, partial $\eta^2 = .152$. Production of all types except for CVV.CVV, which has two long vowels (e.g., *kaakaa*), showed significant improvement although accuracy was greater for /a/ versus /u/.

Nativelikeness Ratings

The above assessment of accuracy used a multiple-choice task; however, the issue is more complex. In a multiple-choice task to determine if a given production is accurate or not, a target long vowel produced with exaggerated duration would still be identified as a long vowel as there is no other option, and thus by default, it would be accurate in this type of task; however, a target short vowel produced with exaggerated duration could be identified as inaccurate (i.e., as a long vowel). To take a finer-grained approach, NSs were asked to rate the nativelike quality of the duration of each of the vowels produced by the learners.

Data for each vowel (/a/, /u/) were tabulated and analyzed separately as there was no theoretical foundation for comparing the two vowels, which represent the longest and shortest vowels, respectively, in the Tokyo dialect (Yoshida 2006). Within each vowel, the short and long durations were also analyzed separately. Three NSs of the Tokyo dialect, who were experienced instructors of Japanese, provided ratings of the nativelikeness of learner vowel durations using a 7-point scale with defined endpoints: The number 1 represented *definitely not nativelike duration*, and 7 represented *definitely nativelike duration*. Raters were instructed to focus only on duration. Practice trials familiarized raters with the task and its focus. Each syllable in a bisyllabic token was played separately for raters to evaluate. Before each sample was played, raters saw what the target was and the syllable (i.e., first or second) that the sample was taken from. Pretest and posttest samples were randomized.

Inter-rater reliability, measured by intraclass correlation coefficients (two-way mixed-effects model with average measure reliability), was over .90 for all tokens; there were many instances of complete agreement. Results for the nativelikeness of the durations are presented per vowel, and begin with the short followed by the long vowels.

Short Vowel /a/

For the nativelikeness ratings for target short vowel /a/, an initial mixed-design ANOVA revealed no significant effect of training group type, $F(1, 30) = .459$, $p = .503$, partial $\eta^2 = .015$; therefore, the data from both groups were combined ($N = 32$) for further analyses. The overall pretest mean rating was 3.827 ($SD = 2.377$; 95% CIs [2.970, 4.684]) and rose to 5.536 ($SD = 1.709$; 95% CIs [4.920, 6.152]) in the posttest. A within-group ANOVA revealed significant improvement in the nativelikeness of the vowels following perception training, $F(1, 31) = 87.333$, $p < .001$, partial $\eta^2 = .738$. There was a significant effect of token type, $F(3, 93) = 16.489$, $p < .001$, partial $\eta^2 = .347$; ratings for cV.cv, in which the target vowel was in the first syllable, were significantly higher. There was a significant effect of preceding consonant, $F(1, 31) = 24.874$, $p < .001$, partial $\eta^2 = .445$; ratings were higher (i.e., judged as more nativelike) for the vowel following /k/. Ratings were also significantly higher when the tokens were produced in isolation (vs. the carrier sentence), $F(1, 31) = 18.905$, $p < .001$, partial $\eta^2 = .379$. Analysis also revealed a significant Token Type x Condition interaction, $F(3, 93) = 9.944$, $p < .001$, partial $\eta^2 = .243$. Simple effects tests indicated that performance was better in the isolated (vs. carrier sentence) condition for token types cvv.cV and cv.cV, where the vowel was in the second syllable.

Short Vowel /u/

Initial analysis of the nativelikeness ratings for short vowel /u/ also revealed no significant effect of training group type, $F(1, 30) = .135$, $p = .716$, partial $\eta^2 = .004$; therefore data were combined ($N = 32$) for the remaining analyses. There was significant improvement in the ratings of nativelikeness for productions of short /u/ from a mean of 4.128 ($SD = 2.438$; 95% CIs [3.249, 5.007]) in the pretest to 5.722 ($SD = 1.719$; 95% CIs [5.102, 6.342]) in the posttest, $F(1, 31) = 77.345$, $p < .001$, partial $\eta^2 = .714$. There was a significant effect of token type, $F(3, 93) = 17.263$, $p < .001$, partial $\eta^2 = .358$; ratings were highest for cV.cv with the vowel in the first syllable. There was also a significant Token Type x Condition interaction, $F(3, 93) = 11.231$, $p < .001$, partial $\eta^2 = .266$; simple effects tests revealed that ratings were higher for the isolated (vs. carrier sentence) condition for cvv.cV and cv.cV. In both cases, the vowel was in the second syllable.

Long Vowel /a/

Initial analysis of the nativelikeness ratings for long vowel /a/ also revealed no significant effect of training group type, $F(1, 30) = .193$, $p = .663$, partial $\eta^2 = .006$; therefore, data were combined ($N = 32$) for the remaining analyses. The mean rating rose slightly from 3.303 ($SD = 2.141$; 95% CIs [2.532, 4.075]) in the pretest to 3.554 ($SD = 1.976$; 95% CIs [2.842, 4.267]) in the posttest; however, the change over time was not significant, $F(1, 31) = 1.654$, $p = .208$, partial $\eta^2 = .051$. There was a significant effect of preceding consonant, $F(1, 31) = 7.566$, $p = .010$, partial $\eta^2 = .196$; ratings were higher for the vowel following /k/. Ratings for long /a/ were higher for tokens produced in the carrier sentence (vs. isolated) condition, $F(1, 31) = 18.892$, $p < .001$, partial $\eta^2 = .379$. There was a significant effect of token type, $F(3, 93) = 4.970$, $p = .003$, partial $\eta^2 = .138$; ratings were higher when the vowel was in the first syllable (e.g., mean = 3.82 for cVV.cv) versus the second syllable (e.g., mean = 3.19 for cv.cVV).

Long Vowel /u/

Initial analysis of the nativelikeness ratings for long vowel /u/ also revealed no significant effect of training group type, $F(1, 30) = .472$, $p = .498$, partial $\eta^2 = .015$; therefore data were combined ($N = 32$) for the remaining analyses. Nativelikeness ratings for long /u/ showed slight improvement after perception training from a mean of 3.030 ($SD = 2.055$; 95% CIs [2.289, 3.771]) in the pretest to 3.221 ($SD = 2.011$; 95% CIs [2.496, 3.947]) in the posttest; however, the change was not significant, $F(1, 31) = 1.046$, $p = .314$, partial $\eta^2 = .033$. There was a significant Token Type x Condition interaction for long /u/, $F(3, 93) = 3.653$, $p = .015$, partial $\eta^2 = .105$. Simple effects tests revealed that for cVV.cv, the ratings for the isolated condition were significantly higher compared to the other token types.

Summary of Nativelikeness Findings

In summary, the nativelikeness of the duration of the short vowels was better following /k/ (vs. /s/), when the vowel was in the second syllable of a token produced in the isolated (vs. carrier sentence) condition, and after perception training. In contrast, production of neither long vowel (/a/, /u/) showed significant improvement in nativelikeness following perception training; however, the duration of both long vowels received higher ratings when produced in the sentence condition, and for the token type cVV.cv.

Duration Measurements of Learners' Vowels

Duration was measured in the expanded waveform display and confirmed with the synchronized spectrogram display and auditory playback. Standard segmentation procedures were applied (e.g., Ladefoged 2003). To measure the duration of a vowel, the beginning was marked at the onset of complex voicing with higher frequency components, and the end was marked at the offset of these components. Vowel durations were analyzed per vowel and are reported in milliseconds (ms). As noted earlier, overall the learners' vowel durations were too long in the pretest; therefore, shorter was the optimal direction for change.

Short Vowel /a/

An initial mixed-design ANOVA revealed no significant effect of training group type, $F(1, 30) = .180$, $p = .674$, partial $\eta^2 = .006$; therefore, data were combined ($N = 32$) for further analyses. The mean duration of short /a/ declined from 146.045 ms ($SD = 46.375$; 95% CIs [129.325, 162.765]) in the pretest to 110.209 ms (*SD* = 32.689; 95% CIs [98.423, 121.972]) in the posttest. A within-group ANOVA revealed a significant effect on duration for preceding consonant, $F(1, 31) = 22.396$, $p < .001$, partial $\eta^2 = .419$; vowel duration was shorter following /k/ (vs. /s/). There was also a significant effect of condition, $F(1, 31) = 20.143$, $p < .001$, partial $\eta^2 = .394$; durations were shorter in the isolated (vs. carrier sentence) condition. There was a significant effect of time, $F(1, 31) = 94.955$, $p < .001$, partial $\eta^2 = .754$ with decreased duration following perception training, and of token type, $F(3, 93) = 18.945$, $p < .001$, partial $\eta^2 = .379$. Following the significant Time x Token Type interaction, $F(3, 93) = 6.901$, $p = < .001$, partial $\eta^2 = .182$, simple effects tests indicated that the decrease in duration (54.97 ms) was greater for token type cV.cvv. Other decreases ranged from a mean of 27.84 ms (cv.cV) to 30.33 ms (cV.cv).

Short Vowel /u/

An initial ANOVA revealed no significant effect of training group type, $F(1, 30) = .174$, $p = .679$, partial $\eta^2 = .005$; therefore, data were combined ($N = 32$) for further analyses. The mean duration of short /u/ declined from 141.716 ms (*SD* = 53.513; 95% CIs [122.422, 161.009] in the pretest to 104.555 ms (*SD* = 31.190; 95% CIs [93.310, 115.799]) in the posttest. There was a significant main effect of time, $F(1, 31) = 75.384$, $p < .001$, partial $\eta^2 = .709$; durations were shorter (optimal direction) following training. There was also a significant Time x Token Type interaction, $F(3, 93) = 6.345$, $p < .001$, partial $\eta^2 = .170$; token type cV.cvv showed the greatest decrease (58.71 ms) in duration following perception training (similar to the findings for short /a/). There was also a significant Time x Token Type x Condition interaction, $F(3, 93) = 3.807$, $p = .019$, partial $\eta^2 = .109$. Simple effects tests revealed that the larger decrease in duration for cV.cvv occurred in the isolated condition.

Long Vowel /a/

An initial ANOVA revealed no significant effect of training group type on duration measurements for long /a/, $F(1, 30) = .323$, $p = .574$, partial $\eta^2 = .011$; therefore, data were combined ($N = 32$) for further analyses. The mean duration of long /a/ declined slightly from 276.101 ms (*SD* = 75.354; 95% CIs [248.933, 303.268]) in the pretest to 270.269 ms (*SD* = 61.831; 95% CIs [247.977, 292.562]) in the posttest. The effect of time (perception training) was not significant, $F(1, 31) = .759$, $p = .390$, partial $\eta^2 = .024$. However, there was a significant effect of consonant, $F(1, 31) = 13.107$, $p < .001$, partial $\eta^2 = .297$; similar to the short vowels, the duration of the target long /a/ was shorter after /k/ (vs. /s/). Durations were significantly shorter for tokens produced in the carrier sentence condition, $F(1, 31) = 6.510$,

$p = .016$, partial $\eta^2 = .174$. There was a significant effect of token type, $F(3, 93) = 3.587$, $p = .017$, partial $\eta^2 = .104$. Pairwise comparisons revealed a significant mean difference of 11.777 ms in the duration of long /a/ between token types cVV.cvv and cVV.cv.

Long Vowel /u/

An initial ANOVA revealed no significant effect of training group type on duration measurements for long /u/, $F(1, 30) = .150$, $p = .701$, partial $\eta^2 = .005$; therefore, data were combined ($N = 32$) for further analyses. Similar to long /a/, the duration of long /u/ showed only a slight decline from 270.852 ms ($SD = 76.323$; 95% CIs [243.335, 298.369]) in the pretest to 265.651 ms ($SD = 66.326$; 95% CIs [241.738, 289.564]) in the posttest. The period of perception training did not result in a significant decrease in the duration of long /u/, $F(1, 31) = .550$, $p = .464$, partial $\eta^2 = .017$. There was a significant Token Type x Condition interaction, $F(3, 93) = 4.571$, $p = .005$, partial $\eta^2 = .129$. Simple effects tests revealed that durations declined more for vowels when they occurred in the first syllable (i.e., cVV.cvv and cVV.cv) in the carrier sentence condition.

Summary of Duration Measurements of Learners' Vowels

In summary, the duration of the vowels produced by learners in both the AV and A-only perception training groups decreased (the optimal direction) following training; however, the change was significant only for the short vowels /a/ and /u/. Tokens involving the short vowels showed a greater decrease in duration when they were produced in the isolated condition; in contrast, measurements revealed that the long vowels were shorter in the carrier sentence condition. The largest decreases in duration in the posttest occurred for the token type cV.cvv for short /a/ and /u/, and for cVV.cv for the long vowels; in both cases, the vowels were in the first syllable. In general, both the target short and long vowels showed a larger decrease in duration when they were produced following /k/ versus /s/.

Correlations between Nativelikeness and Measurement of Learner Vowel Duration

Correlation analysis was conducted to investigate the relationship between the mean rater judgments of nativelikeness and the duration measurements of the learners' vowels. Data were separated by preceding consonant (/k/, /s/), token type (e.g., cV.cv), condition (isolated, carrier sentence), and time (pretest, posttest). For the short vowels /a/ and /u/, all correlations were significant at $p < .001$ and all coefficients were negative; that is, vowel durations that were shorter, which was the optimal direction, were associated with higher nativelikeness ratings. For the long vowels /a/ and /u/, all coefficients were also negative and reached statistical significance although p values were more variable.

Comparison of Vowel Durations Produced by Learners and Native Speakers

The above findings have demonstrated that learners were able to improve their production of Japanese vowel duration toward a more nativelike target following perception training, even in the absence of production instruction. The question arose as to how the improved duration of learners' vowels compared to the duration of the vowels produced by the NSs who had provided the training input, which might provide some insight into the perception-production link. Duration measurements were made of all vowels in the training stimuli to establish ranges for the NSs for comparison with the duration ranges of the learners' vowels.

Table 11.1 presents examples of the results focusing on the short vowels for which learners' productions showed a significant decrease in duration following perception training. The example shown in the first row, *ka̱.kaa* (the measured vowel is underlined), represents token type cV.cvv. As noted earlier, mean duration measurements for this type showed a significantly larger decrease compared to the other token types. The example in the second row, *ka̱.ka* represents token type cV.cv, which showed the next largest decrease in duration in the posttest. As shown in the third row, *ku̱.kuu* represents token type cV.cvv; for short /u/, mean duration measurements showed a larger decrease compared to other types. Note that some of the learners' vowel durations in the posttest approximated those produced by the NSs in the training input.

Table 11.1. Duration Ranges (in milliseconds) for Short Vowels Produced by Learners in the Pretest and Posttest and by Native Speakers (measured vowel is underlined)

Short Vowel	Duration Ranges for Tokens Produced in Isolation			Duration Ranges for Tokens Produced in the Carrier Sentence		
	Learners' Pretest	Learners' Posttest	Native Speakers	Learners' Pretest	Learners' Posttest	Native Speakers
ka̱.kaa	66–327	47–176	45–107	53–282	39–149	34–94
ka̱.ka	62–207	53–128	36–95	50–189	67–142	34–82
ku̱.kuu	48–419	53–178	40–65	48–318	43–155	36–68
ku.ku̱	80–207	57–147	72–133	67–292	56–209	64–148

Source: Hardison and Okuno

DISCUSSION

The current study explored the improvement in L2 Japanese learners' production of vowel duration as a result of perception training with no explicit production instruction. In general, the production pretest revealed that learners' vowel durations were too long. Following perception training, learners were more successful in reducing the duration of the short vowels (/a/, /u/) they produced compared to the long vowels, perhaps the result of focusing attention on one vowel length at a time. Higher ratings of nativelikeness correlated significantly with shorter durations. The duration ranges of some of the learners' posttest vowel productions approximated the ranges of the vowels produced by the NSs they had heard during training.

Although the improvement shown by the learners in both the AV and A-only training groups did not differ to a statistically significant degree, a longer training period with more sessions using waveforms might have allowed a significant difference to emerge as suggested by the findings of two other studies using waveform displays. Olson and Offerman (2021) found greater benefit in VOT training with waveforms in L2 Spanish when learners received more instructional interventions. In addition, Motohashi-Saigo and Hardison (2009) found a significant advantage in L2 production improvement for the group that saw waveforms during perception training involving the duration difference between geminate and singleton consonants in Japanese. Participants in that study reported enjoyment in being able to work with web-based training and found it helpful in understanding the concept of segmental duration. Similar views were reported by the participants in the current study.

IMPLICATIONS FOR TEACHING SEGMENTAL DURATION

Based on the positive views of learners toward the use of technology in the above studies and others, teachers of Japanese as a second or foreign language can easily incorporate waveform displays into in-class listening practice. In a beginning-level Japanese class, it is very common to introduce the topic of vowel and consonant duration (i.e., short and long vowels, singleton and geminate consonants). Teachers usually provide learners with only auditory input and/or orthographic information when introducing the durational contrasts and during listening practice. However, at that point in the curriculum, teachers can also present waveform displays as visual input along with the auditory input.

Sample waveforms could be shown to learners to exemplify target changes in duration. For example, figure 11.4 shows waveforms for the pretest and

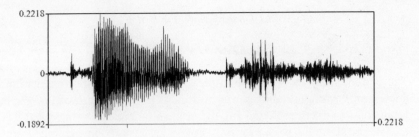

(a) Pretest: *kaka* (judged by NS raters as *kaaka*)

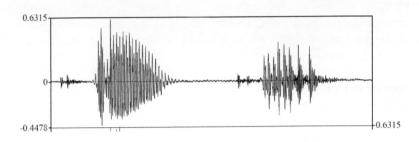

(b) Posttest: *kaka*

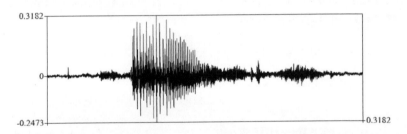

(c) Pretest: *sasa* (judged by NS raters as *saasa*)

(d) Posttest: *sasa*

Figure 11.4. Sample Waveforms of a Learner's Production of kaka (a: pretest, b: posttest), and sasa (c: pretest, b: posttest).

Source: Hardison and Okuno

posttest productions of *kaka* and *sasa* by a learner in the current study. These data are representative of the predominant pretest error pattern for this token type (i.e., CV.CV) in which the vowel in the first syllable tended to have an exaggerated duration leading to the perception by NSs that it was a long vowel. The posttest durations were accurate.

In addition, teachers can assign listening and pronunciation practice outside the classroom because it is not common for a Japanese language textbook to include listening identification and pronunciation practice exercises for the durational contrasts. Simple assignments can be created for practice online using a course management website (e.g., Desire2Learn or CANVAS). The second author uses waveforms in teaching her college-level Japanese classes. When learners practice durational contrasts, they can listen to the words containing the contrasts and see the corresponding waveform displays, respond to an identification task (i.e., listen to a word and choose what they think they hear), and repeat the words to practice their pronunciation. After the learners practice pronouncing the words, they can audio-record their pronunciation and submit the recording to receive feedback. When teachers give feedback on the learners' mistakes, they can show the waveform displays so that the learners can identify their problems visually. In this way, teachers can incorporate into their lessons many simple and useful listening and pronunciation practice opportunities using waveform displays.

CONCLUSION

In conclusion, displays such as waveforms can serve as meaningful visual input for learners to help them improve their perception and production of contrastive segmental duration involving vowels and consonants for languages such as Japanese given the importance of this feature for communication. This input can be a part of in-class activities to ensure learners have the necessary knowledge to use the technology and interpret the displays when they work on assignments outside of class.

NOTE

1. The symbol /u/ is used for typographical ease to represent the high back unrounded vowel in Japanese which is produced with lip compression.

REFERENCES

Banno, Eri, Yoko Ikeda, Yutaka Ohno, Chikako Shinagawa and Kyoko Tokashiki. 2020. *GENKI: An Integrated Course in Elementary Japanese I*, 3rd ed. Tokyo: The Japan Times.

Boersma, Paul, and Weenink, David. 2014. "Praat: Doing phonetics by computer." http://www.fon.hum.uva.nl/praat/

Bradlow, Ann, Reiko Akahane-Yamada, David B. Pisoni, and Yoh'ichi Tohkura. 1999. "Training Japanese Listeners to Identify English /r/ and /l/: Long-term Retention of Learning in Perception and Production." *Perception & Psychophysics* 61, no. 5: 977–985. https://doi.org/10.3758/BF03206911

Bundgaard-Nielsen, Rikke L., Catherine T. Best, and Michael D. Tyler. 2011. "Vocabulary Size Matters: The Assimilation of Second-Language Australian English Vowels to First-Language Japanese Vowel Categories." *Applied Psycholinguistics* 32, no. 1: 51–67. https://doi.org/10.1017/SO142716410000287

Chun, Dorothy M., Yan Jiang, Justine Meyr, and Rong Yang. 2015. "Acquisition of L2 Mandarin Chinese Tones with Learner-Created Tone Visualizations." *Journal of Second Language Pronunciation,* 1, no. 1: 86–114. https://doi.org/10.1075/jslp.1.1.04chu

de Jong, Kenneth, Yen-Chen Hao, and Hanyong Park. 2009. "Evidence for Featural Units in the Acquisition of Speech Production Skills: Linguistic Structure in Foreign Accent." *Journal of Phonetics* 37, no. 4: 357–373. https://doi.org/10.1016/j.wocn.2009.06.001

Field, Andy. 2018. *Discovering Statistics Using IBM® SPSS® Statistics*, 5th ed. Los Angeles: Sage.

Haraguchi, Shosuke. 1999. "Accent." In *The handbook of Japanese linguistics*, edited by Natsuko Tsujimura, 1–30. Malden, MA: Blackwell.

Hardison, Debra M. 2003. "Acquisition of Second-Language Speech: Effects of Visual Cues, Context and Talker Variability." *Applied Psycholinguistics* 24, no. 4: 495–522. https://doi.org/10.1017/S0142716403000250

Hardison, Debra M. 2004. "Generalization of Computer-Assisted Prosody Training: Quantitative and Qualitative Findings." *Language Learning & Technology* 8, no. 1: 34–52. https://www.lltjournal.org/item/2458

Hardison, Debra M. 2005. "Second-Language Spoken Word Identification: Effects of Perceptual Training, Visual Cues, and Phonetic Environment." *Applied Psycholinguistics* 26, no. 4: 579–596. https://doi.org/10.1017/S0142716405050319

Hardison, Debra M. 2012. "Second-Language Speech Perception: A Cross-Disciplinary Perspective on Challenges and Accomplishments." In *The Routledge Handbook of Second Language Acquisition*, edited by Susan M. Gass and Alison Mackey, 349–363. New York: Routledge.

Hardison, Debra M. 2018. "Effects of Contextual and Visual Cues on Spoken Language Processing: Enhancing L2 Perceptual Salience Through Focused Training." In *Salience in Second Language Acquisition*, edited by Susan M. Gass, Patti Spinner, and Jennifer Behney, 201–220. New York: Routledge.

Hardison, Debra M. 2021. "Multimodal Input in Second-Language Speech Processing. *Language Teaching* 54, no. 2: 206–220. https://doi.org/10.1017/S026144482 0000592

Hirata, Yukari, and Spencer D. Kelly. 2010. "Effects of Lips and Hands on Auditory Learning of Second-Language Speech Sounds. *Journal of Speech, Language, and Hearing Research* 53, no. 2: 298–310. https://doi.org/10.1044/1092-4388 (2009/08-0243)

Hirata, Yukari, Spencer D. Kelly, Jessica Huang, and Michael Manansala. 2014. "Effects of Hand Gestures on Auditory Learning of Second-Language Vowel Length Contrasts." *Journal of Speech, Language, and Hearing Research* 57, no. 6: 2090–2101. https://doi.org/10.1044/2014_JSLHR-S-14-0049

Hui, C. T. Justin, and Takayuki Arai. 2020. "Pitch and Duration as Auditory Cues to Identify Japanese Long Vowels for Japanese Learners." *Acoustical Science & Technology* 41, 5. https://doi.org/10.1250/ast.41.796

Inceoglu, Solène. 2016. "Effects of Perception Training on L2 Vowel Perception and Production." *Applied Psycholinguistics* 37, no. 5: 1175–1199. https://doi.org/10.1017/S0142716415000533

Kinoshita, Keisuke, Dawn M. Behne, and Takayuki Arai. 2002. "Duration and F0 as Perceptual Cues to Japanese Vowel Quantity." *Proceedings of the 7th International Conference on Spoken Language Processing*, 757–760.

Koguma, Rie. 2000. "Perception of Japanese Short and Long Vowels by English-Speaking Learners." *Current Report on Japanese-Language Education around the Globe* 10: 43–55.

Kubozono, Haruo. 1999. "Mora and Syllable." In *The handbook of Japanese linguistics*, edited by Natsuko Tsujimura, 31–61. Malden, MA: Blackwell.

Ladefoged, Peter. 2003. *Phonetic Data Analysis: An Introduction to Fieldwork and Instrumental Techniques*. Malden, MA: Blackwell.

Lively, Scott E., John S. Logan, and David B. Pisoni. 1993. "Training Japanese Listeners to Identify English /r/ and /l/. II: The Role of Phonetic Environment and Talker Variability in Learning New Perceptual Categories." *Journal of the Acoustical Society of America* 94, no. 3, Pt 1: 1242–1255. https://doi.org/10.1121/1.408177

Minagawa, Yasuyo. 1997. "Sokuon no shikibetsu niokeru accent-gaga to shiinshu no yooin: kankoku, tai, chuugoku, ei, seigo bogowasha no baai. [Accent Patterns and Segment Places as a Factor for Perceiving Japanese Long and Short Vowels by Native Speakers of Korean, Thai, Chinese, English, and Spanish]." In *Proceedings of the Spring Meeting of the Society for Teaching Japanese as a Foreign Language*, 123–128.

Motohashi-Saigo, Miki, and Debra M. Hardison. 2009. "Acquisition of L2 Japanese Geminates: Training with Waveform Displays. *Language Learning & Technology* 13, no. 2: 29–47. https://www.lltjournal.org/item/2665.

Offerman, Heather M., and Daniel J. Olson. 2016. "Visual Feedback and Second Language Segmental Production: The Generalizability of Pronunciation Gains." *System* 59: 45–60. https://doi.org/10.1016/j.system.2016.03.003.

Okuno, Tomoko, and Debra M. Hardison. 2016. "Perception-Production Link in L2 Japanese Vowel Duration: Training with Technology." *Language Learning & Technology* 20, no. 2: 61–80. https://www.lltjournal.org/item/2947.

Olson, Daniel J. 2014. "Benefits of Visual Feedback on Segmental Production in the L2 Classroom." *Language Learning & Technology* 18, no. 3: 173–192. http://dx.doi.org/10125/44389

Olson, Daniel J., and Heather M. Offerman. 2021. "Maximizing the Effect of Visual Feedback for Pronunciation Instruction: A Comparative Analysis of Three Approaches." *Journal of Second Language Pronunciation* 7, no. 1: 89–115. https://doi.org/10.1075/jslp.20005.ols

Psychology Software Tools, Inc. 2016. *E-Prime 3.0*. Retrieved from https://support.pstnet.com

Tsujimura, Natsuko. 2013. *An Introduction to Japanese Linguistics* 3rd ed. Hoboken, NJ: Wiley- Blackwell.

Wang, Xinchun. 2012. "Auditory and Visual Training on Mandarin Tones: A Pilot Study on Phrases and Sentences." *International Journal of Computer-Assisted Language Learning and Teaching,* IGI Global 2 no. 2: 16–29. https://doi.org/10.4018/ijcallt.2012040102

Wiener, Seth, and Seth Goss. 2019. "Second and Third Language Learners' Sensitivity to Japanese Pitch Accent is Additive: An Information-based Model of Pitch Perception." *Studies in Second Language Acquisition* 41, no. 4: 897–910. https://doi.org/10.1017/S0272263119000068

Yoshida, Yuko. 2006. "Accents in Tokyo and Kyoto Japanese Vowel Quality in Terms of Duration and Licensing Potency." *SOAS Working Papers in Linguistics* 14: 249–264.

Chapter Twelve

Speech Visualization for Pronunciation Instruction

Exploring Instructor Support in L2 Learner Attitudes Toward Visual Feedback

Heather M. Offerman and Daniel J. Olson

INTRODUCTION

With the advent of easily accessible speech visualization software, like Praat (Boersma and Weenink 2018), researchers and second language instructors have begun to leverage this technology for pronunciation instruction, often through visual feedback paradigms. Visual feedback can describe any instruction/training in which second language learners receive feedback on their pronunciation through some type of visual display. Additionally, visual feedback instruction usually consists of learners producing the target stimuli, a visual display of the relevant acoustic features of the learner's production and those of a native speaker for comparison, and an opportunity for learners to produce stimuli again to approximate the native speaker model. A growing body of research has validated the use of visual feedback for pronunciation instruction, with learner improvements in a variety of segmental phonetic features (Okuno 2013; Olson 2014b; Olson and Offerman 2021; Saito 2007). However, considerably less work has addressed student attitudes toward visual feedback in the classroom (c.f., Offerman 2020a), and currently, no research has specifically examined student assessments of the contributions of instructor support in using this technology.

This chapter directly addresses this gap, examining learner attitudes following a variety of visual feedback training-types, and exploring the interplay between instructor support and students' attitudes toward visual feedback. The research aims are addressed through a combination of quantitative and qualitative analyses. Participants included two groups of intermediate-level second language learners of Spanish, all of whom participated in classroom-based visual feedback activities ($n = 69$). Instructor involvement varied from minimal (i.e., inductive paradigm) to significant (i.e., visual feedback coupled with explicit phonetic instruction). Quantitative data are provided from Likert-scale responses from attitude-oriented surveys, with statements addressing both the usability of the technology (see Offerman 2020a) and student satisfaction with speech visualization technology. Qualitative data come from open-ended participant responses. Results demonstrate that learners generally find the technology to be useful and user-friendly with a preference for more direct support from the instructor. The importance of the instructor support is further highlighted in the qualitative analysis, in which participants from both groups regarded instructor involvement as essential to their comprehension and execution of visual feedback tasks. Finally, this chapter provides several practical strategies to consider when implementing visual feedback in the second language classroom.

LITERATURE REVIEW

An Introduction to Visual Feedback

Broadly defined, visual feedback (VF) is the use of visual representations of speech sounds or articulatory movements (or both) as a pedagogical tool for teaching or improving second language (L2) pronunciation. With VF, learners visualize their own speech, and often the speech of native speakers, to facilitate the acquisition process (Olson and Offerman 2021). Drawing on the current literature, the most common approach to VF consists of learners recording their own speech, examining visual representations (i.e., waveforms, spectrograms, intonation contours) with a focus on a particular pre-determined feature, and comparing their production with that of a native speaker. A sample production of the word *pato* (/pa.to/) can be seen below in figure 12.1, displaying the visual features that correlate to each segment.

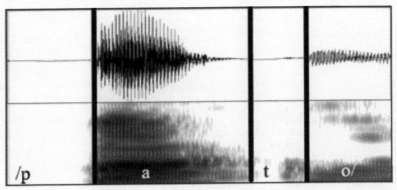

Figure 12.1. Word pato produced by a native speaker of Spanish & segmented.
Source: Heather M. Offerman

From a theoretical perspective, VF draws on the notion of "noticing." According to Schmidt's (1990) Noticing Hypothesis, learners must first notice differences between the first language (L1) and L2 for successful acquisition. Differences that learners notice between the L1 and L2 form 'intake,' which leads to acquisition (Schmidt 1995), and several have noted the importance of noticing in phonetic acquisition (e.g., Derwing and Munro 2005). With respect to L2 phonetics, there is evidence that while some differences between the L1 and L2 are significant and easily noticed (and acquired) by learners, other differences may be subtle and, particularly when processed by an auditory system attuned to the L1, are not easily noticed. For example, the Speech Learning Model (SLM; Flege 1995) suggests that the ability to successfully produce a given sound in the L2 is directly related to the similarity between the new L2 sound and existing sounds in the L1. While L2 sounds that are substantially different from those in the L1 may easily be established as a new category, L2 sounds that are similar to existing sounds in the L1 may be subsumed into the existing L1 category (see also the Perceptual Assimilation Model—L2; Best and Tyler 2007). As such, VF may provide a secondary type of input from the visual modality to allow learners to notice differences between L1 and L2 phonetics and phonology (i.e., pronunciation) not easily perceived otherwise.

As VF encompasses varying methods, several important distinctions should be highlighted. Kartushina et al. (2015), for example, distinguished between direct and indirect VF. Indirect VF, the most common VF approach, consists of providing a visual representation of an acoustic feature, which corresponds to an aspect of the learner's pronunciation. Within indirect feedback, researchers and practitioners have used different types of visual images, depending on the pronunciation feature to be addressed, including intonation contours (de Bot 1980; Chun 1989), waveforms (Akahane-Yamada et al. 1998), spectrograms (Olson 2014b), and representations of the vowel space (Kartushina et al. 2015), to facilitate the acquisition. In contrast, direct VF consists of providing a visual image of the learner's speech articulators, using technology such as ultrasound (Pillot-Loiseau, Antolík, and Kamiyama 2013) or palatography and often requires specialized technology, such as portable ultrasound machines. In contrast, indirect VF can be successfully employed using only a personal computer, microphone, and specialized (free) software.

Several different programs are widely available and adaptable to VF in the L2 classroom, including Praat (e.g., Olson 2014b) Visi-Pitch (e.g., Molholt 1998), My English Tutor (e.g., Tsai 2019), WinPitch (e.g., Sandryhaila-Groth and Martin 2016), Vowel Viewer (e.g., Rehman and Flint 2021), Sonamatch (e.g., Klaus et al. 2019), and Accent Master (Saleh and Gilakjani 2021). To date, Praat (Boersma and Weenink 2018) is the most commonly used software for providing VF, although some authors have noted that Praat is not specifically designed with L2 learners as the target audience (e.g., Olson

2014a). The selection of the features to be addressed and the software program to be used is discussed further in section 2.

Research-basis for VF Use

While VF as a method of pronunciation instruction was initially developed in tandem with access to the personal computer (e.g., de Bot 1980), the body of research on the efficacy of VF has grown significantly in recent years. Taken as a whole, this body of research has demonstrated that VF can be a successful method of teaching pronunciation across a range of different phonetic features and language pairings and is likely to create generalizable, long-lasting improvements.

Considering the features that have been addressed using VF paradigms and cognizant of the role that intuitiveness may play in their outcomes (Olson 2014b), the earliest VF activities addressed sentence-level intonation contours. De Bot and colleagues (e.g., de Bot 1980; 1983; Weltens and de Bot 1984) performed a series of lab-based interventions targeting L2 intonation contours in which participants were given feedback in either an auditory-only or an audio-visual modality. Their results showed an advantage in the acquisition of L2 intonation contours for the groups that received audio-visual feedback. Similarly positive results have been found in the production of novel utterances (e.g., Hardison 2004) and the teaching of discourse-level intonation (Chun 1998; 2002; Levis and Pickering 2004). Improvements in the production of intonation contours have been shown across multiple language pairings, different types of learners (see Sandryhalia-Groth 2019), and different styles of intonation contours (Spaai and Hermes 1993). Although early research focused on suprasegmental features, VF has also been shown to significantly improve various segmental features (e.g., consonants and vowels). For example, Motohashi-Saigo and Hardison (2009) found significant improvement in the perceptual identification accuracy of singleton—geminate distinctions in L2 Japanese (L1 English) following training of waveforms and spectrograms relative to an audio-only control group (i.e., learners only observed waveforms as feedback). Similarly, several studies by Olson and Offerman (Offerman 2020b; Offerman and Olson 2016; Olson 2019; Olson and Offerman 2021) found a significant improvement in the production of voice onset time for voiceless stop consonants for L2 learners of Spanish. Beyond duration-based contrasts, other research has shown promising results for approximants (Olson 2014b), emphatic or pharyngealized consonants (Binasfour, Setter, and Aslan 2017), and stop-rhotic clusters (Hernández Morales 2017). Results for vowel production have been somewhat less consistent, with some studies showing significant improvement in vowel production, specifically location within the vowel space (e.g., Rehman and Flint 2021; Saito 2007), while others have shown mixed results or no effect (e.g., Carey 2004; Ruellot 2011). Similarly, mixed results have been shown for vowel duration, with Okuno (2013) finding a significant improvement in *absolute* L2 vowel durations following VF training, but Olson (2021) failing to find any improvement in *relative* L2 vowel durations (i.e., stressed vs. unstressed). Despite mixed results for vowels, this growing body of research suggests that VF is an effective mechanism for L2 pronunciation instruction across a wide range of suprasegmental and segmental features.

Recent work has also begun to look at the reach (i.e., generalizability) and longevity of such gains, as both are relevant for determining the overall utility. Several studies have established that gains made during a VF paradigm generalize to new stimuli. For example, Offerman (2020b) conducted a VF paradigm focused on word-initial voice onset time in L2 Spanish—L1 English-speaking learners. Following three VF interventions, results demonstrated significant improvement of word-initial voice onset time. More importantly, these results generalized to novel stimuli that were not included in the training paradigms and to productions in a spontaneous speech task. Similar results have been found for suprasegmental features (Hardison 2004). Assessing the generalization of gains in perception, Okuno and Hardison (2016) conducted a VF paradigm focused on improving the perception and categorization of vowel duration in L2 Japanese—L1 English-speaking learners. Following an eight-session intervention with VF (i.e., waveforms), results demonstrated a significant improvement in the perception of L2 vowel duration. Again, these results generalized to novel stimuli and speakers not included in the training paradigm, suggesting that the gains made following VF are linked to the underlying phonological representations, rather than limited to trained items. Moreover, several studies with delayed posttests (see Offerman and Olson 2016; Olson 2014b; Olson 2019; Olson 2021) suggest that the improvements in L2 pronunciation resulting from VF training may be long-lasting, persisting several weeks after instruction.

Finally, research has demonstrated that VF can be easily integrated into the L2 classroom (see Olson 2014a). Some researchers have implemented VF essentially as a stand-alone lesson, with minimal instructor guidance (Olson 2014a), while others have used more significant instructor guidance with the technology (Offerman 2020b) or have included VF as one component of a more multifaceted approach to pronunciation in the classroom (Lord 2005). Although some researchers initially suggested that VF technology, designed for researchers, was ill-suited for learners to use effectively (e.g., Setter and Jenkins 2005), students' assessments of VF technology have been positive, citing both its usability and utility (e.g., Olson 2014a; Offerman 2020a).

Taken as a whole, the current literature shows that VF is an effective method of L2 pronunciation teaching that can be employed to teach a range of suprasegmental and segmental features. Improvements found following VF are both generalizable to novel stimuli and spontaneous conversation, as well as potentially long-lasting. This paradigm has gained a degree of ecological validity, as it has been successfully integrated into the classroom in ways that benefit learners.

L2 Learner Attitudes

While VF paradigms have been shown to be effective for phonetic acquisition, L2 learners' perspectives on these interventions are also relevant. As several researchers have noted, pronunciation is viewed by L2 learners as an important L2 skill, and learners want more direction in developing L2 pronunciation (Drewelow and Theobald 2007; Olson 2014a). In fact, Huensch and Thompson (2017) showed that learners considered pronunciation as more important than other L2 linguistic skills. Other studies suggest that L2 learners believe that pronunciation instruction is crucial to their language learning (Sturm, Miyamoto, and Suzuki 2019) and that pronunciation-focused activities can enhance awareness, or noticing, of features to move toward improvement.

As learners regard L2 pronunciation as essential to their language development, several authors have called for an analysis of both the outcomes and learners' perspectives of different types of pedagogical activities (Jarosz 2019). While several studies have examined learner perspectives on pronunciation instruction more broadly, few studies have comparatively evaluated varying methods. On a smaller scale, Offerman (2020a) looked at learner views on the utility of a VF paradigm, an explicit instructional approach void of any form of VF, and the combination of both the VF and explicit treatments. While results concluded that all groups viewed their specific treatment as useful, it is worth exploring on a larger scale the learner views of a VF-only paradigm and the concept of a more explicit VF treatment that incorporates more instructor involvement.

Research Questions

Addressing this gap, the current study examines student evaluations of VF paradigms in L2 pronunciation training, considering specifically the role of the instructor (inductive vs. explicit) in facilitating such training. The guiding research questions were:

RQ1. Does the degree of instructor support (limited guidance for the inductive approach vs. substantial guidance for the explicit approach) impact learners' evaluations of how useful and enjoyable VF training is?

RQ2. Do learners prefer an inductive VF paradigm, with minimal instructor involvement, or an explicit VF paradigm, with greater instructor involvement?

RQ's 1 and 2 are both addressed via quantitative (i.e., Likert-scale survey) and qualitative (i.e., participant responses to open-ended questions) methods.

METHODS

The current study involved two groups of learners, who differed with respect to the degree of support provided by the instructor. The first group ($n = 52$), henceforth called the Inductive Group (IG), consisted of L1 English—L2 Spanish learners who participated in a VF paradigm with a guided inductive approach (Olson 2014b). This approach included *minimal instructor involvement* and largely relied on learners to draw their own conclusions about the differences between the L1 and L2 pronunciation. The second group ($n = 17$), the Explicit Group (EG), consisted of L1 English—L2 Spanish learners who participated in a VF paradigm with a more explicit approach. In this explicit approach, the instructor played a crucial role, providing detailed explanations of the visual representations and the features under consideration. The participants and methods for the IG and EG groups are further detailed below.

Inductive Group

The IG was drawn from three different studies (Offerman 2020b; Offerman and Olson 2016; Olson 2014b), each considering different features or involving different populations, yet united by the minimal instructor support provided during an inductive VF paradigm. The methods for each of three subgroups are detailed below, although they are collapsed in the analysis.

Inductive Subgroup A (Offerman and Olson 2016)

In Inductive Subgroup A (IG-A), all participants ($n = 17$) were enrolled in a fourth semester Spanish course and completed a language background questionnaire confirming their monolingual status (Offerman and Olson 2016); all participants had begun learning Spanish after the age of 12, had spent no more than six weeks in a Spanish-speaking country, and only had learned

English from birth in and outside of the home. Training consisted of three, 15–20-minute, biweekly interventions involving word-initial voiceless stops (/p, t, k/). Word-initial voiceless stops have long-lag voice onset time (VOT) in English and short-lag VOT in Spanish (Lisker and Abramson 1964). Use of the long-lag variants by English-speaking learners of L2 Spanish is an indicator of accented speech (Lord 2005). Thus, VF was employed with L2 learners in reducing VOT values from the pretest to the posttest. During each of the three interventions, L2 learners compared images of their recorded productions to productions of NSs of Spanish and asked to draw conclusions about cross-linguistic differences. Across four tasks (tokens embedded in a carrier phrase, utterances, short story, and spontaneous speech tasks) participants had significantly improved their productions in Spanish from the pretest to posttest and outperformed a matched control group (see Offerman & Olson 2016 for further analyses).

Inductive Subgroup B (Olson 2014b)

For Inductive Subgroup B (IG-B), participants (n = 22) in a third semester Spanish course took part in a VF treatment, similar to the one described for IG-A. Participants in this group were also considered to be monolingual English speakers. Parallel to Subgroup A, three, 15–20-minute, biweekly VF trainings were conducted. Interventions focused on intervocalic voiced /b, d, g/, which are realized in English as the stops [b, d, g] and Spanish as the approximants [β, ð, ɣ] (Hualde 2005), as English-speaking learners of Spanish typically produce the variants [b, d, g] in their L2 Spanish (Lord 2010). Participants compared their productions to productions by native Spanish speakers, drawing conclusions about cross-linguistic differences. Participants recorded tokens in a carrier phrase and utterances at the pretest and posttest. Across both stimuli types, participant productions significantly improved from the pretest to posttest.

It is worth noting that IG-B differed from the other subgroups and the explicit group in the phonemes under consideration. As the goal of the current paper is to provide a broad investigation into the role of instructor support in VF, the decision was made to include this group, leveraging the additional variability in phonemes to provide a more holistic view of instructor support in VF.

Inductive Subgroup C (Offerman 2020b)

In Inductive Subgroup C (IG-C), participants (n = 13) took part in a VF paradigm similar to Subgroup A. Participants were determined as monolingual English speakers based on the same criteria listed for Subgroup A. Participants took part in three, biweekly trainings focusing on /p,t,k/, comparing their productions to those produced by native Spanish speakers. Results across four tasks (tokens in a carrier phrase, utterances, short story, and spontaneous speech) showed significant improvement of productions at the posttest relative to the pretest. Again, all three subgroups in the IG group are united by the inductive approach of the VF paradigm, with no discussion of the articulatory or acoustic differences between the L1 and L2.

Explicit Group (Offerman 2020b)

Participants ($n = 17$) in the EG were enrolled in a third-semester Spanish course, with all participants considered monolingual English speakers based on the same criteria as the IG. The EG participated in three, biweekly VF paradigms focused on the pronunciation of word-initial voiceless stops /p, t, k/, which differ cross-linguistically between English and Spanish. Parallel to the IG-A and IG-C, participants produced word-initial voiceless stops in four tasks, increasing in complexity (carrier phrase, utterance, short story, and spontaneous speech elicitation tasks).

As with the IG, the VF paradigm consisted of comparing the learners' L2 productions to native speaker productions. The key distinction between the IG and EG is seen in the additional explicit instruction component in the EG. The explicit instruction included discussion of the international phonetic alphabet (IPA) symbols alongside visual representations. Moreover, explicit explanations of the articulatory and auditory differences between English and Spanish word-initial stops were provided by the instructor, along with explicit explanations of the visual displays (i.e., waveforms and spectrograms). Results of this study concluded that participants improved significantly from pretest to posttest across all tasks.

Instruments

While the outcomes (i.e., improvements in pronunciation) in the studies above supported the use of a VF training, it is worth considering the attitudes and views of the participants regarding the two methods (i.e., inductive vs. explicit) employed to teach pronunciation. Following the completion of each of the studies detailed above, participants were asked to complete a brief questionnaire with 17–18 Likert-scale items and several open-ended questions.

For the quantitative assessments, a nine-point Likert scale was employed, with labeled endpoints (1 = Agree, 9 = Disagree) and a midpoint (5 = Neutral).

Participants were asked to indicate their level of agreement with a given statement. A subset of five statements were relevant to the research questions in the current study and addressed three unique categories: (1) usefulness of the VF interventions to the participants (three statements), (2) the "likeability" of the VF method (one statement), and (3) the importance of the instructor role (one statement). The statements are listed in tables 12.1–12.3.

Two minor differences in the questionnaires should be noted. First, the wording of the Likert-scale questions in the IG-B[1] was somewhat different than for the other subgroups, but conceptually similar (see Appendix A). Second, the wording of the statement regarding instructor role (or technology for the IG-B group), differed between one of the three subgroups, as seen in Examples 1 and 2. Given this difference, responses to this statement by the IG-B were reverse scored.

Role of the Instructor

1. IG-A & IG-C Groups: The teacher's guided instruction for this activity was useful for improving my pronunciation.
2. IG-B Group: A program like Praat allows me to improve pronunciation without the instructor correcting me.

For the open-ended questions assessed for the qualitative results, two questions were included, addressing: (1) whether learners thought that the VF paradigm was a good way to improve pronunciation, and (2) whether learners found the teacher or the computer program to be more useful. Worth noting, IG-B answered only the second question, and as such, analysis of the first open-ended question relies on a somewhat smaller set of participants (IG, $n = 30$; EG, $n = 17$).

RESULTS

Quantitative

For the quantitative analyses, descriptive statistics (means and standard deviations) and group comparisons (t-tests) were conducted. Results are presented here for the learner assessments of usefulness of the intervention, likeability, and the importance of the instructor guidance. Table 12.1 is provided below as a reference for statements that correspond to each of the three categories assessed.

Table 12.1. Quantitative Results for Usefulness (1–3), Likeability (4), and Instructor Role (5)

	IG	EG
1. This method is good for understanding ways in which to practice and improve my pronunciation.	2.74 (1.77)	2.72 (1.74)
2. This activity made me think consciously about my pronunciation.	2.57 (1.71)	2.28 (1.71)
3. The visual analysis software we learned about was useful for improving my pronunciation.	3.38 (2.30)	3.10 (2.10)
4. I thought this activity was enjoyable.	3.88 (2.41)	4.39 (1.75)
5. The teacher's guided instruction (IG)/explicit instruction (EG) for this activity was useful for improving my pronunciation.	3.92 (3.54)	2.17 (1.47)

Source: Heather M. Offerman and Daniel J. Olson

Usefulness

Observing the descriptive statistics (table 12.1) for learner assessments of the usefulness of the method, averages show that both groups felt that the treatment they received was beneficial for their learning. Specifically, both groups reported that the pedagogical activity was a good way to improve pronunciation (Statement 1) and helped them think consciously about their own pronunciation (Statement 2). Addressing the software itself (Statement 3), participants from both groups reported that the software was useful for improving their pronunciation, although ratings were somewhat higher (i.e., disagreed more) for this statement than the other two in the category of usefulness.

Comparing the quantitative responses from both groups, a series of independent sample, two-tailed, t-tests were run. While the EG rated Statements 1–3 more positively than the IG, the t-tests showed that there were no significant differences between group ratings for any of the three statements (Statement 1: $t(30) = 0.048$, $p = .962$, $d = 0.011$; Statement 2: $t(30) = 0.048$, $p = .539$, $d = 0.170$; Statement 3: $t(34) = 0.347$, $p = .731$, $d = 0.127$).

Likeability

Considering how much each group enjoyed the pedagogical activity, both groups somewhat agreed that they enjoyed their respective treatments, with the IG collectively indicating that they enjoyed the activities more than the EG (table 12.1). However, the t-test results, once again, reveal no significant differences between group ratings (Statement 4: $t(42) = 1.089$, $p = .282$, $d = 0.242$).

Importance of Instructor Involvement

With respect to importance of instructor (table 12.3), averages indicate that the IG somewhat agreed that the teacher guidance was helpful for their treatment-type, while the EG agreed that the explicit instruction by the teacher was helpful. The t-test revealed a significant difference between group ratings, with the EG holding a more positive view of the instructor role in their treatment-type than the IG (Statement 5: $t(60) = 3.208$, $p = .002$, $d = 0.646$).

Taken as a whole, positive results from both groups suggested that learners found the VF activities, whether inductive or explicit in their approach, were useful and enjoyable. The only notable difference between the groups was found in considering the role of the instructor, with the EG demonstrating more positive views of instructor involvement.

Qualitative

Qualitative results consisted of participant responses to two open-ended questions at the end of each survey, which inquired (1) whether the treatment-type (inductive or explicit) was viewed as a useful way to practice and improve pronunciation, and (2) whether the "computer program" or the instructor was perceived as more useful to their pronunciation learning.[2] For statements about the "computer program" or instructor preference, each statement was categorized as being either the teacher, technology, or both, and examples of these are provided in the analysis below.

Preference of Instructor Importance vs. VF Analysis

With respect to the question "Do you feel like the computer program or the teacher instruction was most useful? Why?," 24 out of 27 IG participants (IG-A and IG-C) indicated that they preferred the teacher instruction over the computer program. Examples, tagged with group, subgroup (for the IG group) and participant number, include:

(1) IG-A 02: "I liked the activity, but I don't think I would have understood without my teacher's guidance."
(2) IG-C 10: ". . . teacher instruction was most useful because she could explain things to me."
(3) IG-A 07: "Definitely the teacher."
(4) IG-C 08: "The teacher instruction was more useful—easier."
(5) IG-A 11: "The teacher—it was really hard to understand the soundwaves and what they meant by themselves."

(6) IG-C 03: "Teacher instruction; it's more personalized/ interactive."
(7) IG-C 05: "The teacher because she speaks Spanish well and helps us."

In examples (1)–(7), each response reveals a positive regard for instructor involvement, reemphasizing the preference of the teacher instruction as opposed to sole use of the computer program in completing and understanding the treatment. Examples (1)–(5) specifically note that the participants relied on further guidance from the instructor and indicate a lack of understanding with respect to the meaning of the visual representations without any instructor assistance. Additionally, examples (6) and (7) express the benefit of interacting with the instructor while taking part in the treatment, indicating that this component is beneficial to them.

Of the EG participants, eight of the 17 participants responded that the instructor guidance was most useful, five participants provided responses indicating the visual analysis was most useful, and four provided comments stating that they believed the combination of the two methods was the most useful to their learning. Examples for each can be found below:

(8) EG 07: "I feel like the teacher's instructions were more helpful because listening to him speak was easier than visualizing it."
(9) EG 12: "Teacher instruction, it was difficult to understand what the visual analysis meant without explanation."
(10) EG 01: "The computer program was more helpful because I could actually see how I was pronouncing the word."
(11) EG 15: "I feel like it was a combination of both. The program allowed us to practice and hear how we sounded, while the teacher taught us the correct pronunciation."
(12) EG 16: "Both were useful to explain how to improve."

Here, examples (8) and (9) provide more insight regarding the preference of the instructor role, with one participant noting their preference for auditory modeling while the other indicated that interpretation of the visual representations was not easily extrapolated without the teacher instruction. Example (10) demonstrates that for some, the visualization of sounds was perceived as more useful than the teacher instruction to make observations about their own pronunciation as well as the opportunity to compare their productions to those of NSs. Further, both components together ("teacher instruction" and the "computer program") were favored, as seen in examples (11) and (12), with one participant specifically stating they found the feedback from the computer program accompanied by the teacher instruction the most useful.

Broadly, the qualitative analysis shows that learners appreciate instructor guidance with VF. Of note, the IG, which completed an inductive VF activity with little instructor involvement, showed the greatest preference or desire for greater instructor involvement, relative to the EG. In other words, while participants believe the VF paradigm to be beneficial, the current results indicate that perhaps a more combined methodology of VF and explicit instruction would provide a more straightforward approach to facilitate L2 learning, similar to the methods employed by Lord (2005) and Kartushina et al. (2015).

Views on Usefulness of Treatment

Of the original 52 IG participants (Subgroups A, B, C), 46 responded to the question, "Do you think this was a good way to practice and improve your pronunciation? Why or why not?" Responses were coded as positive, negative or neutral. A total of 38 of 46 responses were coded as positive, suggesting that participants regarded the VF paradigm as a good way to practice pronunciation. Moreover, three responses were counted as neutral, while five participants' responses were categorized as negative, indicating that they did not find this method useful, with examples below:

(13) IG-A 3: "I liked how we could see the differences between our speech and a native speaker."

(14) IG-A 07: "It helped me see my mistakes."

(15) IG-B 19: "It was useful because it helped me to see the difference between how native speakers and myself say things."

(16) IG-B 21: "It's useful for practicing pronunciation. A lot of times people who are learning Spanish can't be clear to native speakers and it's mostly a pronunciation problem."

(17) IG-C 06: "Yes, because it forced us to practice as well as listen to a native speaker."

(18) IG-C 13: "Yes, because it's important to be understood."

(19) IG-C 14: "Yes, it provides instant feedback."

(20) IG-A 16: "I did think it was helpful, but at first I really struggled to understand what I was looking at without my teacher hinting and a few classmates figuring it out first."

(21) IG-B 02: "In the beginning I thought that it was interesting but not particularly helpful, HOWEVER, the in-class activity was extremely helpful in pointing out my English accent."

(22) IG-B 12: "It was interesting but I don't think my pronunciation will actually improve because of this exercise."

Examples (13)–(22) demonstrate positive thoughts about the VF paradigm, providing evidence that participants who received VF-only treatments did find this method useful. Examples (20) and (21) were categorized as neutral responses, as they reveal that either participants struggled to grasp the goal of the visual representations or thought that the VF treatments provided some information about pronunciation but were not necessarily useful. Finally, example (22) provides a sample response of a participant that did not find the treatment useful by stating that they do not expect any improvement to come from the activity.

EG participant responses, in contrast, were uniformly positive. For perceptions regarding usefulness, all 17 participants stated that they believed this type of activity was useful to their pronunciation learning, as evidenced by examples (23)-(26) below:

(23) EG 04: "Yes, it has us focus on specific, tough sounds to master."
(24) EG 05: "I do think this was a good way to practice and improve my pronunciation because I learned how to specifically say some sounds."
(25) EG 08: "Yes, it forced you to think about how to form words in Spanish."
(26) EG 17: "I think it was a good way because you could tell how you were mispronouncing, which made it easier to improve."

Although in comparison to the IG participants, the EG participants all collectively agreed that their treatment-type was useful, the IG responses were overall positive. Moreover, in relation to finding the VF paradigm useful, one major theme emerged among the IG participants, relating directly to the notion of noticing (Schmidt 1990); multiple participants commented that they were able to see the differences between native speaker productions and their own productions. For example, IG-A 13 commented that they were able to make observations about the differences between their productions and that of a NS, while IG-A 07 added that they *noticed* pronunciation errors. Further, it was found that only one participant of the 46 IG participants reported any difficulty, specifically noting that the software was hard to understand before any instructor-provided guidance.

DISCUSSION AND CLASSROOM IMPLEMENTATION

Discussion

Results from the quantitative analysis suggested that participants from both groups, receiving either more inductive (i.e., less instructor guidance) or explicit (i.e., more instructor involvement) felt that their respective VF activities were useful for developing L2 pronunciation. Qualitative analysis revealed some divergence in the groups, with the EG uniformly finding VF useful for L2 pronunciation development and the IG giving somewhat more mixed evaluations. Specific comments from each group revealed that participants believed their treatment-type aided them in visualizing their mispronunciations, made them aware of their accent, and helped them focus on problematic sounds.

When looking at the importance of the role of the instructor, quantitative results suggest that the EG felt more strongly than the IG that the teacher instruction was beneficial to their pronunciation learning. The qualitative results patterned similarly, with participants broadly highlighting the positive role of the instructor during VF activities. Again, some important group differences emerged; the IG, who received minimal instructor involvement, uniformly believed that instructor support was more beneficial than the VF alone (i.e., preferring teacher instruction to a more inductive approach). In contrast, the EG, who received more instructor engagement, provided more mixed results (although still a majority valued instructor engagement above the VF alone). Five participants from the explicit group responded that the "computer program" was more useful than the teacher instruction. However, it is worth considering whether these participants would have responded the same had there been an absence of an explicit component from their instructor.

Implications for Teaching

Based on the discussion of the results, it is concluded that while both approaches to VF were found to be useful to L2 learners, a preference for more of an active role on the part of the instructor emerged in the data. In other words, L2 learners prefer there to be more instruction provided for the two types of pronunciation instruction as opposed to a more inductive type, namely, the VF paradigm. Although the inductive nature of the VF paradigm is effective for improving L2 learner pronunciation (Offerman and Olson 2016; Olson 2014b) and has been found here to be useful to L2 learners, it is suggested that instructors employ more explicit methods when introducing and working with VF.

Tips for Teaching with Technology

Three different strategies are suggested when implementing VF for pronunciation instruction: (1) the selection of the phonetic feature, (2) software training,[3] and (3) explicit explanations of VF features. Beginning with the selection of the phonetic feature to be addressed using VF, two different factors should be considered when selecting a pronunciation feature for VF instruction: (1) the goals of the learner (comprehensibility vs. nativeness), and (2) the relative "intuitiveness" of the visualization. Considering the goals of the learner, significant advances have been made in the field of L2 pronunciation to distinguish the notions of intelligibility, comprehensibility (i.e., how easily understood an utterance is and the time cost; Derwing, Munro, and Wiebe 1998), and accentedness (i.e., any noticeable pronunciation difference from a local variation; Derwing and Munro 2009). While many VF paradigms rely on a comparison of the learner's production with that of a native speaker, a native-like accent may not necessarily be a practical goal. In selecting a feature to be addressed using VF, instructors should consider what the ultimate goals of the learners may be (see Sturm, Miyamoto, and Suzuki 2019). Further, instructors may highlight the fact that a native-like accent may not be a reasonable or even attainable goal (Birdsong 2007). Second, instructors should explicitly consider the degree to which the visual representation is intuitive to the learner. As noted by Olson (2014b), indirect VF relies on learners being able to interpret a clear relationship between the abstract visual representation (i.e., the sound waves) and the articulatory and perceptual correlates. Some features, such as intonation and duration, may be inherently more intuitive than others (e.g., vowel height as seen in formants). As such, the nature of the feature being addressed, and how easily the visual representation is for learners to understand should be considered. Moreover, given the role of instructor input found in the current study, quality-guided instruction may serve to complement learners' intuitions and expand the range of pronunciation features that can be addressed using VF.

Regarding the second strategy, comments from multiple participants indicated their confusion with the speech analysis software. Introducing learners to the software and guiding them through the initial recordings and analysis may facilitate engagement with the activities. Moreover, this guided approach provides an opportunity for the instructor to have more of an active role in beginning stages so that L2 learners have a clear understanding of what is to be expected on the day of the first VF intervention. Additionally, this will allow for more time to be dedicated to the VF activity rather than being spent on troubleshooting the software.

For the third and final strategy, L2 learners prefer a more explicit approach to a more inductive approach. Within this context, instructors may seek to combine the VF paradigm with: (1) explicit discussions of the differences between the L1 and L2 and (2) a careful demonstration of the visual image, the relevant articulatory gestures, and correlating acoustic/auditory features.

These two key features serve to enhance metalinguistic awareness, which may further enhance noticing. Previous research has demonstrated that metalinguistic awareness of L2 phonetic features may significantly improve L2 pronunciation and perception (e.g., Flege and Wang 1989).

The current study, among the first to examine learner perspectives and the role of instructor support in VF activities, suggests that learners find VF to be useful for the development of L2 pronunciation, but highlight the crucial role that instructors play in supporting learners. Further studies should examine to what extent the instructor should be involved and what effects this has on learner attitudes toward their pronunciation learning and development.

APPENDIX A. OLSON (2014) STATEMENTS

Table 12.2.   Olson (2014) Statements

(1) The Praat activity was useful to me.
(2) The Praat activity was a good way for me to think about my own pronunciation.
(3) The visual analysis software and the explanations of sounds we learned about were useful for improving my pronunciation.
(4) A program like Praat allows me to improve pronunciation without the instructor correcting me.
(5) I liked this activity.

Source: Daniel J. Olson

NOTES

1. Again, while IG-B differed somewhat, the decision was made to include this group to provide a broader response to the research questions. See also Section *Inductive Group B*.
2. IG-B (Olson 2014b) did not respond to this question and was therefore not included in the analysis.
3. While numerous software platforms are available for VF, Praat (Boersma and Weenink 2018) is among the most common. Several resources are available to help instructors become familiar with Praat, including user guidelines and online tutorials (see Beňuš 2021).

REFERENCES

Akahane-Yamada, Reiko, Erik McDermott, Takahiro Adachi, Hideki Kawahara, and John S. Pruitt. 1998. "Computer-based second language production training by using spectrographic representation and HMM-based speech recognition scores." In

Fifth International Conference on Spoken Language Processing: 1–4. http://www
.isca-speech.org/archive

Beňuš, Štefan. 2021. *Investigating Spoken English: A Practical Guide to Phonetics and Phonology Using Praat*. Cham: Palgrave Macmillan.

Best, Catherine T., and Michael D. Tyler. 2007. "Nonnative and second-language speech perception: Commonalities and complementarities." In *Language Experience in Second Language Speech Learning: In Honor of James Emil Flege* edited by Murray Munro & Ocke-S. Bohn, 13–34. Amsterdam: John Benjamins.

Binasfour, Hajar, Jane Setter, and Erhan Aslan. 2017. Enhancing L2 learners' perception and production of the Arabic emphatic sounds. In the *Proceedings of the Phonetics Teaching and Learning Conference*: 16–20. London: Chandler House.

Birdsong, David. 2007. "Native like pronunciation among late learners of French as a second language." In Bohn, O. S., & Munro, M. J. (Eds.). *Language Experience in Second Language Speech Learning: In Honor of James Emil Flege* edited by Murray Munro & Ocke-S. Bohn, 99–116. Amsterdam: John Benjamins.

Boersma, Paul, and David Weenink. 2018. "Praat: Doing phonetics by computer [computer software]." Last modified January 5, 2022. https://www.praat.org.

Carey, Michael. 2004. "CALL VF for pronunciation of vowels: Kay Sona-Match." *CALICO Journal* 21 (3): 571–601. https://www.jstor.org/stable/24149798

Chun, Dorothy M. 1989. "Teaching tone with microcomputers." *CALICO Journal* 7, no. 1: 21–47. https://www.jstor.org/stable/pdf/24147465

Chun, Dorothy M. 1998. "Signal analysis software for teaching discourse intonation." *Language Learning & Technology* 2, no. 1: 61–77. http://llt.msu.edu/vol2num1 /article4/index.html

Chun, Dorothy M. 2002. *Discourse intonation in L2: From theory and research to practice*. Philadelphia: John Benjamins Publishing.

de Bot, Kees. 1980. "Evaluation of intonation acquisition: A comparison of methods." *International Journal of Psycholinguistics* 7: 81–92.

de Bot, Kees. 1983. "VF of intonation: Effectiveness and induced practice behavior." *Language and Speech* 26: 331–350. https://doi.org/10.1177/002383098302600402

Derwing, Tracey M., and Murray J. Munro. 2005. "Second language accent and pronunciation teaching: a research-based approach." *TESOL Quarterly* 39: 379–397. https://doi.org/10.2307/3588486

Derwing, Tracey M., and Murray J. Munro. 2009. "Putting accent in its place: Rethinking obstacles to communication." *Language Teaching* 42, no. 4: 476–490.

Derwing, Tracey M., Murray J. Munro, and Grace Wiebe. 1998. Evidence in favor of a broad framework for pronunciation instruction. *Language Learning* 48, no. 3: 393–410.

Drewelow, Isabelle, and Anne Theobald. 2007. "A comparison of the attitudes of learners, instructors, and native French speakers about the pronunciation of French: An exploratory study." *Foreign Language Annals* 40, no. 3: 491–520. https://doi .org/10.1111/j.1944-9720.2007.tb02872.x

Flege, James E. (1995). "Second language speech learning: Theory, findings, and problems." *Speech Perception and Linguistic Experience: Issues in cross-language research* 92: 233–277.

Flege, James E., and Chipin Wang. 1989. "Native-language phonotactic constraints affect how well Chinese subjects perceive the word-final /t/–/d/ contrast." *Journal of Phonetics* 17, no. 4: 299–315. https://doi.org/10.1016/S0095-4470(19)30446-2

Hardison, Debra M. 2004. "Generalization of computer assisted prosody training: Quantitative and qualitative findings." *Language Learning and Technology* 8, no. 1: 34–52.

Hernández Morales, Ana J. 2017. "Development in pronunciation accuracy through VF and drills: Evidence from stop-rhotic clusters in learners of Spanish as an L2." MA thesis, Purdue University.

Hualde, José I. 2005. *The sounds of Spanish*. New York: Cambridge University Press.

Huensch, Amanda, and Amy S. Thompson. 2017. "Contextualizing attitudes toward pronunciation: Foreign language learners in the United States." *Foreign Language Annals* 50, no. 2: 410–432. https://doi.org/10.1111/flan.12259

Jarosz, Anna. 2019. *English Pronunciation in L2 Instruction: The Case of Secondary School Learners*. Cham: Springer.

Kartushina, Natalia, Alexis Hervais-Adelman, Ulrich H. Frauenfelder, and Narly Golestani. 2015. "The effect of phonetic production training with VF on the perception and production of foreign speech sounds." *Journal of the Acoustical Society of America* 138: 817–832. https://doi.org/10.1121/1.4926561

Klaus, Adam, Daniel R. Lametti, Douglas M. Shiller, and Tara McAllister. 2019. "Can perceptual training alter the effect of visual biofeedback in speech-motor learning?" *The Journal of the Acoustical Society of America* 145, no. 2: 805–817.

Levis, John, and Lucy Pickering. 2004. "Teaching intonation in discourse using speech visualization technology." *System* 32: 505–524. https://doi.org/10.1016/j.system.2004.09.009

Lisker, Leigh, and Arthur S. Abramson. 1964. "A cross-language study of voicing in initial stops: Acoustical measurements." *Word* 20, no. 3: 384–422. http://dx.doi.org/10.1080/00437956.1964.11659830

Lord, Gillian. 2005. "(How) can we teach foreign language pronunciation? On the effects of a Spanish phonetics course." *Hispania* 88, no. 3: 557–567. https://doi.org/10.2307/20063159

Lord, Gillian. 2010. "The combined effects of immersion and instruction on second language pronunciation." *Foreign Language Annals* 43, no. 3: 488–503.

Molholt, Garry. 1988. "Computer assisted instruction in pronunciation for Chinese speakers of American English." *TESOL Quarterly* 22, no. 1: 91–111. https://doi.org/10.2307/3587063

Motohashi-Siago, Miki, and Debra M. Hardison. 2009. "Acquisition of L2 Japanese geminates training with waveform displays." *Language Learning & Technology* 13, no. 2: 29–47. http://llt.msu.edu/vol13num2/motohashisaigohardison.pdf

Offerman, Heather M. 2020a. "Attitudes towards L2 pronunciation instruction: A comparative analysis of usefulness ratings." In *Proceedings of the 11th Pronunciation in Second Language Learning and Teaching conference* Edited by Okim Kang, Shelley Staples, Kate Yaw, and Kevin Hirschi, 270–279. Flagstaff: Northern Arizona University.

Offerman, Heather M. 2020b. "Effects of pronunciation instruction on L2 learner production and perception in Spanish: A comparative analysis." PhD diss., Purdue University.

Offerman, Heather M., and Daniel J. Olson. 2016. "Visual feedback and second language segmental production: The generalizability of pronunciation gains." *System* 59: 45–60. https://doi.org/10.1016/j.system.2016.03.003

Okuno, Tomoko. 2013. "Acquisition of L2 vowel duration in Japanese by native English speakers." PhD diss., Michigan State University.

Okuno, Tomoko, and Debra M. Hardison. (2016). "Perception-production link in L2 Japanese vowel duration: Training with technology." *Language Learning & Technology* 20, no. 2: 61–80. http://llt.msu.edu/issues/june2016/okunohardison.pdf

Olson, Daniel J. 2014a. "Phonetics and technology in the classroom: A practical approach to using speech analysis software in second-language pronunciation instruction." *Hispania* 97, no. 1: 47–68. https://www.jstor.org/stable/24368745

Olson, Daniel J. 2014b. "Benefits of VF on segmental production in the L2 classroom." *Language Learning and Technology* 18, no. 3: 173–192. http://llt.msu.edu/issues/october2014/olson.pdf

Olson, Daniel J. 2019. "Feature acquisition in second language phonetic development: Evidence from phonetic training." *Language Learning* 69, no. 2: 366–404. https://doi-org/101111/lang.12336

Olson, Daniel J. 2021. "Phonetic feature size in second language acquisition: Examining VOT in voiceless and voiced stops." *Second Language Research*: 1–28.

Olson, Daniel J., and Heather M. Offerman. 2021. "Maximizing the effect of VF for pronunciation instruction: A comparative analysis of three approaches." *Journal of Second Language Pronunciation* 7, no. 1: 89–115. https://doi.org/10.1075/jslp.20005.ols

Pillot-Loiseau, Claire, Tanja Kocjančič Antolík, and Takeki Kamiyama. 2013. "Contribution of ultrasound visualisation to improving the production of the French/y/-/u/contrast by four Japanese learners." In *PPLC13: Phonetics, phonology, languages in contact: Contact varieties, multilingualism, second language learning*, 86–89. Paris: General Wallonia-Brussels Delegation.

Rehman, Ivana, and Emily Flint. 2021. "Real-time visual acoustic feedback for non-native vowel production" Presentation presented at *12th Annual Pronunciation in Second Language Learning and Teaching Conference, Brock University, Canada. June 18–19, 2021*. https://brocku.ca/psllt-2021/

Ruellot, Viviane. 2011. "Computer-assisted pronunciation learning of French /u/ and /y/ at the intermediate level." In *Proceedings of the 2nd Pronunciation in Second Language Learning and Teaching Conference* Edited by John Levis and Kimberly LeVelle, 199–213. Ames: Iowa State University.

Saito, Kazuya. 2007. "The influence of explicit phonetic instruction on pronunciation teaching in EFL settings: The case of English vowels and Japanese learners of English." *The Linguistics Journal* 3, no. 3: 16–40.

Saleh, Adeleh J., and Abbas P. Gilakjani. 2021. "Investigating the impact of computer-assisted pronunciation teaching (CAPT) on improving intermediate EFL learners' pronunciation ability." *Education and Information Technologies* 26: 489–515. https://doi.org/10.1007/s10639-020-10275-4

Sandryhaila-Groth, Darya, and Philippe Martin. 2016. "Using a multimedia program in teaching French as a second language. In *8th International Conference on Speech Prosody*, 21–25. doi: 10.21437/SpeechProsody.2016-5

Schmidt, Richard. 1990. "The role of consciousness in second language learning." *Applied Linguistics* 11, no. 2: 129–159. https://doi.org/10.1093/applin/11.2.129

Schmidt, Richard. 1995. "Consciousness and foreign language learning: A tutorial on the role of attention and awareness in learning." In *Attention and awareness in foreign language learning* Edited by Richard W. Schmidt, 1–63. Honolulu: University of Hawai'i.

Setter, Jane, and Jennifer Jenkins. 2005. "State-of-the-art review: Pronunciation." *Language Teaching,* 38: 1–17. https://doi.org/10.1017/S026144480500251X

Spaai, Gerard W., and Dik J. Hermes. (1993). "A visual display for the teaching of intonation." *Calico Journal* 10, no. 3: 19–30. https://www.jstor.org/stable/24147786

Sturm, Jessica, Mayu Miyamoto, and Natsumi Suzuki. 2019. "Pronunciation in the L2 French classroom: Student and teacher attitudes." *The French Review* 92, no. 3: 60–78.

Tsai, Pi-hua. 2019. "Beyond self-directed computer-assisted pronunciation learning: a qualitative investigation of a collaborative approach." *Computer Assisted Language Learning* 32, no. 7: 713–744. https://doi.org/10.1080/09588221.2019.1614069

Weltens, Bert, and Kees de Bot. 1984. "The visualization of pitch contours: Some aspects of its effectiveness in teaching foreign intonation." *Speech Communication* 3, no. 2: 157–163. https://doi.org/10.1016/0167-6393(84)90037-2

Chapter Thirteen

Vowel Visualization for CAPT

A Learner-input Model for Tool Development

Ivana Rehman and Anurag Das

INTRODUCTION

Computer Assisted Pronunciation Training (CAPT) systems come with many advantages, for example, providing language learners extra learning time and material, specific feedback on individual errors, and the possibility for self-paced practice in a private and stress-free environment. As such, CAPT can help address many of the issues a traditional language learning classroom faces when it comes to pronunciation instruction, such as the lack of trained teachers, teachers' limited ability to provide instantaneous and/or individualized feedback due to class sizes, lack of teaching materials, and challenges to pronunciation assessment (Burns 2006; Foote et al. 2011; Isaacs 2013). However, there is still a need for novel approaches to CAPT in providing feedback and in creating new ways to visualize transient aspects of pronunciation (Eskenazi 2009; Hincks 2015).

Although CAPT research has been actively conducted for decades, the tools developed in previous studies have not typically been made available for further use. Additionally, despite calls for more qualitative investigations to inform CALL tool development (Levy 2015), there have been few such efforts in research thus far. When it comes to developing language learning tools, language learners are the direct beneficiaries. Obtaining their perspective can "help ensure that research and practice remain aligned and connected" (Levy 2015, 556). Therefore, learner input should be an integral part of developing CAPT tools. This study introduces a tool for vowel production training called Vowel Viewer, which performs real-time vowel visualization within a vowel plot. First, a qualitative analysis of learners' attitudes toward the use of vowel plots in pronunciation learning was conducted, and the results provided information which was used to inform the development of Vowel Viewer. The study also includes a technical evaluation of Vowel Viewer which tested the accuracy of its formant extraction feature.

LITERATURE REVIEW

Visualization in Pronunciation Learning

The research on the use of technology in pronunciation training has gained considerable attention over the past decades. The potential of certain techniques used in speech analysis technology which provide a visual representation of segmental features, for example, voice onset time (Olson 2014), spectrograms and/or waveforms (Saito 2007), vowel plotting (Carey 2004), has been explored. Each of these techniques follows a similar training pattern when applied to pronunciation learning: (1) learners are provided with a model of target pronunciation, (2) they compare their own production to the model, and (3) they try to improve the pronunciation of the target feature through noticing the differences. Overall, the current body of research reports benefits associated with segmental visualization for pronunciation training.

There are several projects which conducted vowel production training using vowel plots as visual feedback with favorable outcomes. These include studies by Dowd, Smith and Wolfe (1996, 1998). Dowd, Smith and Wolfe (1998) included one-hour long training on six French vowels for 11 monolingual speakers of English with little foreign language learning experience. The researchers instructed the participants to attempt to match the visualized F1 and F2 values which were simultaneously superimposed upon their own vowel production. The training with this setup resulted in an overall significant improvement in both production and perception of vowels. Similar improvement was found in the earlier study (Dowd, Smith and Wolfe 1996) in which the participants used the vowel plot as visual feedback without audio input. Therefore, vowel plots were considered useful for vowel production training.

A more recent study (Kartushina et al. 2015) also showed vowel production improvements due to exposure to vowel plots as visual feedback in vowel production training in a larger-scale training experiment. Specifically, 27 monolingual native French speakers participated in a four-hour training of Danish vowel production as compared to one hour in previous research. The results showed that this training was effective in improving the production accuracy of non-native vowels. Additionally, this study showed production training transferred to perception of the same vowels. The authors suggest that providing this type of articulatory information (i.e., vowel plots) in training can improve both production and perception of the trained vowels.

Furthermore, Sakai (2016) conducted a vowel production training experiment using a program designed for vowel training in singing called Vowel Shapes (Ryan et al. 2015). The program visualizes two vowels, each as a single fixed dot in a graph, one for a model vowel production and one for the user's vowel production. To practice with this program, the learners produced an extended target vowel and tried to reproduce the target (i.e., model in blue). The training lasted a total of two hours, and participants were split into two groups. One had no aural input, including from their own production, while the other had more natural circumstances and could hear their own voice while practicing. The participants in the group with no aural input wore noise canceling headphones while playing "900 Hz low pass filtered white noise at 70 dB" (69). This group showed no improvements in their vowel production, while the group that had aural input showed significant improvements, indicating the training was useful only with natural auditory input.

These studies show that using vowel plotting as visual feedback can be beneficial for vowel production training. They also show that tools investigated in the past are limited in their functionality. Both tools used in Dowd, Smith and Wolfe (1996, 1998) and Kartushina et al. (2015) are limited in providing real-time feedback for a single vowel at a time. Although Vowel Shapes that Sakai (2016) used is an open-source program, it visualizes vowels one at a time which restricts users' vowel space awareness. The visual target vowel provided by these tools is not representative of actual speech, as true vowel production is represented by a range of production, an uneven ellipsis of natural speech variability. However, these tools presented it as a single point in one's vocal tract without evidence of variability. Additionally, previous studies showed that vowel production training with vowel plots can be valuable for a set of vowels rather than a single vowel or a pair (Dowd, Smith and Wolfe 1998).

There have also been several studies that have employed different strategies for formant visualization in tool development. In one such study, Nakamuro et al. developed "KanNon" (Nakamuro et al. 2005), a system that helps deaf individuals visualize speech sounds in real-time. The system displays the spectrogram and spectral peaks in the spectrum, also known as formants. Studying the formants allows deaf individuals to understand language produced by others, who are otherwise restricted to using sign language for communication. In addition to the spectrogram, the system also displays pitch frequency, the loudness of speech, and characters spoken (extracted with a speech recognition system) using a real-time scrolling image. The idea behind their approach is that each phoneme has a unique formant pattern which can be understood by visualizing the spectrogram.

In another work, Dowd, Smith and Wolfe (1998) developed a system that helped speakers pronounce vowel sounds in a second language by providing real-time feedback. Their system measured frequencies of the first two resonances of the vocal tract using an acoustic impedance spectrometer. Although not the same as formant frequencies, the measured resonances share the same relative position in the R1–R2 plane (space for resonant frequencies) as formants in the F1–F2 plane (space for formant frequencies). To test the proposed system, two groups of users were used. Users from the first group had to imitate the productions of eleven non-nasalized French vowel sounds from a native speaker, while those from the other group had the same task but were also assisted by the vocal tract feedback from the system. Interestingly, users who had access to the feedback performed better than those from the other group.

Paganus et al. (2006) developed "Vowel Game," an application for learning pronunciation using vowel charts. Here, participants were presented a Finnish vowel chart which included the target phonemes denoted using circles. Each participant uttered a vowel sound from which formants were extracted. Formants are extracted by first windowing the input speech followed by Linear Prediction (LP) analysis and then Fast Fourier Transform (FFT) to obtain the spectral envelope. The first two maxima on the spectral envelope are then used as the formant frequencies. Once extracted, formant frequencies are mapped to vowels and tracked in real-time. Once the vowel is pronounced correctly, feedback is sent to the participant, asking him to move on to the next vowel. Frostel, Arzt and Widmer (2011) developed a method of visualizing sung vowel sounds, using linear regressions to map vowel sounds to a continuous articulatory space, namely the International Phonetic Alphabet (IPA) vowel chart. The tool displays vowel sounds in real time, and their placement on the vowel chart can be used to measure the quality of the produced vowels. This information can then be used for artistic purposes such as training music.

Tools that visualize speech sounds from already extracted acoustic features have also been developed. As an example, VOIS3D (Wasink 2006) normalizes the formant frequencies and duration of different vowels and then visualizes them. It also finds the spectral overlap between the different vowel sounds. Similarly, Heeringa and Van de Velde (2017) developed "Visible Vowels," a web app that visualizes acoustic measurements such as fundamental frequency, formants, and duration. The system takes as input a spreadsheet containing information of these measurements for different vowels from one or more speakers and then visualizes them. The tool also provides the option to visualize the separation between speakers by comparing distances between them using multidimensional scaling.

Learner Attitudes toward Pronunciation Learning and Technology

Learners' attitudes toward using technology for language learning have been largely positive. Due to the implementation of technology in learning processes, learners may be more engaged and have an overall more positive attitude toward language learning (Golonka et al. 2014). It is also essential to examine existing research on learners' attitudes toward pronunciation learning. Overall, learners seem to be highly interested in pronunciation instruction (Levis and Grant 2003). They also appear to treat pronunciation as a valuable component of their overall language learning (Olson 2014). Other studies (e,g, Huensch and Thompson 2017; Sturm, Miyamoto and Suzuki 2019) noted that learners regarded pronunciation learning higher than other communicative skills. Furthermore, Offerman (2020) reports learners had a positive attitude toward several types of pronunciation instruction, whereas training with visual feedback was regarded as the most useful.

In response to Levy's (2015) call for more qualitative research in CALL, the present study employs a qualitative method to explore learners' attitudes toward visual feedback through the Appraisal Framework (AF) (Martin and White 2005). Previous studies have employed this framework in their evaluations of language learning tools and pronunciation instructors. For example, Huffman (2015) used this framework to look into learners' evaluations of the Research Writing Tutor, a "web-based AWE tool which provides discourse-oriented, discipline-specific feedback on users' section drafts of empirical research papers" (11). Additionally, Lipovsky and Mahboob (2010) used the appraisal framework as a theoretical basis for investigating learners' attitudes toward and perceptions of non-native English-speaking teachers in a pronunciation classroom. Overall, the appraisal framework seems to be suitable for evaluation of a material used for pronunciation learning.

Research Questions

To provide an appreciation analysis as a measure of learners' attitudes, the following research questions are examined:

- What are learners' positively and negatively charged assessments (appreciations) of the usefulness of vowel plots as visual feedback?
- What type of appreciation is present in learners' attitude toward vowel plots as visual feedback?

To examine the acoustic accuracy of Vowel Viewer, the following research question is addressed:

• To what extent are Vowel Viewer's measurements of F1 and F2 values in line with those of Praat?

METHODS—APPRECIATION ANALYSIS

Participants

To address the research questions of this study, a convenience sample of nine participants was chosen because of their enrollment in a pronunciation class in which they were exposed to vowel plots as visual feedback. All participants were male, in their twenties, attending graduate school at a large university in the Midwestern United States, where they were employed as graduate assistants. Although their exact proficiency was unknown, they obtained a sufficient score on a language proficiency exam (e.g., 6.5 on IELTS or 79 on TOEFL) in order to be admitted to graduate programs at a US Research I university. They are from a non-native speaking background with Chinese as their L1.

Materials

While taking part in the pronunciation class, the participants received feedback on their vowel production in the form of a vowel plot. Each participant was trained on how to read vowel plots during student conferences with the instructor. Once they received the first set of vowel plots at the beginning of the semester, which were generated by their instructor, they were asked to compare the vowel plot of their production to that of native American English speaker's production. Students were asked to discuss the differences they noticed between their production and that of a native speaker. At the end of the semester, new vowel plots were generated based on the participants' most recent production. In order to self-assess, and in addition to another comparison to native speakers' vowel plot, participants were asked to also compare their most recent vowel plots to those from the beginning of the semester. Once again, individual conferences were held so participants could practice noticing and understanding the observed differences.

To investigate participants' attitudes toward the use of vowel plots as visual feedback in their pronunciation learning, interview questions were developed to elicit information about appreciation when it comes to using vowel plots as visual feedback in L2 pronunciation learning. The following set of interview questions was asked:

1. How did you like the feedback?
2. What do you think about the usability of the feedback?
3. How useful was the feedback for your learning?

The questions were formed in a way to avoid any type of influence on the participants that would lead them to either a positive or a negative response. Once the participants exhibited positively or negatively charged responses, follow-up questions were asked to reveal details of their attitude.

Procedure

At the beginning of the pronunciation course, the participants were introduced to general information about vowel plots. During the second week of the semester, students were asked to record themselves producing the following words, three times each: <heed>, <hid>, <head>, <had>, <hawed>, <hod>, <hood>, <who'd>, and <hud>. These words elicited nine English monophthongs that were the focus of this study. The consonant environment is the same, that is, preceding consonant is [h] and the following consonant is [d], which allows for the least influence to be exerted on the vowel sound in question. This procedure follows the one suggested by Hillenbrand et al. (1995), which is one of the most cited acoustic analyses that required this type of vowel elicitation. After the recordings were obtained, the instructor calculated the F1 and F2 values in Praat, acoustic analysis software that provides accurate formant values based on the algorithms employed in its extraction (Boersma 2011). Using the calculated averaged F1 and F2 values, the instructor generated the vowel plots using NORM, a web-based software for vowel normalization and plotting. The instructor trained the participants on how to interpret them during student conferences during the third week of the semester. This procedure was repeated at the end of the semester with the second set of recordings (obtained in week 15), and a new vowel plot was created for each student which was given to them during the second in-person conference (week 16).

After the completion of the pronunciation course, the participants were invited to take part in in-person semi-structured interviews to share their attitudes toward the vowel plots. It needs to be noted that both the invitation to participate and the interview took place during the semester after the pronunciation course was completed. The researcher, therefore, had no direct influence on the participants' academic performance at the time of the interviews, and the participants received no incentive for volunteering to take part in the interviews. Follow-up questions were posed for clarification of responses and to request further description or explanation. The interviews were recorded with a voice recorder, and each recording was transcribed for analysis. Coded names were used to protect participants' identities. Each interview session was about ten minutes long.

Analysis

As listed in Huffman (2015), positive appreciation may be revealed through vocabulary such as *useful, helpful, good, great, beneficial*; on the other hand, *wrong, incorrect, issue, problem* may be used to express negatively charged appreciation. Each answer was examined for positively or negatively charged appreciation resources following the guidelines provided in table 13.1. Simply said, positive vocabulary was coded as positively charged, while negative vocabulary was coded as negatively charged. In addition, all responses were annotated to match one of the three aspects of appreciation: reaction (perceptual aspects or aesthetics), composition (balance and complexity), and social valuation (usefulness, worthiness, value). These were further annotated to reflect a positively or negatively charged response. The UAM Corpus Tool (O'Donnell 2007) version 3.0 was used to annotate the transcriptions and calculate the frequencies of the target vocabulary related to appreciation as defined in Martin and Rose (2005). This tool required all interview transcriptions to be exported to text files (.txt),

Table 13.1.   Types of Appreciation

Subcategories	Dimensions	Gloss from UAMCT
Reaction	Impact	How does it strike me? What initial reaction does it make? The perceptual aspects or aesthetics of the item.
	Quality	Do I like it? How do I react emotionally toward it, what are my affectual responses?
Composition	Balance	Did it hang together? Was it harmonious, organised, well-proportioned, logical, or unbalanced, lop-sided, irregular, flawed, discordant, shapeless?
	Complexity	Was it hard or easy to follow? Was it simple, pure, elegant, clear, precise, lucid, coherent, or was it extravagant, byzantine, woolly, arcane, simplistic, etc?
Social-Valuation	n/a	Whether something is 'socially' valued for its usefulness, worthiness, efficaciousness, health-giving properties: its contribution to the community, or its value to the consumer: related to judgment: propriety

Credit: Martin & White 2005

and the already built-in AF provided glosses for each code which made the annotation straightforward. A second coder, an applied linguist experienced with the AF and the UAM Corpus Tool, was involved in peer debriefing to review coding of interview data as a way to provide trustworthiness and avoid biases within the analysis (Mertens 2010).

RESULTS—APPRECIATION ANALYSIS

The transcribed interviews resulted in a total of 276 annotated clauses. More specifically, 74 percent (204) of the annotated clauses were positively charged for appreciation, while 26 percent (72) were negatively charged for appreciation. This result is indicative of an overall positive attitude toward appreciation of vowel plots as visual feedback in pronunciation learning. The participants talked about vowel plots as visual feedback using the following words to express a positive attitude: useful, easy, helpful, visually appealing, intuitive, impressive, good. Participant ID1 said that the vowel chart is of "high quality," that it helped him "improve a lot," and that it gave him "more information about how to produce sounds." Participants ID2 and ID7 expressed their wish to "use them [vowel plots] more frequently." ID7 also noted that "vowel chart helps show [us] progress," and that it is "mostly helpful for evaluation [of pronunciation]." "I did not know there were differences between the vowels, the vowel chart helped me see," said participant ID3 when talking about how vowel charts helped him learn the difference between tense and lax vowels, and ID8 and ID6 shared this experience. Participant ID4 mentioned that not only is the vowel plot good for practicing pronunciation, but it "improves [my] listening ability" as well, stating that if he knows the differences in his own pronunciation it would be easier to hear them, too. The most notable statements by participant ID5 were that the vowel plots "give [us, participants] incentive to practice more," and that "it makes us [participants] more aware of the pronunciation errors." ID9 stated this was his "favorite feedback" received during the class, as it allowed him to directly see how he does in his vowel production.

The negatively charged responses were mainly about two issues: (1) all participants expressed that they did not like the limited exposure to the vowel plots and the inability to create their own when they pleased, and (2) most participants expressed dissatisfaction with the lack of interactive features. A few participants said that they "didn't like using [vowel plots] only twice" (ID2, ID7 and ID9), and some mentioned that they "wanted to use [vowel plots] more" (ID1, ID6, ID7), while the rest of them said that it would be better for students if they "could make the chart on their own" (ID3, ID4, and ID8), so that they can use it more frequently. Some participants noted that they "still had to use Google" (ID2 and ID4) for model pronunciation, and that therefore vowel plots were "not enough" (ID4 and ID5) because they "needed more examples [audio recordings]" (ID2 and ID9) or "looking at the throat and the mouth" (ID5). One of the participants stated that vowel plots are "not a way to teach us" (ID1) but rather show evaluation.

To address the second research question (RQ2), the results show that 76 percent (210) of the annotated clauses were related to social valuation, while only 16 percent (44) and 8 percent (22) were related to composition and reaction, respectively. This is an expected finding considering the use of vowel plots as visual feedback in pronunciation learning is meant to help students in their learning, and social valuation is a tag for something that is valued for its usefulness, worthiness, efficaciousness, etc. (Martin and Rose 2005). The participants said that the vowel plots were "helpful," that they "gave more information" (ID1, ID3, ID7, ID8) about how to produce sounds, and that they "helped them see the differences" (ID2, ID3, ID5, ID7, ID8) between the vowels, which they were unaware of before being exposed to this type of feedback. Additionally, they said that the vowel chart helped them see their own progress, by showing them what they achieved (ID1, ID3, ID4, ID6, ID7). Finally, they noted that the vowel plots helped them find out what exactly to focus on in pronunciation practice (ID4, ID5, ID8, ID9), and that comparing to native speakers' vowel production was extremely helpful (all participants). The responses that were annotated as composition were the ones that described vowel plots as easy to read and intuitive (all participants). This is an important finding as there have been claims that Praat (Boersma and Weenink 2011) and other similar tools and their outputs are too sophisticated for the learners (Derwing 2010). The fact that the participants called vowel plots "intuitive" shows that, with a brief explanation on how to use them, vowel plots may not be difficult for learners and can therefore be introduced in pronunciation learning. Finally, the responses that were marked as reaction said that all participants liked using the vowel plots and would love to use them again in their pronunciation learning.

DISCUSSION

The findings of this study show that learners have mainly positive appreciation of the use of vowel plots as visual feedback in pronunciation learning (RQ1), and that they find it useful (RQ2). The discussion of the two research questions posed in the current study is related—the positive appreciation found in RQ1 might be the direct cause of the fact that the learners found this type of visual feedback useful in their learning which was discovered in RQ2. The largely positive responses were mainly related to raising awareness of pronunciation errors while providing individualized feedback, and the ability to compare one's vowel production with that of a native speaker model. The negative responses were provided in the form of suggestions on how to improve this type of feedback, and even though coded as "negative" according to the AF due to the negative language used by the participants, their meaning was essentially positive. All participants said that they would have liked to have used the vowel plots more frequently, and therefore, that they would have liked it if they were taught to generate one on their own. Additionally, numerous participants stated that they would have appreciated more interactive features within the feedback, such as more examples (audio recordings of example words, and/or visual representations of mouth and/or vocal tract movements). The awareness raising induced by vowel plots is in line with second language acquisition theories. More specifically, Schmidt (2012) stated that "input does not become intake for language learning unless it is noticed, that is, consciously registered" (p. 27), which is known as the noticing hypothesis. Overall, most participants stated that noticing their errors helped them understand their vowel production, and therefore, they were able to direct their own learning toward specific vowel sounds. This type of directed learning helps students self-improve while engaged in an autonomous learning process (Havranek 2002).

The positive attitude may also positively affect learners' improvement of pronunciation, or in this case, vowel production, as previous studies have found a relationship between positive attitudes and language performance (Bidin et al. 2009). This should motivate both researchers and practitioners to increase the use of vowel plots as visual feedback in both research and teaching. The current study shows that learners are mostly satisfied with the way vowel plots aid in their learning of pronunciation. To date, the current literature has yet to examine a dataset as robust as the one offered in this study. The findings of this study encourage the use of this type of feedback, as the learners seem to enjoy employing it in their learning.

The study provides one of the essential components in current CAPT research—learners' voice. The importance of a qualitative component in research on the use of visual feedback is undisputed as it sheds light on learners' attentional focus when engaged in this type of learning (Levy 2015). The learners not only expressed their positive opinion of using vowel plots as visual feedback in pronunciation learning but gave their own observations of what would make vowel plots a more useful and integrated piece of feedback, and this information was used in the development of Vowel Viewer. This information can promote vowel plots to evolve from a mere display of how one's pronunciation should be to how one's pronunciation is and how it develops over time. For learners, vowel plots can serve as a progress map of their own vowel production. The main contribution of this study is that it informs future development of CAPT software. Previous research states that the most useful CAPT tools provide visual feedback and a stress-free autonomous learning environment (Cucchiarini et al. 2009; Levis 2007), and the results of this study inform CAPT developers that vowel plots can serve as a type of individualized visual feedback that is deemed as helpful and useful by L2 learners. Furthermore, if trained, learners can utilize this type of feedback to complement their learning process. Automatizing the process of creating vowel plots via CAPT software would be helpful for both instructors and learners. Having such a tool would enable learners to engage in pronunciation training outside of the classroom, and it would lessen the burden of instructors who oversee a large number of students while working with limited classroom time.

This study also supports the use of multimodal tools to enhance pronunciation training through incorporation of novel technological advances. Pronunciation training has given large importance to the use of oral language (Saz et al. 2011), but implementing visual aids in addition to traditional ways of pronunciation teaching and learning could greatly enhance learners' experience. Instructor feedback often differs from classroom to classroom, and using vowel plots to provide feedback on vowel production would improve feedback consistency and accuracy. Furthermore, the complexity of vowel production training requires as much valuable learning material as possible for optimal learning. This study helps CAPT developers and practitioners consider a beneficial way to use vowel plots for pronunciation learning. Vowel plots easily attend to individual learners' needs and, when combined with audio exemplars, provide useful information to the learner. However, learners require instructor guidance in order to properly navigate vowel plots to inform their pronunciation learning, which confirms the role of instructor in pronunciation learning. Technology can aid but never replace human instruction; however, offering individualized feedback is difficult for any instructor due to time limitations and likely individual variability of learners. With the existence of widely available state-of-the-art tools for acoustic analysis of speech, such as Praat, giving feedback can be accurate, which is why vowel plots should be incorporated in CAPT. Vowel plots are accurate feedback and provide learners with a tangible way of observing progress in their vowel production. As such, including them in pronunciation learning could offer an easy-to-follow progress report.

The findings from this section of the study have been used to inform the development of Vowel Viewer, which is described in more detail in the following section. Overall, as the participants stated that they would enjoy a more interactive platform, we implemented methods for real-time formant reading and vowel plotting. This way, users are able to see their vowel production immediately upon when they utter the target sound. Furthermore, a visual model of native speaker production was inserted so that the users can compare their own production to that of representative native speakers of the target language. Finally, audio examples were inserted for users to be able to have an audio model to imitate in their practice.

METHODS—CREATION AND TECHNICAL EVALUATION OF VOWEL VIEWER

Vowel Viewer Description

Vowel Viewer extracts formant frequencies from vowel sounds and then displays them in a vowel chart in real-time. The vowel chart is a two-dimensional chart with formant frequencies F1 and F2 as the axes. Also shown in the plot are formant frequency regions for different vowel sounds for native speakers. These regions specify the range of native speakers' vowel productions, rather than single points within the vowel plot, to represent authentic language use. We calculate these regions by first extracting formants from the vowel sounds of several native speakers, followed by plotting and drawing contours along the formants that lie along the exterior of each vowel sound.

To calculate formant frequencies, we first split the input speech signal into segments and then feed them to Parselmouth (Jadoul, Thomson and De Boer 2018), a Python based library that internally uses Praat's code and allows us to calculate formants. Calculating formants on speech segments containing only silence or those devoid of vowel sounds is not of interest to us. To remove such segments, we first calculate the number of voiced frames in each speech segment using Parselmouth. If the number of voiced frames is less than a threshold, we reject the entire speech segment. By default, we set the threshold for the number of voiced frames to five.

We set the analysis window for extracting formants to 0.5 seconds. In piloting, we found that using a smaller analysis window led to spurious formant frequencies whereas a longer analysis window increased the time delay between the words spoken and the displayed formants and therefore affected the real-time nature of the tool. An analysis window of 0.5 seconds was therefore a sweet spot in the trade-off between the accuracy of the formants extracted and the real-time behavior of the tool.

The formant visualization occurs within a panel that already visualizes native speakers' production in the form of colored dots where each vowel is represented by a unique color. To include this visualization, 100 recordings of American English native speakers (50 male and 50 female) from the Speech Accent Archive (Weinberger 2015) were randomly chosen, and the F1 and F2 values for eight vowels were manually calculated via Praat. Selected NS participants were monolingual adults from the United States in order to model general American English pronunciation. This way, the model is up to date as it represents the state of recent American English vowel production. The vowel plot panel is represented in figure 13.1.

To start recording, the participant clicks play and the interface automatically starts capturing the formant frequencies of their productions. Since this happens in real time, it can be difficult to keep track of the formants particularly if there is a lot of variation between them. Therefore, we only display the five most recent formants connected using lines and remove the previous ones. This visualization appears over the native speaker model examples (colored dots) as a bigger, bright blue dot. In addition to visualizing their vowel sounds, they can also compare their productions to the same exemplars produced by native speakers, available just below the vowel chart.

Below the vowel plot (figure 13.1), a panel of native samples of exemplar word productions is included to provide native speaker auditory input, along with a sample vowel plot which represents General American English pronunciation. The word exemplar audio recordings were collected by recording two native English speakers, one male and one female. All words are one

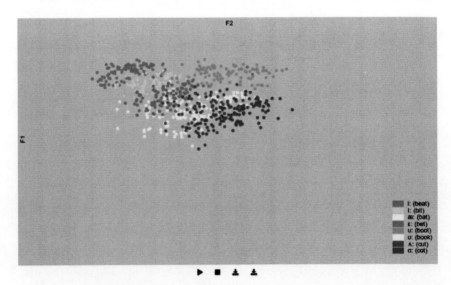

Figure 13.1.   Vowel Viewer's vowel plot panel.
Source: Rehman & Das

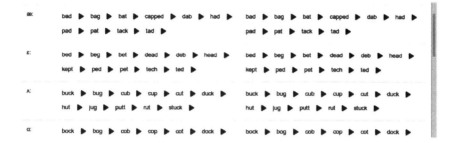

Figure 13.2. Vowel Viewer's exemplar panel.
Source: Rehman & Das

syllable words to allow the learners to focus on a single vowel per exemplar. Each vowel is produced in a consonant environment which least affects the formant frequencies, such as consonants /h/ and /d/, as to provide an acoustically optimal environment for the vowels. In this particular example, /h/ is a voiceless consonant with low acoustic energy which does not affect the adjacent vowel (Lučić 2015). Consonant /d/ is a stop sound which makes it easy to determine the offset of the preceding vowel (Khalil 2014). The screenshot of the exemplar panel is shown in figure 13.2.

Researchers have agreed upon the necessity of explicit pronunciation instruction, as it helps create phonological awareness, which plays a key role in L2 speech intelligibility (Saito 2011), and technology may be a useful facilitator of awareness. Creating and modifying software that allows for learning specific pronunciation features with meaningful feedback is useful for L2 learners. Developing this software allows for focusing on specific linguistic characteristics of target language, in this case the acoustic characteristics of vowels, and makes that feature the main focus of the software. Considering that research has found visual feedback as beneficial to L2 learners, providing a visual representation of vowel production in form of a vowel plot could be a dynamic way of engaging learners in pronunciation training. Vowel Viewer provides both native speaker models and individualized visual feedback of their own vowel production.

Technical Evaluation

While some researchers use the term "evaluation" to talk about the usefulness of a CALL tool for language learning (Kumar et al. 2011), others have used the same term to discuss technical accuracy (Bennett and Black 2005). While the former test their tools on language learners, the latter mostly use a human evaluator's manual measurements as a point of comparison to confirm accuracy, despite the differences in their functionality. These evaluations show how different procedures are applied to a variety of CALL applications, even if their end goal is ultimately the same. To ensure that Vowel Viewer is accurate, its formant values were compared directly with those obtained manually using Praat. Both sets of formant values were extracted on the same set of speech samples.

Speech Samples

In order to perform the sanity check of the accuracy of Vowel Viewer's acoustic feature extraction, a set of speech samples from George Mason University's Speech Accent Archive was used. The recording features participants reading the following elicitation paragraph, designed to elicit all vowels of English:

> Please call Stella. Ask her to bring these things with her from the store: Six spoons of fresh snow peas, five thick slabs of blue cheese, and maybe a snack for her brother Bob. We also need a small plastic snake and a big toy frog for the kids. She can scoop these things into three red bags, and we will go meet her Wednesday at the train station.

Speech samples of six male and six female non-native speakers of English were randomly chosen from the GMU Speech Accent Archive. All speech samples were produced by learners of English as an L2 in an academic setting. Each participant was of a different L1 background, to confirm Vowel Viewer's ability to function accurately for learners of all language backgrounds. Each participant provided a token to represent each of the eight vowels included in pronunciation training with Vowel Viewer ([i], [æ], [u], [ɑ], [ɛ], [ɪ], [ʌ], and [ʊ]), for a total of 96 tokens. This sample size was sufficient to perform statistical analysis of measurement reliability between Vowel Viewer and Praat.

Procedure

For checking the accuracy of the acoustic feature extraction, the formant values given by Vowel Viewer were compared with the values manually collected through Praat. Praat has been widely used for acoustic analyses and provides accurate formant values which are the main acoustic features of interest in this project. To extract the formant values, the middle 60 percent (approximately) of the target vowel was manually located. This was done to ensure no surrounding consonants exerted acoustic influence on formant measurements. Then, an average F1 and F2 were extracted. Vowel Viewer formant values were obtained automatically. More specifically, a Python script was used with audio files as input, applied the same pipeline that Vowel Viewer uses for formant extraction, and provided written output of the formant values.

Analysis

In order to determine whether Vowel Viewer provides reliable formant value measurements as compared to Praat, intra-correlation coefficient (ICC) was calculated using SPSS. ICC is a measure of reliability of measurements or ratings which compares the variability of different ratings of the same subject to the total variation across all ratings and all subjects (Shrout and Fleiss 1979). For this sanity check, consistent agreement (Landers 2015) was the choice of comparison between the two sets of values, and single measurement reliability is considered as the point of comparison. Considering the same two tools were used for all measurements obtained, and individual values were compared (cell by cell agreement), a two-way mixed effects model with single measures was used in which participants' effects are random (due to their random selection), and measures' effects are fixed (as Vowel Viewer and Praat were used on all tokens). An estimate is that the ICC needs to be above 0.7 to claim reliability (Shrout and Fleiss 1979).

RESULTS—TECHNICAL EVALUATION

Using SPSS, the ICC value was calculated with its 95 percent confidence interval for each F1 and F2 value. The reliability results for F1 are reported in table 13.2.

The ICC values were .895 with 95 percent confidence interval of .844–.930, and .873 with 95 percent confidence interval of .812–.915 for F1 and F2 values, respectively. These values are indicative of the high reliability of Vowel Viewer. The reliability analysis confirmed that Vowel Viewer's speech processing function agrees with that of Praat. This result in the initial evaluation of the tool is critical because the rest of the research conducted

Table 13.2.   ICC Value and Its 95 Percent Confidence Interval for F1 and F2

ICC F1	95% CI	ICC F2	95% CI
.895	.844–.930	.873	.812–.915

Source: Rehman & Das

with Vowel Viewer is dependent on the accuracy of the formant extraction. This study conducted a technical evaluation of Vowel Viewer, and the results presented in this technical evaluation show that Vowel Viewer is a viable tool when it comes to its speech processing function.

GENERAL DISCUSSION AND CONCLUSION

This study presents a newly-developed CAPT tool for vowel production training. The qualitative analysis of learners' attitudes toward the use of vowel plots as visual feedback discovered positive appreciation through articulating the usefulness of vowel plots as feedback in their learning of pronunciation. Vowel Viewer was then developed combining the knowledge obtained via qualitative analysis and previous research findings.

The results serve as a beneficial contribution to the current investigation on the use of visual feedback in pronunciation learning, as this is a gap in current research. A significant contribution is also the fact that a part of the AF analysis was successfully employed to investigate attitudes for visual feedback of pronunciation, which expands the possibilities for future qualitative investigation of pronunciation-related topics. The results obtained in this study are relevant to pedagogy, as instructors can obtain pertinent information as to what type of feedback is successful for learners in their learning of pronunciation. Such a tool is especially useful for pronunciation teachers with no training in acoustics as implementing it in the classroom is possible with simple instructions. However, it is important to note that all tools used in the first part of the study (e.g., Praat and Norm) are freely available and include extensive tutorials to help users, acousticians or not, access these resources. Therefore, these tools are currently available worldwide for use by teachers and learners alike.

This chapter also informs materials developers and their approaches to generation of pronunciation textbooks by including similar feedback as a part of the included exercises. Additionally, with constant technological advancements, the knowledge provided by this study could advise future efforts of CAPT development. Such learner-centered approach to software development helps align research and practice. Additionally, such a CAPT tool offers more opportunities to language learners for beneficial pronunciation training. This tool can be implemented as a part of a curriculum where students would engage in pronunciation learning in class or it could be used as a supplement to pronunciation instruction where students could be instructed to engage with it in their private environment. It is also important to note that, although this study focused on L2 English, Vowel Viewer is easily adaptable to other languages as well, as formant measures are language-independent. Overall, this chapter provides beneficial information for both pedagogy and language learning software development.

REFERENCES

Bennett, Christina L., and Alan W. Black. 2005. "Prediction of pronunciation variations for speech synthesis: A data-driven approach." In *Proceedings (ICASSP'05) IEEE International Conference on Acoustics, Speech, and Signal Processing.* vol. 1, pp. I–297.

Bidin, Samsiah, Kamaruzaman Jusoff, Nurazila Abdul Aziz, Musdiana Mohamad Salleh, and Taniza Tajudin. 2009. "Motivation and attitude in learning English among UiTM students in the northern region of Malaysia." *English Language Teaching* 2, no. 2: 16–20.

Boersma, Paul. 2011. "Praat: doing phonetics by computer [Computer program]." http://www.praat.org

Burns, Anne. 2006. "Integrating research and professional development on pronunciation teaching in a national adult ESL program." *TESL Reporter* 39: 8–8.

Carey, Michael. 2004. "CALL visual feedback for pronunciation of vowels: Kay Sona-Match." *Calico Journal*: 571–601.

Cucchiarini, Catia, Ambra Neri, and Helmer Strik. 2009. "Oral proficiency training in Dutch L2: The contribution of ASR-based corrective feedback." *Speech Communication* 51, no. 10: 853–863. https://doi.org/10.1016/j.specom.2009.03.003

Derwing, Tracey M. 2010. "Utopian goals for pronunciation teaching." In *Proceedings of the 1st pronunciation in second language learning and teaching conference*, pp. 24–37.

Dowd, Annette, John Smith, and Joe Wolfe. 1998. "Learning to pronounce vowel sounds in a foreign language using acoustic measurements of the vocal tract as feedback in real time." *Language and Speech* 41, no. 1: 1–20.

Dowd, Annette, John Smith, and Joe Wolfe. 1996. "Real time, non-invasive measurements of vocal tract resonances: application to speech training." *Acoustics Australia*: 53–60.

Eskenazi, Maxine. "An overview of spoken language technology for education." *Speech Communication* 51, no. 10 (2009): 832–844. https://doi.org/10.1016/j.specom.2009.04.005

Foote, Jennifer A., Amy K. Holtby, and Tracey M. Derwing. 2011. "Survey of the teaching of pronunciation in adult ESL programs in Canada, 2010." TESL Canada: 1–22. https://doi.org/10.18806/tesl.v29i1.1086

Frostel, Harald, Andreas Arzt, and Gerhard Widmer. 2011. "The vowel worm: Real-time mapping and visualisation of sung vowels in music." In *Proceedings of the 8th Sound and Music Computing Conference*, pp. 214–219.

Golonka, Ewa M., Anita R. Bowles, Victor M. Frank, Dorna L. Richardson, and Suzanne Freynik. 2014. "Technologies for foreign language learning: A review of technology types and their effectiveness." *Computer Assisted Language Learning* 27, no. 1: 70–105. https://doi.org/10.1080/09588221.2012.700315

Havranek, Gertraud. 2002. "When is corrective feedback most likely to succeed?." International *Journal of Educational Research* 37, no. 3–4: 255–270. https://doi.org/10.1016/S0883-0355(03)00004-1

Heeringa, Wilbert, and Hans Van de Velde. 2017. "Visible Vowels: A Tool for the Visualization of Vowel Variation." In *Proceedings of INTERSPEECH*, pp. 4034–4035.

Hillenbrand, James, Laura A. Getty, Michael J. Clark, and Kimberlee Wheeler. 1995. "Acoustic characteristics of American English vowels." *The Journal of the Acoustical Society of America* 97, no. 5: 3099–3111. https://doi.org/10.1121/1.409456

Hincks, Rebecca. 2015. "Technology and learning pronunciation." In *The Handbook of English Pronunciation*, edited by Marnie Reed and John Levis, 505–519. Malden, NY: Wiley- Blackwell. https://doi.org/10.1002/9781118346952.ch28

Huensch, Amanda, and Amy S. Thompson. 2017. "Contextualizing attitudes toward pronunciation: Foreign language learners in the United States." *Foreign Language Annals* 50, no. 2: 410–432. https://doi.org/10.1111/flan.12259

Huffman, Sarah Rebecca. 2015. "Exploring learner perceptions of and interaction behaviors using the Research Writing Tutor for research article Introduction section draft analysis." PhD diss., Iowa State University.

Isaacs, Talia. 2013 "Pronunciation." In *Cambridge English centenary symposium on speaking assessment*, pp. 13–15. Cambridge English Language Assessment.

Jadoul, Yannick, Bill Thompson, and Bart De Boer. 2018 "Introducing parselmouth: A python interface to Praat." *Journal of Phonetics* 71: 1–15. https://doi.org/10.1016/j.wocn.2018.07.001

Kartushina, Natalia, Alexis Hervais-Adelman, Ulrich Hans Frauenfelder, and Narly Golestani. 2015. "The effect of phonetic production training with visual feedback on the perception and production of foreign speech sounds." *The Journal of the Acoustical Society of America* 138, no. 2: 817–832. https://doi.org/10.1121/1.4926561

Khalil, Samar. 2014. "Comparative study of the acoustic vowel space of Egyptian English vowels and general American English vowels." *Linguistic Portfolios* 3, no. 1: 8.

Kumar, Anuj, Anuj Tewari, Seth Horrigan, Matthew Kam, Florian Metze, and John Canny. 2011."Rethinking speech recognition on mobile devices." In *Proceedings of 2nd International Workshop on Intelligent User Interfaces for Developing Regions*, Palo Alto, CA: 10–15.

Landers, Richard. 2015. "Computing intraclass correlations (ICC) as estimates of interrater reliability in SPSS." *The Winnower*, 2, https://dx.doi.org/10.15200/winn.143518.81744

Levis, John. 2007. "Computer technology in teaching and researching pronunciation." *Annual Review of Applied Linguistics* 27: 184–202. https://doi.org/10.1017/S0267190508070098

Levis, John M., and Linda Grant. 2013. "Integrating pronunciation into ESL/EFL classrooms." *TESOL Journal* 12, no. 2: 13–19.

Levy, Mike. 2015. "The role of qualitative approaches to research in CALL contexts: Closing in on the learner's experience." *Calico Journal* 32, no. 3: 554–568. http://dx.doi.org/10.1558/cj.v32i3.26620

Lipovsky, Caroline, and Ahmar Mahboob. 2010. "Students' appraisal of their native and non native English-speaking teachers." *WATESOL NNEST Caucus Annual Review, 1:* 119–154.

Lučić, Ivana. 2015. "Acoustic Analysis of Montenegrin English L2 Vowels: Production and Perception." *Linguistic Portfolios, 4*, no. 1: 77–91.

Martin, James, and Peter White. 2005. *The Language of Evaluation: Appraisal in English*. Palgrave Macmillan, London.

Mertens, Donna. 2010. *Research and evaluation in education and psychology: Integrating diversity with quantitative, qualitative, and mixed methods*. Sage Publications, Thousand Oaks, CA.

Nakamuro, Ken, Katsuhiro Haruki, and Sueo Sugimoto. 2005. "The KanNon system-Real time speech visualization." *International Journal of Innovative Computing, Information & Control* 1, no. 3: 561–547.

O'Donnell, Mick. UAM Corpus Tool. [Computer software]. Retrieved from http://www.corpustool.com/, (2007)

Offerman, Heather M. 2020. *"The effects of pronunciation instruction on L2 production and L2 perception in Spanish: A comparative analysis."* PhD diss., Purdue University Graduate School.

Olson, Daniel J. 2014. "Phonetics and technology in the classroom: A practical approach to using speech analysis software in second-language pronunciation instruction." *Hispania*, 97, no. 1: 47–68.

Paganus, Annu, Vesa-Petteri Mikkonen, Tomi Mäntylä, Sami Nuuttila, Jouni Isoaho, Olli Aaltonen, and Tapio Salakoski. 2006. "The vowel game: continuous real-time visualization for pronunciation learning with vowel charts." In *International Conference on Natural Language Processing* (in Finland), pp. 696–703. Springer, Berlin, Heidelberg.

Ryan, Cynthia, Katherine Ciesinski, and Mohammed Hoque. 2015. "Vowel shapes: an open-source, interactive tool to assist singers with learning vowels." In *Proceedings of the 2015 ACM International Joint Conference on Pervasive and Ubiquitous Computing*, pp. 1179–1183.

Saito, Kazuya. 2011. "Examining the role of explicit phonetic instruction in native-like and comprehensible pronunciation development: An instructed SLA approach to L2 phonology." *Language Awareness* 20, no. 1: 45–59. https://doi.org/10.1080/09658416.2010.540326

Saito, Kazuya. 2007. "The influence of explicit phonetic instruction on pronunciation in EFL settings: The case of English vowels and Japanese learners of English." *Linguistics Journal* 2, no. 3: 16–40.

Sakai, Mari. (Dis)connecting perception and production: Training native speakers of Spanish on the English/i/-/I/distinction. Georgetown University, 2016.

Saz, Oscar, Victoria Rodríguez, Eduardo Lleida, W-Ricardo Rodriguez, and Carlos Vaquero. 2010. "The use of multimodal tools for pronunciation training in second language learning of preadolescents." *Language Teaching: Techniques, Developments and Effectiveness*. Nova Science Publishers, Hauppauge (NY), USA.

Schmidt, Richard. 2012. "Attention, awareness, and individual differences in language learning." In *Proceedings of CLaSIC 2010*, Singapore: 721–737. Singapore: National University of Singapore, Centre for Language Studies.

Shrout, Patrick E., and Joseph L. Fleiss. 1979. "Intraclass correlations: uses in assessing rater reliability." *Psychological Bulletin* 86, no. 2: 420–428.

Sturm, Jessica L., Mayu Miyamoto, and Natsumi Suzuki. 2019. "Pronunciation in the L2 French classroom: Student and teacher attitudes." *The French Review* 92, no. 3: 60–78. https://doi.org/10.1353/tfr.2019.0182

Wassink, Alicia Beckford. 2006. "A geometric representation of spectral and temporal vowel features: Quantification of vowel overlap in three linguistic varieties." *The Journal of the Acoustical Society of America*, 119, no. 4: 2334–2350. https://doi.org/10.1121/1.2168414

Weinberger, Steven. 2015. "Speech Accent Archive. George Mason University." Online:< http://accent.gmu.edu

Part 5

CORPUS-BASED APPROACHES

Chapter Fourteen

Spoken Corpora in Pronunciation Research and Instruction

The Case of the Corpus of Teaching Assistant Classroom Speech (CoTACS)

Idée Edalatishams

INTRODUCTION

International Teaching Assistants (ITAs) in North American universities are master's or doctoral students who are assigned teaching responsibilities such as lecturing, holding office hours, and grading, while completing their own studies as graduate students. They teach many of the introductory and foundational undergraduate courses and therefore play a key role in staffing instructional positions and educating undergraduate students. ITAs are often non-native speakers of English and are generally thought to speak differently from TAs who are native speakers of American English (ATAs). These perceived differences have been less about ITAs' knowledge of their fields or their teaching performance, and more about their speaking and pronunciation ability (Kaufman and Brownworth 2006).

Speech prosody is one area of pronunciation in which ITAs and ATAs differ. Prosodic features such as intonation that function at the level of discourse have been found to play an important role in undergraduate students' comprehension of ITA speech (Kao et al. 2016; Tyler, Jefferies, and Davies 1988; Lindemann and Clower 2020). ATAs clearly mark topic development in their lectures through intonational paragraphing, an organizational tool realized by a high pitch at the beginning and a low pitch at the end of a sequence of semantically coherent clauses. ITAs, on the other hand, have shown weaker levels of control over the intonational structure of their speech, resulting in little or no signaling of information structure (Pickering 2004; Wennerstrom 1998). ITAs have also been found to struggle with employing rising and falling tones to project involvement with their class and develop rapport with their students (Pickering 2001).

Prominence or sentence stress, realized by a higher pitch, lengthened vowel, and increased intensity in speech, can help TAs signal the structure of information presented in the lecture and assist students in understanding what information is given and what is new information (Pickering 1999). Given information refers to information that is shared between the speaker and the hearer and is recoverable from previous linguistic information, immediate context, or general cultural knowledge. While given information is typically marked with low pitch and is non-prominent, new, emphatic, or contrastive information is marked with high pitch and prominence (Chun 2002; Levis and Wichmann 2015; Pickering 1999). ATAs typically employ prominence to signal information structure in their lectures; ITAs, however, have been found to place prominence on multiple content words or struggle with using a high pitch to mark contrastive information (Tyler, Jefferies, and Davies 1988). ITA speech is also characterized by limited pitch range and correspondingly limited degrees of pitch increase and decrease to mark the status of information as new, given, or contrastive (Levis, Levis, and Slater 2012; Wennerstrom 1994). Limited pitch variation in ITA speech has also been found to impact undergraduate students' evaluations of ITAs' status traits like education and intelligence, and solidarity traits like kindness and politeness (Lindemann and Clower 2020).

Most of these previous studies on ITA pronunciation have been exploratory in nature, using either elicited speech or small extracts of speech from classroom or test contexts. However, elicited speech is often not ideal for identifying patterns of errors that compromise intelligibility and comprehensibility (Gray and Levis 2019; O'Brien et al. 2018). Employing corpora in pronunciation research can help the field move toward the use of data in more naturalistic environments, resulting in the collection of data that can provide a realistic view of patterns of error that interfere with non-native speakers' intelligibility and comprehensibility in real life. Spoken corpora also enable examination of a larger number of observations of nuanced aspects of language, such as "sounds in particular environments, prosodic variations, [and] comparative L1 [first language] performance" (Gray and Levis 2019).

Prosodic features, in particular, behave differently in naturally occurring discourse than they do in isolated speech examples. Speakers' choices of prominence placement heavily depend on the ongoing larger discourse, and directly impact the information structure at the level of discourse. Such a level of interaction between prosody and discourse demands research in this area that moves away from the structural viewpoint on intonation, where prosodic markers of given/new information are directly mapped into syntactic markers (Gray and Levis 2019). Therefore, corpus methods may be better suited for studies of prosody than traditional methods, because prosodic features work at the discourse level where they are associated with functional patterns of use (Gray and Levis 2019).

Finally, although the size and scope of previous studies of ITA prosody indicate the difficulty of collecting large samples of ITA speech in non-testing environments, large-scale analyses using corpus-based techniques enable more principled analyses (Baker 2006) and allow for better linguistic representativeness, making it possible to generalize the results to a larger population. Data driven from a corpus of classroom speech by TAs from a wide range of disciplinary and L1 backgrounds provide a larger number of data points for a target intonation feature such as prominence, enabling the generalization of the results to a larger population of TAs from the same L1 background. For instance, a corpus analysis indicating that L1 Thai speakers place prominence on a certain syllable at significantly higher rates than speakers of other languages, can lead to generalizations about prominence placement by L1 Thai speakers even in contexts other than the one in which the data was collected. In addition to benefiting research on ITA pronunciation, a prosodic corpus of ITA speech can also be used in training ITAs.

Pedagogical Uses of Spoken Corpora

The potential of corpus linguistics in informing and improving pedagogical practice is undeniable. Corpora have long informed teaching by improving descriptions of linguistic features to be taught, but they also serve as tools for teachers and learners to analyze language (Cobb and Boulton 2015). In a survey Römer (2009) conducted to understand the needs of language teachers, two types of needs were identified: (1) the need for teaching materials that are based on authentic language and cover variation among different speakers; and (2) the need for reference tools and native speakers available to answer language-related questions. These needs are most likely to be addressed through the use of large databases of authentic language that are produced in natural environments and cover some level of variation. Such corpora are searchable and can answer a range of questions both teachers and learners may have about language use. Corpora can also be used to identify teaching targets and create data-driven learning materials to increase learners' language awareness and engagement with the learning materials (Cobb and Boulton 2015; Römer 2009).

However, pedagogical applications of spoken corpora in pronunciation are in their infancy, having been explored mostly over the last two decades (Mauranen 2004). Limited numbers of teachers and learners report use of spoken corpora in their pronunciation teaching and learning (Chen and Tian 2020), due to reasons such as a general discomfort with technological innovations

(O'Brien et al. 2018) and lack of familiarity with corpus tools and search techniques (Mauranen 2004). Nevertheless, research on the applications of spoken corpora in language instruction has yielded promising results in the teaching of prosody.

One example is in an English for Specific Purposes (ESP) context, where Staples (2019) created a pronunciation curriculum for internationally educated nurses, relying on corpus-based needs analysis, material development, and assessment. A corpus was created and teaching materials were developed using data from the corpus, based on the differences found in pitch range, tone choice, and prominence placement between US and international nursing discourse. Corpus-based teaching materials included images captured from speech analysis software along with audio files later created to accompany those pictures. Use of these corpus-based materials resulted in measurable improvements in learners' pronunciation for pragmatic purposes. After taking the pronunciation course, the internationally trained nurses showed an increase in their pitch range and a decrease in their use of falling tones to empathize with patients. They also responded well to the training regarding prominence placement, stressing fewer key words when conveying information to patients.

Using a phonologically annotated corpus of Mandarin composed of read and free speech, Chen and Han (2020) identified common areas of segmental and suprasegmental difficulties in the speech of L1 Cantonese learners of Mandarin and developed a platform to provide learners with perception and production activities on these areas. The platform made the annotated corpus data and practice activities available for teachers' and learners' use, along with useful guides, online resources, and a Praat beginners' manual. Learners enrolled in university-level Mandarin courses and instructors from K–12 and university contexts who used the corpus-based pronunciation platform evaluated it as effective in helping them identify patterns of pronunciation error and learning/teaching to improve in those areas more efficiently than when using non-corpus-based methods.

Corpora have also been used in the training of pronunciation teachers. In a workshop for pre-service pronunciation teachers in an EFL context, Chen and Tian (2020) introduced these teachers to a number of English learner corpora and corpus-based lesson plan and activity development. Some of these teachers were then provided with more extensive training on using corpora in their teaching, including the development of listening tasks using corpus examples. These tasks aimed at helping language learners assess the intelligibility of an accent and identify mispronunciations of speakers from different L1 backgrounds. The teachers that were later interviewed reported a strong willingness to incorporate examples from corpora in their lessons to raise language learners' awareness of their mispronunciations. Spoken corpora also increased these teachers' motivation to teach pronunciation. The vast majority of learners who evaluated a lesson provided by two of the trained pronunciation teachers reported that they learned correct pronunciations of target sounds and developed the ability to identify words they mispronounced.

Even though the benefits of corpora for language instruction have been emphasized by many (e.g., Kettemann and Marko 2002), it is extremely time-consuming to collect spoken corpora or ask teachers to collect a corpus themselves for use in each class they teach. The need for developing spoken corpora and making them available to language teachers and learners has been frequently emphasized (Mauranen 2004; O'Brien et al. 2018), but corpora that can be used in pronunciation instruction are still rare (Gut 2014). Considering the benefits that corpus data offer for studying characteristics of TA speech and training ITAs, corpora that consider TAs as a target group need to be developed and made available. Some existing spoken corpora, such as the British Academic Spoken English Corpus (BASE) and the Michigan Corpus of Academic Spoken English (MICASE), include a small number of TA classroom speech files. However, those data are not prosodically annotated and/or accompanied by audio files, rendering them unusable for research or teaching of pronunciation. On the other hand, those corpora that are prosodically annotated, such as the Spoken English Corpus (SEC), the Hong Kong Corpus of Spoken English (HKCSE), and the London-Lund Corpus, in addition to not offering audio files, do not include TA speech. The Corpus of English for Academic and Professional Purposes (CEAPP) is the only corpus with instructional speech as its target domain that has audio and transcriptions available on their website, once users create an account. However, the main goal for this corpus has been to collect data from a broad range of instructional contexts (from K–12 and ESL to university level courses) and the annotations are conducted from a conversation analysis viewpoint. Therefore, the Corpus of Teaching Assistant Classroom Speech has been developed with university-level TA classroom speech as its target domain and prosodic features as the focus of its annotations. The following section describes this corpus in detail.

THE CORPUS OF TEACHING ASSISTANT CLASSROOM SPEECH (COTACS)[1]

The Corpus of Teaching Assistant Classroom Speech (CoTACS) is a prosodically annotated corpus that has been developed to provide (1) researchers with data to conduct studies on pronunciation and discourse features of TA speech, and (2) teachers and learners with materials for pronunciation instruction. CoTACS contains recordings of speech by 10 ATAs with American English as their L1 and 20 ITAs from a range of non-English L1s, including Farsi, Chinese, Bengali, Spanish, Korean, Nepali, and Bahasa Indonesia. TAs were recorded using a non-intrusive wearable recorder while teaching lectures, labs, problem-solving, and studio sessions in a range of disciplines including English, Engineering, Chemistry, Biology, Arts, Business, Computer Science, and Mathematics. For each speaker, the corpus includes an audio file (Mean length = 54 minutes) and a TextGrid file that can be opened in Praat (Boersma and Weenink 2009) to show the aligned transcription and annotations. Orthographic transcriptions are aligned with the audio at the level of sounds, words, and tone units. Prosodic annotations include tone units, prominence, and pauses based on Brazil's (1997) discourse intonation framework. Metadata is available for each speaker, including self-reported information about gender, L1, native-speaking status, course title, major, degree, department, year in the program, number of semesters as a TA, and length of residence in an English-speaking country. Figure 14.1[2] shows a segment of an ATA's speech in Praat. From the top, this figure displays the waveform, pitch movement, aligned words, aligned sounds, syllables, orthographic transcription, tone unit and prominence markup, the student speech tier,[3] and a comments tier for any additional notes. Tone unit boundaries are marked with double slashes (//) and prominence is marked using capital letters. The annotations were done based on auditory analyses of phonetic cues such as pause, vowel lengthening, and pitch direction shift (Pickering 1999).

   Linking research in technology for pronunciation learning and practical applications for teaching, the next two parts of this chapter discuss the re-

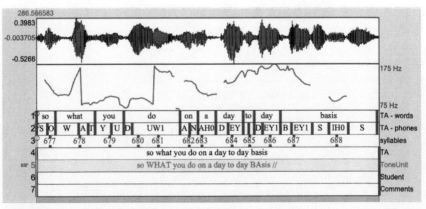

Figure 14.1.   Sample CoTACS file opened in Praat.
Credit: Edalatishams 2022

sults of a study using data from CoTACS to examine ATAs' and ITAs' use of prominence and to introduce suggestions for employing data from CoTACS in pronunciation instruction.

QUALITATIVE ANALYSIS OF
TA PROMINENCE PLACEMENT

In this part of the chapter, an analysis of speech by six CoTACS speakers will be presented using examples from the data, with the aim of showcasing the types of differences that can be found in the prosodic structure of ITA and ATA speech and impact listeners' understanding of the discourse. The research question here is: How do the differences in ATA and ITA tone unit and prominence marking impact the information structure of their speech?

Methods

The speech analyzed in this section comes from four ITAs teaching courses in Math, Computer Science, and Business and two ATAs teaching courses in English at a large Midwestern university. These speakers were chosen from the total of 30 speakers in CoTACS with the goal of examining lectures and problem-solving sessions in humanities, sciences, business. In the lectures, the TAs are mostly the sole speakers and students talk occasionally during discussions and activities. In the problem-solving sessions, the TAs are mostly solving math problems on the board as part of a new lesson or a previous assignment or exam. In these sessions, students do not generally speak unless when they have questions or are prompted by the TA to answer questions. At the time of data collection, all six TAs in this analysis reported being at least in their second semester of a doctoral program and having lived in an English-speaking country for at least two years. They also reported having experience teaching as a TA for a minimum of four semesters, with teaching responsibilities including stand-alone teaching, grading, office hours, lab supervision, and proctoring exams. Table 14.1 summarizes the speakers' demographic characteristics.

For this analysis, the audio recording and annotated TextGrid file for each of these six speakers were used. Thirty tone units from the beginning of each speaker's class (excluding the greetings and housekeeping matters) were used as the basis for this analysis. I focused on the aligned transcriptions, tone unit boundaries, and prominence markups to identify patterns of differences between ATA and ITA speech that could impact the information structure and therefore the overall comprehensibility of their speech at the discourse level.

Table 14.1. Demographic Characteristics of Speakers

Code	L1	Gender	Age	Discipline	Class Type	Course Title
ATA2	English	M	35–45	English	Lecture	Written, Oral, Visual, and Electronic Communication
ATA3	English	M	35–45	English	Lecture	Technical Communication
ITA2	Farsi	F	25–35	Computer Science	Problem Solving	Discrete Mathematics
ITA7	Farsi	M	25–35	Business	Lecture	Strategic Management
ITA9	Chinese	F	25–35	Math	Problem Solving	Elementary Differential Equations
ITA16	Chinese	F	25–35	Computer Science	Problem Solving	Design and Analysis of Algorithms

Source: Edalatishams 2022

Results

Results of the qualitative analysis of ATA and ITA prominence placement are discussed in this section, using examples from the six TAs' speech.[4]

Prominence on Given Information

ATAs are found to segment their speech into tone units in such a way that enables undergraduate student listeners to easily identify pieces of information that are expected to be highlighted due to their information status as new. Prominence is placed on new information, clearly marking what students should pay more attention to. The ATA in example (1) is discussing the topic of the class, research methods. Students have already read about quantitative and qualitative research methods, and the ATA is reviewing these two methods right before stating the sentence in the example. In this sentence, the ATA is describing the research projects that these students must carry out for this class.

(1) *ATA3:* // ALL of the research that you're DOing // for OUR class // is QUANtitative //

ATA3 is uttering this sentence in three tone units, each with meaningful information and at least one prominent syllable. In each tone unit, prominence is placed on all words that the speaker considers new or contrastive information. He is emphasizing that *all* of their research and not only their current project, for *this* class and not necessarily for other classes, is quantitative and not qualitative. All given information already accessible to the students (e.g., words such as *research* and *class*) is non-prominent, signaling to the listeners to pay attention to the new pieces of information.

ITAs, however, often place prominence on words that are already known to the listener. The ITA in example (2) has just mentioned that there are three characteristics that control water flow: precipitation rate, evaporation rate, and surface characteristics. She is explaining the first two in this example.

(2) *ITA9:* //precipitation RATE is LARger than infiltration RATE //

While the word *rate* is previously introduced and is therefore known to the listener, her placing prominence on both instances of this word signals to the listener that *rate* is new information. This can make listeners think that *rate* is being presented in contrast with another concept like frequency, making the statement more difficult to understand. Similarly, when she introduces the third factor that impacts water flow, she places prominence on another word which is also not new information (example 3).

(3) *ITA9:* // and SURface characteRIstic also affects water FLOW //

Flow is the topic of the lesson and therefore already known to the listeners. However, its being marked as prominent signals that it is new information, diverting the listener's attention from the actual new information that needed to take focus. With *flow* stated as prominent, it sounds like *surface characteristics* affect multiple things including *flow*. In addition to this prominence marking issue, the word *characteristic* used in singular form is a syntactic issue that can potentially result in more confusion for the listener.

Multiple Prominences

In addition to misplacement of prominence, one of the other patterns found in this data is that ITAs place prominence on multiple syllables within the same tone unit when those words neither present new information nor are contrastive. Example (4), spoken by an ITA whose L1 is Farsi, illustrates this point.

(4) *ITA2:* // SO I'M going to SHOW HOW they're EQual //

Similar levels of prominence are placed on five words in this tone unit, several of which are function words. This makes it difficult to identify the main information, which is *how* the two items previously discussed are equal. In example (5), another ITA with the same L1 is discussing the business strategies of the chain grocery store, *Aldi*. He is placing prominence on both the adverb *very* and the adjective *good*.

(5) *ITA7:* // because i I think ALdi's case is a [*pause*] uh is a VEry GOOD case //

Placing prominence on both of these words makes it sound like contrastive information, as if he has previously talked about a *good* case and is now evaluating *Aldi*'s case as *very* good. Also, prior to this sentence there has been no discussion of *Aldi*'s *case* or *any other case* being a *bad* case. This speaker is emphasizing that this case is a good one, but by placing prominence on the modifying adverb as well, signals a contrast. Farsi speaking ITAs seem to have this tendency to produce all or several words with similar levels of prominence, possibly because Farsi is a syllable-timed language (example 6).

(6) *ITA7:* // if there is ANYthing important that you want to SHARE //

In this example, all words are fully enunciated, no syllable is shortened, and there are no contracted forms, resulting in every word sounding as prominent. However, the ITA compromises this by placing more emphasis on the words that are expected to be prominent: *anything* and *share.* By doing so, the speaker creates the difference in pitch level that the listener expects to hear on new information. The ITA in example (7) also places prominence on two words toward the end of the tone unit.

(7) *ITA16:* // SO today I'm gonna review several PROBlems in the reVIEW [*pause*] LIST //

The word *review* in this example is lengthened and followed by an unfilled pause right after it, making the listener think that she is done speaking. Placing a pause right before the last word, although common in native speech, is usually not followed by a prominent word. In example (8) from an ATA, no prominence is placed on the last word, *one.*

(8) *ATA2:* // a LOT of you all did NOT remember Ethos // and this is by FAR the most POWerful [*pause*] one //

Multiple prominences are sometimes caused by a problem with word stress. In example (9), the ITA is discussing two possible routes rainfall can take: infiltration and run-off.

(9) *ITA9:* // and YOU have RAINfall here // and SOME water will INfiltrate into GROUND become GROUNDwater // and SOME will uh become RUNOFF //

In the last tone unit, the word *run-off* is a compound noun, and the stress usually falls on the first word in a compound noun. This ITA, however, is placing similar prominences on both parts of this compound word, resulting in problems with both lexical prosody and phrasal prosody. A similar interreference of stress at the word level and at the sentence level can be seen in example (10) from the same ITA.

(10) *ITA9:* // over TIME // STREAM // uh eRODES landSCAPE //

While the stress in *landscape* (also a compound noun) generally falls on the first word, this ITA places stress on *scape*, resulting in the sentence prominence falling on that syllable as well. Example (11) shows the complete sentence, where this ITA is now missing prominence on new information.

(11) *ITA9:* // over TIME // STREAM // uh eRODES landSCAPE // move and dePOSits SEDiment //

In this sentence, the topic seems to be the three actions that *stream* takes. *Moving* is one of those actions and should therefore be prominent, just like *erode* and *deposit* are prominent. As a result of not marking *move* as prominent, it becomes difficult to identify *moving* as having a similar information status as the two other actions. This prominence placement issue is even more complicated by the syntactic issue of subject-verb agreement: *move* needs to be in singular form to agree with the singular subject *stream*. Occurrence of multiple issues with lexical prosody, phrasal prosody, and syntax within the same sentence makes this difficult to follow.

Several other differences in prominence placement were observed between ITA and ATA speech, including ITAs marking new information as non-prominent or misplacing lexical stress in ways that further complicate sentence prominence. All of these prosodic anomalies impact the information structure of ITAs' speech. As a result, comprehending the speech becomes more difficult because "similar intonation weight is given to items with unlike informational status" (Wennerstrom 1994, 416).

These issues should also be seen in reference to the concept of mental representation. In addition to common knowledge and the background knowledge of the topic that speakers and listeners share, there is information in their short-term memory about what ideas are already mentioned and which ones are new (Wennerstrom 1997). Since prominence is an important signal for information structure in native speech, listeners unconsciously expect new information to be prominent and given information to be non-prominent. When listener expectations are violated, they need to "make continual adjustments to their representation of the text and predictions as to what will follow" (Pickering 1999, 256). Therefore, receiving misleading prosodic signals about the status of information causes more processing load for the listener (Engelhardt, Ferreira, and Patsenko 2010), impacting their comprehension of the ITA's speech (Hahn 2004).

PEDAGOGICAL IMPLICATIONS

In the fourth and last part of this chapter, I discuss how spoken corpora like CoTACS can serve as instructional tools. A discussion of contexts in which CoTACS data can be used in teaching is provided along with some notes on training instructors and learners on how to use corpus data for pronunciation instruction. I then introduce five possible scenarios for using CoTACS in teaching prosody. Two of these scenarios refer to the examples presented in the results section and provide a list of steps for creating activities that target perception and production of prominence.

Since CoTACS is composed of TA speech, it can be argued that it is best suited for use in TA training. CoTACS data can be used in developing training for both ITAs and ATAs to prepare them for communication tasks required in the classroom context, such as effective strategies for lecturing, responding to students' questions, and asking questions. For lessons targeting such general communication tasks, instructors can explore the audio files in CoTACS and use segments of discourse they identify as useful for their teaching objectives. CoTACS can also be used to provide data for lessons and activities at the level of discourse, paragraph, sentence, tone unit, word, and sound, particularly designed for training ITAs in comprehensible pronunciation. Potentials of CoTACS for teaching, however, are by no means limited to TA training. CoTACS provides a great amount of language data for teaching pronunciation to language learners at different proficiency levels. The prominence annotations make the corpus readily usable for lessons on prominence placement and its role in information structure.

Before a corpus can become a useful resource for language teachers and learners, guidance and training need to be provided on using the corpus to achieve linguistic and pedagogical goals (Staples 2019). Pre-service language teachers who were introduced to corpora for the first time showed only limited development of competencies in working with corpus tools, using corpus analysis techniques, and applying corpora in their teaching (Leńko-Szymańska 2017). It appears that familiarizing teachers with corpora through workshops or short-term trainings can be beneficial only to a limited degree, indicating that continuous support may be needed for language teachers to gradually develop technical, analytical, and pedagogical skills related to using corpora in their teaching. Learners also need support in understanding the structure of the corpus they are provided with and developing the necessary technical skills to use corpus data (Mauranen 2004). While detailed instructions and guidelines for using CoTACS in pronunciation teaching can be accessed along with the corpus data, some general recommendations are listed here:

1. Prior to the lessons, learners need to be familiarized with basic pronunciation concepts related to prosody, especially thought grouping or tone units. This will prepare them for analyzing other intonational features that occur within a tone unit, such as prominence and tone choice.
2. Before tasking learners with exercises using corpus data, instructors need to introduce them to the speech analysis software, Praat, and how its basic features work.
3. Instructors should also provide learners with guidance about the conventions used in the corpus annotations, such as double slashes for tone units and capital letters for prominence, and what information is presented in each tier of the TextGrid files.

For pronunciation-focused courses, corpus data can be employed at different stages of curriculum development and lesson planning (see Staples 2019). Before developing a course, CoTACS can be used by ITA trainers to conduct needs analysis aimed at identifying language functions that ITAs are expected to perform in the target situation, that is, teaching undergraduate courses ("Target Situation Analysis," Flowerdew 2013). Instructors can also benefit from CoTACS in assessing the gap that exists between learners' current stage of knowledge and what is expected at the end of the course ("Present Situation Analysis," Flowerdew 2013). Similarly in teacher training, CoTACS can be used to introduce instructors to the linguistic objectives ITAs are expected to reach by the end of the course, as well as areas of pronunciation that ITAs from different L1 backgrounds may need to focus on.

Finally, in developing content for pronunciation lessons, CoTACS offers a wide range of speech data to choose from depending on the learners' needs and the instructional context. Segments of speech that include the target pronunciation features for each lesson can be extracted from both the native and non-native samples of the corpus. While native speech samples can help illustrate prosodic patterns that facilitate listeners' understanding, it is also important for pronunciation teachers to make use of non-native speech samples to illustrate correct uses of pronunciation features. This suggestion is supported by almost three decades of pronunciation research, which has shown the importance of intelligibility over native-like pronunciation (Levis 2005; 2020; Munro and Derwing 1995). Therefore, instructors should consider using intelligible non-native speech samples in their teaching and open up discussions of why being intelligible should be prioritized over reaching native-speaker standards. Pronunciation instructors can use the corpus audio files either with screenshots of Praat to provide a visual representation of the target pronunciation feature, or with short TextGrid files extracted from the original TextGrid files. The latter provides learners with the opportunity for a more in-depth analysis of speech and is recommended with advanced learners who have received extensive training on how to use speech corpora. The following is a non-exhaustive list of teaching targets that can be determined using CoTACS data:

Prominence Placement on New or Given Information

To provide learners with practice in their perceptive skills, an instructor can prepare excerpts of speech where correct prominence placement on new information can facilitate listeners' understanding and incorrect prominence placement on given information can interfere with meaning. Learners can benefit from comparing different speech samples with correct, misplaced, or missing prominence (Hahn 2004). Learners can work individually or in pairs to identify prominent syllables in each speech sample, and then share their answers with class. The instructor can then open a discussion of the differences in meaning caused by correct, misplaced, or missing prominence. This activity can be used early on in a series of lessons targeting different prosodic features but can also be used along with activities focused on production after learners develop their perceptive skills to a considerable level. Example (1) in the results section (illustrating a segment of speech with correct prominence) and example (2) in the results section (illustrating a speech segment with misplaced prominence) can be used in a lesson aimed at comparing prominence placement on new or given information, with suggested steps as follows:

1. The instructor provides a lesson about prominence, explaining the auditory cues for prominence such as higher pitch, lengthened vowel, and loudness.
2. The instructor briefly provides the context for each of these excerpts, plays each audio file, and asks learners to circle the words that the speakers uttered with prominence.
3. Learners compare their answers in pairs and share with class.
4. The instructor asks the class if they think prominence placement should be different in either of these samples, starting a discussion of how the meaning would be different with prominence placed on different words.
5. The instructor then asks learners to produce the statement in the non-native sample with correct prominence placement.

Prominence Placement by Speakers of Different L1s

In a class where learners' L1s are represented in CoTACS, the instructor can prepare excerpts of speech by CoTACS speakers from the different L1 backgrounds and task small groups of learners in class with working together to identify patterns of prominence marking in each L1. Learners will then share their groups' findings with class. With a focus on learners' perceptive skills, this activity can raise all learners' awareness of possible patterns of prominence placement in English speech by different L1 speakers, potentially facilitating communication between non-native speakers of English. Learners who speak the same L1s as represented in the activity can further practice their productive skills by reproducing the tone units spoken by the CoTACS speakers and focusing on modified prominence placement to convey different meanings. Example (4) in the results section illustrates equal prominence placement on multiple words and can be used in an activity aimed at both perceptive and productive skills in this regard. Suggested steps are as follows:

1. The instructor provides a lesson about prominence, explaining the auditory cues for prominence such as higher pitch, lengthened vowel, and loudness.
2. The instructor provides the transcription for this segment (along with the surrounding context, if needed) and asks learners to underline words that they think should be prominent.
3. The instructor then plays the audio for this segment and asks learners to circle the words that the speaker uttered with prominence.
4. The instructor then draws learners' attention to the annotations in the *ToneUnit* tier in the Praat file or a screenshot of this segment and asks learners to compare the words they underlined and circled with the words marked in capital letters in that tier.
5. The instructor then leads a discussion on how equal prominence placement on multiple words within the same tone unit may interfere with the meaning the speaker intends to convey.
6. The instructor then asks learners to produce this tone unit out loud with correct prominence placement.

Thought Grouping for Increasing Fluency

Learners can be provided with transcripts of short segments of native and non-native speech from CoTACS and asked to mark tone units (thought groups) on the transcripts while listening to the audio. They can then compare their observations of the differences between thought grouping in native and non-native speech. More advanced learners can be asked to mark thought groups on the transcripts before listening to the audio, allowing them to assess their understanding of the concept before focusing on their perceptive skills. This can be followed by an activity focused on correctly producing the non-native examples in thought groups.

Pause Placement and Length in Native and Non-native Speech

Learners can be asked to open excerpts of TA speech in Praat, identify short and long pauses, measure their length, and compare these traits between different speech samples. This can be followed by a discussion of the impact of pause length on how listeners understand speech. Advanced learners can also be prompted to examine pause placement as it relates to thought grouping.

Use of Tones and Pitch Contours

Instructors can provide a lesson focused on how falling, rising, and level tones can be used in interactions to indicate friendliness and build rapport. In the case of ITAs, for example, the instructor can provide examples from CoTACs to explain how tone choice can help elicit linguistic or non-linguistic response from undergraduate students, resulting in more interaction in the classroom. In such a lesson, ITAs learn about or improve their understanding of using a rising tone to raise a question or to speak a statement in such a way that elicits students' response.

CONCLUSION

Application of corpora and corpus linguistics methods in pronunciation research and teaching has helped the field move toward examining speech in more naturalistic settings, resulting in implications for teaching that emphasize the role of pronunciation features in discourse. Such an emphasis can translate into integration of more activities on pronunciation features like discourse intonation into course development and lesson planning at different levels. Drawing attention to pronunciation features that contribute to comprehensibility of speech beyond words and sentences, corpus data can help inform training in ways that traditional pronunciation teaching and research methods have not.

Spoken corpora can provide instructors with a large amount of information to draw from, not only to understand the needs of different groups of learners, but also to design materials and content for pronunciation-focused courses. For the teaching of prominence, as one pronunciation feature that acts at the discourse level, Hahn (2004) recommends making use of longer stretches of discourse and learners' own discourse in designing activities. Spoken corpora like CoTACS can provide longer stretches of discourse produced in real teaching situations, with the added value of opening a window to how courses on different topics are taught by other instructors. The qualitative analysis presented in this chapter revealed some differences between ATAs and ITAs in terms of prominence placement and its role in information structure. Future research using speech corpus data can explore other pronunciation features that contribute to the comprehensibility of discourse, suggest ways for implementing findings in pronunciation instruction, and develop materials for training instructors and learners in using corpora for pronunciation teaching and learning.

NOTES

1. Development of COTACS was partially funded by a grant from the *Language Learning* journal. The corpus can be accessed at https://sites.google.com/view/cotacs along with descriptions of its components and guidelines for use in teaching and research. Transcriptions and prosodic annotations continue to be added to the files. Users are welcome to provide teaching materials they develop from CoTACS to become available on the website.

2. This figure is a screenshot of an audio file and a TextGrid file opened in Praat, zoomed in to capture a complete segment of speech. As a result, the text in some intervals may not be entirely visible, although Praat users can view it by further zooming in.

3. Students' voices are removed from the audio files in CoTACS for confidentiality purposes; but to provide context for TAs' speech, words spoken by students are transcribed in this tier.

4. The examples presented in this section are not intended as representative of ITA or ATA speech and the results do not indicate any statistically significant difference between the two groups. These examples are specifically selected to showcase patterns of prosodic differences between the two groups. The corpus includes many instances of correct prominence placement by non-native speakers, which are not presented here.

REFERENCES

Baker, Paul. 2006. *Using Corpora in Discourse Analysis*. New York, NY: Bloomsbury Academic.

Boersma, Paul, and David Weenink. 2009. *Praat: Doing Phonetics by Computer*. www.fon.hum.uva.nl/praat.

Brazil, D. (1997). *The communicative value of intonation in English*. Cambridge, UK: Cambridge University Press.

Chen, Hsueh Chu, and Qian Wen Han. 2020. "Designing and Implementing a Corpus-Based Online Pronunciation Learning Platform for Cantonese Learners of Mandarin." *Interactive Learning Environments* 28, no. 1: 18–31. https://doi.org/10.1080/10494820.2018.1510422

Chen, Hsueh Chu, and Jing Xuan Tian. 2020. "Developing and Evaluating a Flipped Corpus-Aided English Pronunciation Teaching Approach for Pre-Service Teachers in Hong Kong." *Interactive Learning Environments*, 1–14. https://doi.org/10.1080/10494820.2020.1753217

Chun, Dorothy M. 2002. *Discourse Intonation in L2: From Theory and Research to Practice.* Vol. 1. Philadelphia: John Benjamins Publishing.

Cobb, Tom, and Alex Boulton. 2015. "Classroom Applications of Corpus Analysis." In *The Cambridge Handbook of English Corpus Linguistics*, edited by Douglas Biber and Randi Reppen, 478–97. Cambridge, UK: Cambridge University Press.

Engelhardt, Paul E., Fernanda Ferreira, and Elena G. Patsenko. 2010. "Pupillometry Reveals Processing Load during Spoken Language Comprehension." *Quarterly Journal of Experimental Psychology* 63, no. 4: 639–45. https://doi.org/10.1080/17470210903469864

Flowerdew, Lynne. 2013. "Needs Analysis and Curriculum Development in ESP." In *The Handbook of English for Specific Purposes*, edited by Brian Paltridge and Sue Starfield, 325–46. West Sussex, UK: John Wiley & Sons.

Gray, Bethany, and John Levis. 2019. "A Pronunciation Researcher and a Corpus Linguist Walk into a Bar." Presented at the Pronunciation in Second Language Learning and Teaching Conference, Flagstaff, AZ, September 13.

Gut, Ulrike. 2014. "Corpus Phonology and Second Language Acquisition." In *The Oxford Handbook of Corpus Phonology*, edited by Jacques Durand, Ulrike Gut, and Gjert Kristoffersen, 286–301. Oxford, UK: Oxford Handbooks in Linguistic.

Hahn, Laura D. 2004. "Primary Stress and Intelligibility: Research to Motivate the Teaching of Suprasegmentals." *TESOL Quarterly* 38, no. 2: 201–23. https://doi.org/10.2307/3588378

Kao, Sophia, Jiwon Hwang, Hyunah Baek, Chikako Takahashi, and Ellen Broselow. 2016. "International Teaching Assistants' Production of Focus Marking." *The Journal of the Acoustical Society of America* 139, no. 4: 2161–2161. https://doi.org/10.1121/2.0000356

Kaufman, Dorit, and Barbara Brownworth, eds. 2006. *Professional Development of International Teaching Assistants.* Case Studies in TESOL Practice Series. Alexandria, VA: Teachers of English to Speakers of Other Languages, Inc.

Kettemann, Bernhard, and Georg Marko. 2002. *Teaching and Learning by Doing Corpus Analysis: Proceedings of the Fourth International Conference on Teaching and Language Corpora, Graz 19–24 July, 2000.* 42. Rodopi.

Leńko-Szymańska, Agnieszka. 2017. "Training Teachers in Data Driven Learning: Tackling the Challenge." *Language Learning & Technology* 21, no. 3: 217–41. https://doi.org/10125/44628

Levis, John. 2005. "Changing Contexts and Shifting Paradigms in Pronunciation Teaching." *Tesol Quarterly* 39, no. 3: 369–77. https://doi.org/10.2307/3588485

———. 2020. "Revisiting the Intelligibility and Nativeness Principles." *Journal of Second Language Pronunciation* 6, no. 3: 310–28. https://doi.org/10.1075/jslp.20050.lev

Levis, John, Greta Levis, and Tammy Slater. 2012. "Written English into Spoken: A Functional Discourse Analysis of American, Indian, and Chinese TA Presentations." In *Working Theories for Teaching Assistant Development: Time-Tested & Robust Theories, Frameworks, & Models for TA & ITA Learning*, edited by Greta Gorsuch, 529–72, Stillwater, OK: New Forums Press.

Levis, John, and Anne Wichmann. 2015. "English Intonation: Form and Meaning." In *The Handbook of English Pronunciation*, edited by John M. Levis and Marnie Reed, 139–55. West Sussex, UK: John Wiley & Sons, Inc.

Lindemann, Stephanie, and Amy Clower. 2020. "Language Attitudes and the 'ITA Problem': Undergraduate Reactions to Instructors'(Non) Nativeness and Pitch Variation." *International Journal of Applied Linguistics* 30, no. 1: 127–43. https://doi.org/10.1111/ijal.12271

Mauranen, Anna. 2004. "Spoken Corpus for an Ordinary Learner." In *How to Use Corpora in Language Teaching*, edited by John Sinclair, 12:89–105. Philadelphia: John Benjamins Publishing.

Munro, Murray J., and Tracey M. Derwing. 1995. "Foreign Accent, Comprehensibility, and Intelligibility in the Speech of Second Language Learners." *Language Learning* 45, no. 1: 73–97. https://doi.org/10.1111/j.1467-1770.1995.tb00963.x

O'Brien, Mary Grantham, Tracey M. Derwing, Catia Cucchiarini, Debra M. Hardison, Hansjörg Mixdorff, Ron I. Thomson, Helmer Strik, et al. 2018. "Directions for the Future of Technology in Pronunciation Research and Teaching." *Journal of Second Language Pronunciation* 4, no. 2: 182–207. https://doi.org/10.1075/jslp.17001.obr.

Pickering, Lucy. 1999. "An Analysis of Prosodic Systems in the Classroom Discourse of Native Speaker and Non-Native Speaker Teaching Assistants." PhD Thesis, Gainesville: University of Florida.

———. 2001. "The Role of Tone Choice in Improving ITA Communication in the Classroom." *TESOL Quarterly* 35, no. 2: 233–55. https://doi.org/10.2307/3587647

———. 2004. "The Structure and Function of Intonational Paragraphs in Native and Nonnative Speaker Instructional Discourse." *English for Specific Purposes* 23, no. 1: 19–43. https://doi.org/10.1016/S0889-4906(03)00020-6

Römer, Ute. 2009. "Corpus Research and Practice: What Help Do Teachers Need and What Can We Offer?" In *Corpora and Language Teaching*, edited by Karin Aijmer, 33:83–98. Philadelphia: John Benjamins Publishing.

Staples, Shelley. 2019. "Using Corpus-Based Discourse Analysis for Curriculum Development: Creating and Evaluating a Pronunciation Course for Internationally Educated Nurses." *English for Specific Purposes* 53: 13–29. https://doi.org/10.1016/j.esp.2018.08.005

Tyler, Andrea, Ann A. Jefferies, and Catherine E. Davies. 1988. "The Effect of Discourse Structuring Devices on Listener Perceptions of Coherence in Non-Native University Teacher's Spoken Discourse." *World Englishes* 7, no. 2: 101–10. https://doi.org/10.1111/j.1467-971X.1988.tb00223.x

Wennerstrom, Ann. 1994. "Intonational Meaning in English Discourse: A Study of Non-Native Speakers." *Applied Linguistics* 15, no. 4: 399–420. https://doi.org/10.1093/applin/15.4.399

———. 1997. "Discourse Intonation and Second Language Acquisition: Three Genre-Based Studies." PhD Thesis, Seattle: University of Washington.

———. 1998. "Intonation as Cohesion in Academic Discourse: A Study of Chinese Speakers of English." *Studies in Second Language Acquisition* 20, no. 1: 1–25. https://doi.org/10.1017/S0272263198001016

Chapter Fifteen

Innovation in ITA Course Design

Incorporating Student-designed Field-specific Corpora

Mai M. Eida and Suzanne Franks

INTRODUCTION

Thirty-one percent of all international students from approximately one hundred countries at the University of Illinois at Urbana-Champaign are appointed as teaching assistants based on their English Proficiency score from IELTS, TOEFL, or the university's English Proficiency Interview (EPI) (Graduate College n.d., Graduate College 2019).[1] If students do not meet the minimum TOEFL or IELTS speaking score established by the university to become Teaching Assistants, they are required to take the EPI. If they do not receive a passing score on the EPI, they are recommended to enroll in a course for International Teaching Assistants (ITAs) offered by the ESL program at the same university. Due to the ever-changing needs of ITAs, the course Oral Communication for ITAs has undergone some recent changes to ensure the accommodation of all ITAs of various linguistic and academic backgrounds. One of the focal assignments introduced to respond to student needs has been "*The (Mini-)corpus project*," where students are encouraged to base some of their in- and out-of-class assignments on terminology and content extracted from their own field and subdiscipline. This has been the first time to explore the use of student-generated mini-corpora in an ITA course, which will be further introduced and explained in this chapter. In this chapter, we will begin by justifying the need for a mini-corpus in our ITA courses, then review the theoretical background around ITA pedagogy and use of corpora in the classroom, followed by an illustration of integrating a mini-corpus into the course and utilizing it for pronunciation instruction and practice. After providing tasks and assignment examples, the chapter will present an outline for creating an ITA course based on student experiences and responses.

CONTEXT

In the ESL program of the University of Illinois at Urbana-Champaign in the United States, international students are recommended to take an International Teaching Assistants (ITA) course either (1) to prepare for an oral English assessment (EPI) to be able to TA; (2) to improve their points of weaknesses because they scored low on an oral English assessment and thus seek instruction, and finally; (3) to improve their oral communication skills, thus enroll in the course as an elective. The overall goal of this course is to provide international graduate students the tools to become a more successful TA in a US academic context. Those who become TAs need more than microteaching practice, therefore, the course focuses on linguistic skills, teaching skills, and cross-cultural communication skills (Ross & Dunphy 2007). The goal regarding linguistic skills in an EAP setting includes a focus on learning and communication strategies, vocabulary usage, suprasegmental features of language including thought groups, rhythm, linking, word and phrase stress, and adjusting speech rate and loudness adjustments, to account for classroom conditions. The teaching skills goals include lecturing skills, questioning strategies, student and teacher responses to questions, discussion techniques, interactive teaching techniques, and peer- and self-assessment strategies. In regard to cross-cultural communication, these goals include topics such as non-verbal communication, eye contact and gestures in the classroom, cross-cultural differences between the academic settings in the United States and other countries, and other strategies for being an effective TA in a US classroom.

ITA classes usually meet twice a week for 80 minutes per session (face-to-face), for 16 weeks throughout each semester. For the Spring 2020 through the end of Summer 2021, due to COVID-19, ITA courses had been offered in a hybrid online format, which included two 50-minute synchronous sessions and 33 percent of course material delivered asynchronously. Class size does not exceed 14 students, and they come from varying linguistic and academic backgrounds, mostly Chinese, but also including Arabic, Hindi, Korean, Persian, and Spanish. Until the Fall of 2019, the course included four microteaching assignments each with a different theme, a practice English Proficiency Interview (EPI), where students take part in a mock interview with a peer, complete peer- and self-assessments, and individual conferences with their instructor. The materials previously taught in this course were heavily influenced by a required textbook.

In Spring 2020, a redesign for this course began with the purpose of accommodating the diverse needs and academic background of ITAs, and to strengthen the curriculum to outstand the changing needs of ITAs throughout the years. A mini-corpus created by the student containing articles in their subdisciplines to serve as a basis for practicing pronunciation and teaching skills appeared to satisfy the gap. The new curriculum's major assignments in the ITA class still included microteaching assignments, a classroom observation assignment, self- and peer-assessments, as well as a mock EPI assignment, however, some of the major assignments and smaller pronunciation assignments were built using the mini-corpus.

Before the course redesign which piloted the corpus project, major assignments included four microteaching assignments: introduce a syllabus, teach an extended definition, explain a process, and give an interactive lecture. Assignments also included EPI practice, individual conferences after three of the microteaching assignments, and activities based on a required textbook. In the course redesign, the "Explain a Process" microteaching was removed, the textbook was no longer required due to its limited and outdated material in the face of the students' current needs, a classroom observation was retained, and other assignments were personalized to the student's discipline through the use of student-generated mini-corpora.

A major change to the curriculum arose from the need to move beyond general academic word lists when practicing suprasegmental features and microteaching to include more field-specific terms drawn from each individual student's research subfield. Considering the diversity of subfields and specificity of vocabulary needs in graduate-level academics, it would be difficult for instructors to curate field-specific terms for each student's subdiscipline or use a general academic word list while maintaining the assignments and tasks assigned to improve their pronunciation and fluency. For example, students were asked to build some of the microteaching assignments using field-specific terms and concepts and they often had struggled with how to make the selection of an important term or concept to introduce in their field. Moreover, finding academic field-specific terms relevant to each student's discipline by instructors in the mock EPI assignment proved to be a challenge. Through the creation of a mini-corpus from a major journal in each student's discipline, students are able to determine the field-specific terms they will use in several homework and in-class assignments. As electronic textbooks become more readily available, students can add textbooks for introductory courses in their fields of study to their mini-corpus. Such additions would increase ecological validity to the language samples they have to work with. The use of a mini-corpus provides students the opportunity to direct their own learning through "data-driven learning," a term used by Johns (1991a in Boulton 2010, p. 18). Instructors also have access to each student's word list generated from their mini-corpus to inform the design of some classroom activities.

Microteaching has been one of the most popular major assignments among instructors and students, as this assignment gives the students opportunities to gain procedural knowledge while practicing the strategies they learned throughout the course. For example, after delivering content related to body language, suprasegmentals, lecturing strategies and other skills, microteaching is a chance for students to demonstrate their understanding and application of these strategies in a familiar classroom environment, while receiving feedback from their peers and teachers related to linguistic skills, teaching techniques, and cross-cultural aspects of their presentations. Students are encouraged to use their mini-corpus as a guiding tool in selecting the topics for microteaching which is especially helpful for first-semester students who have not yet begun working on their research papers. Moreover, students are required to reflect on their performance before meeting with their instructor during each individual conference after at least two of the microteaching assignments.

Given that each academic discipline varies in classroom instruction and teaching methods, a classroom observation assignment was introduced in the new syllabus.[1] ITAs are required to observe a class which they might TA in the future, in their department, or any other tertiary classroom at the student's institution. The classroom observation is an opportunity to reflect on teaching strategies and other behaviors among students and teachers. This assignment informs an in-class round-table discussion about the US classroom and cross-cultural communication in academic settings.

THEORETICAL BACKGROUND

Responding to ITA Needs

When ITAs teach undergraduate lecture-discussion or lab classes, the language proficiency requirements for these assistantships are often higher than those for graduate school admissions, especially regarding oral English proficiency. Thus, the overarching goal of ITA courses is to help international students attain the needed proficiency to become successful TAs. Communicative competence is one of the most important models of language proficiency of late which has been applied to language pedagogy and assessment. Communicative competence is frequently divided into four dimensions or types of competencies: grammatical or linguistic, strategic, sociolinguistic, and discourse (Celce-Murcia, Dornyei, & Thurrell 1995; Canale & Swain 1980). Linguistic competence refers to the accuracy of lexis, syntax, morphology, and phonology. Strategic competence is defined as the skills to negotiate meaning or repair communication breakdown. Sociolinguistic competence, sometimes divided into sociocultural and actional competencies, refers to the ability to use appropriate communication norms in different social situations

(Celce-Murcia et al. 1995). Discourse competence involves the use of various linguistic and organizational tools to achieve cohesive and coherent stretches of discourse. As the dimensions of communicative competence overlap with each other, language instruction often addresses more than one competency at a time. Nonetheless, some competencies receive more attention than others in ITA courses and in the discussion that follows.

Before Course Redesign

The existing course already addressed common gaps in student linguistic, sociolinguistic, and strategic competencies. The most frequent linguistic deficiencies identified in our student population were not lexical, syntactic, or even morphological in nature, but phonological or morphophonological. Sociolinguistic competencies have been covered topically in lessons on US academic culture, teaching expectations, and similar cross-cultural communication topics. Components of strategic competence mentioned by Celce-Murcia and colleagues (1995), such as the use of circumlocution, stalling, and comprehension checks, have been encouraged in the context of oral interview practice. Furthermore, the course has aimed to teach another form of strategic competence, which is student autonomy, by promoting metaphonological awareness through in- and out-of-class assignments.

Principles Guiding Course Redesign

The course revisions described in this chapter sought to address more fully specific aspects of communicative competence that fall under the categories of strategic and discourse competencies. One way to enhance strategic competence is to foster the development of learner autonomy, which is the ability "to monitor and be aware of [the students' own] learning," so that students are more "effective and independent" language learners and users (Nation & Macalister 2010, 38–39). Although strategic competence is applicable to all language skills, the main focus of strategies in this course is on strategies for improving pronunciation and oral communication. Another aspect addressed in the course redesign, referred to as *textual competence*, falls under discourse competence (Canale and Swain 1980). Textual competence is defined as a learner's knowledge of and ability to use "well-known and taken-for-granted 'scripts' in a language," which are frequent phrases or terms, often not present in general dictionaries or grammar books (Gorsuch 2015, p. xi). These aspects of discourse competence deserved special attention in ITA course design. Knowing and accessing these common academic or field-specific scripts would make the task of explaining concepts or processes to undergraduate students in an introductory-level science course easier and more automatic. For example, knowing that the four most frequent verbs that appear with the word *energy*, in general American English (Davies 2008–2022) are *produce, reduce, release*, and *generate* would help build mental scripts for talking about *energy* in everyday settings. Furthermore, the knowledge that verbs, such as *emit* and *radiate,* appear frequently in academic texts about *energy* would give TAs quicker access to common vocabulary or phrases used in academic discourse, which increases oral fluency. Practice using such scripts provides opportunities to practice features of connected speech, such as linking. Because ITAs are likely to teach undergraduate courses, general and academic textual competence as well as the ability to readily produce such language intelligibly are crucial.

The redesigned course seeks to provide more meaningful context in which to practice procedural knowledge, which is accomplished through the use of student-generated corpora. *Propositional knowledge* is contrasted with *procedural knowledge*. The former is defined as facts about the world and the latter is the ability to perform processes to accomplish a desired goal. Traditionally, language instruction, including for ITAs, has been better at teaching propositional knowledge. For ITAs, necessary procedural knowledge includes how to perform the act of teaching in the target language, while accessing content knowledge and teaching skills that TAs may already possess in their primary language and home country's cultural context (Gorsuch 2015, xiii). In addition to procedural knowledge about teaching, ITAs often need to gain procedural knowledge in the target language. When learning any new skill, such as a sport, the athlete requires a great deal of *practice.* One expected outcome of practice is increased *self-efficacy*, which is "an individual's beliefs in his/her ability to perform a designated task or complete an activity and [self-efficacy] may be used as a predictor of future performance" (Mills 2014, p. 8). Thus, both components of the learning process, practice and self-efficacy, are needed for growing procedural knowledge. In the context of language learning, practice is described as the "cognitive process that transforms declarative (or propositional) knowledge into procedural knowledge" (DeKeyser 2007 cited in Gorsuch 2015 xv). For the ITA, procedural knowledge is gained through experiences doing things, such as teaching or engaging in academic discourse. The course described in this chapter, Oral Communication for ITAs, attempts to address the theoretical implications of academic and field-specific textual competence and procedural knowledge within the target language and teaching context. These are gained through increased self-efficacy, that is, through increased confidence in one's abilities and plentiful opportunities to practice the procedural skills that ITAs need to succeed in their teaching assignments. Some of the tools used in this course that aim to respond to these theoretical implications involve corpus linguistics techniques.

Corpus Linguistics in ITA Courses: Theory Meets Practice

A common theme in literature about language pedagogy is the lack of communication between teaching practice and theory. Corpus linguistics offers many applications in language teaching. A large and balanced general corpus, such as the Corpus of Contemporary American English (Davies 2008–2022) provides multifaceted pictures of how language is used in real life. Empirical data, such as word frequencies and collocations, can be extracted from corpora leading to more evidence-based decisions about language curricula and textbooks. Teachers and students can search a corpus to answer questions about lexico-grammatical conventions, such as which prepositions are most often used with specific noun phrases. However, corpus linguists have also lamented the disconnect between their academic discipline and teaching practice. Aijmer (2009) and Boulton (2010) have stated that corpora have had little impact on the English as a Foreign Language (EFL) classroom. Boulton and colleagues agree, declaring "the application of corpora to university English for Specific Purposes (ESP) courses is a rarity, and the independent exploitation of specialized language corpora by non-linguist academics themselves (scientists, economists, etc.) is all but non-existent" (Boulton et al. 2012, 2). Thus the disconnect between theory and practice persists, but why? Some teachers and students may view the inclusion of corpus techniques and the software needed for carrying out tasks as overly technical, and they misunderstand the value of investigating real-world language, or simply resent what is perceived as extra work (Boulton et al. 2012; Granger 2009; Lee & Swales 2006). It is easy to see why teachers and students shy away from assignments requiring the use of a corpus. One way to minimize these misgivings is to make assignments as user-friendly as possible by stating clear objectives, limiting the size of assignments, and providing easy-to-follow instructions.

Many different types of corpora have been generated and used for linguistics and pedagogical purposes. Some types of corpora that are relevant to ITAs are those that are made up of academic texts (Coxhead 2000), corpora created to address the needs of specific learner audiences (Granger 2009), and student-generated corpora (Lee & Swales 2006). An example of a corpus-focused English for Academic Purposes (EAP) course that made use of student-built corpora, using students' own writing is discussed by Lee and Swales (2006). This course, called "Exploring your own discourse world," primarily targeted advanced academic writing while carrying a secondary focus on academic speaking (Lee & Swales 2006, 58). Courses that target primarily oral communication and make use of corpora are hard to find or nonexistent in EAP literature.

In a large university setting for which it would be impossible to maintain contact with all the departments an ITA program serves, a corpus project can act as a proxy, albeit small, for knowledge about the language needs of each academic field represented in any given ITA course. In his resource book for EAP educators, Hyland (2006) strongly supports the use of corpora:

> The value of corpus work lies in the fact that it can both replace instruction with discovery and refocus attention on accuracy as an appropriate aspect of learning. This methodology not only provides an open-ended supply of language data tailored to the learner's needs rather than simply a standard set of examples, but also promotes a learner-centred approach bringing flexibility of time and place and a discovery approach to learning. (Hyland 2006, 93)

The course described in this chapter uses a different kind of student-generated corpora than the kind that was described in Lee and Swales (2006). Rather than collect students' own writing, each student collects texts from an academic subfield by selecting articles from an important academic journal in their field of study. Braun (2010) supports the use of this technique by stating that students and teachers have expressed the need for smaller, more homogeneous corpora, ones that correspond with genres that are pedagogically relevant and are easier to use when compared to traditional and broader corpora. The diversity and specificity of academic fields of the students enrolled in ITA courses further support the inclusion of this corpus technique. Therefore, the goal of this chapter is to explore how student-based corpora encourage learner autonomy, afford learners opportunities for meaningful language and teaching practice, and expand their academic discourse repertoire, which leads us to the research question. How does integrating a corpus-based project into an ITA course:

a. accommodate the diverse and versatile academic needs of students while improving pronunciation?
b. address the communicative competence needs of students?

Other important components in the course described in this chapter address the previously mentioned theoretical underpinnings. Practice for building procedural knowledge involves teaching simulations, through microteaching assignments and audio or video recorded homework assignments. Self-efficacy is addressed through a focus on negotiating language learning goals with students, as well as lessons about and opportunities for performing self- and peer-assessments throughout the semester. Due to space limitations, this chapter zooms in on the mini-corpus project and then provides an outline of the entire course. Student reactions through survey results are discussed in the procedures and results section. A more detailed course description and sample activities can be found on the website.[2]

MINI-CORPUS CREATION

This section will explain the steps taken by students to create their own mini-corpus and how student corpora are integrated into the ITA curriculum. Then selected samples of corpora and their implementation in ITA and pronunciation teaching are used to illustrate various aspects of the mini-corpus project. Some of the details about this project are listed in a way that an instructor could design a similar assignment to fit their own teaching context. In the ITA course described in this chapter, students begin creating their own mini-corpus in the fourth week of instruction. Since the first steps of this project are relatively tech-intensive, students are provided with detailed tutorial videos on how to create their own mini-corpus, with a handout detailing the steps below. Two of the tutorial videos can be found on the website under The Corpus Project.[3]

A. Contents of the Mini-Corpus

  1. Students determine the best journal for their field or subfield (the more specific to their interests the better).
  2. Students download all articles from this journal's latest issue. A minimum of 5 articles must be downloaded; however, the more articles they use the more useful results they will extract from their mini-corpus.
  3. After downloading the articles, students are instructed to convert all articles into ".pdf" files, if applicable. While the corpus tool, AntConc (Anthony 2020), is compatible with ".word" and ".txt" files, it is recommended to use ".pdf" to avoid unplanned errors that will create an obstacle to creating the mini-corpus.

B. Creation of the Mini-Corpus:

  4. Students are instructed to download the corpus tool AntConc from the official website.
  5. They then are directed to open the AntConc application, click on "file," and "create quick corpus" to upload the collection of downloaded articles in ".pdf" format.

C. Navigation of the Mini-Corpus:

6. The course learning management system (LMS) website has a corpus project wiki with a separate wiki page for each student to use for documenting the results of their corpus assignments. Students are taught how to navigate the mini-corpus and extract the most frequently used words (while learning to exclude function words such as demonstratives and articles as well as any general academic terminology). They learn how to view the context in which they are used and identify the most common preceding and following collocations. They are also encouraged to use a combination of word frequency and their own intuition about their fields when creating their personalized word list.

7. Students build their corpus wiki page in the LMS by stating their discipline, the journal(s) from which they selected their articles, and the number of words in the mini-corpus. Then they are asked to select the 10 most frequently used field-specific terms from the mini-corpus and list them in their corpus wiki. This is further illustrated in the student sample that appears in figure 15.1. The corpus wiki is completely student generated since instructors provide feedback on a separate assignment page instead of directly on the student's corpus wiki. Though this is explained in the next section, it is important to note that the final line in figure 15.1 lists the collocation "linear interpolation" which is labeled as having vowel-to-vowel linking. In most North American dialects, this phrase would likely have consonant-to-vowel linking.

Figure 15.1. Corpus Project Wiki (Student Sample).
Credit: Eida and Franks

However, in r-less dialects, *linear* may end in a vowel, thus the student's label is understandable even though this phrase does not fit the vowel-to-vowel linking patterns they were taught.

INTEGRATING MINI-CORPUS CONTENT INTO PRONUNCIATION PRACTICE AND ASSIGNMENTS

Practicing Word Stress Using the Mini-corpus

After students create the mini-corpus, the instructor can utilize the mini-corpus to ask students to practice word stress, especially in relation to relevant field-specific terms in their own field. This is also a good opportunity for instructors to explore lexical stress patterns based on word class, suffixation, and compounding. After explaining the definition and importance of word stress in speech, students are instructed to record themselves saying the 10 field-specific terms from their Corpus Project Wiki. Moreover, they are asked to provide a written equivalent of their recorded field-specific terms by capitalizing the syllable with the primary stress. First, they record the field-specific term itself, and then they record a sentence they created that includes the field-specific term (sentences may be from their mini-corpus or they may make up their own). For example, if their field-specific term is "translanguaging," they would write the field-specific term as "transLAN-guaging" highlighting the primary stress placement, then record their pronunciation of the field-specific term, followed by the sentence "Bilinguals often use translanguaging when talking to bilingual peers." In order to foster interaction between students as they complete this word stress pronunciation task and improve their ability to not only correctly pronounce word stress but also recognize it, we conduct this task in three steps, using a forum tool in the course LMS. In the first step, students record the 10 most frequently used field-specific terms in their mini-corpus, as explained above, and submit their written equivalent marking the primary stress. In the second step, we ask students to peer-review a classmate's recording, giving feedback after listening to their peer's recording, writing down the words while capitalizing the syllable they heard as stressed. After this, they check the word stress on their peer's Corpus Wiki page or in an online dictionary. Peers comment on any of the terms that are not pronounced correctly or are hard to understand. They also explain why the term is mispronounced or hard to understand (stress, consonants, vowels, too fast, etc.). In the final step, the student takes their peer's feedback into consideration as they re-record their 10 field-specific terms in sentences.

Common Phrases and Linking Using Mini-corpus

After students have practiced word stress, we then introduce the concept of linking. After scaffolding the concept, students are tasked with identifying two to three common collocations (phrases) for at least three words in their list of the field-specific terms on their Corpus Project Wiki. They are asked to mark instances of consonant-to-vowel, consonant-to-consonant, and vowel-to-vowel linking. Detailed instructions are provided on how to extract collocations from their mini-corpus using AntConc. Students are instructed to update their corpus wiki page. Some examples are illustrated in figure 15.1 and the following teacher sample is provided for students:

> "3) Bi.'lin.gual/Multilingual—source https://www.merriam-webster.com/dic tionary/bilingual Common collocations include: bilingual_education (consonant to vowel), dual-language (consonant to consonant) bilingual programs, emergent bilingual"

Since we supplement this step with other activities unrelated to the mini-corpus, we do not ask them to record themselves in this activity. However, future instructors may ask students to record themselves pronouncing the collocations they selected and give peer feedback on one other's recordings.

Two Fake and One Real Definition Using Mini-corpus

To provide the students with further pronunciation practice that includes an application of both phrase stress and linking, students are asked to use their mini-corpus to extract academic field-specific terms they consider important in their field and record themselves providing three different definitions for one of the terms they select. One definition should be real, while the other two definitions need to be fake. Students are allowed to use the same definition yet add or remove crucial information each time. After this, their peers listen to the recording, record themselves repeating the same three definitions, and then try to determine which definition is the real one. This provided opportunities for students to practice their pronunciation, and for their peers to practice their listening and understanding of the recordings. In a third step, the student who posted the original definitions records a longer version of the correct definition. This peer activity takes place asynchronously in a forum but could easily be modified to do in class.

Marking and Shadowing Using Mini Corpus

Students have a chance to practice what they learned about connected speech, phrase stress, and some features of intonation, such as final falling and rising intonation, in the "Two Fake and One Real Definition" task. After this task, students are introduced to more intonation patterns, such as final and non-final intonation. After practicing these concepts in and out of class, they use the mini-corpus to select one of their field-specific terms from their corpus wiki page. Using Youglish.com, students are asked to do a search for the term, or a short phrase containing the term, then they identify a video that they like, either because the speaker is very good or they like the topic. They select a portion that is at least 20 seconds long to transcribe and are given the opportunity to use the "Open Transcript" command in YouTube to obtain an existing transcript. After this, they are asked to copy and paste about one paragraph of spoken text onto the corpus wiki page. They are asked to mark the transcribed spoken paragraph as following:

- Mark all the pauses they hear with using a forward slash '/'
- Bold any words that have primary phrase stress (one or two words per thought group)
- Use the ↘ for falling intonation, the ↗ for rising intonation, and nothing if the intonation seems flat at the end of a thought group.
- Finally, students are asked to record themselves imitating the speaker as closely as possible.

Using the field-specific terms selected from their mini-corpus ensures that they will search for videos on topics they are highly interested in as they practice their pronunciation and intonation. This task is implemented as a three-step peer activity as the ones described above. Another option is to skip the peer feedback step and simply have students submit directly to the teacher their recordings along with the link to the video they used. Figure 15.2 illustrates a "Marking and Shadowing" corpus wiki entry teacher sample to show students what this assignment should look like on their own corpus wiki page.

Other Applications of the Corpus Project

In addition to the pronunciation-specific applications of the mini-corpus, the students are encouraged to explore the corpus and select the materials used for their mock EPI and material for their microteaching assignments from the mini-corpus itself. This is illustrated in the next section as we describe in detail the outline of the ITA course offered and how the mini-corpus is utilized in the class syllabus.

Marking and shadowing task

Edit section

Transcription:

Further, / I use **translanguaging** ↗/ as a theoretical **framework**, ↗/ and for those of you that are not familiar with this **term** / or this **notion** of translanguaging, ↘ / it's the **idea** that / the **term** ↗/ and the notion of language shifts from a ↗ **noun** to a **verb**. ↘ / Right? ↗/ Because language is something we **do**, / it's not something we **own**. ↘ Right? ↗/ And **so**, / these children not only **language**, ↘ / but they **translanguage** ↘ / because they go ↗ **in** and **out** ↗ / and they **blend** ↗/ the different **ways** ↗ / of **using** language ↘ / and the different experiences they **have** with language ↘ / in their everyday **practice**, ↘ / and / positioning translanguaging or bilingualism as a **normal** ↗ / **language** ↘ / **practice**. ↘

Source: Emergent bilingual children at play, colloquia with Dr. Mileidis Gort

(11:23–12:05).

My shadowing audio:

Figure 15.2.   Marking and Shadowing (Teacher Sample provided on course LMS).
Credit: Eida and Franks

STUDENT RESPONSES TO ITA COURSE

After preparing the course with the changes detailed above, the course was piloted in Spring 2020. Due to the COVID-19 pandemic, this course was moved to a synchronous online format in March 2020. The course continued following the redesigned syllabus, with some necessary adjustments to accommodate the sudden change in teaching mode and to decrease the workload of the instructors and students. For example, the classroom observation assignment was made optional to relieve the pressure on the students as well as the instructors being observed.

To gauge student satisfaction of the course and ensure the course redesign met student needs, students were asked to take a course satisfaction survey to report on their experience. Survey questions were organized by the sections of the course, therefore, the survey examined student reactions regarding their satisfaction with the course generally as well as regarding microteaching, preparation for the EPI, and the classroom observation assignment. The survey contained 72 items ranging from closed-ended items to open-ended items. The first 15 items were questions about students' academic background, 10 items about general satisfaction with the course, 12 items related to the EPI assignment, 19 items related to microteaching and American classroom culture, and 8 items on the use of the corpus project. Closed-ended items were assigned the scores from 1–4, 1 reflecting "strongly disagree" and 4 reflecting "strongly agree." Thirteen students from two sections participated in the survey at the end of the semester. Students enrolled in this course at the time of survey distribution differed in language backgrounds which included Chinese, Spanish, Korean, and Bengali. Students who participated in the survey reflected the Graduate College population of international TAs in their backgrounds and disciplines. Student majors included computer science, electrical and computer engineering, economics, finance, mathematics, microbiology, chemical and biomolecular engineering, political science, statistics, geology, and landscape architecture. The majority of the students had never taught in the United States, but seven students had experience teaching in their home country, and two students had experience teaching in the United States. All students who participated in the survey were doctoral students. All students had been living in the United States at the time of the survey, varying between a semester to more than three years. The data collected will not be used to make generalizations about the corpus project or the course, but to receive feedback on the ongoing course and plan further improvement accordingly.

Since the survey was created to gauge student satisfaction as a guide and not for research purposes, we report with caution that the responses we received to the open-ended question of which major assignment was most helpful, eight students enrolled in the course indicated that the most helpful assignment was microteaching, and they reported preferring to use the words and phrases from the mini-corpus over using a general academic word list. Four students reported self- and peer-assessment as the most helpful, and one student reported the corpus project was the most helpful as it "gives the fundamental materials of many oral presentations." Eleven students reported their appreciation for self- and peer-feedback, illustrating that the process of recording themselves before and after feedback was extremely beneficial. Student responses also indicated that watching other microteaching presentations had helped them improve and reflect on their own teaching, and that they enjoyed listening to presentations from other disciplines. However, five students indicated in the open-ended questions that the least helpful assignment was the corpus project as they lacked understanding of the purpose of the mini-corpus. They also believed it was time-consuming to gather and conduct a mini-corpus project and one student did not agree that the most frequently used words were the most important words in their field. However, in the multiple-choice items, ten students agreed that using the mini-corpus helped them select field-specific terms and utilize them in other assignments, that the corpus project helped them prepare for microteachings and the EPI, and that they preferred using field-specific terms selected from their mini-corpus than field-specific terms from a general academic list. As for the pronunciation features, ten students agreed that linking helped their pronunciation inside and outside the classroom, while twelve agreed that word stress, rhythm and intonation strategies helped them enhance their fluency.

DISCUSSION

The results of the survey show general satisfaction with the course redesign. To address the first research question, it seems that the corpus project addressed the field-specific and versatile needs of students. Students reported the mini-corpus had helped with microteaching term selection as well as other assignments, yet the students did not show high enthusiasm about the corpus project. This is because students could not see that they could transfer the skills of creating a corpus to other academic situations and complained that it was a long and tech-intensive process. Additionally, some did not agree that the most frequently used words were the most important words in their field. This finding reflects similar results found in the literature; the complexity of doing corpora as well as the students' failure to perceive the purpose of using corpora has been an obstacle in integrating corpus techniques in classroom instruction (Boulton et al. 2012; Granger 2009; Lee & Swales 2006). However, the goal of the corpus project is to provide students with a student-centered, flexible, and field-specific approach to replace the general academic list, which, given the survey results, this goal has been somewhat accomplished even if not all students' perception agree with this assessment. As Hyland (2006, 93) illustrated, the purpose of creating a corpus is to "replace instruction with discovery" and to provide the student with "an open-ended supply of language data tailored to the learner's needs." The students will get the option to create a resource from which they can choose the core of their assignments (microteaching, pronunciation practice, EPI practice) rather than choosing from a general academic list provided by the instructor. The criticism of the concept that word frequencies do not equate the most important words in a field is correct; however, the mini-corpus provides students with the power to control this deficiency by selecting different articles, journals, or not necessarily selecting from the top 10 most frequently used field-specific words. The student can use a combination of word frequency and their own intuition about their fields when creating their personalized word list. More-over, this lifts the weight off the instructor to curate the academic word list by discipline for each student, and it gives the student an authentic opportunity to explain and practice concepts from their discipline to an unfamiliar audience. As the corpus project was designed to alleviate the instructor of the weight of curating academic word lists by discipline for each student as well as accom-modate the diverse academic disciplines, it is important to note that a large part of helping students understand the purpose of the corpus is the respon-sibility of the instructor. Since the students' complaint was on how long and tech-intensive the process is, yet still reported their frequent use of it in their assignments and reported their preference for choosing from a corpus in their field to a general academic list, this should only further our efforts to better create and facilitate the process through more handouts, office hours, and video tutorials. This supports Lee & Swales's (2006, 71) report that "some felt that having access to corpora was better than using reference books or grammar books." This allowed students to access different phrases and struc-tures used in their disciplines; this is especially true in large, diverse depart-ments where each sub-discipline uses different academic jargon than others. Students' lack of understanding of the purpose of creating a mini-corpus could be explained by personal preference or the difficulty of demonstrating how the project facilitates fulfilling course objectives.

A positive reaction to the mini-corpus project was perceived by subsequent instructors. Since the course was piloted in Spring 2020 during the start of the COVID-19 pandemic and sudden transition to online instruction, it could be that the comfort with technology before and after the COVID-19 online instruction period has affected student perception of the corpus project in subsequent semesters. In the pilot semester, our experience showed us that our students were generally technologically savvy enough so that the creation and execution of the corpus project was not hindered by technical difficulties. All three instructors who taught the course online due to the pandemic com-mented that none of their students expressed difficulty with the technology, however, they did not appreciate that the process was long and tedious. It is important to note that the AntConc software only started accepting .pdf files in December 2021, which led to the shortening of the process by two steps. As students at the time of the corpus project pilot had to convert .pdf files into .txt files, which required uploading files to an online converter if they did not have access to software such as Adobe® Acrobat®, and finally, open the files in AntConc, it is understandable that they would consider the pro-cess tedious. Fortunately, two steps were eliminated from the process since they can now download the article .pdf files and directly upload them to the corpus tool AntConc. Another factor that might contribute to the success of the corpus project in subsequent semesters could be that the actual building of the corpus and assignments most closely tied to it account for a small portion of the course grade but enriches the course content as it makes the class more student-centered.

Regarding the second part of the research question, "How does integrating a corpus-based project into an ITA course address the communicative needs of students?" Textual competence, which is classified under discourse competence (Gorsuch 2015; Canale and Swain 1980), is addressed in at least two of the new assignments directly linked to the student-designed mini-corpus. In the "Identifying linking in collocations" assignment (see figure 15.1), students search for words that appear before and after their field-specific terms and add common phrases or collocations in their corpus wiki. Their search for common phrases forces students to notice those phrases as well as apply what they learned about linking to those phrases. This assignment is one of the steps that builds up to the "Defining Field-Specific Terms" microteaching. Another assignment that contributes to textual competence is the "Marking and Shadowing" assignment. Since in this assignment students are instructed to search videos using field-specific terms from their corpus, the results for these searches have often been academic in nature, which means students are being exposed to academic discourse in their field or in closely related fields. The second author observed that student's recordings resulted in close imitations of the video clips they submitted, which is further evidence that students took this assignment seriously and practiced the oral text sufficiently. Another important concept that was identified in this study is procedural knowledge, which is perhaps most closely tied to discourse and sociolinguistic competencies (Gorsuch 2015). Procedural knowledge is gained through continual practice doing specific tasks. Although procedural knowledge with a sociolinguistic focus had already been addressed through assignments such as microteaching, several new assignments in the redesigned course added many more opportunities to practice field-specific discourse through recorded homework, peer activities, and a wider range of vocabulary practice in and out of class. Therefore, discourse competence was the dimension that was most enhanced in the course redesign. However, pronunciation was not ignored as either fluency building or specific pronunciation features were quite frequently intertwined with the corpus tasks.

While the technical component of creating the corpus was difficult, the more difficult task was communicating the value of the corpus tools and techniques to enhance language learning and student autonomy during and after the completion of the ITA course. Another aspect that instructors struggled with was the integration of diverse course goals and activities with the corpus project activities. An important principle in the use of technology for teaching is that the objectives should guide the choice and implementation of technology rather than the technology drive the course objectives. Therefore, lessons learned from this project are summarized in the following lessons for using the corpora to teach ITAs:

Lesson 1: Keep assignments influenced by the mini-corpus as simple as possible. While large corpora are preferred in linguistics, for the purposes of the ITA course described in this chapter, each student builds their own mini-corpus, often ranging from as small as 5,000 words, perhaps in a field where academic articles are very short, to more than 500,000 words. While a much larger corpus would have been better, even a small student-built corpus can yield a sufficient sample of language in each student's field that instructors, students, and their classmates can use for a variety of language practice (Braun 2010). However, overwhelming students with several requirements that are based upon their use of the corpus could lead to confusion and frustration; therefore, it is important not only to keep the assignments limited to one pronunciation feature observed in the corpus at a time, but also provide detailed step-by-step instructions.

Lesson 2: Whenever possible, integrate corpus-based assignments into larger course objectives and goals. Instructors must clearly explain the value of an assignment or project and ensure that students understand how each step of a task leads to another and ultimately connects to course objectives and real-world results.

Lesson 3: Video tutorials and written step-by-step instructions are essential to help students get started. Providing clear and specific assignment parameters, sample assignments, and grading rubrics (when applicable) are useful ways to ensure that students know what a successful assignment looks like.

Lesson 4: Weigh assignment grades appropriately based on proportionate workload and importance relative to other coursework. Because the corpus project naturally related to a relatively small portion of the pronunciation and oral communication goals of the course and because only a few class sessions and about five homework assignments were directly linked to the corpus project, only about 5 percent of the course grade was derived from these project activities. However, the 5 percent does not account for other assignments that may have been informed by the corpus project, such as a microteaching in which students define field-specific terms found in their mini-corpus.

We acknowledge that this course is difficult to design and implement due to the diversity of the students and departments that it serves, and while students may not enthusiastically embrace the corpus project as a novel assignment, the overall effectiveness of the course has been improving continuously and instructors continue finding new ways to address student needs. It is important to note that more extensive surveys that are created to gather data should be conducted specifically on the use of the corpus project on pronunciation.

CONCLUSION

Using field-specific corpora to teach oral communication for future TAs is not a simple undertaking and teachers may shy away from the technology needed to accomplish such a project. In agreement with Nation and Macalister's (2010) principles of language curriculum design, this course redesign has strengthened the use of student strategies and autonomy. Through an examination of students' ongoing needs, the course continues evolving and we plan to keep the mini-corpus project for the foreseeable future, however, we also plan to further conduct surveys and other research projects to determine the efficacy of student-created corpora in teaching pronunciation.

NOTES

1. The authors would like to thank past instructors of the course described in this chapter for their many contributions to designing and improving course materials. Their informal comments were invaluable throughout the process of designing surveys, assignments, tutorials, and so forth. Colleagues we would like to thank individually are Dr. Hugh Bishop, Crystal Bonano, Beth Carroll-Curry, Joshua Dees, Ever Miller, Eva Miszoglad, Linda Sims, Dr. John Young. We would also like to thank our anonymous reviewer and book editor Shannon McCrocklin for their insightful comments and suggestions. Any mistakes or omissions are our own.
2. https://bit.ly/ITACourseDesign.
3. https://bit.ly/ITACourseDesign.

REFERENCES

Aijmer, Karin, ed. 2009. Corpora and language teaching. Vol. 33. *John Benjamins Publishing*.

Anthony, Laurence. 2014. "AntConc (Version 3.4. 3)[Computer Software]. Tokyo, Japan: Waseda University.."

Boulton, Alex. 2010. "Data-Driven Learning: On Paper, in Practice." In *Corpus Linguistics in Language Teaching*, edited by Tony Harris and María Moreno Jaén, 17–52. Linguistic Insights: 128. Bern, Switzerland: Peter Lang Publishing Inc. https://search-ebscohost-com.proxy2.library.illinois.edu/login.aspx?direct=true &db=mzh&AN=2011902760&site=eds-live&scope=site.

Boulton, Alex, Shirley Carter-Thomas, and Elizabeth Rowley-Jolivet, eds. 2012. *Corpus-informed research and learning in ESP: Issues and applications*. Vol. 52. John Benjamins Publishing.

Braun, Sabine. 2010. "Getting Past 'Groundhog Day': Spoken Multimedia Corpora for Student-Centred Corpus Exploration." In *Corpus Linguistics in Language*

Teaching, edited by Tony Harris and María Moreno Jaén, 75–97. Linguistic Insights: 128. Bern, Switzerland: Peter Lang Publishing Inc. https://search-ebsco
host-com.proxy2.library.illinois.edu/login.aspx?direct=true&db=mzh&AN=20119
02762&site=eds-live&scope=site.

Canale, Michael, and Merrill Swain. 1980. "Theoretical bases of communicative approaches to second language teaching and testing." Applied linguistics 1, no. 1: 1–47.

Celce-Murcia, Marianne, Zoltan Dörnyei, and Sarah Thurrell. 1995. "Communicative competence: A pedagogically motivated model with content specifications." *Issues in Applied linguistics* 6, no. 2: 5–35.

Coxhead, Averil. 2000. "A new academic word list." *TESOL quarterly* 34, no. 2: 213–238.

Dörnyei, Zoltán, and Tatsuya Taguchi. 2009. *Questionnaires in second language research: Construction, administration, and processing.* Routledge.

Gorsuch, Greta. 2015. "Introduction: International teaching assistants learning to talk in academic departments." *Talking matters: Research on talk and communication of international teaching assistants* Stillwater, OK: New Forums.

Graduate College. n.d. University of Illinois at Urbana-Champaign. Retrieved from https://grad.illinois.edu/.

Granger, Sylviane. 2009. "The contribution of learner corpora to second language acquisition and foreign language teaching." *Corpora and language teaching* 33: 13–32.

Hyland, Ken. 2006. *English for academic purposes: An advanced resource book.* London: Routledge.

Lee, David, and John Swales. 2006. "A corpus-based EAP course for NNS doctoral students: Moving from available specialized corpora to self-compiled corpora." *English for specific purposes* 25, no. 1: 56–75.

Mills, Nicole. 2014. "Self-efficacy in second language acquisition." *Multiple perspectives on the self in SLA,* edited by Sarah Mercer and Marion Williams, 6–22. Blue Ridge Summit, PA: Multilingual Matters.

Macalister, John, and IS Paul Nation. 2019. *Language curriculum design.* New York: Routledge.

Ross, Catherine, and Jane Dunphy, eds. 2007. *Strategies for teaching assistant and international teaching assistant development: Beyond micro teaching.* Vol. 114. San Francisco: Jossey Bass.

Index

About the Editor

Shannon McCrocklin (PhD, Iowa State University) is associate professor of Applied Linguistics/TESOL in the Department of Linguistics at Southern Illinois University. Her research focuses primarily on second language pronunciation and computer-assisted language learning.

About the Contributors

Karen Acosta (PhD, University of Kansas) is associate professor of Spanish in the Department of Modern and Classical Languages at Valdosta State University. Her areas of interest include Spanish-English bilingualism and biliteracy, reading comprehension, the integration of technology in the foreign language curriculum, digital literacies, and the development of intercultural understanding.

Hsueh Chu Chen (PhD, National Kaohsiung Normal University) is associate professor at the Department of Linguistics and Modern Language Studies, the Education University of Hong Kong. She is currently serving as Head of Centre for Language in Education. Her research interests cover computer-assisted pronunciation teaching, interlanguage phonology, and third language phonological development.

Julia Choi (MA, Ohio University) has a background in Applied Linguistics and over eight years of experience working with English as a Second Language Learners. Her research interests include Computer Assisted Language Learning, English for Academic Purposes, and corpus linguistics. She currently works for a nonprofit as an online education specialist.

Anurag Das (Bachelor of Technology, National Institute of Technology, Silchar) is a graduate student in Computer Engineering at Texas A&M University with experience in speech recognition and synthesis, and machine learning for human clinical data. He is interested in leveraging these technologies to solve real-life engineering and language-learning problems.

Idée Edalatishams (PhD, Iowa State University) is currently the Faculty ESL Specialist at George Mason University's Writing Center. Her research interests include corpus linguistics and pronunciation, focusing on technological resources for supporting language learners' speaking and pronunciation.

Mai M. Eida (MA, University of Illinois at Urbana Champaign) has been an ESL educator since 2016. She has worked both in EFL and ESL contexts, and she is currently a Computational Linguistics PhD student at UIUC.

Vivian Flanzer (PhD, University of Texas at Austin) is professor of Instruction and Director of the Portuguese Language Program at the University of Texas at Austin. She is the author of the Open Educational Resource *Clica-Brasil: Portuguese Language and Culture for Intermediate Students,* and the coauthor of the ESL podcast series *Slice of Life.* Her research interests include foreign language education; language teaching, culture, and technology; and cross-culture pragmatics.

Suzanne Franks (PhD, University of Georgia), is teaching assistant professor and ESL Pronunciation and ITA Coordinator at the University of Illinois Urbana-Champaign. Her research interests include how phonetics and phonology can inform the teaching of second language pronunciation.

Atsushi Fukada (PhD, University of Illinois at Urbana-Champaign) is professor of Japanese and Linguistics at Purdue University. His research interests include all areas of Japanese linguistics, pragmatics, technology, and language pedagogy.

Debra M. Hardison (PhD, Indiana University) is faculty member in the Department of Linguistics, Languages, and Cultures at Michigan State University. Her research focuses on auditory-visual integration in spoken language processing, learner variables affecting oral communication skill development, co-speech gesture, and the applications of technology in perception and production training.

Solène Inceoglu (PhD, Michigan State University) is senior lecturer at the Australian National University where she teaches French courses and supervises postgraduate students in Applied Linguistics. Her research interests include the effects of instruction on pronunciation development, individual differences in L2 speech perception/production, and technology in L2 pronunciation teaching/learning.

Di Liu (EdD, Boston University) is assistant professor of Instruction and the coordinator of the TESOL MS.Ed. program and the English Language Teaching (ELT) Certificate program at Temple University. His research focuses on Complexity Theory, Applied Phonology, and Technology-Enhanced Language Learning. He has published in *Frontiers in Communication* and *Journal of Second Language Pronunciation.*

Eugenie Mainake (MA, Southern Illinois University) graduated with an MA in TESOL from the Department of Linguistics at Southern Illinois University. He is currently an English language teacher in Indonesia. His research interests include CALL/ Technology enhanced Language Teaching and Learning, Teacher and Student Technology Literacy, Bilingualism, and Sociolinguistics.

Mayu Miyamoto (PhD, 2019, Purdue University) is assistant professor of International Japanese Studies at Nagoya University of Foreign Studies in Japan. Her research interests are applied linguistics, language pedagogy, and language assessment.

Aurore Mroz (PhD, The University of Iowa) is assistant professor of French with a concentration in Second Language Acquisition Teacher Education at The University of Illinois at Urbana-Champaign. She investigates the role of Computer-Assisted Language Learning in affording relevant simulations that can promote the learning of oral skills in a foreign language.

Michelle Ocasio (PhD, University of Missouri) is associate professor of Spanish and TESOL in the Department of Modern and Classical Languages at Valdosta State University. Her areas of interest include Garífuna historical linguistics, contact linguistics and the use of virtual and augmented reality as vehicles for conversation practice in the target language.

Heather M. Offerman (PhD, Purdue University) is assistant professor of Spanish at the University of Arkansas. Her research includes phonetics and phonology, specifically focusing on methods for pronunciation instruction with the use of technology. Additionally, she focuses on second language acquisition, second language perception, the relationship between second language production and perception, learner attitudes, and second language pedagogy.

Tomoko Okuno (PhD, Michigan State University) is faculty member in the Residential College at University of Michigan. Her research focuses on L2 speech perception and production, L2 pronunciation instruction, L2 perception training, and foreign and second language pedagogy.

Daniel J. Olson (PhD, University of Texas at Austin) is associate professor at Purdue University. His research focuses on phonetics and psycholinguistics in bilingual populations, including second language learners. He is interested in the cognitive mechanisms and pedagogical methods that facilitate the acquisition of second language phonetics.

Marnie Reed (EdD, Boston University) is professor of Education and director of the graduate TESOL program at Boston University where she teaches linguistics and applied phonology. She is coeditor, with John Levis, of the *Wiley Handbook of English Pronunciation* and coeditor, with Tamara Jones, of the TESOL Press edited volume, *Listening in the Classroom*.

Ivana Rehman (PhD, Iowa State University) is applied linguist passionate about language technology. Her research interests include L2 pronunciation learning and teaching, computer assisted language learning, and oral communication assessment. She is especially interested in automated visual feedback for pronunciation learning and computer assisted pronunciation training.

Veronica G. Sardegna (PhD, University of Illinois at Urbana-Champaign) teaches teacher education courses, and conducts research on English pronunciation teaching, intercultural learning, and instructional technology at Duquesne University, United States. Her work has appeared in many peer-reviewed journals and books. She is also coeditor of *Theoretical and Practical Developments in English Speech Assessment, Research, and Training* (2022, Springer).

Rachel Stuckel (MA, Southern Illinois University) has interest and research experience in L2 pronunciation, CALL, VR and language learning, and L2 literacy acquisition. Her thesis research during her MA in TESOL explored how frequency of corrective feedback may affect ESL pronunciation learning. She hopes to continue gaining teaching experience and pursue a PhD program in TESOL or Linguistics.

Jessica L. Sturm (PhD 2008, University of Illinois at Urbana-Champaign) is associate professor of French and Applied Linguistics at Purdue University. She conducts research on classroom acquisition of L2 French pronunciation and teaches courses on French language and culture.

Jing Xuan Tian (MA, Education University of Hong Kong) is PhD student at the Department of Linguistics and Modern Language Studies, the Education University of Hong Kong. She is specialized in English Language Education.

Namiko Uchida (MA 2015, Purdue University) is assistant lecturer of Japanese at Ball State University. Her research interests include all areas of Japanese linguistics, technology, and language pedagogy.

Lara Wallace (PhD Ohio University) is the founder of English for Sustainability, LLC, and helps people communicate effectively in English. With over two decades of university-level teaching experience, she examines ways that technology enhances pronunciation learning and shares this tech and the techniques for using it with her coaching clients as well as through publications and presentations. She is a coauthor of "Technology for Teaching Pronunciation" in *TESOL['s] Encyclopedia of English Language Teaching.*

Mariko M. Wei (PhD 1998, Georgetown University) is associate professor of Japanese and Linguistics at Purdue University. Her research interests include first and second language acquisition, Japanese pedagogy, and psycholinguistics.